P9-CLF-132

JACK LONDON

JACK
LONDON

—————

A LIFE

Alex Kershaw

St. Martin's Press ♏ New York

A THOMAS DUNNE BOOK.
AN IMPRINT OF ST. MARTIN'S PRESS.

ISBN 0-312-18119-1

First published in Great Britain by HarperCollins Publishers

First U.S. Edition: January 1998

10   9   8   7   6   5   4

APR 2 6 1999

FOR ROBIN

CONTENTS

ILLUSTRATIONS

'San Francisco is gone.' Street scene after the 1906 earthquake. (*Courtesy of the California Department of Parks and Recreation*)

Captain Jack and his Mate aboard the *Snark* in Oakland, 1907. (*Courtesy of the California Department of Parks and Recreation*)

Between pages 228 and 229

Charmian, Jack, Martin Johnson and others in Pendruffyn, Solomon Islands, 1908. (*Courtesy of the California Department of Parks and Recreation*)

Jack and friend in fancy dress, Pendruffyn, 1908. (*Courtesy of the California Department of Parks and Recreation*)

Mate Woman among the 'savages'. (*Courtesy of the California Department of Parks and Recreation*)

Jack and Charmian return from the South Seas aboard the *Tymeric*, 1909. (*Courtesy of the California Department of Parks and Recreation*)

The Master looking over his Valley of the Moon. (*Courtesy of the California Department of Parks and Recreation*)

Jack, Charmian and Laurie Smith aboard the *Roamer*. (*Courtesy of the California Department of Parks and Recreation*)

Jack amongst the *Roamer*'s sails. (*Courtesy of the California Department of Parks and Recreation*)

Jack with his old adversary, French Frank. December 1914. (*Courtesy of the California Department of Parks and Recreation*)

Jack sculling a boat, with Possum aboard, past Petaluma bridge. (*Courtesy of the California Department of Parks and Recreation*)

The 'nature-faker' at rest. (*Courtesy of the California Department of Parks and Recreation*)

Jack aboard the *Roamer*, photographed by Charmian in 1914. (*Courtesy of the California Department of Parks and Recreation*)

Jack with old colleagues in Mexico, 1914. (*Huntington Library, San Marino, California*)

Jack bandaged because of chronic toothache, aboard the *Roamer* (*Courtesy of the California Department of Parks and Recreation*)

Jack hunting for duck with a Winchester .22 rifle. (*Courtesy of the California Department of Parks and Recreation*)

BOOKS BY JACK LONDON

1900   *The Son of the Wolf* (Boston, Houghton Mifflin)

1901   *The God of his Fathers* (New York, McLure, Phillips)

1902   *Children of the Frost* (New York, Macmillan)
The Cruise of the Dazzler (New York, Century)
A Daughter of the Snows (Philadelphia, J.B. Lipincott)

1903   *The Kempton–Wace Letters* (with Anna Strunsky) (New York, Macmillan)
The Call of the Wild (New York, Macmillan)
The People of the Abyss (New York, Macmillan)

1904   *The Faith of Men* (New York, Macmillan)
The Sea Wolf (New York, Macmillan)

1905   *The War of the Classes* (New York, Macmillan)
The Game (New York, Macmillan)
Tales of the Fish Patrol (New York, Macmillan)

1906   *Moon-Face and Other Stories* (New York, Macmillan)
White Fang (New York, Macmillan)

1907   *Before Adam* (New York, Macmillan)
Love of Life and Other Stories (New York, Macmillan)
The Road (New York, Macmillan)

1908   *The Iron Heel* (New York, Macmillan)

1909   *Martin Eden* (New York, Macmillan)

1910   *Lost Face* (New York, Macmillan)
Revolution and Other Essays (New York, Macmillan)
Burning Daylight (New York, Macmillan)

1911   *When God Laughs and Other Stories* (New York, Macmillan)
Adventure (New York, Macmillan)
The Cruise of the Snark (New York, Macmillan)
South Seas Tales (New York, Macmillan)

1912   *The House of Pride and Other Stories* (New York, Macmillan)
        A Son of the Sun (New York, Doubleday, Page)
        Smoke Bellew (New York, Century)

1913   *The Night-Born* (New York, Century)
        The Abysmal Brute (New York, Century)
        John Barleycorn (New York, Century)
        The Valley of the Moon (New York, Macmillan)

1914   *The Strength of the Strong* (New York, Macmillan)
        The Mutiny of the Elsinore (New York, Macmillan)

1915   *The Scarlet Plague* (New York, Macmillan)
        The Star Rover (New York, Macmillan)

1916   *The Little Lady of the Big House* (New York, Macmillan)
        The Turtles of Tasman (New York, Macmillan)

1917   *The Human Drift* (New York, Macmillan)
        Jerry of the Islands (New York, Macmillan)
        Michael, Brother of Jerry (New York, Macmillan)

1918   *The Red One* (New York, Macmillan)

1919   *On the Makaloa Mat* (New York, Macmillan)

1920   *Hearts of Three* (New York, Macmillan)

1922   *Dutch Courage and Other Stories* (New York, Macmillan)

ACKNOWLEDGEMENTS

This book would not have been possible without the kind help and advice of many individuals. I would first like to thank Milo Shepard, executor of the Jack London Estate, for his generosity and invaluable advice, and for allowing me permission to quote from materials copyrighted by the Trust of Irving Shepard, from other sources held at the Huntington Library in San Marino and other collections, and from Charmian London's *The Book of Jack London*.

I am also indebted to Sue Hodson at the Huntington Library and to its staff for their help over a two-year period in my research of the Jack London collection. Similarly, I am grateful to staff at the Bancroft Library in Berkeley, at Utah State University and the University of Southern California for their permission to quote from materials held in their collections. Glenn Burch, state historian at the California State Park offices in Santa Rosa, provided great assistance in sorting through several hundred photographs. He also granted me permission to use many of those that appear in this book.

I would also like to thank Winnie Kingman at the Jack London Research Center and bookstore in Glen Ellen for reading the manuscript and providing answers to many questions. Her late husband, Russ Kingman, is one of several biographers whose studies aided me considerably in my assessment of Jack London's life. Others whose work I found both inspiring and helpful include the pre-eminent London scholar Earle Labor, Andrew Sinclair, Carolyn Johnston, Clarice Statz, David Hamilton, Kevin Starr, Richard O'Connor, Irving Stone, Franklin Walker, James McClintock, Philip Foner, A. Grove Day, John Perry and Joan London.

Nettie DeBill of Stanford University Press kindly helped in locating sources and saved me considerable time in other areas. I would also like to thank the Board of Trustees of the Leland Stanford Junior University for their permission to quote from *The Letters of Jack*

London, three volumes, edited by Earle Labor, Robert C. Leitz and I. Milo Shepard.

My agents, Derek Johns and Nick Marston of A.P. Watt, and Robert Bookman of CAA, gave tremendous help and encouragement, and I was also very fortunate to have Richard Johnson and Robert Lacey as my editors at HarperCollins. Their patience and consummate professionalism are much appreciated.

Finally, there are several others without whose friendship and support in recent years this book would not have been completed: Paul Spike, Chris Littleford, David McBeth, Tessa Souter, Lindsay Stirling, my wife Robin Loerch and her family and, last but not least, my own.

Alex Kershaw, Los Angeles, 1997

MAPS

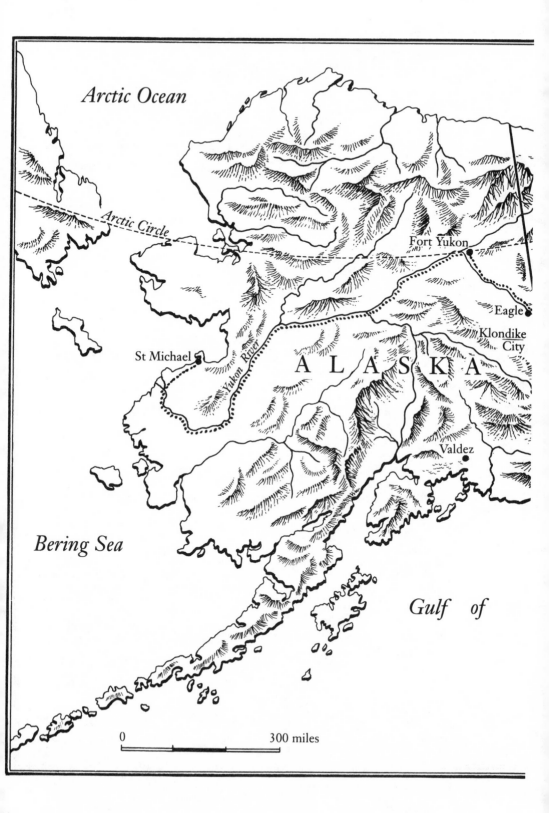

Arctic Ocean

Arctic Circle

Fort Yukon

Eagle

Klondike
City

St Michael

Yukon River

A L A S K A

Valdez

Bering Sea

Gulf   of

0   300 miles

Jack London's Klondike

Forty Mile
Klondike R.
Dawson
Upper
Island
Stewart
River
Thirty
Mile R.
Chilkoot
Pass
Skagway
Juneau

CANADA

Rockies

Rockies

Alaska

Vancouver

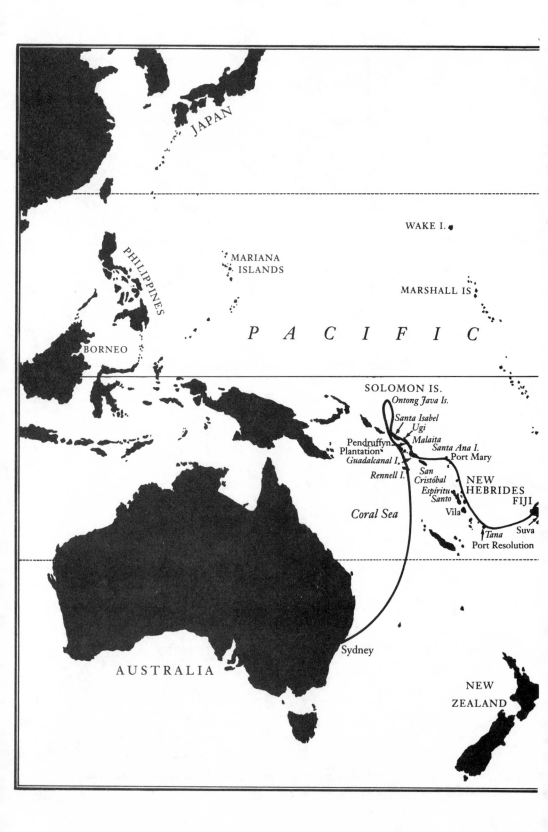

JAPAN

WAKE I.

MARIANA
ISLANDS

PHILIPPINES

MARSHALL IS

P   A   C   I   F   I   C

BORNEO

SOLOMON IS.
Ontong Java Is.

Santa Isabel
Ugi

Pendruffyn
Plantation
Guadalcanal I.

Malaita
Santa Ana I.
Port Mary

San
Cristóbal

Rennell I.

NEW
HEBRIDES

FIJI

Espíritu
Santo

Vila

Coral Sea

Tana
Port Resolution

Suva

Sydney

AUSTRALIA

NEW
ZEALAND

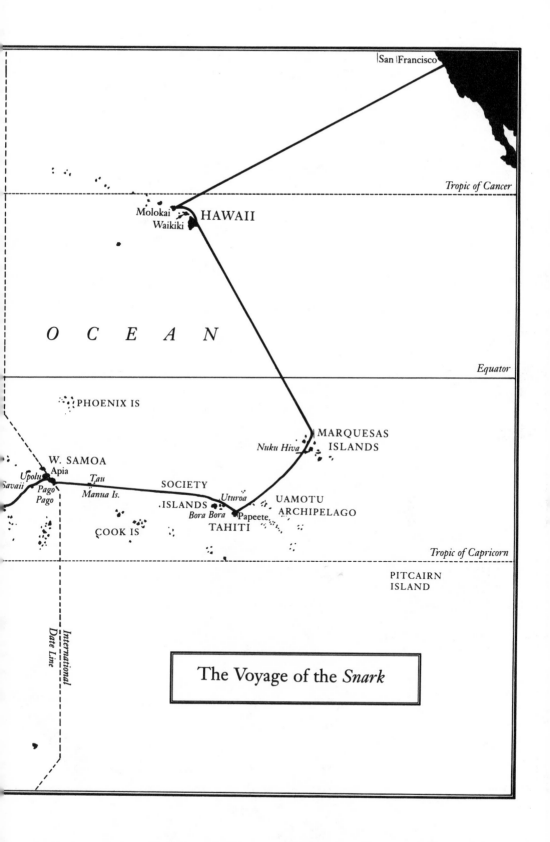

San Francisco

Tropic of Cancer

Molokai
Waikiki
HAWAII

O C E A N

Equator

PHOENIX IS

MARQUESAS
ISLANDS
Nuku Hiva

W. SAMOA
Apia
Upolu
Savaii
Pago
Pago
Tau
Manua Is.
SOCIETY
ISLANDS
Uturoa
Bora Bora Papeete
TAHITI
UAMOTU
ARCHIPELAGO

COOK IS

Tropic of Capricorn

PITCAIRN
ISLAND

International
Date Line

The Voyage of the *Snark*

The Valley of the Moon

There's not a joy the world can give like that it takes away,
When the glow of early thought declines in feeling's dull decay;
'Tis not on youth's smooth cheek the blush alone, which fades so fast,
But the tender bloom of heart is gone, ere youth itself be past.

LORD BYRON, 'There's not a Joy'

One August afternoon I drove out of San Francisco, across the Golden Gate Bridge and through the vine-flanked valleys of northern California. Eventually, as the sun began to set, bathing the countryside in golden light, I found him. The final resting place of Jack London is deep in a grove of oak trees a short walk from the ruins of a great stone house.

A mile away, Jack's study has been preserved in a museum. On his desk are his pencils, and against a wall are stacked his boxes of clippings and research. Above his roll-top desk, a photograph has been mounted. I still cannot erase it from my mind.

Following that visit, as I struggled to enter this man's psyche, and as I read his love letters and marvelled at the raw passions and anger that drove him, my thoughts often returned to this image of Jack London – of a man in pain, paunchy in a light suit and soft open-necked shirt. It is a disturbing portrait to anyone with a sense of tragedy. For we have all seen the look on that bloated but still handsome face elsewhere: in the mirror, if we are not cautious, and always in the expressions of people who have lost the fight against disillusionment. As I read his final letters and imagined the pain of his last years, his agonised stare kept reminding me of the central tragedy of his life:

that he failed to realise, until it was too late, that the soul can never be satisfied by wealth and fame alone.

Often I returned to Glen Ellen, half-hoping to meet London's ghost. In his perfectly preserved office, I examined the tools of one of America's first celebrity writers. I saw the souvenirs of a great explorer: tribal art from the South Seas, objects brought back from deepest Alaska. Here also were some of the notes, letters and manuscripts of a legend who came to believe in his own mythology.

How few, how precious, are our heroes. They do not have to be perfect in order to gain our respect. Far from it. But they must be fighters – men who strive and may even lose, but who recognise the battle as worth fighting. What animated Jack London's life, above all, was a hope that one day poverty and social injustice would decrease, not increase; that the environment would not continue to be regarded as a resource to be endlessly exploited; that humanism would, one day, triumph.

Jack London embodied the promise of socialism. He exposed capitalism's evils; its decimation of the workforce through ruthless profit-making. In some of his most powerful prose, he showed how expendable people are to the process of increasing a governing elite's wealth. To his last breath, he championed the underdog. He did more to increase class-consciousness than any other writer of his time. Yet he ended his life sipping cocktails with the colonial bosses of Hawaii.

The short but relentlessly dramatic life of Jack London spans exactly the period between the American Civil War and the First World War, the age in which contemporary America took shape. He would witness the arrival of the lightbulb, the electric tram, the telephone, radio, motion picture, skyscraper, automobile and aeroplane. His was an epoch of 'technological miracles and of profound cultural and spiritual instability'.

More than any other American writer, Jack London had an insatiable appetite for life. He often said he preferred living to writing, and he was true to his word. By the age of sixteen he had experienced more than most men do in a lifetime. His curiosity and lust for life never dulled. He was forever exploring new ideas, hungry to extend his knowledge in an astonishing variety of fields. His wanderlust was unequalled; his 'adventure path', as he labelled the journey of life, took him across several continents and provided the inspiration for all of his best fiction.

The best of Jack London's writing has a raw power and lyrical brilliance which resonates to this day. Written off during his lifetime by America's literary elite, he remains popular among readers. Few, however, realise the extent of his output or of his interests. In just eighteen years he produced more than two hundred short stories, four hundred non-fiction pieces and twenty novels. His subjects ranged from alcoholism, revolution, eugenics and lunatic asylums to bull-fighting, boxing and surfing. Hardly any aspect of the human condition escaped his attention.

In recent decades, a number of academics have performed detailed post-mortems of Jack London's works. While these have been overdue, they have often overlooked the powerful drama of his life. In the popular imagination he remains the shadowy author of a couple of dog stories; yet if any American writer deserves a reassessment, it is Jack London. Viewed from the distance of almost a century, his quest for faith in a godless world, his existential angst, his belief in technology and his violent fictions all have resonance for contemporary man.

In an age when culture is increasingly homogeneous, when mass media and technology have dulled our senses, we yearn as never before for authentic experience. We live in a time of slick anti-heroes and cynicism, in which nihilism masquerades as art and the realm of adventure, of exploration, is a distant mirage. More than ever, we need to look to history for a sense of continuity, yet the past is becoming ever more obscure as we are swamped by digital information, by a relentless obsession with the detail of the present.

As long as we strive to make sense of the world, and of our place within it, Jack London will remain an inspirational figure. As the English critic Stephen Graham has written, London is 'a living writer. His books will be read when many that are greater works of art will be dust-collecting ... He wrote for "the unfinished and the not finished America".'

1

1

Aloha Hawaii

Somehow, the love of the Islands, like the love of a woman, just happens. One cannot determine in advance to love a particular woman, nor can one so determine to love Hawaii. One sees, and one loves or does not love. With Hawaii it seems always to be love at first sight.

JACK LONDON, 'My Hawaiian Aloha'

DURING HIS PREVIOUS VISIT to Hawaii, at the height of his fame, Jack had learned to surf, to ride the waves that batter the island's golden shores. Ten years later, in 1916, the sands in front of his beloved Seaside Hotel have washed away. Razor-sharp coral is all that remains. Now his Pacific paradise soothes neither his body nor his brain.

In pain from his rheumatic joints, Jack begins to shave. Once a 'blond beast', with the face and body of a 'Greek god', he is not yet forty but feels like an old man: his ankles are swollen, his deep blue eyes are bloodshot and lifeless. Months ago, he stopped exercising – he who once prized his image as the he-man of American letters, who boxed, surfed, fenced and swam to the peak of fitness for so many years. Now it hurts even to look in the mirror. The face that gazes back, ravaged by serious illness, is surely not that of America's greatest ever literary hero.

Jack sips his fruit juice and begins to pick at his breakfast. The juice is essential for washing out the poisons in his body. Suddenly, he feels sick. He runs to the toilet and vomits. When he returns to the veranda, ghostly white, he lights another cigarette and watches the sun appear from behind the palm trees lining Waikiki Beach.

He can hear the first rumble of traffic passing behind his bungalow;

even here, in the middle of the unending Pacific, Ford's damned automobile has arrived. So this is what his century has brought: rubber tyres and prophylactics and the stink of gasoline. It seems to him now that the world, not just his body, has become old and tired. 'The world of adventure is almost over now,' he has recently written. 'Even the purple ports of the seven seas have passed away, and have become prosaic.'

He turns to the *Pacific Commercial Advertiser*, the newspaper his Japanese valet, Sekine, leaves by his desk every morning. As he reads about the latest carnage in Flanders' poppy fields, he is suddenly filled with rage. The mad dog of Europe – Germany – must be stopped. In France, tens of thousands are dying like cattle in the genocide they are already calling the Great War. Had he not predicted the horrors of trench warfare? The maze of mud, stinking of death, awash with the blood of a doomed generation.

His wife is awake. She is walking about the beach-house. Catching her eye, he mouths her a kiss. A few minutes later she is at his side, rubbing his swollen ankles. Can she fetch him anything?

'I'm all right – don't bother,' he says. 'You're never up in time to see the huge breakfast I tuck away – three cups of coffee, with heavy cream, two soft-boiled eggs, half a big papaia.'

Jack loosens his royal-blue kimono and moves his chair towards the shade to protect his sickly skin from the sun. He dare not tell her that he throws up his breakfast every morning, nor that he seldom changes out of his bathing trunks and sandals because it takes too much effort to dress.

His wife is calling to him. She still has slim ankles, an innocent face, the snub nose of a small child. 'Are you going to swim with me today?' she asks.

'Yes – I believe I will . . . No, I'm right in the thick of this new box of reading matter from home. Oh, I don't know – the water looks so good . . . But no; I'll go out in the hammock where I can read and watch you.'

All his life, Jack has looked to books for a philosophy of life, and to take him away from the 'fever of living'. As an idealistic young man, he read everything he could about the great thinkers of the late nineteenth century: Nietzsche, Darwin and Marx. Now he is immersed in Jung's seminal *Psychology of the Unconscious*. He has discovered the most significant of twentieth-century sciences.

Through reading Jung's earliest writings, Jack is beginning to examine his own life, a story far more dramatic than any of his fifty books which line a shelf in his study. At last, he is studying his addictions and terrors. It is too late for denial.

'Personality is too vague for any of our vague personalities to grasp,' he once believed. 'There are seeming men with the personalities of women. There are plural personalities. There are two-legged human creatures that are neither fish, flesh, nor fowl. We, as personalities, float like fog-wisps through glooms and darknesses and light-flashings. It is all fog and mist, and we are all foggy and misty in the thick of the mystery.'

Now the mists are being blown away. Slowly, Jack is turning his back on the beliefs of his youth, the mistaken philosophies that have damned his life. How naive of him to have thought that knowledge of the external world is all that counts, that the soul is not to be trusted . . .

Time to write. Time to begin his daily therapy. For twenty years his routine has never altered. Every day a thousand words before lunch, without fail, whether caught in a gale rounding Cape Horn, waiting for cannibals to attack, or lying hungover in bed in an expensive hotel in New York.

Jack picks up a blunt pencil, lights another filterless Russian Imperiale cigarette, one of sixty he smokes a day, and begins to scribble on the envelopes of several letters from his readers. He still receives hundreds each week, many from aspiring writers. He has rarely refused them advice, and still takes great pleasure in helping young men achieve success.

'I assure you, in reply to your question,' he writes, 'that after having come through all of the game of life, and of youth, at my present mature age of thirty-nine years I am firmly and solemnly convinced that the game is worth the candle. I have had a very fortunate life, I have been luckier than many hundreds of millions of men in my generation have been lucky, and, while I have suffered much, I have lived much, seen much, and felt much that has been denied to the average man. Yes, indeed, the game is worth the candle. As a proof of it, my friends all tell me I am getting stout. That, in itself, is the advertisement of spiritual victory.'

Here in Hawaii, Jack feels distant from his past. The cobalt waters seem to wash much of it away. Yet when he turns his eyes to the shade, he still sees images he can never erase: of the frozen Arctic wastes, heavy with the 'white silence', where wolves had called his name; of gold nuggets glinting in the half-light; of great fires and storms that destroyed his dreams; of smoke-filled halls and red-flag-waving crowds; of fist-fights in dockside bars and midnight hours spent with twittering Oriental whores.

This afternoon, after he completes his thousand words, perhaps he will play high-stakes poker with the entrepreneurs who have turned Hawaii into a tourist destination for the rich. He used to threaten to string such men up in the streets. Once, he agreed with Karl Marx: 'Accumulation of wealth ... is at the same time accumulation of misery, agony of toil, slavery, ignorance, brutality, mental degradation ...'

The sun is unbearably hot. It has wrapped the snow-capped volcanoes in haze. Jack wants to spend this afternoon doing more than lounging in a hammock under a palm tree or marvelling at the genius of Charlie Chaplin in a muggy movie theatre. He aches to feel the soothing, milky waters, to surrender himself to the Pacific, the ocean he tried to master in his youth.

His wife looks concerned. In the distance she sees the heavy surf, yet she follows her husband into the water and towards the 'smoking curlers', her forty-five-year-old body still that of a woman ten years younger, supple and slim as ever in her clinging wool bathing suit. Beyond the shallows, through thick wracks of seaweed they crawl, the crashing of the waves on the reef growing louder at every stroke.

'Keep flat, keep flat,' Jack commands as the breakers tower above them.

They swim on, past the surf into the calmer, deeper waters, below them strange marine life, coral all the colours of the rainbow. For half an hour they idle in the cobalt-blue ocean. Then Jack begins to sink. His ambition has outreached his strength yet again. He grabs at her, as a drowning man might grab at a piece of flotsam in an empty ocean. She goes under, swallows water, loses her swimming-cap, and then surfaces, blinded by her red hair, gasping for air.

'Relax,' she soothes. 'Make yourself slack – slack in your mind; and your body will slack. Yield. Remember how you taught me to yield to the undertow.'

Mercifully, men on surfboards suddenly appear from behind a wave. In an instant, it seems, they lay Jack on a board, massage his cramped muscles, and then his wife ferries him to the shore.

For a few hours, he manages to hide his humiliation from her. 'You're so little,' he finally says. 'So frail, little white woman.'

Jack takes hold of her arm. 'Look at that arm, with its delicate bones,' he smiles proudly. 'I could snap it like a clay pipe-stem, and yet your arms never failed in the sea today.'

He points to his head. 'That's where it comes from,' he says. 'That's where it resides – that's what makes the trivial flesh and bone able to do what it does.'

As the sun begins to set, Jack retires for cocktails. There is a long night ahead, and he must fortify himself well in advance. Three years ago he wrote a book, *John Barleycorn*, which he called his 'alcoholic memoirs'. To the last page he catalogued a life of heavy drinking and then denied that he was an alcoholic.

But look at him now – feeling like a saint because only a couple of glasses get him jingled. Because his kidneys no longer process the alcohol.

'Sometimes I think I'm saturated with alcohol, so that my membranes have begun to rebel,' he says. 'See! How little in the glass, and this is my first drink today.'

At dinner, against doctors' orders, he gorges on raw aku, a Pacific fish. Like a ravenous wolf, he adores barely cooked meat: roast duck, lamb chops, tuna steaks. Any still-bloody flesh will do. His favourite midnight snack used to be a 'cannibal sandwich': raw beef chopped fine with small onions.

He has always had a great appetite, and can remember writing to his first girlfriend about the hunger he felt as a boy. He was so starved for meat, he claimed, that he stole from lunchboxes at school: 'Great God, when those youngsters threw chunks of meat on the ground

because of surfeit, I could have dragged it from the dirt and eaten it
. . . This meat incident is an epitome of my whole life . . . Hungry!
Hungry! Hungry! From the time I stole meat and knew no call above
my belly, to now when the call is higher, it has been hunger, nothing
but hunger.'

Jack swallows another chunk of raw fish and begins to rave about
Psychology of the Unconscious. His wife listens patiently. She has learned
that she must stand by 'night and day, for his instant need'. For the
next few hours, until he burns himself out, she struggles to get a word
in edgeways. He is argumentative, and often pushes a point too far
before exploding with resentment. Soon, she knows from experience,
he will become less bullish, and will begin to rant about his current
pet hate: East Coast socialists, the bleeding-heart liberals wearing their
social conscience on their starched sleeves, whose beliefs now taste
like ashes in his mouth.

A few weeks ago, after a decade as America's highest-profile revolutionary, Jack resigned from the Socialist Party in disgust. His brothers
wouldn't support his call for America to go to war against the Kaiser.
They had no guts. Now they accuse him of betrayal, of going soft.
He has become, they sneer, one of the fat capitalists he once despised.

'Radical!' Jack snorts, lurching about in his chair. 'Next time I go
to New York, I'm going to live right down in the camp of these
people who call themselves radicals. I'm going to tell them a few
things, and make their radicalism look like thirty cents in a fog! I'll
show them what radicalism is!'

They think he's finished. The critics write him off as a hack, a
tragic sell-out, the author of a couple of brutal stories about dogs.

'Just wait!' he cries. 'Wait until I've got everything going ahead
smoothly, and don't have to consider the wherewithal any more. Then
I'm going to write some real books!'

A few drinks later, Jack changes tack again. He loosens his black
tie and unbuttons his white silk shirt.

'My mistake was opening the books,' he almost whispers. 'Sometimes, I wish I had never opened the books.'

His wife smiles. One day, she has already resolved, she will tell the
world about her husband. His has been the story of 'a princely ego
that struggled for full expression, and realised it only in a small degree'.

It is now pitch black. Late at night, Jack often becomes maudlin and sentimental.

'You are the only one in the world who could live with me,' he says. 'Bear with me. Please. You're all I've got.'

'I will,' she soothes. 'I will.'

After dinner, at 10.30, Jack retires to his sleeping-porch fronting the ocean. He and his wife have slept apart for several years because of her nightly battles with insomnia.

Until 2 a.m., as every night, he reads his mail. Then the quest for a few hours' peace begins in earnest. To help him through the night he consults his medicine chest, the most important object in his life. It contains an array of pain-killers: strychnine, strontium sulphate, aconite, belladonna, morphine, and that sweetest of all escapes – opium.

'Oh, have no fear, my dear,' he reassures his wife whenever he reaches for his stash of narcotics. 'I'll never go that way. I want to live a hundred years.'

Jack is now his own anaesthetist. He prescribes himself enough to stop the pain, just as he used to down bottles of whiskey.

He takes out a silver hypodermic needle and with practised precision mixes the correct amounts of pain-killers, then pulls back the plunger. The skin breaks clean – a good vein. The drugs begin to work, jolting his heart and bladder muscles and making him drowsy at last.

2

The Cruel Seas

Once a sailor, always a sailor. The savour of the salt never goes away. The sailor never grows so old that he does not care to go back for one more wrestling bout with wind and wave.

JACK LONDON, quoted in *The Book of Jack London*

JACK CLUNG TO SLEEP, 'fighting for its oblivion as the dreamer fights for his dream'. He made feeble swipes at the air; they were intended for his mother, Flora, but she avoided them as she shook him by the shoulder.

'Lemme 'lone!'

Jack's cry began, 'muffled, in the deeps of sleep, that swiftly rushed upward, like a wail, into passionate belligerence, and that died away and sank down into an inarticulate whine. It was a bestial cry, as of a soul in torment, filled with infinite protest and pain.'

Flora remained unmoved. She was a sad-eyed woman, less than five feet tall, and too tired to chivvy her fourteen-year-old son into waking up. She got a grip on the bedclothes and tried to strip them down, but Jack still clung to them desperately.

'All right,' he finally mumbled.

Flora grabbed the lamp and left the room, leaving him in darkness.

'You'll be docked,' she called back to him.

Jack shivered and then dressed, groped his way to the kitchen sink and splashed himself with ice-cold water. For a few minutes he sat at the kitchen table, wolfed down some stale bread and sipped the dirty brown liquid his mother called coffee.

Emerging into the cold morning, the stars still shining above him,

Jack jogged to another day's work in Hickmott's Cannery in Oakland, across the bay from San Francisco. For the next twelve hours he counted cans and watched the clock, trapped in a stench of gutted salmon and cod roe. Beside him at the production line other children buckled down and accepted their fate, resigned to a future of mind-numbing labour. Older men appeared even more imprisoned. Only death would release them from wage-slavery.

'My wages were small, but I worked such long hours that I sometimes made as high as fifty dollars a month,' Jack would later recall. 'Duty – I turned every cent over. Duty – I have worked in that hell hole for thirty-six straight hours, at a machine, and I was only a child. I remember how I was trying to save the money to buy a skiff – eight dollars. All that summer I saved and scraped. In the fall I had five dollars as a result of absolutely doing without all pleasure. My mother came to the machine where I worked and asked for it. I could have killed myself that night.'

All his life, Jack would nurture a deep resentment of his mother. She had not been born into poverty. She had not been forced into child labour. She had grown up the youngest child in a wealthy household in Massillon, Ohio, and had been pampered by her father, Marshall Wellman, a wheat merchant. But then tragedy hit hard – she was 'stricken with typhoid fever which not only ruined her looks and damaged her eyesight but stunted her growth'. She lost her hair and would wear a wig for the rest of her life, as well as a size twelve child's shoe.

The fever caused bouts of depression and left her permanently unhinged: always, she ranted about the racial purity of her ancestors. She raised Jack with the belief that 'dark-skinned races are not to be trusted'. He will never be able to shake this monkey off his back. All his life, he will believe, like most of his generation, that the Anglo-Saxon is the superior breed.

When she was about twenty-five, Flora left home. After a brief stay in Seattle she moved to San Francisco, then a boom town where rich gold prospectors and railroad magnates were beginning to erect an imperial city which would, in just a few years, boast some of the most lavish mansions and most beautiful civic architecture in all America. In the 1870s the city attracted tens of thousands of immigrants, for

whom it promised a new beginning on the cusp of the Pacific. By
the time Flora arrived, San Francisco was already the most cultivated
metropolis west of the Rockies, with a thriving social scene and a
growing artistic community.

At first, Flora gave piano lessons to support herself. In 1874 she
moved in with a man named William Chaney, an itinerant astrologer
who encouraged her fascination with spiritualism. Together, Flora and
Chaney ran an 'astrology parlour'. Smart hostesses dared not even hire
a housekeeper without first consulting spiritualists such as Flora who,
for a price, acted as a primitive psychotherapist, offering to communi-
cate with the dead and to send messages to former loved ones.

But fleecing the superstitious did not pay the rent. William Chaney,
who liked to call himself 'The Professor', had a day job with *Common
Sense* magazine, which advertised itself as the only 'free thought' magazine west of the Rockies. On the side he gave private readings in
horoscopes, dashed off articles, and delivered sociological lectures for
a group called the Philomathean Society. He was irrevocably convinced
that astrology was a science, not quackery, and that it could, for
example, help a man and woman produce a 'biologically superior child'.

On 12 January 1876, Flora produced such a child, a small boy whom
she named John. Pregnancy had shattered her hopes of striking it
rich. Now she was saddled with an unwanted child – her 'badge of
shame'. The birth itself had almost killed her. She was left so weakened
by it that a local doctor recommended a wet-nurse, a local black
woman, Virginia Prentiss, known as 'Mammie Jennie', who had just
lost her own baby in childbirth. Baby John was taken to Mrs Prentiss's
home where, for eight months, he was suckled and cared for as if he
were her own child.

Meanwhile, William Chaney deserted Flora. A few months after
Jack's birth, she met and quickly married a middle-aged Civil War
veteran, John London, a widower who had recently arrived from the
midwest with two young daughters, Eliza and Ida. They made their
first home in a cramped apartment on Folsom Street, in a relatively
safe and well-to-do neighbourhood of San Francisco.

When Jack, now known as John London, was finally returned to his
family in late 1876, it was his stepsister Eliza, not Flora, who took on the
duties of a mother. Eliza would continue to act as a surrogate mother

for the rest of Jack's life, and would become the one woman he would trust and love more than any other. It was Eliza, not Flora, who read to him at bedtime. When he cut his forehead Eliza, not Flora, 'calmly treated the wound by smearing it with a mixture of cobweb and tar'.

John London the elder was just as kind, caring for Jack as if he were his own son; and indeed Jack believed that he *was* John's son. But his health was so impaired – he had lost a lung during the war – that he had difficulty finding work to support his new family. He was also incapable of standing up to Flora, whose restlessness and mood swings would blight Jack's childhood and the remaining years of her husband's life.

Jack was her only child, yet, he later claimed, she showed him no affection. He would tell of being frightened by the séances she held in which she dealt with a medium called Plume, an Indian chief. He would never forgive her for making John London beat him, nor would he ever forget her hysterical breakdowns, her feigned heart attacks and her temper tantrums.

When Jack and Eliza came down with diphtheria, the family doctor recommended that the Londons move out of San Francisco, and so John London moved his family across San Francisco Bay to Oakland, a small community which was beginning to flourish due to its growing reputation as the pre-eminent railroad terminus in California and because it skirted a natural harbour.

Though San Francisco was only thirty minutes from Oakland by steam-ferry, the cities seemed far more distant from each other. While San Francisco was seen as a decadent city of *nouveau riche* excess and civic corruption, Oakland was a gritty, no-nonsense town built on true pioneer values of hard work and honesty. It had begun as a logging town, and soon became a centre where the vast natural resources of northern California – particularly its enormous redwood trees – could be exploited and then exported by rail and sea to the rest of America and the world. In Jack's childhood it was a settlement of clapboard houses surrounded by poppy fields and meadows teeming with wildlife. Because it nestled alongside San Francisco Bay, the local diet was rich in seafood and wildfowl.

John London acquired a couple of acres and started a market garden. Within months, his produce was known as the finest in the region.

But then the family fortunes began to change. Flora urged John to move to a small farm in San Mateo County, south of San Francisco. On 12 January 1883 he reluctantly piled his family's belongings onto a cart, tied a lone cow behind, and moved on to a new life. At first, his success as a smallholder continued. With the profits from his San Mateo farm, he bought an eighty-seven-acre ranch in nearby Livermore, to the east of Oakland. Once again, Flora was behind the move.

While John planted olive trees and vineyards, Jack settled into the life of a hard-working farm-boy. With his dog, Rollo, as his only friend, he would wander the desolate surrounding countryside, hunting with his stepfather for duck. Aged five, Jack swallowed some ale which he was taking to John as he laboured in the fields, and became dreadfully ill. Two years later, he was given red wine at an Italian wedding. Again, he became delirious with the alcohol. 'I was a sick child,' he later recalled, 'and despite the terrible strain on my heart and tissues, I continually relapsed into the madness of delirium. All the contents of the terrible and horrible in my child's mind spilled out . . . All the inconceivable filth a child running at large in a primitive countryside may hear men utter was mine . . . My brain was seared for ever by that experience. Writing now, thirty years afterwards, every vision is as distinct, as sharp-cut, every pain as vital and terrible.'

Though the Livermore ranch was a success, Flora was still not satisfied. Having grown up in a wealthy family, she would not be content until her circumstances matched those of her childhood. On a whim, she offered to board Captain J.H. Shepard, a widowed Civil War veteran like her husband. He had three children.

Eliza, already a full-time mother to Jack, now took on responsibility for Shepard's brood. Though he was old enough to be her father, Shepard seemed a romantic figure to Eliza, who was by now sixteen and who had spent all her life in drudgery, caring for others. In 1884 they eloped and moved back to Oakland. Eight-year-old Jack was devastated. Losing Eliza felt like losing a mother.

A few months later, an epidemic wiped out John London's chicken coops. One misfortune followed another as John struggled to pay the interest on the farm's mortgage. The potato wagon was once again loaded and John took his family back to Oakland, his hopes of establishing a profitable farm dashed forever.

Jack was delighted by the move. The new family cottage was only a couple of blocks from Eliza's house and also within walking distance of Mammie Jennie, his old wet-nurse, who still treated him as her own son, providing the affection denied by his mother. In the neighbouring streets he learned how to defend himself from local bullies on his way home from the Garfield Elementary School. He was not a strong fighter, but even though he looked more like a cherub than a wiry brawler, he had soon earned a reputation among the local gangs, as a cunning fighter best left alone.

The family fortunes continued to deteriorate. When a scheme to house Scottish girls who worked in the local cotton mills fell through, the Londons lost their home and were forced to move to the least desirable part of town: West Oakland, a poverty-stricken community of immigrant Italians and brutally exploited Chinese. Flora was soon so preoccupied with her life's obsession – spiritualism – that she continued to overlook Jack's hunger for her love.

In 1890, aged fourteen, Jack graduated from Cole Grammar School in West Oakland. Because his family could not afford to put him through high school, Jack was sent to work at Hickmott's, the local canning factory.

There had been no attempt to outlaw child labour in California, nor was there health and safety legislation, nor any limits on hours worked. Jack and his peers were at the mercy of ruthless employers. Fortunately, Jack's physique was more than equal to the hard labour as a result of his years ranging the marshes and rugged coastline in the San Francisco Bay area. His muscles had grown lean and strong as he learned to fish, hunt and trap. He had also become skilled in sailing small boats, and often took great risks in trying to beat larger yachts in races across the bay. He had, however, developed his physical strength on his own. His had been a lonely childhood, with books as his companions and the local library in Oakland as his sole sanctuary. Jack would always worship its librarian, Ina Coolbrith, the first person of culture to enter his life. She had been a loyal friend to the writers Mark Twain and Bret Harte, and had helped found the *Overland Monthly* magazine, which had published Twain himself and several of California's best writers, including John Muir, Bret Harte and Joaquin Miller.

Later to become California's first Poet Laureate, Ina Coolbrith quickly warmed to Jack. He read everything she recommended: dime novels about Viking heroes and blonde goddesses; Horatio Alger's rags-to-riches stories; *The African Adventures of Paul du Chaillu*, which would remain at his bedside even in his dying days; and Washington Irving's novel *Alhambra*, with its images of a vast Moorish palace. All of these books opened up his mind to a world beyond Oakland.

The more jars Jack stuffed with pickles at Hickmott's Cannery, the more he hungered for escape, for a life of excitement and adventure – for a world he knew existed because he had read about it. He began to fear that his mind was becoming as numb as those of his workmates, and he sensed that his ambition and wanderlust were dying.

As Jack would write in his most autobiographical short story, 'The Apostate', there was no pleasure in his life. 'The procession of the days he never saw. The nights he slept away in a twitching consciousness. The rest of the time he worked, and his consciousness was machine consciousness. Outside this his mind was a blank.'

To escape his fate, at least for a few hours, Jack got drunk. In saloons along the Oakland and San Francisco waterfronts, which he had first visited when John London worked briefly as a special constable, he was treated like a prince if he bought a round of whiskey. His fellow drinkers did not sneer at his shabby appearance and his pittance of an income from the cannery. With a few shots settled in his stomach, Jack felt less at odds with his environment, and his sense of isolation melted away. 'In the saloons life was different,' he would later write in a confessional novel, *John Barleycorn*, his account of his lifelong association with alcohol. 'Men talked with great voices, laughed great laughs and there was an atmosphere of greatness.'

While several biographers were to claim that Jack's 'alcoholic memoirs' were exaggerated, he insisted that in fact he had toned down the full extent of his debauches in the book, for fear of repelling editors and readers. Alcohol closed the divide between his sensitive side, that of the bookish, shy boy, and the man he thought he should be. It seared its way into his brain, 'melting his shyness, talking through him and with him and as him, his adopted twin brother and alter ego'.

After stumbling along Oakland's wharves, sailors from every port in the world gathered in Jack's favourite bar, Johnny Heinold's First and Last Chance Saloon. Among the spittle and sawdust, Jack sat in rapture and listened to the tales of whalers, sealers, harpooners, every one an expert in killing. These were true men, not factory fodder, who had lived 'big' and who recounted their adventures with wry smiles, one hand grasping a bottle, the other caressing the stem of a whalebone pipe. Not one of them would have settled for a life filling cans, chained to a production line.

Jack heard about certain occupations open to young men with ambition, and about oyster pirates who stole from private beds and sold their booty for enormous profits. In one bar he discovered that one of the pirates, 'French Frank', was willing to sell a sloop, the *Razzle Dazzle*, for just $300.

Jack furiously set about trying to raise money to buy his escape. Finally, he turned in desperation to Mammie Jennie, now working as a nurse. According to him, she handed her 'white child' the $300, he dashed to meet French Frank in the First and Last Chance Saloon, handed over the glinting $20 gold pieces, and closed the deal with a swift whiskey before sprinting to the dock where he found a group of 'wharf-rats' sitting on the *Razzle Dazzle*'s deck around a jug of wine. Among them were two sisters, Mamie and Tess, and two oyster pirates, 'Whiskey Bob' and 'Spider Healey'.

Mamie was known as 'the queen of the oyster pirates'. A pretty waif, she went with the boat, providing 'comfort' to its skipper. And, sure enough, on his first day as captain, she took Jack on deck, while the others swigged their wine, and made love to him.

There were other rites of passage to be undergone. To become a man among men, Jack was forced to prove his masculinity not only through getting laid, but also by brawling, drinking and standing up to any tough who threatened him. On one occasion French Frank tried to run down the *Razzle Dazzle* in his schooner, so jealous had he become of Jack's conquest of Mamie. Never one to turn and run, Jack stood defiantly on deck, steering with his feet, a double-barrelled shotgun cocked in his hands, and forced French Frank to give way.

Jack's recollections of his days as an oyster-pirate, recounted twenty years later in *John Barleycorn*, were perhaps clouded by a desire to romanticise his youth. He was also inclined to exaggerate the poverty

of his childhood – one contemporary, Frank Atherton, insisted that
Flora in fact cooked steaks for the family's dinner.

The morning after an oyster raid, saloon-keepers and hoteliers
bartered for the finest pickings. One night's work brought Jack at
least $25 – far more than he would have earned in a month at Hick-
mott's Cannery. He was soon able to repay Mammie Jennie her
investment with interest. And his mother received more money from
him than ever.

Jack was now the family's sole breadwinner. John London had
suffered from weak lungs since returning from the Civil War, and his
health was failing rapidly. Shortly before Jack had begun work at
Hickmott's, John had been badly injured in an accident in the Oakland
railroad yards. Now any kind of physical labour was beyond him.

Although Jack believed his means of supporting his family was 'raw
and naked, wild and free', at times he felt the need to escape it. The
countless dollars he blew at the bar didn't give him half as much
pleasure, he said, as a night with his books. What he enjoyed most
was escaping to his candle-lit cabin where he could be alone with
Flaubert's *Madame Bovary*, Kipling's *The Light That Failed* and Melville's *Typee*.

The reality of Jack's new profession was that death always stalked
close by. Every night, he had to navigate without lights, his oarlocks
muffled in case he alerted armed guards protecting the oyster beds.
Often, his only guidance was gunfire lighting up the sky. Life was
even cheaper on San Francisco's Barbary Coast and Oakland's estuary,
where Jack spent afternoons drinking before the night's adventure,
and where his new associates thought nothing of stabbing a man in
the back for a sack of rotting shellfish. The area was so violent that
the police patrolled in pairs, armed to the teeth, their preferred weapon
a knife more than a foot long with which they sometimes severed the
hands of assailants.

Few places in America were as brutalising. Indeed, some parts of
San Francisco and Oakland, even at the close of the nineteenth century, still deserved to be called the Wild West. Only three decades
before Jack's birth, the city beside the bay had been a small settlement
of a few hundred hardy inhabitants. Then, in 1849, gold was found
in the nearby hills. From across America and beyond came hordes

of prospectors, cowboys, desperadoes all. Within a year of the gold rush, the boom town's population mushroomed into the tens of thousands.

By the mid-1850s very little of the city's wealth 'remained in the hands of the men who had dug it from the earth'. Almost all of it had been consumed by the Barbary Coast; or rather by the unscrupulous owners of the bars, brothels and casinos to which the area was dedicated.

Until 1917, when its brothels and most of its bars were shut down by God-fearing politicians, the Barbary Coast remained the most depraved dockside in America, if not the world. In Jack's youth, it enjoyed a golden age. Chinese gangs and exotic whores crammed the alleyways; syphilitic 'hostesses' opened doors to the most infamous bars and casinos in the west. Greenbacks bought any perversion imaginable. Murder was commonplace, as were vicious press-gangs.

In this environment, Jack was fortunate to survive. Several of his colleagues were killed in fights along the waterfront. Others were arrested and sent to the infamous San Quentin Prison. In *John Barleycorn*, Jack recounted how he himself was once knocked unconscious for seventeen hours in a fight.

His three months as an oyster pirate ended, Jack later claimed, when a fellow hoodlum, 'Scotty', tipped over a lantern and set the mainmast of the *Razzle Dazzle* ablaze. Jack joined forces with another wharfside youth, 'Scratch Nelson', and went sailing for a couple of weeks around San Francisco Bay. But he was still caught between two fates: either he remain a criminal or he return to wage-slavery. Unable to contemplate going back to a factory, he tried his hand at salmon fishing for a week. Then, without qualms, he decided to switch sides. Accepting a job with the local Fish Patrol, Jack would now pursue his former associates.

In the 1880s, San Francisco Bay was infested with Chinese shrimp raiders and Greek salmon thieves. The Fish Patrol's objective was to catch these rogue fishermen and impose stiff penalties. Jack would receive half the fines collected from those he captured. In his 1902 book *Tales of the Fish Patrol*, he was to portray himself as a swashbuckling youth who fought off marauding Chinamen and proved himself far more courageous than his fellow officers. As in *John Barleycorn*, the adventures he recounted were without doubt reworked for an audience of young readers. On the flyleaf of one copy of *Tales of the Fish Patrol* he would write: 'Find here, sometimes hinted, sometimes told, and sometimes made different, the days of my boyhood.'

He quickly discovered that his new colleagues drank even more than the oyster pirates did. One night, after a particularly long binge, Jack staggered onto a sloop at the end of a wharf to sleep it off. He lost his footing, fell overboard into the lethal Carquinez Straits at the northern end of the bay, and was swept away by the current.

Coughing and spluttering, the tang of salt water sobering him, he decided not to fight the pull of the tide, and so he drifted further and deeper into the bay. The gaslights of San Francisco flickered in the distance. The stars shone brighter, more clearly than he had ever noticed before. Some 'maundering fancy' of going out with the tide suddenly obsessed him. He had never been morbid. Thoughts of suicide, he wrote, had never entered his head. But now he thought it 'fine, a splendid culmination, a perfect rounding off of his short but exciting career'.

Just as rapidly as it deserted him, Jack's will to live returned. But now, as he tried to swim to safety, the ice-cold water began to cramp his muscles. About to sink for good, he was hauled to safety by a Greek fisherman who took him back to his hut, wrapped him in blankets and poured steaming soup down his throat.

Sobered by this experience, Jack realised he wanted more from life than an endless round of theft, brawling and drinking. His hunger for experience was now so great that any escape route from Oakland, no matter how dangerous, would do. Sailing one day up the Sacramento River, he came across a group of boys swimming naked. Instantly he hitched himself to the gang of homeless youths, and for a couple of weeks he learned the ways and means of young hobos. By 'riding the rods' – jumping from one train to another – he beat his way across the Sierra Nevada, the mountain range that had protected California for so long from pioneers.

The adventure was short-lived. Having earned the moniker 'Sailor Kid', Jack returned to Oakland as soon as he began to go hungry, and joined one of the many waterfront gangs that preyed on Chinese immigrants. Again he fell into a life of binge drinking and gang activity. Local barmen now gave him a year to live before he fatally overdosed on their cheap booze.

They were almost right. Late in 1892, Jack had possibly his worst experience with alcohol. One afternoon he and Scratch Nelson learned that local politicians were buying votes with free booze. Extra bar-keepers couldn't keep up with the demand, and within hours Jack had drunk himself into oblivion. His head reeled, his heart pounded, his lungs gasped for air. Finally he was carried semi-conscious to a train bound for Oakland. 'I often think that was the nearest to death I have ever been. I was scorching up, burning alive internally, in an agony of fire and suffocation, and I wanted air – I madly wanted air. My efforts to raise the window were vain, for all the windows in the car were screwed down. Nelson had seen drink-crazed men, and thought I wanted to throw myself out. He tried to restrain me, but I fought on. I seized some man's torch and smashed the glass.'

The sound of breaking glass sparked a frenzied fist-fight. Jack was the first to be knocked unconscious. 'Heavens! That was twenty years ago and I am still very much and wisely alive; and I have seen much, done much, lived much, in the intervening score of years; and I shudder when I think how close a shave I ran, how near I was to missing that splendid fifth of a century that has been mine since.'

Truly sobered, Jack considered his options. His way of life would have to change. 'It made toward death too quickly to suit my youth and vitality,' he would later explain. 'And there was only one way out of this hazardous manner of living and that was to get out.' By coincidence, a sealing-fleet was wintering in San Francisco Bay. In one saloon Jack met a seal-hunter, Pete Holt, and after several drinks he agreed to be his boat-puller and to sign on any schooner he signed on.

'Rolling and climbing the moving valleys', the *Sophie Sutherland* fought her way farther and farther into the heart of the Pacific. As he later described it in *The Sea Wolf*, Jack could hear the wind whining. It came to his ears as a muffled roar. Now and again feet stamped above his head. An endless creaking was going on about him, 'the woodwork and the fittings groaning and squeaking and complaining in a thousand keys'.

The *Sophie Sutherland* was one of the last sealers to leave San

Francisco Bay, and was now headed for the Bering Sea and ninety days of harpooning. The boat's forecastle, into which Jack dropped his hold-all eight days after his seventeenth birthday, was lined on either side by bunks; on the walls hung oilskins, sea boots, and lanterns. When none of his fellow crew was watching, Jack stowed his most valuable belongings: books by Flaubert and Melville and a copy of *Anna Karenina*. He then rushed on deck to wave San Francisco goodbye.

As the *Sophie Sutherland* ploughed through the Golden Gate Strait, Jack's spirits soared. At last he was headed for the strange and exotic lands he had read about, over and over, in *Moby-Dick*. He was a man among men. Life had begun.

To sign on as an able-bodied seaman, Jack needed to be nineteen or to have three years' experience. He had neither qualification, but such was his reputation along the waterfront that an exception had been made for 'young Johnnie'. By contrast, his new shipmates were old hands to a man, mostly callused Scandinavians who had spent years before the mast. In their eyes, Jack was an impostor, a callow boy pretending to be a sailor.

Jack quickly realised he would have to prove himself at least their equal if the nine-month voyage were not to become an insufferable ordeal. From the first day at sea, he was careful to pull his weight so his shipmates would not resent his presence. Early in the voyage he discovered that he would also have to resort to violence if he was not going to be abused by the older men. One day, as he sat on his bunk weaving a mat of rope-yarn, a bullying Swedish sailor swore at him. Jack answered back. The older sailor dropped the coffee-pot he was carrying and made to slap Jack for his insolence. Before he could land a blow, Jack smacked him right between the eyes. Choking with rage, the Swede lunged again at Jack, this time with a 'sledge-hammer fist', but again Jack managed to dodge aside. A split-second later, he vaulted onto the sailor's back. His fingers were soon clamped around the Swede's windpipe. He'd rip it out, he screamed, if the sailor didn't back off.

The Swede 'bellowed and charged like a mad bull, and with every frenzied jump, his head knocked against the deck beams'. A lamp fell to the floor; the rest of the crew jumped out of their bunks and gathered round. Jack looked as if he was being throttled to death. His eyes bulged, his face streamed blood, yet he continued to dig his fingers deeper into the Swede's throat.

'Will you promise to let me alone? Eh? Will you?' Jack screamed.

The Swede, by now purple in the face, 'gurgled an assent', and when Jack's 'vise-like grip on his throat lessened, reeled and stumbled to his knees like a felled bullock. The sailors, jamming their way through a wild clutter of food and broken dishes, crowded around the jubilant hero of the hour with friendly offers of assistance and a noticeable increase of respect.'

When he wasn't swinging his fists, Jack buried his head in his books, keeping the oil lamp burning through the night, and learning how Flaubert's Madame Bovary had mythologised her childhood to find social acceptance. When a whining cockney – 'the Bricklayer' – died during a storm and was dropped overboard, Jack commandeered the dead man's bunk, despite the superstition of his shipmates. The bunk was better lit than his former berth, but for years he would be haunted by the memory of the Bricklayer's corpse bobbing in the *Sophie Sutherland*'s wake.

Several weeks into the voyage, Jack's turn came to take the wheel. Could a seventeen-year-old greenhorn handle the eighty-ton schooner in high seas? After watching him for a few minutes, the captain nodded and went below. Jack was left alone, the gale whipping his salted, bleached hair into his eyes. For an hour, he kept the ship on course: 'In my grasp the wildly careering schooner and the lives of twenty-two men . . . With my own hands I had done my trick at the wheel and guided a hundred tons of wood and iron through a few million tons of wind and waves . . . When I have done some such thing, I am exalted. I glow all over. I am aware of a pride in myself that is mine, and mine alone. It is organic. Every fibre of me is thrilling with it. It is very natural. It is a mere matter of satisfaction at adjustment to environment. It is success.'

Fifty-one days into the voyage, the *Sophie Sutherland* neared the Bonin Islands south-east of Japan. As they came into view, it was as if a scene from Melville's *Typee* or Stevenson's *Treasure Island* had come to life. Jagged volcanoes skirted by jungle greeted Jack, and as the *Sophie Sutherland* crossed the reefs, native canoes and

Japanese sampans surrounded her. 'It was my first foreign land; I had won to the other side of the world, and I would see all I had read in the books come true,' Jack later recalled. 'I was wild to get ashore.'

He was also gasping for a drink. With Victor, a Swedish sailor, and Axel, a Norwegian, he had planned his shore leave. First they would toast their arrival in paradise, then they would explore it. Leaving their boat on a white beach of coral sand, they walked under the coconut palms and into town. To their amazement, they found several hundred 'riotous seamen from all the world, drinking pro-digiously, singing prodigiously, dancing prodigiously – and all on the main street to the scandal of a helpless handful of Japanese police'. They had stumbled across other crews who had put in to port with the same intentions as their own.

Jack and Axel wandered from drink to drink before separating, and then Jack drifted alone 'downing more drinks, getting hazier and hazier'. He sat in a circle with 'Japanese fishermen, kanaka boat-steerers from our own vessels', and with 'due and proper and most intricate Japanese ceremonial' drank 'sake, pale, mild, and lukewarm, from tiny porcelain bowls'.

He would always remember his first sight of 'runaway apprentices – boys of eighteen and twenty, of middle class English families, who had jumped their ships and apprenticeships in various ports of the world and drifted into the forecastles of the sailing schooners. They were healthy, smooth-skinned, clear-eyed, and they were young – youths like me, learning the way of their feet in the world of men. And they were men. No mild sake for them, but square-faces illicitly refilled with corrosive fire that flamed through their veins and burst into conflagrations in their heads.'

Jack eventually staggered back to the *Sophie Sutherland*, now bound for northern waters. Three weeks later he caught sight of his first seal herd as it barked its way to the rookeries of the Bering Sea. The fun was over. For the next three months, Jack joined the daily routine of butchery. Within minutes of beginning the cull, the *Sophie Sutherland* was a floating slaughter-house, her decks 'covered with hides and bodies, slippery with fat and blood, the scuppers running red, masts, ropes, and rails splattered with sanguinary colour; and the men, like butchers plying their trade, naked and red of arm and hand, hard at work with ripping and flensing knives, removing the skins from the pretty creatures they had killed.'

For several weeks, Jack slept no more than three hours at a stretch before climbing down a flimsy rope-ladder to a small boat bobbing in the ice-floes. He would row to within a few yards of the icebergs while a harpooner took careful aim. So greatly had the value of seal fur declined on the international market that the *Sophie Sutherland* could only return to port when her holds were brimming with hides.

The *Sophie Sutherland*'s decks were a brutal place for any man who did not pull his weight and loudly revel in the slaughter. Here, in the most unpredictable waters in the northern Pacific, Jack first witnessed the lengths man will go to in killing animals for profit. The butchery seemed to make his fellow sailors as bestial as the animals they culled in the name of greed.

The long weeks at sea did, however, provide one unexpected bonus: time for self-reflection. Though Jack had fallen in with his shipmates, he now felt more detached than ever from the men of his own class as he waded through blood and blubber. He realised he was still a callow outsider, mingling without real ease with the killers around him. But he later wrote of how he quickly developed an ability to adapt to different environments. Among drinkers, he got drunk. Among sailors, he swore. This knack was essential, not to social advancement, but survival. Yet it bore a price: Jack never developed a robust sense of self, and he would enter adulthood with little self-esteem. His enthusiasms would be too easily encouraged. He would define himself in opposition to other classes and races, and be swayed too quickly by the prejudices of others.

In a letter to a lover in 1903, he wrote:

> My child life was uncongenial. There was nothing responsive around me. I learned reticence, an inner reticence. I went into the world early, and I adventured among many different classes. A newcomer in any class, I naturally was reticent concerning my real self, which such a class could not understand, while I was superficially loquacious in order to make my entry into such a class popular and successful. And so it

went, from class to class, from clique to clique. No intimacies, a continuous hardening, a superficial loquacity so clever, and an inner reticence so secret, that the one was taken for the real, the other never dreamed of.

While he was on board the *Sophie Sutherland* Jack heard of Alexander McLean, the notoriously brutal captain of another sealing ship, whom he would later portray as Wolf Larsen in his novel *The Sea Wolf.* 'McLean had a big record as a rough character,' Jack recalled, 'and was known as the worst man, so far as physical violence was concerned, among the seal hunters.' In 1906 he disappeared in a storm at sea.

In early summer 1893, the *Sophie Sutherland* headed for home with a heavy catch, docking en route at Yokohama on the east coast of Japan. Yokohama was a maze of docks and modern buildings with a population of a quarter of a million. Back on dry land, he took a rickshaw to the nearest saloon and for a fortnight repeated the excesses of the Bonin Islands. Drunk, day and night, on warm sake, he saw nothing but the inside of bars. At the end of this binge, he wrote in *John Barleycorn*, chased by port police, he dived into the harbour and swam a mile back to the *Sophie Sutherland* to escape arrest. He was apparently registered as drowned. On the voyage back to San Francisco he did almost die, of a sudden attack of the shingles.

On 26 August 1893 the *Sophie Sutherland* dropped anchor in San Francisco Bay. The voyage had lasted almost eight months. After finding his land legs, and again getting blitzed with his shipmates on the Barbary Coast, Jack crossed the bay to Oakland and home.

Flora was genuinely pleased to see him. But if he was to stay a sailor, he must ensure an effective means of getting his earnings to her. He could adventure to his heart's content, so long as he remembered his true role: as a breadwinner with dependants. He must never forget his responsibilities, whether he was breaking the law to put bread on the table or was up to his waist in blood and guts in the perilous waters of the northern Pacific.

In Jack's absence, the bay area had sunk further into depression.

Capitalism's cycle of boom and bust was wreaking havoc across America. It was impossible to find a job with even half-decent pay. Back where he had started, Jack did not avoid the fate of his peers for long.

3

On the Road

Idleness so called, which does not consist in doing nothing, but in doing a great deal not recognised by the
dogmatic formularies of the ruling class, has as good a
right to state its position as industry itself. It is admitted
that the presence of people who refuse to enter in the
great handicap race for sixpenny pieces, is at once an
insult and a disenchantment for those who do.

ROBERT LOUIS STEVENSON, *An Apology for Idlers*

DURING HIS MONTHS AT SEA Jack resolved to change his way of
life, and to become a respectable young man. On returning to Oakland
in August 1893, he discovered the fate of his former associates: his old
oyster-pirate friend Scratch Nelson had been riddled by policemen's
bullets during a drunken brawl, and many of those still alive were
stewing in San Quentin.

Jack's fascination with the waterfront was now quite dead; he no
longer cared for 'the drinking, nor the vagrancy of it'. He wandered
back to the Oakland Free Library and 'read the books with greater
understanding . . . Then, too, my mother said I had sown my wild
oats and it was time I settled down to a regular job. Also, the family
needed the money. So I got a job at the jute mills – a ten-hour day
at ten cents an hour. Despite my increase in strength and general
efficiency, I was receiving no more than when I worked in the cannery
several years before.'

Jack was again imprisoned in a noisy factory. The stench of the
cannery had been replaced by a mist of lint and an ear-piercing din.
'It was humdrum machine toil,' he later recalled. 'I wanted life. I
wanted to realise myself in other ways than at a machine for ten cents

an hour. And yet I had had my fill of saloons. I wanted something new. I was growing up.'

In an attempt to distance himself from the past, Jack joined the YMCA, seeking more wholesome company. But he failed to fit in among the 'clean-minded' boys. 'The life there was healthful and athletic, but too juvenile. For me it was too late. I was not boy, nor youth, despite my paucity of years. I had bucked big with men. I knew mysterious and violent things. I was from the other side of life so far as concerned the young men I encountered at the YMCA. I spoke another language, possessed a sadder and more terrible wisdom. (When I come to think it over, I realise, now, that I have never had a boyhood.)'

After several weeks in the jute mill, a promise of escape glimmered briefly. His mother noticed that the *San Francisco Morning Call* had announced a competition for a descriptive sketch written by a young reader, and she pushed her son to enter. As soon as Jack put pen to paper, word after word flowed from his store of mental imagery, tumbling onto the page faster than he could scribble them. By dawn he had finished four thousand words.

At just seventeen, Jack had produced a work of great vitality. He had not seen the inside of a classroom for three years, but he had read more books than his schoolmates would probably read in a lifetime. By his own reckoning, there were few novels in the Oakland Library which had not been checked out under his name.

Jack's first published sentences swelled with the rhythm of the ocean itself:

> Each mighty sea, all phosphorescent and glowing with the tiny lights of the myriad animalculae, threatened to overwhelm us with a deluge of fire. Higher and higher, thinner and thinner, the crest grew as it began to curve and overtop preparatory to breaking, until with a roar it fell over bulkwards, a mass of soft glowing light and tons of water which sent the sailors sprawling in all directions and left in each nook and cranny little specks of light that glowed and trembled till the next sea washed them away, depositing new ones in their places.

According to the *San Francisco Morning Call*, the most striking aspect of Jack's story 'Typhoon off the Coast of Japan' was 'the largeness of grasp and steady force of expression that shows the young artist'. Jack was awarded the first prize of $25, with second and third prizes going to men in their early twenties studying at the University of California and at Stanford University.

Jack's first literary success began to change his relationship with his mother. Should he succeed at writing, she would be the first to benefit. She had not forgotten her bitter disappointment on arriving in San Francisco: the city had not offered a new beginning, but had condemned her to poverty far removed from the comfort of her childhood. She longed to be accepted by San Francisco society, and to experience the glamour it had held for her as an unembittered young woman. Through her son, Flora might at least enjoy it vicariously. But for now he would have to return to the jute mill, she insisted. His wages from the *Sophie Sutherland* had not settled the family debts, and his prize from the newspaper would keep the larder stocked for a few weeks at best.

Now, on Sunday afternoons in local parks, Jack found time to discover the fairer sex, egged on by a young apprentice blacksmith, Louis Shattuck. 'Louis was handsome and graceful, and filled with love for the girls,' Jack later recalled. 'I didn't know anything about girls. I had been too busy being a man. This was an entirely new phase of existence which had escaped me. And when I saw Louis say goodbye to me, raise his hat to a girl of his acquaintance, and walk on by her side down the sidewalk, I was made excited and envious. I, too, wanted to play this game.'

His first sweetheart, he wrote in *John Barleycorn*, was called Hydee, a sixteen-year-old with soft brown eyes and a slender oval face. Jack, who was a year older, met her at a Salvation Army meeting and within weeks was kissing her nervously during strolls beneath the apple boughs in local orchards. He shared his sweets with her, and tried not to smoke in her presence, nor to betray any of the other habits he had picked up as an oyster pirate: spitting, telling dirty jokes and proving his masculinity by picking fights on the slightest pretext. For a year, he dated Hydee. Ever after, he was convinced that true love was possible at first sight.

But was Hydee flesh and blood, or a figment of Jack's imagination? As he rewrote his past, he may have invented her so as to represent a virgin figure, a romantic ideal. It is more likely that his first fixation was with one of the female 'wharf-rats' he associated with as an oyster pirate. But to mention such a liaison in his memoirs would have meant acknowledging a less palatable start to his romantic life.

Meanwhile, back at the jute mill, a promised raise to $1.25 a day did not materialise. Jack finally quit. He would learn a trade instead, as a way of avoiding unskilled labour, which could only crush his spirit. 'I believed in the old myths which were the heritage of the American boy when I was a boy. A canal boy could become president. Any boy, who took employment with any firm, could, by thrift, energy, and sobriety, learn the business and rise from position to position until he was taken in as a junior partner. After that the senior partnership was only a matter of time.'

Jack applied for work at the power plant of the Oakland, San Leandro, and Haywards Electric Railway, and was offered a job shovelling coal. He believed his new employer when he said the path was clear to 'great success', and that within a decade or two he could be one of the bosses. Though Jack later said he rejoiced in the 'dignity' of this work, it was physically demanding; since his sealing trip, he had begun to suffer from weak joints. Now he was forced to use tight straps to protect his wrists.

During a break in one shift, several weeks into the job, a co-worker pointed to a newspaper story. It was about an ex-employee, married with three children, who had killed himself because he could not find a job. To his dismay, Jack discovered that he had replaced the man. He had been doing two men's work for half the dead man's pay.

Jack threw down his shovel. He was finished with wage slavery. He would not play the bosses' game. He would never become a scab, some wretch who fills dead men's shoes. But he had chosen the worst possible time to make his own way. America, having only recently become an industrial nation, was in the throes of its first great economic depression. Unemployment had decimated the workforce in its squalid industrial cities; Wall Street had collapsed; bankruptcy had reached epidemic proportions, throwing tens of thousands of workers onto the streets in every major city.

1894 was a watershed for radical politics in America. Across the
nation there was bitter and bloody industrial unrest. In West Virginia,
at least twenty-one miners were killed in clashes with strike-breakers
and police. In Chicago, the union leader Eugene Debs began a six-
month prison term for leading a rail-workers' strike. The Populist
Party, which expressed the American working class's increasing mili-
tancy, was growing into a major political force. Even the right-wing
press talked of a coming 'nationwide insurrection'.

The state of the labour market was so grave that a man by the
name of Jacob S. Coxey, based in Masillon, Ohio – the birthplace of
Jack's mother – was organising an army of unemployed men to march
on Washington and demand that Congress issue $5 million with which
to put men to work building roads. Groups sympathetic to Coxey's
cause had formed across the United States. In Oakland, the self-styled
'General' Charles T. Kelly, a young printer, assembled a detachment
of two thousand men who would travel to Washington in box-cars
provided free of charge by railroad companies anxious to shunt them
east and thereby rid the region of potential trouble-makers.

Jack could not wait to join Kelly's army. The possibility of
again beating his way down 'the adventure path', as he later referred
to his travels in search of new drama, was too good to pass up.
Anything was better than white slavery. Now, at least, he would see
America.

Throughout his days on the road, Jack kept his first diary. By turns
lyrical and full of a sense of wonder, its eighty-three pages of notes
included thoughts about suicide, and would later form the basis of
his non-fiction book *The Road*, published in 1907.

'Every once in a while, in newspapers, magazines, and biographical
dictionaries, I run upon sketches of my life, wherein, delicately
phrased,' Jack wrote in *The Road*, 'I learn that it was in order to study
sociology that I became a tramp. This is very nice and thoughtful of
the biographers, but it is inaccurate. I became a tramp – well, because
of the life that was in me, of the wanderlust in my blood that would
not let me rest . . . I went on "The Road" because I couldn't keep
away from it; because I hadn't the price of the railroad fare in my
jeans; because I was so made that I couldn't work all my life on "one

same shift"; because – well, just because it was easier to than not to.'

By the time Jack heard of Kelly's army, it had already left Oakland for Sacramento. Desperate to catch up, he rode the rails again, clinging to the platform boards beneath the trains. It was a suicidal way to save on fares. On one occasion a spark from the engine set fire to his clothes. Frantically he tore off his coat, which was sucked in a split second beneath the clattering wheels.

After ten days of playing Russian roulette on the tracks, Jack joined a rear detachment of Kelly's army high in the Sierra Nevada mountains. Caught in a blizzard, suffering the first symptoms of exposure, he pushed his way into a cattle truck crowded with men who were 'keeping warm by telling jokes and sipping from flasks of whiskey'. To pass the hours, they also groaned about unemployment and sadistic bosses.

Around 2 a.m. on 17 April 1894, Jack caught his first glimpse of Jacob Coxey's Industrial Army. Sixteen hundred men were huddled together in a field near Reno with little protection from the pouring rain. Fatigue, hunger and a sea of mud had weakened their solidarity. It was futile to try to keep a fire burning in the downpour, and fist-fights broke out over the few blankets that could be found.

The next morning, despite torrential rain, the army set out, marching east. By now Jack was forced to beg food at back doors. He began to fall behind, hobbling along on swollen and blistered feet. At night the army set up camp in open fields and, by a blazing fire, Jack rested his feet. The talk often turned to politics, and Jack was impressed by the intelligence of his fellow marchers. Many were drifters like himself, but others had been broken, after many years in good jobs, by capitalism. Some had wit, were self-educated and articulate about society's problems. Many could quote their hero Eugene Debs: 'The issue is Socialism versus Capitalism. I am for Socialism because I am for humanity. We have been cursed with the reign of gold long enough. Money constitutes no proper basis of civilisation. The time has come to regenerate society – we are on the eve of universal change.'

For the first time, Jack began to think deeply about politics. The debates he heard at firesides made him question the faults in a system which seemed oblivious to human need. They also underlined what he had learned from bitter experience as a 'work beast'. But it was not only fireside debates which had roused his political consciousness.

Throughout his time on the road, Jack was to witness cruelty and suffering at almost every turn.

One afternoon he came across a gipsy camp. The head of the camp was a sadist who forced the children to work in the fields all day, and brought out a whip when any of them showed signs of flagging. Jack watched the brute beat a small boy. 'The whip hissed through the air, and I caught myself with a start of surprise at the severity of the blow. The thin leg was so very thin and little. The flesh showed white where the lash had curled and bitten, and then, where the white had shown, sprang up the savage welt, with here and there along its length little scarlet oozings where the skin had broken.'

When Kelly's army reached Des Moines, Iowa, it finally ground to a halt. The town could feed the two thousand men for a few days, but no longer. Councillors tried to persuade the railroads to keep the army moving but they refused. Stranded, Jack and his comrades camped in a disued stove works.

It was suggested they take to the water now that the railways were forbidden. They would float down the Des Moines River to the Mississippi and from there paddle up the Ohio to Wheeling, West Virginia, only a few hundred miles from their destination, Washington. Jack was now in his element. The army built several rafts, and he took control of one, christening it *The Pirate*. He quickly forged ahead of the other parties, and whenever he reached a town he told welcoming parties he was captain of the 'advance boat' sent ahead to reconnoitre supplies. He then took the pick of whatever was offered.

Within days, however, 'General' Kelly sent word ahead that Jack and his fellow pirates were not to be helped. Deprived of the richest pickings, Jack began to go short of food. The march had lost its magic – it was now a desperate trek to find food and water, and somehow to reach Washington. When it finally arrived on 30 April, the army would number just four hundred men. The next day, Coxey was arrested for trespassing on the Capitol's lawn as he tried to present a petition to Congress, and the army disbanded in chaos.

Jack, like many others, had meanwhile decided to desert, and headed for the nearest big city. In Chicago he visited the post office, where he hoped to find mail from his mother, who had promised to send small amounts of money to various cities along his route. To his relief, he was welcomed by a letter containing $7. He found a flea-market and bought a new pair of boots, went to the theatre, saw the sights, and slept in a bed for the first time in weeks. He then took a boat across Lake Michigan to St Joseph, where his mother's sister Mary Everhard lived with her husband and children. For several weeks he stayed with the Everhards, updated his diary and entertained the family with accounts of his recent adventures. He also met a cousin, Ernest Everhard, whose name he would later give to a hero in the most political of his novels, *The Iron Heel*.

Jack hitched rides to New York, where he roamed for a few days around the city's notorious slums. Conditions there had recently been highlighted by the campaigning journalist Jacob A. Riis in his classic study *How the Other Half Lives*. Riis's photographs revealed squalid sweatshops, ill-lit opium dens and whole families huddled in filthy rooms. The ghettos which Jack toured were crowded with an unprece-dented influx of recent immigrants. Having fled poverty and repression in Europe, and been fed, deloused and processed by the authorities on Ellis Island, the newcomers became scapegoats as well as citizens. The flood of cheap labour infuriated American trade unions, and led to violent clashes between immigrant groups. In 1893 America's 'melt-ing pot' of races was a simmering, bitter-tasting gruel.

Within days of arriving in Riis's new Sodom, Jack was again begging for food, and was spending the afternoons in a small park by City Hall. For a few cents he bought second-hand books and lounged on the grass drinking glasses of milk. One afternoon police raided the park and Jack was beaten over the head with a night-stick. The blow intensified his long-standing loathing of all authority.

Cities could never hold Jack for long. It was the countryside, the real America, which he longed to explore. From New York he jumped onto a freight train headed for Niagara Falls. Overawed by the thun-dering water, he forgot even to eat. He remained long into the evening, then climbed a fence and bedded down for the night. At five o'clock the next morning he woke and began to make his way back to the falls, but a policeman stopped him. Unable to provide proof of a local address, Jack was arrested for vagrancy and taken to Niagara Falls jail. The next morning, along with sixteen other prisoners, he stood in the dock of a local courthouse. A judge sentenced him and his fellow vagrants to thirty days' hard labour. Jack protested his innocence, rambled about his constitutional rights and was told to button his lip.

He was handcuffed, chained to a group of men and taken to the Erie County Penitentiary. There he had his head clipped and his 'budding mustache' shaved, was given convict stripes, deloused, made to 'march the lock-step, and put to work under the eyes of guards armed with Winchester rifles – all for adventuring in blond-beastly fashion'.

'On June 29, 1894,' his prison record read, 'one John London, age 18: Single: Father & Mother Living, Occupation – Sailor; Religion – Atheist; – was received at the Erie County Penitentiary, for a term of 30 Days, charge of Tramp, sentenced by Police Justice Charles Piper – Niagara Falls, New York; and was released on July 29, 1894.'

On his way to prison, Jack shared his tobacco with a man who had been locked up many times and who knew the ropes. Jack became the man's 'meat', a young inmate protected by an old hand. Within two days, Jack had been promoted to 'hall man', one of thirteen prisoners who 'dominated and exploited the other five hundred inmates'. He was now among those who 'ruled by fear, the fist, and the club'. He managed to get 'magnificently jingled' on illicit booze. He also witnessed all the horrors of the jail.

Jack was 'no spring chicken in the ways of the world and the awful abysses of human degradation', but what he saw in the Erie County Pen would stay with him for the rest of his life. The prison was 'filled with the ruck and the filth, the scum and the dregs, of society – hereditary inefficients, degenerates, wrecks, lunatics, addled intelligences, epileptics, monsters, weaklings, in short, a very nightmare of humanity'.

In the 1890s, American prisons were the most dangerous institutions any young man could expect to find himself in. There was no sense that imprisonment should be accompanied by basic human rights. Society wanted to be rid of law-breakers, and did not care about the fate of young men like Jack, suddenly at the mercy of a system ruled by unrelenting brutality. Any man deemed weaker or more effeminate than the average was gang-raped or beaten, and often killed.

Fearing for his life, Jack adapted to his new circumstances as if he had been dropped in the middle of a savage wilderness. All he wanted was for the nightmare to end with as little damage to his mind and body as possible. He had seen his first real sociopaths, and he was terrified. The prison was a microcosm of capitalism at its worst, except that the currency was not the dollar but tobacco and moonshine – a gut-rotting schnapps made from potatoes, or smuggled in by a bribed warder. Older men, protected by rampaging inmates, acted as bosses. They organised who received what food or privileges, and whether a man should be abused or 'promoted'.

Powerless to intervene, Jack watched a 'handsome young mulatto' prisoner thrown down five flights of steel stairs because he had 'stood up for his rights'. The man hit the floor near where Jack was watching. Somehow he managed to get to his feet. As he stood upright, he flung his arms wide and uttered a scream of 'terror and pain and heartbreak'. The shreds of his clothing fell from him, 'leaving him wholly naked and streaming blood from every portion of the surface of his body. Then he collapsed in a heap, unconscious. He had learned his lesson, and every convict within those walls who heard him scream had learned a lesson.'

At last the day of his release arrived. Jack and his 'pal' left the prison together and began to walk towards Buffalo, several miles away. As soon as they reached the main street they headed for a bar. 'I'd have liked to say good-by,' Jack later wrote. 'He had been good to me. But I did not dare. I went out through the rear of the saloon and jumped the fence. It was a swift sneak, and a few minutes later I was on board a freight and heading south on the Western New York and Pennsylvania Railroad.'

It took several months for Jack to cross the three thousand miles of Canadian railroads back to the west coast. Many nights he spent in icy box-cars and at dawn, numb from the cold, he would crawl out to beg for food. At one point he rode the same carriage for a thousand miles, watching the Canadian landscape slip past as the sun rose and set. He now lied when questioned by the police, convincing them he was anything but a tramp. Finally he reached Vancouver on the Pacific coast, found a job on the steamer *Umatilla*, and worked his way back to San Francisco. His days of lawless freedom were over.

*   *   *

When Jack later wrote about his days on the road, he did not mention what really happened in prison. But he did dedicate *The Road* to Josiah Flynt – 'the real thing blowed in the glass'. In an article for a book by Havelock Ellis, the pioneering sexologist, Flynt had described in harrowing detail the reality of life on the road. He had witnessed the gang rape of a black boy in a freight car, and the fate of 'pretty' young men such as Jack in jail was often similar.

Jack had suffered all manner of 'unthinkable horrors' in prison. For the first time, he had lived 'down in the cellar of society, down in the subterranean depths of misery about which it is neither nice nor proper to speak', 'the pit, the abyss, the human cesspool, the shambles of our civilisation. That is the part of the edifice of society that society chooses to ignore.'

Jack concluded *The Road* by admitting that the things he saw at the base of the pit gave him a 'terrible scare'. Such a fright, in fact, that he resolved once again to make his peace with society and, as soon as possible, settle into its groove. By the time he arrived back in Oakland in autumn 1894, he had sworn to escape the cellar for good. He would not be part of the human filth and slime. He would succeed. His life now depended on it.

4

The Boy Socialist

Then began a frantic pursuit of knowledge. I returned to California and opened the books . . . Other and greater minds, before I was born, had worked out all that I thought, and a vast deal more. I discovered that I was a Socialist. JACK LONDON, *John Barleycorn* (1913)

JACK LOOKED AS IF he had just come ashore after months at sea. He was wearing an ill-fitting dark blue suit. His face was sunburned and his hair dishevelled and he was chewing tobacco, a habit he had picked up on the road and continued because it numbed the pain of cavities in his teeth. The other pupils at Oakland High were dumbfounded. Could this possibly be their new classmate?

On returning from his adventures on the road in late 1894, Jack had again found himself back in his mother's kitchen in East Oakland, penniless and depressed. He had told his mother of his travels, leaving out the cruder details, and about his plans to make her genuinely proud of him. He would no longer be her 'badge of shame' – the delinquent son whom neighbours gossiped about, who swore at her and reacted bitterly whenever she encouraged him to find a career. He was determined to stay under one roof until he had 'developed his brain'. He had dropped out of the school system for five years. Now he intended to make up for the loss in two. At nineteen, he would return to high school, joining pupils four years younger.

Though he pretended not to care as he swaggered into class, Jack was painfully aware of his separation from his fellow pupils. As soon as he sat down in the classroom, he felt the yawning gap open even wider. They were mere infants, so naive and so carefree, with none of his responsibilities.

As the man of the house, Jack now had to earn a living as well as study. And so he mowed lawns and beat carpets at weekends, and when the janitor of Oakland High needed an assistant, his stepsister Eliza got Jack the job. After school, he remained behind to scrub the floors and mop up his classmates' splashed urine. 'I was working to get away from work, and I buckled down to it with a grim realisation of the paradox.'

Only to a young man yet to conform to adult society's rules was this a paradox; and it was only weeks, in fact, before he discovered a new set of his own. On the road, he had heard about a pamphlet called *The Communist Manifesto*. In Oakland Library he came across a dog-eared copy. From the first syllable, it was a revelation, as if a blindfold had been flung from his eyes. Marx's logic was faultless.

In a notebook, Jack jotted: 'The whole history of mankind has been a history of contests between exploiting and exploited; a history of these class struggles shows the evolution of man; with the coming of industrialism and concentrated capital a stage has been reached whereby the exploited cannot attain its emancipation from the ruling class without once and for all emancipating society at large from all future exploitation, oppression, class distinctions and class struggles.'

Flicking quickly through the pamphlet, Jack discovered that socialism meant the 'abolition of private property, and that the means of production, communication and transportation should be owned by the state'. Above all, he was stirred by Marx's call to arms: 'Let the ruling classes tremble at the socialistic revolution. The proletarians have nothing to lose but their chains. They have a world to gain. Working men of all countries, unite!'

Jack's experiences made socialism a compelling belief. He had felt real poverty and hunger, and he had seen the fate of the working class: to be discarded when spent, like so much carrion in a society in which Darwinian principles had been taken to their logical extreme.

But only some of his suffering had been caused by capitalism. There was another source of his political ire. Socialism provided him with an outlet for the resentment he felt because of his mother's indifference to him. Jack's anger at having suffered loneliness and lack of affection as a boy was channelled into what would become a lifelong commitment to righting social injustices and an unerring support for the underdog.

By the time Jack discovered Karl Marx, socialism in America already had a distinct history of its own. Imported from Europe through mostly German immigrants who arrived in the 1840s and fifties, socialism had confronted unique obstacles in America: the Civil War, which had pitted the working class against itself; the United States's relative lack of class-consciousness yet high degree of racial division due to slavery and widespread antagonism to new immigrant groups; and an all-powerful capitalist class.

Nevertheless, socialism quickly put down strong roots. In October 1857 the Communist Club of New York was formed, and throughout the next decade hundreds of thousands of Americans became familiar with the organisation's guiding principles through reading Karl Marx's contributions to the *New York Tribune*, the most widely circulated newspaper in the country.

The publication of Edward Bellamy's *Looking Backward* in January 1888, at the end of a decade of bloody industrial dispute across America, catalysed nationwide interest in creating a new social system based on social and economic equality: the book sold over a million copies. Daniel De Leon was one of many who were inspired by Bellamy's utopian prediction of a 'cooperative commonwealth' in America by the year 2000. As editor of the *People*, the newspaper of the Socialist Labor Party, De Leon managed to transform his party from a German-speaking band of revolutionaries into an organisation with popular appeal. Within just a decade, the party would be able to mount a credible challenge in presidential elections.

Before Jack could lead the assault on the barricades, he needed to arm himself with academic qualifications. As his entry into the vanguard of the revolution, Jack chose the University of California in Berkeley, the most prestigious college on the west coast, a short streetcar ride from his mother's home in Oakland.

But Berkeley, if Jack took the standard route, was still at least three years off. In the meantime, he again became a regular visitor to Oakland Library, his preferred classroom. He still revered its librarian, Ina Coolbrith. More than ever, she realised that her young protégé required stimulus and encouragement – Jack needed to mix with similar minds. And so she introduced him to another young man hungry for knowledge, Fred Jacobs, who worked as an assistant in the reference room.

In his spare time, Jacobs avoided saloons, opting instead for the serious sobriety of the Henry Clay Debating Society run by the nearby Cole Grammar School. It was not long before he invited Jack to one of the meetings. The debaters were mostly professionals and university students, but they accepted Jack immediately. For the first time he was judged solely by the quality of his mind.

Within weeks, Jack had taken another step up, entering 'onto the parlour floor' of society, visiting the homes of Fred Jacobs and his fiancée Bess Maddern, a mathematics teacher, and fellow debaters Ted Applegarth and his ethereal sister Mabel, who was studying English at the University of California at Berkeley. At first sight, Jack was besotted. Twenty-one-year-old Mabel was a fragile girl with wide 'spiritual blue eyes' and a mass of golden hair. Her porcelain skin, refined diction and ability to quote whole sonnets from the Romantic poets made her seem a goddess to him.

Here, at last, was a girl he could talk to about what really stirred his mind and heart. She had class. Her family were British, well bred and educated at the best private schools. Framed oil paintings hung from the walls in their home in a prosperous suburb of Oakland. A piano took centre stage in their elegant drawing-room with its book-shelves of leather-bound classics.

In Mabel, Jack had found a member of the opposite sex, the first he had met, who was both attractive and intellectual, who could understand, if not where he had come from, at least where he wanted to go. She was a 'pale gold flower upon a slender stem'. Jack did not yet know his new princess was slowly dying of tuberculosis. He would later immortalise Mabel as Ruth Morse in *Martin Eden*. While critics are still divided over that novel's literary merits, it is clear that Martin is Jack's alter ego in many respects. Above all, the book reveals Jack's emasculation as he moves from his working-class peer group to the middle-class world of Ruth and its feminised values. It shows how his need to belong made him cast aside the validity of the gritty experiences which had shaped his character.

The first time he visited the Applegarths for dinner, as he described the experience in *Martin Eden*, Jack was probably terrified. The array of knives and forks must have bewildered him: 'They bristled with unknown perils, and he gazed at them, fascinated, till their dazzle became a background across which moved a succession of forecastle pictures; wherein he and his mates sat eating salt beef with sheath-knives and fingers, or scooping thick pea soup out of pannikins by means of battered iron spoons.'

Jack glanced around the table. 'How they loved each other, the members of this family! . . . He had starved for love all his life. His nature craved love. It was an organic demand of his being. Yet he had gone without, and hardened himself in the process. He had not known that he needed love. Nor did he know it now.'

The Applegarths did not appear to notice Jack's gaucheries, his rough language and the holes in his clothes. When he returned to his draughty bedroom on the other side of town, he felt as if he had come from a different galaxy, one whose comforts and tastes he had now sworn to make his own. He may, like Martin Eden, have asked himself: 'Where do you belong? . . . You belong with the legions of toil, with all that is low, and vulgar, and unbeautiful. You belong with the oxen and the drudges, in dirty surroundings among smells and stenches. There are the stale vegetables now. Those potatoes are rotting. Smell them, damn you, smell them.'

And yet Jack had dared to open the books, 'to listen to beautiful music, to learn to love beautiful paintings, to speak good English, to think thoughts that none of his kind thought, to tear himself away from the oxen . . . and to love a pale spirit of a woman who was a million miles beyond him and who lives in the stars!'

For better or worse, the Applegarths changed Jack. Encouraged to talk about the *Sophie Sutherland* and his tramping days, he glamorised his youth for his supper, quickly burrowing into his middle-class friends' lives, mimicking their manners and gestures, repeating their cadences in private until the callused vowels dropped away. He even managed not to pepper his most passionate rants with the usual 'darn'. He bought a dictionary and vowed to learn twenty new words each day.

Jack had always been quick to recognise short-cuts to success, and his journey from poverty to the book-lined drawing-rooms of Oakland

was accelerated, above all, by his decision to become actively involved
in local politics. In early 1896, at the same time as he was learning to
endear himself to nice middle-class girls such as Mabel Applegarth,
Jack joined the local Socialist Labor Party in Oakland. It had been
founded four years earlier by a group of well-to-do intellectuals, among
them several ministers who believed socialism offered the best hope
for Christianity, a group of exiled German socialists and a couple of
former members of the British Socialist Labour Party. One of the
latter, Herman 'Jim' Whitaker, who had encouraged Jack to join the
party, would soon become a close friend, even though he was a decade
older and already married with six children. It was not only a passionate
commitment to social reform which they had in common. They shared
a love of combative sports, and Whitaker taught Jack to box. Both
also hoped one day to become successful writers, and would chat
about their ambitions. Eventually Whitaker would write seven novels,
including *The Planter* and *The Settler*, and become a celebrated war
correspondent.

At first, Jack thought it odd how few genuinely working-class lads
like himself attended meetings of the party. But that didn't matter.
If anything, he could play up his proletarian pedigree. This was a
party for the 'caring bourgeoisie', numbering less than a hundred
members, among whom Jack soon gained kudos for his address alone.
Yet he was no backroom debater. Smoke-filled rooms were for boozing
among real men, not preaching to the converted. Already signing his
letters 'Yours for the Revolution', he preferred the adrenal rush of
taking the revolution onto the streets, of mounting the soapbox and
parrying all comers.

While Jack's involvement in politics provided an entree into intellectual circles, it did not alter his essential beliefs. What he learned in
debates was theoretical. What he learned on the streets was a more
militant politics. He recognised that socialism was a futile concept
without the full support of the working class, yet his own conversion
was completed among the bourgeoisie, whose attitudes he would later
hold in contempt.

But as a rabble-rouser, prosecuting a 'holy war' in the name of Karl
Marx, Jack showed great promise. On 16 February 1896, the *San
Francisco Chronicle* reported:

Jack London, who is known as the boy socialist of Oakland, is holding forth nightly to the crowds that throng City Hall Park. There are other speakers in plenty, but London always gets the biggest crowd and the most respectful attention . . . The young man is a pleasant speaker, more earnest than eloquent, and while he is a broad socialist in every way, he is not an anarchist. He says on the subject when asked for his definition of socialism, 'It is an all-embracing term – communists, nationalists, collectionists, idealists, utopians . . . are all socialists, but it cannot be said that socialism is any of these – it is all.' Any man, in the opinion of London, is a socialist who strives for a better form of government than the one he is living under.

To the end of his life, Jack would struggle to explain the exact nature of socialism. His own beliefs would modify as his finances prospered. Although he would become adept at spouting the party's latest dogma, his views would often, in later years, vary dramatically from the official party line. As he saw it, socialism was essentially a vehicle for bringing greater and fairer opportunity to the downtrodden, and a means of providing institutions which would ameliorate the social ills which blighted the lives of tens of millions of his fellow Americans. Although his allegiance to the party would later wane because of his disappointment at its inability to set the pace of progress, his loyalty to its founding principles of social and economic equality would never diminish.

On 10 February 1897, Jack discovered that socialism was not as popular as he had thought. He was the main speaker on a Lincoln's Birthday meeting organised to protest against Oakland Ordinance No. 1676, which forbade addressing a public meeting on any public street without the written permission of the mayor. After hectoring a crowd of several hundred for a few minutes he was arrested and taken to Oakland jail. He demanded a jury trial (held on 18 February), spoke in his own defence, and won a widely reported acquittal.

Despite this victory, Jack's social standing was shattered by his arrest. Members of the Henry Clay Debating Society withdrew invitations to their homes and stopped asking him to their *soirées*. Direct action jarred with their genteel sensibilities. He could talk all he liked about revolt, but to incite it was going too far.

Jack was not shunned by the Applegarths, however, and the week-end bicycle rides, picnics and boating trips with Mabel continued. He was by now infatuated with her, as only 'God's own mad lover' could be. He made it clear that he wanted to marry her when he was in a position to support her in the style her parents would expect.

One of the subjects of their passionately cerebral conversations was Jack's literary ambition. Ten of his articles and short stories had been published in his school magazine, the *Aegis*. All showed a natural command of narrative structure and a raw talent for expressing vividly what he had experienced himself. But these tales of skinning seals and tramping the roads shocked Mabel and horrified his classmates. When Jack launched into a lecture on the evils of capitalism in a mid-term debate, parents and staff were even more outraged. Instantly, the Parent and Teachers' Association demanded something be done about the 'boy socialist' before Jack further poisoned young minds.

Before the school could act to censure him, Jack dropped out. He was impatient. He was already twenty, and it would take him two more years to graduate and then four more at college – a short cut was needed. His stepsister Eliza provided him with the means, loaning him the tuition fee necessary to enrol at a nearby crammer, the University Academy in Alameda. Jack stayed just five weeks at the 'academy' before its principal returned his money. Jack had been asked to leave, he later maintained, because he had covered two years' work in two months.

Jack threw himself into cramming for the entrance examinations on his own, and was soon studying nineteen hours a day without rest. His teacher friend Bess Maddern, with whom he often took long bicycle rides, helped him with mathematics, and Fred Jacobs coached him in physics; Ina Coolbrith provided moral support.

After three months of intense cramming, with ragged nerves Jack sat the three-day Berkeley entrance exams on 10 August 1896. They were far more exacting than he'd expected – the university had raised its standards in order to cut down its intake. He nevertheless passed with distinction.

After the examinations, Jack later recalled, 'I didn't want to see a book, I didn't want to think nor to lay eyes on anybody who was liable to think. There was but one prescription for such a condition, and I gave it to myself – the adventure path.' He stowed a roll of blankets and some cold food into a borrowed boat and set sail. But he had not gone far when he came across some fishing barks moored along the waterfront. Without a second thought, he headed for the shore. He knew what he wanted. He wanted to get drunk.

Jack arrived at Berkeley in autumn 1896, in high spirits. He was there, above all, to learn how to write, and set out to take every English course the university provided. At first he felt at home among the middle-class students, almost all of them supported by wealthy parents. Even though they thought it bizarre that he paid his fees through steeplejacking, they quickly warmed to the brusque but extremely bright young man who dressed so casually and yet argued so intensely it seemed he was delivering truth from the bottom of his heart.

When not climbing tall buildings, Jack was often to be found in the college gymnasium wearing boxing gloves and inviting all comers to go a few rounds with him. Few of his fellow students dared – they had heard rumours about Jack's days on the waterfront. Once, however, Jack managed to persuade a young freshman to put on the gloves. He began to fight using the 'windmill' technique he had learned on the waterfront, and within minutes he had knocked his opponent out. Another student, a year older and from a wealthy family, then stepped forward and told Jack he should be ashamed of fighting a boy who weighed less than him.

'Go to hell,' sneered Jack. 'Or you'll get some of the same stuff yourself.'

'Oh, I don't think so,' the wealthy student replied.

Without warning, Jack lunged at him. His opponent ducked, escaping a powerful blow. 'As you wish,' he said calmly, and slipped on a pair of gloves. Again Jack pounced, but to his amazement, the student 'put up a guard like a stone wall and, until he was ready, made no attempt to land a blow . . . Fast and furious Jack went at him only to wear himself out while the crowd of students who had now gathered looked on silently.'

Then two blows 'struck like lightning'. One found Jack's nose, the other his jugular. For a few seconds, Jack counted stars, sprawled out on the floor. A couple of bystanders helped him to his feet. Some tried to lead him to the washroom to clean up. Jack refused, threw down his gloves, grabbed his coat and ran off without washing.

Another student, James Hopper, one of Berkeley's best athletes and later a talented short-story writer, was perhaps Jack's closest friend at Berkeley. The 'dominating quality' of Jack's character was 'bigness', Hopper wrote. 'His clothes were floppy and careless; the forecastle had left a suspicion of a roll in his broad shoulders; he was a strange combination of Scandinavian sailor and Greek god, made altogether boyish and lovable by the lack of two front teeth, lost cheerfully somewhere in a fight . . . He was going to take all the courses in the natural sciences, many in history, and bite a respectable chunk out of the philosophies.'

Bite as he did, Jack did not fully digest the philosophies. He chose only that which tasted good, and then wolfed it down. The tastiest morsel was Herbert Spencer's *Philosophy of Style*. From its first pages, he was mesmerised – 'here was all knowledge, classified and organised, proving that all was law and everything was related'. Life, sex, emotions – all could be explained as if in a mechanic's handbook.

Jack, like Martin Eden, had been 'mastered by curiosity all his days . . . He wanted to know, and it was this desire that had sent him adventuring over the world. But he was now learning from Spencer that he never had known, and that he never could have known had he continued his sailing and wandering forever . . . There was no caprice, no chance. All was law. It was in obedience to law that the bird flew, and it was in obedience to the same law that fermenting slime had writhed and squirmed and put out legs and wings and become a bird.'

It is difficult, almost a century later, to comprehend the earth-shattering nature of Spencer's writings. Along with Charles Darwin, he was responsible for a set of intellectual ideas which turned conventional thinking on its head. In 1859, Darwin rocked the foundations of religion by challenging the notion of divine creation in *On the Origin of Species*. While Darwin developed scientific theories to explain evolution, Spencer provided a philosophy to accompany the biological rules of existence. As the American critic Charles Child Walcutt has written: 'Spencer asserted that evolution is the fundamental law of social as well as physical process: from simple and relatively uniform materials evolve increasingly complex and specialised structures . . .and thus he saw the social struggle for existence as leading up to the ultimately perfect and stable society. The evils of child labour, poverty, unemployment, and industrial warfare which were rampant in Western Europe and America were justified because they were the means to the perfect society. The fit would survive.'

Jack read Spencer's book in one sitting, throughout the night and well into the next day. In his haste, he understood little except that it offered the meaning of life. Certainly he did not see the contradiction in adopting Marxism as well as Spencer's philosophy of 'the survival of the fittest'.

An idealistic student in search of answers, so impatient to succeed that he still had time only to skim the surface of life, Jack was bowled over by Spencer. By contrast, his fellow students found the English philosopher heavy going. Jack had begun to feel the same about Berkeley. He was still doing odd jobs to pay his way. A few weeks after the mid-term vacation, he decided to give up the battle to study and support his family at the same time. It would have taken another three years to graduate. Life called too fiercely, his hunger was too great, to wait such an eternity. And so, four months after arriving, on 4 February 1897, Jack again dropped out. Everything of importance he had learned he had discovered for himself. He already knew more about the world than any of his professors, and he had lived twice their lives.

'Do you know what happened to me over there, in the State university at Berkeley, supported by the taxes of the people?' he blustered more than a decade later. 'I was called out before a whole regiment of students undergoing, as I was, enforced military drill, and I was publicly humiliated by an officer of the regular army because my uniform was shabby, because I lacked forty dollars to buy a new one.'

If Jack still sounded bitter over a decade after dropping out, he may have been pained by a lesson he did not learn at Berkeley, but across the bay in a dusty newspaper office in San Francisco. From an early age he may have suspected that he was illegitimate, and that

John London was not his real father. But it was not until he was at Berkeley that he took steps to ascertain his parentage. It was in a room stacked with yellowing back issues of the *San Francisco Chronicle* that he learned of the murky events surrounding his birth. Flicking through back copies, he found the following announcement, dated 13 January 1876:

BIRTHS

Chaney – In this city, January 12, the wife of W.H. Chaney, of a son.

He then flipped back seven months to an article in the *Chronicle* of 4 June 1875:

A DISCARDED WIFE

Day before yesterday Mrs Chaney, wife of 'Professor' W.H. Chaney, the astrologer, attempted suicide by taking laudanum. Failing in the effort she yesterday shot herself with a pistol in the forehead. The ball glanced off, inflicting only a flesh wound, and friends interfered before she could accomplish her suicidal purpose.

The incentive to the terrible act was domestic infelicity. Husband and wife have been known for a year past as the center of a little band of extreme Spiritualists, most of whom professed, if they did not practise, offensive free-love doctrines. To do Mr Chaney justice, he has persistently denied the holding of such broad tenets. He has been several times married before this last fiasco of the hearthstone, but it is supposed that all his former wives have been duly laid away to rest, and now repose, like Polonius, in rural churchyards,

> At their hearts a grass-green turf
> At their backs a stone.

The last marriage took place about a year ago. Mrs Chaney, formerly Miss Flora Wellman, is a native of Ohio. She came to this coast about the time the Professor took the journey overland through the romantic sagebrush, and for a while supported herself by teaching music. It is hard to see what attracted her toward this man, to whom she was united after a short acquaintance. The union seems to have been the result of a mania like, and yet unlike, that which drew Desdemona toward the sooty Moor.

The married life of the couple is said to have been full of self-denial and devoted affection on the part of the wife, and of harsh words and unkind treatment on the part of the husband. He practised astrology, calculated horoscopes for a consideration, lectured on chemistry and astronomy, blasphemed the Christian religion, published a journal of hybrid doctrines, called the *Philomathean*, and pretended to calculate 'cheap nativities' on the transit of the planets for $10 each, for all of which he obtained but slender pecuniary recompense . . .

She says that about three weeks ago she discovered, with a natural feeling of maternal pleasure, that she was enceinte. She told her husband, and asked to be relieved for two or three months of the care of the children by means of which she had been contributing to their material support. He refused to accede to the request and some angry words followed.

Then he told her she had better destroy her unborn babe. This she indignantly declined to do, and on last Thursday morning he said to her, 'Flora, I want you to pack up and leave this house.' She replied, 'I have no money and nowhere to go.' He said, 'Neither have I any to give you.' A woman in the house offered her $25, but she flung it from her in a burst of anguish, saying, 'What do I care for this? It will be no use to me without my husband's love.'

This show of sincere affection had no effect on the flinty-headed calculator of other people's nativities. He told the poor woman that he had sold the furnishings (for which she had helped to pay) and it was useless to think of her remaining there any longer. He then left her, and shortly afterwards she made her first attempt at suicide, following it by the effort to kill herself with a pistol on the following morning, as already stated.

Failing in both endeavours, Mrs Chaney was removed in

a half-insane condition from Dr Ruttley's on Mission Street to the house of a friend, where she still remains, somewhat pacified and in a mental condition indicating that she will not again attempt self-destruction. The story given here is the lady's own, as filtered through her near associates.

Chaney's reputation had spread across America, and after a brief search Jack got hold of his Chicago address from a fellow astrologer. Jack wrote to Chaney on 28 May 1897, using Ted Applegarth's address so that his mother would not know about his enquiries. He wanted to know what kind of woman his mother was, and whether Chaney really was his father. Chaney replied, addressing Jack as 'Dear Sir':

I was never married to Flora Wellman but she lived with me from June 11, 1874, until June 3, 1875. I was impotent at that time, the result of hardship, privation, and too much brain work. Therefore I cannot be your father, nor am I sure who your father is.

He then linked Flora's name with two other men in spring 1875, and added:

There was a time when I had a very tender affection for Flora; but there came a time when I hated her with all the intensity of my intense nature, and even thought of killing her myself, as many a man has under similar circumstances. Time, however, has healed the wounds and I feel no unkindness toward her, while for you I feel a warm sympathy, for I can imagine what my emotions would be were I in your place . . .

The Chronicle published that I turned her out of doors because she would not submit to an abortion. This was copied and sent broadcast over the country. My sisters in Maine read it and two of them became my enemies. One died believing I was in the wrong. All others of my kindred, except one sister in Portland, Oregon, are still my enemies and denounce me as a disgrace to them.

I published a pamphlet at the time containing a report from a detective given me by the Chief of Police, showing that many of the slanders against me were false, but neither the Chronicle nor any of the papers that defamed me would correct the false statement. Then I gave up defending myself, and for years life was a burden. But reaction finally came, and now I have a few friends who think me respectable. I am past seventy-six, and quite poor.

Jack wrote back demanding further clarification. Still denying he was his father, Chaney sent one last letter:

The cause of our separation began when Flora one day said to me, 'You know that motherhood is the great desire of my life, and as you are too old – now some time when I find a good, nice man are you not willing for me to have a child by him?' . . . A month or so later she said she was pregnant by me. I thought she was only trying me and did not think she was pregnant. So I made a great fuss thinking to warn her not to make the attempt.

This brought on a wrangle that lasted all day and night. After daylight I got up and told her she could never be a wife to me again. She was humbled in a moment, for she knew I was in earnest. She crawled on her knees to me, sobbing, and begged my forgiveness. But I would not forgive her, although I still thought she was merely pretending to be in a family way. But her temper was a great trial, and I had often thought before that time that I must leave her on account of it.

Chaney may have denied he was Jack's father because to admit otherwise would awaken long-repressed guilt and invite paternal duties he had always shunned. But when Jack gazed at the picture of Chaney contained in the Chronicle report, he could not help but be struck by his own resemblance to the man staring balefully back at him. At first glance, age and a grey beard obscured their similarity. But there was no denying the sensation of staring at a man whose face foretold how Jack might look in thirty years' time. He had the same light hair, high forehead, deep-set eyes and sturdy torso.

The effect on the twenty-one-year-old Jack of reading the newspaper report and Chaney's letters must have been a sense of bewilderment, as well as anger that Chaney could be so callous as to cloud the circumstances of his birth even further.

Chaney's second letter, demeaning Flora and describing his parting from her, would be his last communication with Jack. During his final decade, spent in freezing penury in Chicago, Chaney would devote himself for sixteen hours a day to astrology – it was all he had left. When Jack embarked on his one undisputed masterpiece, Chaney lay dying, a forgotten man.

Jack did not rejoin the 'wage-slaves' after dropping out of college. In a Sunday newspaper supplement he had read that magazines paid contributors two cents a word – he could expect only ten cents an hour on the shop floor. He had long complained to Mabel Applegarth that the stories in popular magazines lacked all vitality. If only he could get down on paper the images in his mind, he could surely make a go of it as a serious writer.

Again he returned to his cramped room and laid siege to 'the citadel of knowledge'. This time he would escape through writing fiction, not by trying to act out what he had read as a boy. He would earn a living by creating his own fantasy worlds, just as his heroes had done. If he could not be Rudyard Kipling or Mark Twain, he would try to write like them.

Jack rented a typewriter and threw himself, body and soul, at his objective, believing that mental effort alone would bring him success. For fifteen hours a day, for weeks without a break, the words gushed from him. 'Heavens, how I wrote!' he recalled. 'Never was there a creative fervour such as mine from which the patient escaped fatal results. The way I worked was enough to soften my brain and send me to a mad-house.'

As soon as he completed a story, Jack would mail it with a self-addressed envelope to the editor of a local newspaper or a juvenile magazine such as the *Black Cat*. Inevitably, they came back, as if returned by some impersonal machine. Yet the higher the pile of rejection slips grew, the more stubborn Jack became.

Convinced he was sending the magazines what they wanted, despite the evidence to the contrary, Jack hammered away on his typewriter, which would only print in capitals, until the blisters on his fingers burst. He wrote essays (uncannily similar in style to those of 'Professor' Chaney); short stories; and, like every literary aspirant, insipid poetry:

The Lover's Liturgy

For a whim of bubble-blowing,
Perhaps to while an empty day,
For a whim of stubble-sowing,
For a game at godlike play.
Shall the bubbles in the drifting
Pay the whim of Him who played?
Shall the seedlets in the sifting
Of the sifter be afraid?

But energy and determination would not yet be enough. Jack was spreading himself too thin, desperate for any acceptance at all, and writing, he would later accept, for the wrong market. Yet for two months longer he pawned his books and clothes to buy stationery and postage, and still the 'impersonal editorial machine' on the East Coast sent back the 'Thank you for thinking of us' slips. Soon there was nothing left to put in hock, and Flora lost patience. With bitter reluctance, Jack gave up trying to live as a writer in the spring of 1897. His creative frenzy had come to nothing.

He found a job in the laundry of the Belmont Academy, a military school south of San Francisco, similar to the crammer he had been asked to leave. For ten hours a day he sweated in a steaming hell, ironing and starching rich kids' shirts and collars. He had little time to see Mabel Applegarth – her family had recently moved to San Jose, fifty miles from Oakland, and he lacked the energy to cycle to see her on his Sundays off. He loved her, and she had told him she had the same feelings for him. But Mrs Applegarth would not allow her daughter to marry beneath her station; only if Jack became a salaried success would he be in a position to propose.

Was his destiny simply to make do with his lot? After all the adventures and attempts to make his own fate, there seemed no way forward, no escape from wage-slavery. The game had so far not been worth the candle. There was no time for books, just an endless round of hot irons and starched corsets. His literary ambitions defeated, pulling in just $30 a month as a shirt-presser, Jack began to give up all hope. Would he ever escape into the bourgeoisie?

5

The White Silence

It is not pleasant to be alone with painful thoughts in
the White Silence. The silence of gloom is merciful,
shrouding one as with protection and breathing a thousand intangible sympathies; but the bright White
Silence, clear and cold, under steely skies, is pitiless.

JACK LONDON, 'The White Silence' (1899)

BY 1896, GEORGE CARMACK had been in northern Canada for
several years and was still battling on in the increasingly faint hope
that the numbing winters, the hunger and physical pain would be
rewarded. Now, once again, winter was looming, its icy threat growing
nearer with every gust of wind from the north.

In pain, Carmack struggled over fallen trees and forced his way
through the razor-sharp thorns. Breaking out of dense forest, he and
his two Indian guides 'floundered into a swamp that marked the
headwaters of Rabbit Creek'. At last, the ground became firmer. By
a riverbank, they paused to prospect for gold. As Carmack began to
swill the muddy water around in his pan, he saw a tell-tale glint of
metal. His first pan, to his amazement, yielded a quarter of an ounce
of gold – at least a week's wages for the average workman back in
America, where twenty-one-year-old Jack London was sweating in a
laundry for a beggar's pickings.

Carmack flung down the pan and let out a cry of euphoria. He
then smoked a cigarette and began to pan out more gravel. By nightfall
he had collected enough raw gold to fill a shotgun shell. As he drifted
off to sleep before a blazing fire, he pictured a suitcase full of gilt-edged
securities, and rivers of gold. Below him in the permafrost, as he

dreamt golden dreams, lay one of the richest finds in the history of gold prospecting, worth tens of millions of dollars today.

It took a year for the news of Carmack's strike to reach the outside world. Within weeks of his find, winter had descended so rapidly that he was stranded until spring thawed the Klondike, a region named after a tributary of the Yukon where the richest finds would soon be made. When his strike was finally reported, America went gold-crazy. News reports such as James S. Easby-Smith's for *Cosmopolitan* aggravated the frenzy:

> Early in July '97 there sailed through the Golden Gate and up the docks of San Francisco a treasure-ship bearing a motlier crowd than ever swarmed upon a buccaneer's deck and greater riches than ever lay hidden in the hold of a Spanish galleon. The human freight was two score men, young and middle-aged, ragged, unkempt and weather-browned; but in their eyes shone the light of triumph, and smiles of anticipated pleasures lighted up their rugged faces. The treasure consisted of more than a million dollars' worth of virgin gold in dust, flakes and nuggets, wrapped in blankets, tied up in canvas bags and the skins of animals, and poured into bottles and cans.

Around the globe, men and women were soon deserting careers and families to join the most dramatic gold rush of them all. In London, the *Daily Chronicle* published its very own ode to what was, by mid-July 1897, a world stampede:

> Klondike! Klondike!
> Libel yer luggidge 'Klondike'!
> Theers no chawnce in the street ter-dye
> Theers no luck darn Shoreditch wye
> Pack yer traps and be orf I sye,
> An' orf an' awye ter Klondike!

It was not only the promise of untold wealth, and the urging of the press, which would in just two years draw over a hundred thousand people to one of the most merciless regions of the planet, a barren place where a man can go insane after a winter of solitude. What also attracted many was the need to escape the grind of their daily lives. The Klondike promised gold. It guaranteed adventure.

How little these argonauts knew of what lay ahead. Although the goldfields lay entirely in Canada, the mighty Rockies barred the way. The shortest route was through Alaska, but any man who tried that would find himself confronted by the dreaded Chilkoot Pass, a mountain trail so steep that in places it was almost vertical. And even if he climbed the Chilkoot, he would then need to construct a boat from felled trees and brave the lethal rapids and gorges.

The news of Carmack's find lifted many areas of the Pacific north-west out of the economic depression which had lingered on since the early 1890s. Life savings were cashed in as thousands went on spending sprees to equip themselves for the long, hazardous journey north. Everyone, it seemed, was liquidating assets or borrowing small fortunes to put together a 'grubstake', as prospectors called the often prohibitive amount of money required to make an official claim to a plot of land in the goldfields. In Seattle, a man dying of lung disease decided to make the trek north, announcing that he would rather gasp his last panning for gold than rot in poverty in America.

Jack could not have agreed more. When he read of the Klondike finds in July 1897, he immediately asked local newspapers for credentials as a correspondent. Turned down, he went to his stepsister Eliza, who had helped him so often before. Eliza was still married to Captain Shepard, now past sixty and suffering from a failing heart. As luck would have it, he had also been infected with 'Klondikitis', and eagerly offered to grubstake Jack by mortgaging his and Eliza's home. There was one condition: Jack would have to take Shepard with him. Jack argued that he would need all his strength to get his own supplies over the Chilkoot Pass. Nevertheless, desperate for funds, he reluctantly agreed.

Eliza drew $500 from her savings and added a $1000 mortgage for good measure. Her money flowed through Jack's hands 'like water' as he bought fur-lined coats, caps, heavy high boots, thick mittens, red flannel shirts, underwear of 'the warmest quality', a year's supply of 'grub', tents, blankets, Klondike stoves and tools to hew boats and cabins from fir trees. Before long, Jack's kit weighed nearly two thousand pounds.

Mabel Applegarth's mother wrote begging Jack to abandon the trip:

> Oh, dear John, do be persuaded to give up the idea, for we
> feel certain that you are going to meet your death, and we
> shall never see you again ... Your Father and Mother must
> be nearly crazed over it. Now, even at the eleventh hour, dear
> John, do change your mind and stay.

But the glitter of gold blinded Jack's senses, along with those of
hundreds of others who left San Francisco aboard the *Umatilla* on 25
July 1897. Every profession, race and creed was among Jack's 471
fellow passengers (the *Umatilla*, crack steamer of the Pacific Steamship
Company, was licensed to carry only 290). Jack was among the youngest and most gold-fevered on board. 'I had let career go hang, and
was on the adventure path again in quest of fortune.'

Though the *Umatilla* was scheduled to leave at 9 o'clock in the
morning, it was 10.30 before her big engines started up. The crowd
thronging the dockside cried, 'God speed you!' and Jack and his fellow
dreamers shouted back, 'Hurray for the Klondike!', waving madly
until they were out of sight of the well-wishers.

The eight-day trip to Juneau in Alaska passed without incident.
From there, small boats ferried the prospectors to Dyea Beach, which
marked the start of the infamous Chilkoot Trail. As soon as he was on
dry land, Jack joined an anarchic scramble of thousands of prospectors
desperate to reach Dawson City, fifty miles from the goldfields.

On 8 August 1897, Jack found a spare moment to write to Mabel
Applegarth:

> We lay several days in Juneau, then hired canoes and paddled
> 100 miles to our present quarters. The Indians with us brought
> along their squaws, papooses and dogs. Had a pleasant time.
> The 100 miles lay between mountains which formed a
> Yosemite Valley the whole length, and in many places the
> heights were stupendous. Glaciers and waterfalls on every side.
> Yesterday a snow slide occurred and the rumble and roar
> extended for fully a minute.

The sands at Dyea resembled an invasion beach. Everywhere men bartered with Indian porters, trying to persuade them to haul their goods for reasonable prices. Jack's ageing partner Shepard took one look at the glittering white wall of the Chilkoot Pass and decided to turn back. Within weeks he would be joined by thousands more. In retreat, they would find abandoned kit littering the coastline for forty miles.

Despite the Chilkoot Pass's back-breaking nature, by the autumn of 1897 twenty-two thousand men and women had reached the other side. Jack was among them. But only after a struggle which tested his stamina to the limit.

Crippled horses littered the trail, 'broken-boned, drowning, abandoned by man'. They died 'like mosquitoes in the first frost . . . they snapped their legs in the crevices and broke their backs falling backwards with their packs; in the sloughs they sank from sight or smothered in the slime . . . men shot them, worked them to death, and when they were gone, went back to the beach and brought more. Some did not bother to shoot them – stripping the saddles off and the shoes and leaving them where they fell. Their hearts turned to stone – those which did not break – and they became beasts, the men on Dead Horse Trail.'

Surrounded by rotting flesh, Jack somehow managed to find perverse pleasure in the backbreaking climb. Having padded his shoulders, he was soon outpacing most of the white men and, he later maintained, some of the hundreds of Indians who were working as carriers. The higher Jack climbed, the more debris of human failure cluttered his way. But finally, after a week, he crossed over.

Now he had to haul his kit nine miles through a steep canyon to Lake Linderman, one of five that still separated him from Dawson. Here ingenuity, not brute strength, was required; there was no visible means of crossing the lake, and carrying his supplies around would take far too long. Again, many men fell by the wayside. But not Jack. On 8 September 1897 he began to cut down trees and knock up two boats.

He named one of them the *Yukon Belle*. If she was not as watertight as he had hoped, he did not care. It was now a fight against the clock, for the bite of winter was already in the rising wind. Every dawn Jack saw a fresh film of ice forming on the lake. He suspected he had already cut things too fine. Yet Lake Linderman was only the first obstacle, and a relatively placid one at that. Having crossed it, Jack found himself at Fifty Mile River, which canyoned into the already legendary White Horse Rapids. Almost all the men who had tried to shoot them had failed or disappeared without trace. Those who had survived were too frightened to try again.

Jack felt his stomach knot as he gazed at the thundering white water which formed a foaming ridge along the centre of the canyon. Three men had accompanied him from the *Umatilla*, over the Chilkoot and across Lake Linderman to this point: Fred Thompson, Jim Goodman and Merrit Sloper. Now Jack asked them to join him in what would be the riskiest moments of their lives. His plan was to ferry their supplies through the gorge and then walk back along the sheer cliffs to pick up the rest. Before they could back out, he assigned each man a position in the *Yukon Belle*, the thunder of white water muffling his barked orders. Sloper, fresh from adventures in South America, had some experience of rafting and sat in the bow with a paddle. Thompson and Goodman took up the oars. Jack cast off.

'Keep on the ridge in the middle,' cried the bystanders.

The water had an 'oily appearance' until they neared the edge of the first series of rapids, where it began to 'foam and rage'. Concerned that his rowers might capsize, Jack called the oars in, glimpsing spectators fringing the brink of the cliffs above as he did so. A split-second later, the canyon's rock walls were dashing by 'like twin lightning express trains'.

Jack's entire energy was concentrated on 'keeping to the ridge', which was now serrated with stiff waves through which the boat, 'dead with weight, jabbed her nose every few seconds'. Suddenly, Sloper's paddle snapped in two as he tried to avoid a cluster of rocks which then ripped at the *Yukon Belle*'s hull. But they made it through in one piece, with Jack timing the passage at exactly two minutes – the longest two minutes of his life. The most dangerous section of the river was, however, yet to come. With Jack steering, the *Yukon Belle* again approached the swift current in the middle of the canyon and lunged down yet more rapids, narrowly missing a bank of rocks.

Then the 'makeshift craft' shot into an unexpected whirlpool. From every side, water rushed on board, threatening to swamp the crew. Worse still, the *Yukon Belle* began to lurch in the direction of the jagged left bank. Although Jack strained against the tiller until it cracked, he could not turn the *Yukon Belle*'s nose downstream.

The thunder of the water was deafening. Then, as rapidly as they entered the whirlpool, they escaped it. Now they were nearing the wildest stretch of the river, dubbed 'The Mane of the Horse'. 'When we struck the Mane,' Jack would later write, 'the *Yukon Belle* forgot her heavy load, taking a series of leaps almost clear of the water, alternating with as many burials in the troughs. To this day I cannot see how it happened, but I lost control. A cross current caught our stern and we began to swing broadside.' For a few seconds their lives flashed before them, but then, miraculously, they found themselves floating on calmer waters, their hearts pounding in their ears.

Sensing that it was only a matter of days before the great 'freeze-up' began, Jack pushed on with his three colleagues down the swift Thirty-Mile River, into the valley of the Yukon River, and then onto the 'Nile of Alaska' itself. But as they reached the mouth of the Stewart, a tributary near Upper Island, a mere seventy-five miles from Dawson, time ran out. Jack would later describe how the race to beat the seasons in Alaska almost always ended for even the most intrepid prospectors: 'Their speed began to diminish and cakes of ice to up-end and crash and smash about them . . . Then all movement ceased. At the end of half an hour the whole river picked itself up and began to move. This continued for an hour, when again it was brought to rest by a jam. Once again it started, running swiftly and savagely, with a great grinding. Then they saw lights ashore, and, when abreast, gravity and the Yukon surrendered, and the river ceased for six months.' Jack and his colleagues were forced to hole up for the long winter in an abandoned fur-traders' log cabin.

'There's no drama up here, no comedy, no warmth. Life is as pale and as cold as the snow . . . we'll never read any great stories about Alaska and the Klondike. This country is too drab and weary.' So reported Rex Beach, a journalist who had got as far as Jack and who later became a celebrated author of novels set in the region. But there was drama and comedy in Jack's log cabin. His new home fast became the centre of social life on Upper Island. When he needed to escape to his books again, Jack could turn to Darwin's *Origin of Species*, Spencer's *Philosophy of Style*, a translation of Marx's *Das Kapital*, Haeckel's *Riddle of the Universe* and Milton's *Paradise Lost*.

W.B. Hargrave was one of several prospectors upon whom Jack would leave an 'indelible impression'. 'His personality would challenge attention anywhere,' Hargrave would write. 'Not only in his beauty – for he was a handsome lad – but there was about him that indefinable something that distinguishes genius from mediocrity, he displayed none of the insolent egotism of youth; he was an idealist who went after the attainable, a dreamer who was a man among strong men; a man who faced life with superb assurance and who could face death serenely imperturbable.'

The greed for gold blinded most men to their seemingly lifeless surroundings. Jack, by contrast, was already developing a deep empathy for Alaska. Outside the cabin was a 'world of silence and immobility. Nothing stirred. The Yukon slept under a coat of ice three feet thick. No breath of wind blew. Nor did the sap move in the hearts of the spruce trees that forested the river banks on either hand . . . The weather was sharp and clear; there was no moisture in the atmosphere, no fog nor haze; yet the sky was a grey pall. The reason for this was that there was no cloud in the sky to dim the bright of the day, there was no sun to give brightness.'

When Jack left the safety and warmth of his cabin to explore the local snowfields, he was struck by the sense of insignificance he felt. With nothing but endless white, broken here and there by a ridge of trees, as his horizon, he was often overawed by the spiritual pull of the land. The emptiness of it all – what he called 'the white silence' – left a deep and lasting impression.

There were more visitors to Jack's cabin than to any other that winter: trappers, hardened sourdoughs (prospectors) and Indians all dropped by. Jack compiled a rogues' gallery of them in his mind, a bonanza of images and people, memories and anecdotes which he hoarded as Carmack had his gold.

With the exception of an occasional squaw, Jack saw only one woman that winter. She had a 'smoke-tarnished complexion', her voice was soft and caressing, 'like the south wind in the moonlight, and there was music in her laugh . . . her small, well-rounded figure showed soft and yielding in the tight, dilapidated dress'.

When she came to Jack's cabin she was not alone. A man named Stevens, who made it clear that she belonged to him, was with her. Stevens had seen and done it all: in the jungles of the upper Amazon, he had 'made it a rule to kill on sight, man or beast; and women he took where he found them . . . Always in his wake there was blood, for he must kill if he would live.'

Stevens regaled Jack with tales of the jungle. Jack was hypnotised, 'blind to everything about him, even the woman, whose eyes seldom wandered from Jack's young and handsome face'. It was almost dark when Stevens and his woman left the cabin. As they stepped through the cabin door, she invited Jack and his companions to visit them.

'Come soon!' she said, her eyes on Jack.

Three days later, in spite of a warning that 'baby eyes in a woman of her age spells trouble', Jack crossed the frozen river to the couple's cabin. For a few minutes they shivered and talked, then Stevens suddenly asked, 'Have you ever seen straight shooting, Mr London?' He rose from the edge of the bed where he had been sitting and pulled a Winchester rifle from a hook above the stove. Jack buttoned up his coat, pulled the fur on his cap around his ears, and followed him out of the door.

Stevens nailed a piece of tin, about the size of a man's hand, to a tree. In what seemed like a couple of seconds, he holed it perfectly – ten times.

It would be several months before Jack again braved the elements in search of female company. According to Fred Thompson, who had crossed the Chilkoot with him, he did make another foray that winter, but this time it was not for women. Despite the freezing conditions, Jack and Thompson decided to look for gold in a nearby riverbed. Digging among the rock and gravel, Jack came up with a shovel of earth streaked with a heart-stopping glitter. Thompson said that Jack staked a claim, then rushed back to Upper Island to break the news. But when old hands examined his find it turned out to be iron pyrites – it looked like gold to the inexperienced eye, but was worthless.

On the shortest day of the year, Jack dared not even stir from his cabin. A temperature of minus 60 degrees and nothing outside but week-long blizzards kept him and his bearded companions huddled together, betting on when spring would arrive. Jack panned the memories of the old-timers who sought refuge in his cabin. He heard that those who hunted to fend off starvation often did not return. He was told about a man, caught in a blizzard miles from a settlement, whose fingers had frozen before he could light a fire. Warned, Jack was careful not to leave his fur-lined gloves off for long. A man's fingers often froze before he was even aware they were cold.

Jack later wrote: 'It was in the Klondike that I found myself. There, nobody talks. Everybody thinks. You get your perspective. I got mine.' There, huddled in his furs in the ancient forest, he thought of the life he had left behind. In Alaska, man's stature was far greater than in the cities. His nobility increased, it seemed, the further he stepped from the factory gates. It was here also, Jack believed, that white men proved Darwin's theory of evolution. Anglo-Saxons were surely the fittest of men, destined to survive any other race, for had they not won the battle to survive by adapting to the harshest conditions a man could find?

'When a man journeys into a far country,' Jack would write, 'he must be prepared to forget many of the things he has learned, and to acquire such customs as are inherent with existence in the new land; he must abandon the old ideals and the old gods, and oftentimes he must reverse the very codes by which his conduct has hitherto been shaped ... It was better for the man who cannot fit himself to the new groove to return to his own country; if he delay too long, he will surely die.'

Eventually, winter did turn to spring, though every man in the settlement, faced with snowdrifts in mid-May, had doubted it would. The greatest spectacle of the north had arrived – the breaking up of the Yukon ice. In his first novel, *A Daughter of the Snows*, Jack would describe the scene:

The whole river seemed to pick itself up and start down the stream. With the increasing motion the ice-wall broke in a hundred places, and from up and down the shore came the rending and crashing of uprooted trees ... great blocks [of ice] were spilled inland among the thrown and standing trees and the slime-coated flowers and grasses like the titanic vomit of some Northland monster. The sun was not idle, and the steaming thaw washed the mud and foulness from the bergs till they blazed like heaped diamonds in the brightness, or shimmered opalescent-blue.

Jack dismantled an abandoned cabin, built a raft out of the logs and sailed down the still-creaking Yukon to Dawson City. He had to keep a watchful eye open for sweepers – branches and roots of ice-felled trees which could catch a man unawares and leave him to drown in the ice-cold eddies of the snow-melt.

As he swung round a bend in the river, Jack came across another unforgettable sight: a boom town at its height. And what a tantalising oasis it was, with its broken promises and frostbitten whores to warm the nights and its bank vaults heaving with gold dust. If you prospected the streams of sewage running in the streets, they said, you'd find nuggets the size of eggs.

According to Frank Canton, a US marshal sent to keep the peace in Dawson, the town was 'a wild, picturesque, lawless mining camp. The like had never been known, never would be seen again. It was a picture of blood and glittering gold-dust, starvation and death ... If a man could not get the woman he wanted, the man who did get her had to fight for her life.'

A city of flimsy buildings and tents, knee-deep in mud, Dawson was a fetid settlement where all but a few dreams of unending riches finally turned to nightmare. Vast fortunes were won and lost in its makeshift twenty-four-hour casinos, where a man had to hold onto his cards to prevent icy drafts from scattering them across the green baize of rickety card tables.

Jack soon learned that he needed to be worth his weight in gold to survive in Dawson. During the Klondike gold rush, an estimated $60 million was spent by prospectors, but only $10 million was extracted from the earth. The difference now lay in the pockets of entrepreneurs – saloon-keepers and madams – who fed off failure like vultures. There was little prospect of Jack being able to afford Dawson for more than a couple of weeks. All the better claims had been staked in the first six months after Carmack's summer 1896 claim. What little of his stepsister's money he had left soon disappeared in buying basic goods, so exorbitant was the cost of living.

Looking for gold was impossible, because Jack did not have enough cash even for a grubstake. He was now faced with three stark options: he could stay and starve, work in a local sawmill or mine, or head for home. Yet for a few weeks longer, he remained true to the adventure path.

Jack spent the nights in bars, laughing at old-timers' jokes and slugging back cheap spirits. Again storing up memories, he watched the 'Eldorado Kings', prospectors who had struck gold, strutting around and frittering vast fortunes away. Of particular fascination were the women who danced and sang for a living. One of them in particular would linger in his memory, a Greek, Freda Maloof, who called herself 'The Turkish Whirlwind Danseuse'. Her trick outside the bedroom was the belly dance, or hootchie-kootchie, which she had performed at the 1892 Chicago World Fair.

In search of female company, Jack trawled Dawson's many dance-halls. In *A Daughter of the Snows* he would describe the interior of one such establishment:

> The crowded room was thick with tobacco smoke. A hundred men, dressed in furs and warm-coloured wools, lined the walls and looked on. But the mumble of their general conversation destroyed the spectacular feature of the scene and gave to it the geniality of common comradeship . . . Kerosene lamps and tallow candles glimmered feebly in the murky atmosphere, while large stoves roared their red-hot and white-hot cheer. On the floor a score of couples pulsed rhythmically to the swinging waltz-time music. The men wore their wolf and beaver skin caps, with the grey-tasselled ear-flaps flying free, while on their feet were the moose-skin moccasins and walrus-hide of the north. Here and there a woman was in moccasins, though the majority danced in frail ball-room slippers of silk and satin. At one end of the hall a great open doorway gave

glimpse of another large room where the crowd was even denser. From this room, in the lulls in the music, came the pop of corks and the clink of glasses, and as an undertone the steady clink and clatter of chips and roulette balls.

Two men in particular were later to recall Jack's time in Dawson: Marshall and Louis Bond, Yale-educated sons of a prominent Santa Clara, California judge. It was their mongrel dog which Jack would later immortalise in a work of true genius, *The Call of the Wild*. Marshall Bond vividly remembered his first meeting with Jack: 'His face was masked by a thick stubby beard. A cap pulled down low on his forehead was the one touch necessary to the complete concealment of head and features, so that part of the anatomy one looks to for an index of character was covered with beard and cap. He looked as tough and uninviting as we doubtless looked to him. On a box, out of the circle of light from the lamp, he sat in silence one night, a confused blur of cap, mackinaw [coat], and moccasins.'

One morning when Jack pressed his fingers to his leg he saw with horror that the fingerprints remained indented in the grey flesh. Like thousands of others, his winter diet of 'the three Bs' – bread, beans and bacon – had been insufficient to fend off scurvy. He had not packed dried vegetables or fruit, and now his face was ashen. His teeth began to loosen, and soon he was bent double in constant pain.

Jack hobbled to a makeshift hospital run by Father William Judge. A gaunt man in a tattered cassock, 'the Saint of Dawson' provided a bed and some vitamin-rich food. After a week Jack was back on his feet. Father Judge had probably saved his life. But what next? Fortunately, the perfect survival route snaked between soaring mountains, right before his eyes – the mighty Yukon.

It was 4 p.m. on 8 June 1898 when Jack cast off from the riverbank, leaving Dawson behind. Alongside were 'big-bodied, big-hearted' John Thorson, and Charley Taylor, fellow prospectors eager to return to civilisation before another winter descended. Jack and his new companions had stumped up enough for a small boat, 'home-made, weak-kneed, and leaky'. In the stern rocked a Klondike stove, hidden by a canvas covering where they would sleep between watches and shifts at steering.

His strength fast ebbing as scurvy returned, Jack had only one destination: St Michael, the salt-water port on the Bering Sea at the mouth of the Yukon, 1800 miles away. 'The three of us had sworn to make this a pleasure trip, in which all labour was to be performed by gravitation, and all profit reaped by ourselves. And what a profit it was to us who had been accustomed to pack great loads on our backs or drag all day at the sleds for a paltry twenty-five or thirty miles. We now hunted, played cards, smoked, ate and slept, sure of our six miles an hour, of our 144 a day.'

Jack began to keep a journal. As each dawn greeted him with swirls of mist, the trip became more and more a surreal drift down the main artery of Alaska. Everywhere were sights and sounds which he never imagined could exist so near the Arctic. It was summer, the couple of months a year when life in Alaska blazes with all the intensity one would expect if a southern summer were compressed into half its normal timespan.

First the Yukon carried Jack and his companions five hundred miles north, then, just as it crossed the Arctic Circle, it veered south in a great bend. A few miles after this stretch, as the river divided and a land of a thousand islands emerged, dense fog shrouded the boat each morning. Death was close at hand. They were now in a treacherous stretch of the Yukon called the Flats, 'a vast area of low country, extending for hundreds of miles in every direction, into which the Yukon plunges and is practically lost'. Men had been known to lose their way and wander for weeks in 'this perplexing maze'.

Here, among the powerful currents, the days of easy drifting came to a swift end. The ordeal began with a low humming and then a brutal onslaught of buzzing insects. They had arrived in a breeding area for mosquitoes. Jack knew only too well the stories of unprotected men who had been driven to suicide by such attacks. Even caribou and horses had been killed by the insects. In seconds, Jack and his companions dived beneath netting and closed every gap in their clothing. Not until they made it to salt water, still a thousand miles away, would they be free of the mosquito menace. Jack's journal soon included such passages as: 'put up netting and fooled mosquitoes . . . One night badly bitten under netting – couldn't vouch for it but John watched them and said they rushed the netting in a body, one gang holding up the edge while a second gang crawled under. Charley swore that he has seen several of the larger ones pull the mesh apart and let a small one squeeze through. I have seen them with their proboscis bent and twisted after an assault on the sheet iron stove.'

Days after the first assault, almost mad from itching, they landed the 'heavy craft amid the litter of some flimsy bark canoes which lined the Yukon's banks'. They had arrived in an Indian fishing camp. Picking his steps among the tents and wading through the sprawling babies and fighting dogs, Jack made his way to a large log building.

After much pushing and shoving, he forced an entrance through a cluster of children. The long, low room he entered was packed with dancers. There was 'no light, no ventilation, except through the crowded doorway'. In the semi-darkness, 'strapping bucks and wild-eyed squaws' sweated, howled and revelled in a dance which defied description. With the elation of the 'traveller who scales the virgin peak', Jack prepared to enjoy 'the novelty of the situation'. What he saw next stunned him. At the back of the crowded room, 'dizzy with heat and the smell of bodies', he suddenly made out 'the fair bronzed skin, the blue eyes, the blond mustache of the ubiquitous Anglo-Saxon'. Here, where he least expected it, was evidence of how thoroughly some sourdoughs had acclimatised to the wilds of Alaska and assimilated with the native Indian culture, often taking Indian women as their brides.

In the popular imagination, the Indians had been demonised as the savage enemy in the battle to win the West. The trail to the Klondike and, fifty years earlier, to California, had been cut through Indian lands, territory which the Anglo-Saxon saw as his 'manifest destiny' to subjugate and civilise.

The further Jack and his companions ventured along the Yukon, the more bizarre their journey became. A hundred miles below a village called Nuklukyeto, their 'midnight watch was disturbed by a wild chant which rose and fell as it floated across the water'. An hour later they rounded a bend and landed at another fishing village 'so engrossed in its religious rites' that their arrival was not noticed. 'Urged on by the chief medicine men, women had abandoned themselves to the religious ecstasy, their raven hair unbound and falling to their hips, while their bodies were swaying and undulating to the swing of the song.'

Further, deeper into the limitless forests of central Alaska they drifted. At intervals deserted villages, abandoned human belongings and ancient bones bleached by the sun broke the endless horizon of trees. At four o'clock one morning Jack watched Indian 'bucks' dance with their 'maidens' on the riverbank; the squaws were gathered in gossiping huddles, their babies rolling in the mud with 'tawny beasts half wolf and half dog'.

By the time Jack reached Anvik, a few hundred miles from the mouth of the Yukon, the horror of scurvy had returned. His teeth clattered whenever he opened his mouth. A stranger saved his life by giving him raw potatoes and a can of tomatoes – worth more to Jack, at this stage, 'than an Eldorado claim'.

After Anvik, the Yukon's brown current ran swiftly out of the heart of darkness, bearing Jack and his companions down towards the sea. As the river's delta appeared in the distance, they made their first contact with the ancient Malemute race, a part-Eskimo tribe living near the Bering Sea. Jack was deeply impressed by their ingenuity and resilience in the struggle to survive. They neither raped the environment nor pillaged its resources, taking only what they needed for food, shelter and clothing.

They were almost at journey's end, yet still the most dangerous section of the Yukon was to come: the treacherous channels of the Great Delta, a myriad of lethal currents that empty into the Bering Sea. After several hours of nervous navigation, Jack found the correct passage, finally reaching St Michael twenty-one days after leaving Dawson.

It was as if he had woken from a dream. The end of his journey was no more than a couple of shacks beside depressing mud flats. Later, he would only remember the sight of a rusting cannon and the smell of rotting fish. In his journal, Jack made his last entry: 'Leave St Michael – unregrettable moment.'

Jack took a job stoking on a boat bound for British Columbia. After eight days shovelling coal, he was badly burnt and had to quit. Fortunately he still had enough money to buy a steerage ticket to

Vancouver, from where he returned to Oakland by again riding freight trains.

Jack came back from the Klondike a changed man. In the brutal northland, his mind had expanded. He had read *Paradise Lost* and Dante's *Inferno* for the first time, and his determination to become a writer had grown. Above all, the Klondike had taught him that dreams are made real at often terrible costs. In the years that followed he would live as if climbing an unending Chilkoot Pass, convinced that he could overcome any obstacle.

The gold rush had also provided Jack with the stuff of great fiction. The north, with all its yearnings and tragedy, was the richest metaphor any writer could want for life itself. 'I never realised a cent from any properties I had an interest in up there,' he would later concede. 'Still, I have been managing to pan out a living ever since on the strength of the trip.'

6

Superman

Nietzsche rejected the democratic idea of equal rights
for all men as hampering natural leaders from realising
their full capacities . . . He saw the dominant weight of
mass tastes, opinions and moral prejudices as a 'slave
morality'. Mankind's leaders should live by a 'master
morality' above common concepts of good and evil.
The goal of human evolution was the *Ubermensch*, the
higher man, the 'artist-genius' who would be to ordinary
man as ordinary man was to the monkey.

BARBARA W. TUCHMAN, *The Proud Tower*

'SOME ARE BORN TO FORTUNE and some have fortune thrust upon
them. But in my case I was clubbed into fortune, and bitter necessity
wielded the club.' Only Jack London could have described the most
remarkable accomplishment of his life so violently. But for once he
did not exaggerate. His climb in only a couple of years to the literary
summit of America has yet to be matched in speed and drama.

No contemporary could claim, as Jack did, that he had pulled
himself up so rapidly by his own bootstraps. 'Critics have complained
about the swift education one of my characters, Martin Eden,
achieved,' he later complained. 'In three years, from a sailor with a
common school education, I made a successful writer of him. The
critics say this is impossible. Yet I was Martin Eden. At the end of
three working years, two of which were spent in high school and the
university and one spent at writing, and all three in studying
immensely and intensely, I was publishing stories in magazines such
as the *Atlantic Monthly*, was correcting proofs of my first book (issued

by Houghton Mifflin Co.), was selling sociological articles to *Cosmopolitan* and *McClure's*, had declined an associate editorship proffered me by telegraph from New York City, and was getting ready to marry.'

These achievements were even more notable given that he had returned from the Klondike a wreck, soot-soiled from riding the freights again, and near death from scurvy. All he had to show for his adventure was $4.50 in gold dust and the journal he kept while floating down the Yukon. Mention of Alaska would, for several months, make Jack swear like a disgruntled sourdough. It was a hellish place and had ruined his health. He had gone there to get rich and all he'd brought back was a bad case of skin-rot. Damn gold country!

Never would Jack publicly concede that the wild had beaten him. It had provided adventure, and the crucible of his best fiction. But in fact it had defeated him just as it had crushed thousands of gold-blind Anglo-Saxons who did not return alive. Although his journal had included the observation that 'the Indian seems unable to comprehend the fact that he can never get the better of the white man', in such an environment evolution had made of the Malemutes by far the more successful men.

It was indeed a bitter homecoming. His family were in worse straits than when he had left: his stepfather, John London, had died, and Flora was in dire need of support, having adopted Johnny Miller, the son of Jack's stepsister Ida, who could not cope with the child. After looking in vain for work, Jack tried to cash in on his experiences in the Klondike. The local papers were full of stories about the gold rush – here was a market, and Jack had goods to sell.

Flora watched in silence as her son pulled out his typewriter again. Even if he were to sell a couple of pieces, the pay would not be enough to live on. She preferred quick, easy cash: in her son's absence, she had spent some of the housekeeping on lottery tickets. And so she may have grimaced as her son knocked off a story about his journey down the Yukon and posted it, with a covering letter, to the editor of the *San Francisco Bulletin*:

September 17th 1898
Dear Sir

I have just returned from a year's residence in the Klondike
entering the country by the way of Dyea and Chilcoot Pass.
I left by the way of St Michael, thus making altogether a
journey of 2,500 miles on the Yukon in a small boat. I have
sailed and travelled quite extensively in other parts of the world
and I have learned to seize upon that which is interesting, to
grasp the true romance of things, and to understand the people
I may be thrown amongst.

I have just completed an article of 4,000 words describing
the trip from Dawson to St Michael in a row boat. Kindly
let me know if there would be any demand in your columns
for it – of course thoroughly understanding that the acceptance
of the manuscript is to depend upon its literacy and intrinsic
value.

Yours very respectfully,
Jack London

A few weeks later, the letter returned with a note scribbled at the
bottom: 'Interest in Alaska has subsided in an amazing degree. Then
again so much has been written that I do not think it would pay us
to buy your story.'

Undeterred, Jack dashed off a twenty-one-thousand-word story
which he targeted at a juvenile magazine, *Youth's Companion*. Again,
he began to push himself to his mental limits, pausing only to sleep
for three hours each night. To be a writer, he had decided, was all
he had ever wanted. Surely, though, it was a crazy dream? He had
many liabilities and no assets, no income, and two other mouths to
feed.

Jack knew none of the rules of the writing game, and lived in
California, far from the publishing centres in the east. He had little
idea what editors were looking for. But if it killed him, he had vowed,
he would succeed. 'If I die I shall die hard, fighting to the last,' he
told Mabel Applegarth, 'and hell shall receive no fitter inmate than
myself . . . If I were a woman I would prostitute myself to all men
but that I would succeed – in short, I will.'

As Jack saw it, two things were essential to success: a clear philosophy of life, and extensive study of how the 'greats' had risen to the top. In the Klondike and as a tramp, he had continued to skim nineteenth-century philosophy. At college he had become dangerously enamoured of the theories of Herbert Spencer. From the history of ideas he had grabbed what he found most attractive, and with little time to ruminate, had swallowed many a spurious idea whole.

But Jack was still looking for a system, a set of rules to clear his confusion, by which to plot the route ahead. If Marx, Darwin and Spencer had given him a rudimentary belief in a scientific approach to life, what he still lacked was a philosophical motivation for living.

In coming years, Jack would find inspiration in several philosophers, including Benjamin Kidd and Schopenhauer. But it would be the German Friedrich Nietzsche whose ideas would affect him most. Like countless others of his time, Jack would be seduced by Nietzsche's genius for the incendiary phrase: 'Egoism is the very essence of a noble soul . . . Live dangerously. Build your cities on the slopes of Vesuvius . . . All truths are for me soaked in blood . . . All idealism is falsehood in the face of necessity . . . Faith means not wanting to know what is true . . . The most common lie is that with which one lies to oneself: lying to others is relatively an exception.'

Above all, Nietzsche provided Jack with an argument to validate egotism. For it was through him that Jack would discover the theory of the 'superman' – better, stronger, wiser than other men, who would overcome all obstacles. In his quest for power, the superman would speed the selection of the fittest.

'Such an individual,' the historian Richard Tarnas has written, 'had to transform life into a work of art, within which he could forge his character, embrace his fate, and recreate himself as heroic protagonist of the world epic. He had to invent himself anew, imagine himself into being. He had to will into existence a fictive drama into which he could enter and live, imposing a redemptive order on the chaos of a meaningless universe without God . . . Truth was not something one proved or disproved; it was something one *created*.'

Surely, Jack was such a man? Was it not his destiny to rise from obscurity and one day inspire – as an 'artist-genius' – the masses to revolution? Had he not survived his mother's neglect, the Barbary

Coast, jail, the Chilkoot Pass, scurvy? Had not Nietzsche spoken like an oracle? 'To be a man was to write man in large capitals on my heart,' was Jack's new credo. 'To adventure like a man, and fight like a man and do a man's work (even for a boy's pay) – these were things that reached right in and gripped hold of me as no other thing could. And I looked ahead into long vistas of a hazy interminable future in which, playing what I conceived to be a man's game, I should continue to travel with unfailing health, without accidents, and with muscles ever vigorous . . . This future was interminable. I could only see myself raging through life without end like one of Nietzsche's blond beasts, lustfully roving and conquering by sheer superiority and strength.'

One of Jack's contemporaries, Austin Lewis, later wrote: 'In 1899, Jack London was young, vigorous, with a sure sense of emotional values and a mind which was beginning to show marks of cultivation and development. One would have predicted for him a wholesome, beautiful existence. But even then there were other concepts and theories of life attracting him, seducing him, destroying him, really . . . Jack stood with one foot planted in the soil of social democracy, but the other foot was already being clogged in the morasses of the philosophical teachings from which have sprung fascism.'

Having adopted a philosophy of life, Jack next cast about for literary role-models. His favourite 'artist-geniuses' were an eclectic bunch: Robert Louis Stevenson, who had lived in San Francisco, Zola, Flaubert, Turgenev and Montesquieu. But he drew most inspiration from the British journalist turned poet and adventure-writer, Rudyard Kipling, then the best-selling author in the world, an *Ubermensch* among writers. So effectively did Kipling strike the 'perfect combination of noble destiny and unselfish mission' that his poems were known throughout the English-speaking world, including 'The White Man's Burden', published in *McClure's* magazine in 1899:

> Take up the White Man's burden –
> Send forth the best ye breed –
> Go bind your sons to' exile
> To serve your captives' need;
> To wait in heavy harness

On fluttered folk and wild –
Your new-caught sullen peoples,
Half-devil and half-child.

Determined to acquire Kipling's style, Jack copied out story after story until he felt Kipling's cadences were his own. In a letter, he later acknowledged his debt to the Englishman: 'As for myself, there is no end of Kipling in my work. I have even quoted him. I would never have possibly written anywhere near the way I did had Kipling never been. True, true, every bit of it.'

Night and day, Jack hunched over his battered typewriter, by his side a line of roll-your-own cigarettes to get him through a night of wandering, lost, in a Yukon blizzard; of crossing vast snowfields behind a team of yelping huskies; of hearing the wolves calling to each other beneath the midnight sun. With enough effort, enough digging, he would strike paydirt. He knew it.

'Dig is the arcana of literature,' he wrote. 'There is no such thing as inspiration and very little genius. Dig, blooming under opportunity, results in what appears to be the former, and certainly makes possible the development of what original modicum of the latter one may possess. Dig is a wonderful thing, and will move more mountains than faith ever dreamed of. In fact, Dig should be the legitimate father of all self-faith.'

Eventually, however, this homespun philosophy was not enough. By late 1898, Jack was numbing his mind with overwork, and rewards were as distant as ever. Hope again withered as money disappeared; the editorial offices in the east, bastion of elitism and dour convention, continued to respond to his efforts with rejection slips.

Jack began to nurture a deep resentment of editors which would last until the end of his life. Like Martin Eden, his alter-ego, he grew to believe that 'the chief qualification of ninety-nine per cent of all editors is failure. They have failed as writers ... And right there is the cursed paradox of it. Every portal to success in literature is guarded by those watch-dogs, the failures in literature.'

Jack's anger at the mediocrities who stood between him and success only increased his determination to escape failure. He pushed on, certain that he could achieve the impossible. He began to lose weight.

His nerves became jagged, his skin sallow from lack of sunlight. But still he kept up his Spartan regime. Every morning the alarm clock would wake him at five o'clock sharp; all day he would sit and type away, lifting his stooped shoulders from the writing-desk only to find out more about the world he wanted to fictionalise.

The door to fortune seemed to crack open, only to slam shut again when Jack won two prizes of $10 each for essays in a contest organised by the Oakland Fifth Ward Republican Club for campaign songs, essays and cartoons. Jack was not paid for these contributions to the Republican cause – contributions he would later conveniently forget.

'Well, well, plenty of dig, and an equal amount of luck may enable me some day to make perhaps a small livelihood out of the pen,' he wrote to Mabel Applegarth. 'But what's the diff? I get so hungry sometimes, hungry for all I have not, that I'd rather quit the whole thing and lie down for the good long sleep, did I not have my mother to look out for. This world holds so much, and it takes but such a little to get a fair share of it.'

Jack was aware that he had not lived up to his ideal of the superman. Now, sheer discipline would be his lifeline. He would also adopt Kipling's work ethic. Work! Work! And so he established a routine, which was to last a lifetime, of writing a thousand words a day. If he fell behind his daily quota, he compensated the following morning.

Yet he could not live off his imagination and memories alone. Finally forced to look for work in December 1898, again the gods were against him. 'I had my name down in five employment bureaus. I advertised in three newspapers. I sought out the few friends I knew who might be able to get me work; but they were either uninterested or unable to find anything for me.'

When an old schoolfriend, Frank Atherton, visited him one morning, Jack admitted that he had contemplated suicide. 'I could see nothing to live for. All I could see was failure. If I failed to succeed in writing, there would be nothing else for me to do. I recalled all the various jobs I had worked at in the past, way back to my paper route. And the only bright spot in all my past experience was the open sea. But how could I go to sea again when my mother and Johnny Miller were depending on me?'

Atherton asked how he could be of any assistance to them if he were dead.

'Oh, I know I was crazy,' Jack admitted, 'but that was the way I felt about it. I had it all planned, the farewell letters all ready to mail . . . I'm going to stick to my writing,' he insisted, 'and the publishers are going to accept it whether they like it or not. And some of these days they'll be glad to take the stuff they've rejected and pay me a good price for it; you just wait and see.'

Just as Jack considered giving up the game, a letter magically arrived. It was from the editor of the *Black Cat*, a Boston magazine dedicated to juvenile adventure stories, who wanted to run one of Jack's pieces, 'A Thousand Deaths', on condition that it was cut by half, in which case a cheque for $40 would soon be on its way. 'I was at the end of my tether,' Jack recalled, 'beaten out, starved . . . Literally, and literarily, I was saved by the *Black Cat* story.'

On 16 January 1899, an even better reprieve from the abyss landed on the doormat: a letter from the local post office offering Jack a job that would pay enough to support his family and spelt security for life. But he was now in the 'snares of writing' – ambition pulsed through him. Yet he had earned just $40, a few cents more than he had spent on paper and postage.

Jack called the post office manager. Could he wait a few months for him to make his mind up?

'Then you don't want the job?' the manager asked coldly.

'But I do,' Jack replied. 'Don't you see, if you pass me over this time . . .'

'If you want it,' the manager snapped, 'you will take it.'

His mother made the decision. She had not forgotten the prize Jack had won back in 1893. Through her son, perhaps she might have the social life she had dreamed of when she first moved to San Francisco, her very own Dawson City of spiritual riches. She suggested he keep fighting. She was always up for a gamble, whether on a lottery ticket or in the hope of vicarious fame.

Her faith was soon rewarded. Within just six months of returning from Alaska, the *Overland Monthly*, the west's most prestigious literary magazine, accepted the first of Jack's Klondike stories, 'To the Man on Trail'. Ecstatic, Jack quickly submitted a second, one of his best short stories, 'The White Silence', which appeared in the February 1899 issue. Its narrative raced along like a sled with new runners, driven by Jack's most evocative prose to date:

> Nature has many tricks wherewith she convinces man of his finity – the ceaseless flow of the tides, the fury of the storm, the shock of the earthquake, the long roll of heaven's artillery – but the most tremendous, the most stupefying of all, is the passive phase of the White Silence. All movement ceases, the sky clears, the heavens are as brass; the slightest whisper seems sacrilege, and man becomes timid, affrightened at the sound of his own voice. Sole speck of life journeying across the ghostly wastes of a dead world, he trembles at his audacity, realises that his is a maggot's life, nothing more. Strange thoughts arise unsummoned, and the mystery of all things strives for utterance ... then, if ever, man walks alone with God.

The story featured the Malemute Kid and his sidekick Mason, who are struggling to survive in minus 65 degree temperatures, with 'two hundred miles of unbroken trail in prospect' and only six days' food left for themselves and none for their dogs. With them is Ruth, Mason's pregnant Indian wife. One morning Mason is crushed by a falling tree. His arm, leg and back are broken; an 'occasional moan' is only sign of life. If Ruth and the Malemute Kid wait for him to die, they could also perish. Mason begs the Malemute Kid to take his wife and unborn child to safety. In an act of tragic mercy, the Malemute Kid puts Mason out of his misery and carries out his wishes.

'The White Silence' was remarkably accomplished, introducing several facets that would come to distinguish Jack's fiction from that of his contemporary adventure writers: lyrical descriptions of the elements and landscape, a life-or-death situation, and characters who appeared authentic to those who had never experienced life in the remoter regions of the planet.

The story established Jack as the most talented young writer in town, and certainly the most invigorating. George Hamlin Fitch, literary critic of the *San Francisco Chronicle*, concluded: 'I would rather have written "The White Silence" than anything that has appeared in fiction in the last ten years.'

The story also marked the beginning of a lifelong friendship. Cloudesley Johns, a young postmaster at a small desert office in Harold, California, and an apprentice writer, sent Jack his first fan letter after 'The White Silence' appeared. Jack immediately replied to thank him, and within weeks the pair were writing to each other almost daily.

'The White Silence' had won Jack a loyal ally and considerable local prestige, but very little else. To his outrage, he was paid just $7.50 for the piece. Had he not read that the standard rate for magazines was two cents per word? Yet he had received only a fifth of that. With most of his possessions already pawned, he was further than ever from making enough to keep his family, however intense the thrill of seeing his name in print.

Jack later claimed that he was forced to visit the *Overland Monthly*'s offices in person to obtain payment, so shoestring was the magazine's budget. While he wrangled with the managing editor, Roscoe Eames, a secretary working for the magazine caught his eye. Eames introduced his niece, Charmian Kittredge. Charmian would always remember the meeting.

In a letter written on Christmas Day 1898, Jack had revealed his frustrations to Mabel Applegarth:

About the loneliest Christmas I ever faced ... Well, the FIRST BATTLE has been fought. While I have not conquered, I'll not confess defeat. Instead, I have learned the enemy's strongholds and weak places, and by the same I shall profit when the SECOND BATTLE comes off; and by what I learn through that, I will be better for the Third Battle – and so on, ad infinitum ... Are you aware of the paradox entailed by progress? It makes me both jubilant and sad. You cannot help feeling sad when looking back over work and realising its weak places, its errors, its inanities, and again, you cannot but rejoice at having so improved that you are aware of it, and feel capable of better things ... There are numerous paths to earthly happiness; but to find them, skill in geography or typography is worse than useless. I shall forsake my old dogmas, and henceforth, worship the true god. 'There is no God but Chance, and Luck shall be his prophet!'

Neither God nor Luck rescued Jack. He was richer in material than he knew, and a natural-born writer. Impressed by his first stories, the *Overland Monthly* offered him a contract for six more, promising that though the fee would still be only $7.50 each, the stories would be given prominence in the magazine and were bound to attract the attention of reviewers and higher-paying publications on the East Coast.

Although the *Overland Monthly* could only provide Jack with barely enough to live, it was an ideal showcase for his talents. The magazine vigorously promoted young western writers. Charles Warren Stoddard, Bret Harte, and Ina Coolbrith no less – known as the 'Golden Gate Trinity' – had all written for the magazine. Because of his association with it, Jack would be taken seriously as a fiction writer.

Jack told Mabel Applegarth the good news. At last he was on his way. Soon he would be financially secure, and they could be married. To his dismay, Mabel told him that a handful of acceptances from one magazine meant little. It would take a decade, perhaps longer, for him to arrive. Suddenly, Jack realised that she did not understand him or his aspirations. Despite her love of Byron and Shelley, she was as bound by convention as her mother.

It was not only Mabel's cool response to his early success which made Jack re-evaluate his ethereal goddess. Absence had already made his heart grow colder. In the Yukon he had met women with all the qualities Mabel suddenly appeared to lack: strength, courage, and unreserved faith in him. On his return to Oakland, in the middle-class society which Mabel personified, Jack had to struggle to conceal his contempt for those who preened and posed in the parlours.

'It was a great love, at the time,' he would write to a close friend in 1901 of his infatuation with Mabel. 'I mistook the moment for the eternal . . . Time passed. I awoke, frightened, and found myself judging. She was very small. The positive virtues were hers, and likewise the negative vices. She was pure, honest, true, sincere, everything. But she was small. Her virtues led her nowhere. Works? She had none. Her culture was a surface smear, her deepest depth a singing shallow. Do you understand? Can I explain further? I awoke, and judged, and my puppy love was over.'

*   *   *

At last, in November 1899, Jack's big break arrived. He had written a long story, 'An Odyssey of the North', and sent it to the *Atlantic Monthly*, the most haughty literary magazine in the United States, published in New York. He fully expected his manuscript to be returned with a condescending note, but instead the editor praised the story, asked him to cut three thousand words from the opening section, and offered him $120. The story's hero, Alex Grunderson, is 'a king of Eldorado', a six-foot superman: 'To bear his three hundred pounds of bone and muscle, his snowshoes were greater by a generous yard than those of other men. Rough-hewn, with rugged brow and massive jaw and unflinching eyes of palest blue, his face told the tale of one who knew but the law of might.'

'An Odyssey of the North', Jack later wrote, marked the beginning of his career – its publication in January 1900 brought him to the attention of East Coast book publishers. Houghton Mifflin were the first to approach him, with the idea of collecting his Alaska tales in book form. The result was *The Son of the Wolf* (the Alaskan Indians' name for the white man), published in April 1900. The collection included some of Jack's finest short stories, including 'The White Silence'; 'In a Far Country', about two men holed up together throughout a brutal winter who end up trying to kill each other; and 'An Odyssey of the North'.

The critics praised the stories' virility and vivid descriptions. 'His work is as discriminating as it is powerful,' said *The Critic*. 'It has grace as well as terseness, and it makes the reader hopeful that the days of the giants are not yet gone by.'

If readers wanted to know more about the twenty-four-year-old author of these stirring tales, which read as if the author had lived them himself, they could write to Houghton Mifflin for a biographical report. Like his stories, however, the biography Jack had provided for his publishers was part fact, part fiction.

He had begun to create his own mythology. Because he could not tell the full truth about his background, he tried to erase his suspected illegitimacy by adopting a heroic ancestry, the genealogy of a great Californian. His father, John London, he told Houghton Mifflin, was 'Pennsylvania born, a soldier, a scout, backwoodsman, trapper, and wanderer'. To even have hinted at the circumstances surrounding his birth would have been to admit to neuroses Jack had yet to realise fully; it would be many years before he began to exorcise such demons. In the meantime, he would tell his own story as if it were a Horatio Alger parable of rags-to-riches success. That, Jack sensed, was what his mass readership wanted to hear.

To a great degree, this version of his life was the truth. Only eighteen months ago, he had returned from the Yukon delta penniless and physically broken. Yet in 1899 alone he had published twenty-four pieces, and had sold stories to the most discerning magazine and publishing house in America. It had taken him less than two years to cast his shadow as a writer. 'With one foot in the past and the other in the future', he had 'noisily straddled two centuries, last of the writers to celebrate the American frontier, first to trumpet the battles on the frontier of social justice'.

'That's the way it is,' Jack would tell his daughter Joan fifteen years later. 'You look back and see how hard you worked, and how poor you were, and how desperately anxious you were to succeed, and all you can remember is how happy you were. You were young, and you were working at something you believed in with all your heart, and you knew you were going to succeed!'

In 1903, Jack would explain in detail the secrets of his success. In an article, 'Getting into Print', which appeared in *The Editor* magazine, he gave advice which has since inspired countless young writers:

> Don't quit your job in order to write unless there is no one dependent upon you. Fiction pays best of all, and when it is of fair quality is more easily sold. A good joke will sell quicker than a good poem, and, measured in sweat and blood, will bring better remuneration. Avoid the unhappy ending, the harsh, the brutal, the tragic, the horrible – if you care to see in print the things you write. (In this connection don't do as I do, but do as I say.) Humour is the hardest to write, easiest to sell, and best rewarded. There are only a few who are able to do it. If you are able, do it by all means. You will find it a Klondike and a Rand rolled into one. Look at Mark Twain.
>
> Don't write too much. Concentrate your sweat on one

story, rather than dissipate it over a dozen. Don't loaf and invite inspiration; light out after it with a club, and if you don't get it you will nonetheless get something that looks remarkably like it. Set yourself a 'stint', and see that you do that 'stint' each day; you will have more words to your credit at the end of the year. Study the tricks of the writers who have arrived. They have mastered the tools with which you are cutting your teeth. They are doing things, and their work bears the internal evidence of how it is done. Don't wait for some good Samaritan to tell you, but dig it out for yourself.

See that your pores are open and your digestion is good. That is, I am confident, the most important rule of all. And keep a notebook. Travel with it, sleep with it. Slap into it every stray thought that flutters up into your brain. Cheap paper is less perishable than grey matter, and lead pencil marking endures longer than memory. And work. Spell it in capital letters, WORK. WORK all the time. Find out about this earth, this universe, this force and matter, and the spirit that glimmers up through force and matter from the maggot to the Godhead. And by all this I mean WORK for a philosophy of life. It does not hurt how wrong your philosophy of life may be, so long as you have one and have it well. The three great things are: GOOD HEALTH, WORK and a PHILOSOPHY OF LIFE. I may add, nay, must add, a fourth – SINCERITY. Without this, the other three are without avail. With it you may cleave to greatness and sit among the giants.

Jack did not mention the key factor which explained his rapid rise through the ranks of jostling hacks: he appeared on the literary scene at a time of enormous demand for adventure stories. Inexpensive paper manufacture and new printing techniques had helped magazine publishing become a highly profitable industry. By appealing to mass tastes, George Horace Lorimer had increased the circulation of the *Saturday Evening Post* from less than two thousand to more than a million. Frank Munsey of *Munsey's* magazine explained what all editors aimed for: 'Good easy reading for the people – no frills, no fine finishes, no hair splitting niceties, but action, action, always action.'

Jack offered action and plenty more: stories of violence, heroism and virility. 'His work was realism,' he later wrote of his alter ego in *Martin Eden*, 'though he endeavoured to fuse it with the fancies and beauties of imagination. What he sought was an impassioned realism, shot through with human aspiration and faith. What he wanted was life as it was, with all its spirit-groping and soul-reaching left in.'

As well as appearing in print at the dawn of the golden age of the magazine, Jack was writing for an era now known as the 'Strenuous Age', a time when America believed it needed to reclaim the ethos of its pioneer past. The turn-of-the-century immigration of millions of poverty-stricken Europeans to America's newly industrial cities had turned the dream of a New World into a nightmare of squalor, rampant crime and mass unemployment. Many Americans longed to return to the days before urbanisation – before 1893, the year in which the historian Frederick Jackson Turner declared the frontier closed.

By the time Jack tramped across America, the new frontier was urban. The immigrants from Europe who had flocked to America's mushrooming cities were joined by countless farmworkers affected by the agricultural depressions of the 1880s. These cities seethed with the new energies of mass commerce, embodied by fantastically powerful and wealthy tycoons, 'robber barons' such as Rockefeller, Frick, Carnegie and Morgan, who made their fortunes from oil, railroads, steel and the new religion of high finance.

Since 1879, a new form of American literature had started to emerge. In that year Henry Adams had published his bitter novel *Democracy*, about the 'corrupt new political order'. One of the major influences on this 'muckraking literature' was Emile Zola, who believed that literature should be a form of reportage in which 'the study of abstract, metaphysical man is replaced . . . by the study of natural man, subject to psycho-chemical laws and determined by the effects of his milieu'.

By the time Jack enjoyed his first success as a writer, a decade-old tradition of naturalism existed in American literature. Zola's views found eager advocates among writers in the New World who sought a way of recording the rapid changes in American society through the lens of ordinary citizens' lives. Stephen Crane mastered the technique to harrowing effect in *Maggie: A Girl of the Streets* (1893), set in New

York's Lower East Side, but the naturalist movement's most popular author was Frank Norris, who had studied art in Paris and who returned to the University of California with a suitcase full of Zola's works. His novel *McTeague: A Story of San Francisco* (1899), about working-class life in Jack's native city, has been described by Alfred Kazin as 'the first great tragic portrait in America of an acquisitive society'.

In his earliest fiction, set in the Klondike, Jack would turn naturalism into 'a romantic popular and populist celebration – away from a philosophy of despair or ironic victimisation toward a celebration of will and vitalism'. He would reflect an American psyche forged by the frontier, whose characteristics were, in Frederick Jackson's words, 'coarseness and strength . . . acuteness and inquisitiveness . . . restless, nervous energy . . . buoyancy and exuberance which comes with freedom'.

The reader's report for Houghton Mifflin on *The Son of the Wolf,* which would be one of the company's best-selling books of 1900, shows how well Jack's writing suited the nostalgic yearnings of the age: 'He uses the current slang of the mining camps a little too freely, but his style has freshness, vigour and strength. He draws a vivid picture of the terrors of cold, darkness, and starvation, the pleasures of human companionship in adverse circumstances, and the sterling qualities which the rough battle with nature brings out.'

Jack did not need a reader's report, however, to tell him what he already knew from reading his reviews: his prose was so dynamic that it had exploded onto the literary scene with all the brute force needed to usher in a new century. His muscular lyricism had left readers with their nerve-ends jangling and ravenous for more.

Such was his confidence in his abilities that in December 1900 he turned down an offer of employment which a year earlier he might have accepted without hesitation. After winning first prize in a competition sponsored by *Cosmopolitan*, Jack was offered a position as an assistant editor and staff writer on special projects. 'Of course,' he wrote to Cloudesley Johns, 'I shall not accept it. I do not wish to be bound . . . I want to be free, to write what delights me. No office work for me; no routine; no doing this set task and that set task. No man over me.'

All his life, there would be no man over him, except perhaps

Friedrich Nietzsche. But would he ever be free? How much further could he go if he ignored convention and lived life his way? He would, from now on, live the Big Life. He would 'rather be ashes than dust! I would rather that my spark should burn out in a brilliant blaze than it should be stifled by dry rot. I would rather be a superb meteor, every atom of me in magnificent glow, than a sleepy and permanent planet. The proper function of man is to live, not to exist. I shall not waste my days in trying to prolong them. I shall use my time.'

He would write like a superman *pour encourager les autres*, and wait for the inevitable revolution, jogging it along with brilliant sideswipes at the system that had denied him, and millions of others, their birthright.

'I should like to have socialism,' he told Cloudesley Johns, 'yet I know that socialism is not the very next step; I know that capitalism must live its life first, that the world must be exploited to the utmost first; that first must intervene a struggle for life among the nations, severer, more widespread than before. I should much prefer to wake tomorrow in a smoothly-running socialist state but I know I shall not; I know it cannot come that way. I know that the child must go through the child's sickness ere it becomes a man. So, always remember that I speak of things that are; not of things that should be.'

The Oakland Socialist Party were the first to exploit Jack's growing activism, just as factory owners had once exploited his physical strength. He began to lecture on the significance of strike action and the destructive powers of capitalism. Realising that his growing literary cachet would draw desperately-needed publicity, he agreed to run for Mayor of Oakland on the socialists' ticket. There was not the faintest hope that he would be elected, but his name alone would attract attention to the party and its cause.

On 26 January 1901, the *San Francisco Evening Post* reported:

Jack London is announced as a candidate for Mayor of Oakland ... I don't know what a socialist is, but if it is anything like some of Jack London's stories, it must be something awful. I understand that as soon as Jack London is elected Mayor of Oakland by the Social Democrats the name of the place will be changed. The Social Democrats, however, have not yet decided whether they will call it London or Jacktown.

In the autumn 1901 mayoral elections, Jack received just 246 votes (the victor, John L. Davie, a wealthy populist, received 2,548). But he did succeed in his objective – to bring the principles of socialism to a wider audience through his exposure in the local press.

It was not only a political revolution that Jack advocated. He also urged that human relations be viewed more scientifically, according to the same laws of attraction that existed among other species. He had long since discovered the pleasures of sex without becoming tied by the hypocritical moralities of the repressed middle class. Along the waterfront he had become a man. There, sex carried no obvious psychological burden.

There were two types of women, either 'wonderful and unmoral and filled with life to the brim', or offering the promise of being 'the perfect mother, made pre-eminently to know the clasp of the child'. The first kind he called the 'Mate Woman', with whom he might just, from the 'strictly emotional and naturalistic viewpoint', find real love. The second was the 'Mother Woman', 'the last and highest and holiest in the hierarchy of life' – the ideal housewife, a mother who would never nag, who would love him without fail – unlike Flora.

Typically of his contradictory nature, while promoting sexual freedom, Jack had also been increasingly drawn to the idea of marriage. The union he envisaged, however, was far from a permanent bond of love and mutual support. Marriage would speed his biological destiny.

According to one of his first biographers, Jack wanted a mother to 'seven sturdy Anglo-Saxon sons'. And he already knew a woman who matched his specifications perfectly: Bessie Maddern, a forthright, voluptuous, raven-haired Irishwoman in her twenties who had once dreamed of going on the stage, but, forbidden by her family, had settled for tutoring mathematics instead. Her cousin Minnie Maddern Fiske was a celebrated actress who had played several of Ibsen's heroines in New York. As one contemporary, the journalist Joseph Noel described her, Bess was 'slender and, no doubt because she had her hair in the Pompadour mode, looked nearly as tall as Jack. Her face, strong, well-modelled, was enhanced by grey eyes fringed by chorus-girl lashes. When she smiled she was at her best. The surroundings were brightened.'

Until recently, she had also planned to marry. But her fiancé, Fred Jacobs – Jack's old friend from the Oakland Library – had died. He had enlisted in the army at the beginning of the Spanish–American war of 1898, but on his way to the Philippines on a troopship, before he got to fire a single shot, he had come down with a tropical fever and died before his boat docked at Manila. Four thousand other Americans – twenty times the number killed in battle – would die of disease during what the politician John Hay called a 'splendid little war', which ended with the Spanish ceding the Philippines to America in December 1898 for a $20 million indemnity.

Bess was flattered by Jack's approaches immediately following Fred's funeral. She was well-educated, and had read Jack's short stories. Though she found them a touch too brutal, she had always assured Jack, since his first attempts to write, that he would succeed one day.

No one knew better than she how far Jack had come. She had tutored him while he was cramming for entry to Berkeley, and since 1895, on his return from the *Sophie Sutherland*, she had spent many afternoons cycling with him to picnics with the Applegarths. As their relationship developed, she began to edit his manuscripts, correcting spellings and smoothing out the cruder sections, the raw phrases and clumsy grammar. As a secretary, too, she had just the qualities Jack was looking for.

'You know I do things quickly,' Jack wrote on 3 April 1900 to Ninetta Eames, editor of the *Overland Monthly*. 'Sunday morning, last, I had not the slightest intention of doing what I am going to do . . . Sunday evening I opened transactions for a wife; by Monday evening had the affair well under way; and next Sunday morning I shall marry . . . "the rash boy", I hear you say. Divers deep considerations have led me to do this thing; but I shall override just one objection – that of being tied. I am already tied. Though single, I have to support a household just the same . . . As it is, I shall be steadied, and can be able to devote more time to my work. One only has one life, after all, and why not live it? Besides, my heart is large, and I shall be a cleaner, wholesomer man because of a restraint being laid upon me instead of being free to drift wheresoever I listed. I am sure you will understand.'

Despite the fact that Jack later claimed in a letter that he had told Bess he did not love her, after a week's engagement the couple were married – on 7 April 1900, the same day his first book, *The Son of the Wolf,* was published.

A photograph of the 'Mother Woman' and her 'Daddy Boy' was taken in the garden of the Maddern home before the couple left on their bicycles for a three-day honeymoon in northern California. It shows Jack wearing knickerbockers and grinning with a cigarette dangling from his mouth. Bess looks far more sober in her long skirt, and seems to be smiling with some hesitation.

After their brief honeymoon, husband and wife moved into a large house at 1130 East Fifteenth Street in Oakland – spacious enough to accommodate Flora and young Johnny Miller as well. Although Bess and Flora argued bitterly for several weeks, eventually a harmony of sorts prevailed. Flora, encouraged by Jack's stepsister Eliza, grudgingly accepted her new rival. Bess, also placated by Eliza, tried to ignore her mother-in-law by throwing herself into her new duties. When not tutoring students in mathematics, at night she continued to correct Jack's manuscripts, and she read books in which he was interested so that she could share his intellectual passions. She copied out his favourite poems, binding hundreds of them between red cardboard covers, and set up a darkroom in the house where she taught him the basics of photography. Even if Jack had said he did not love her, she was certain that before long he would reciprocate her feelings. As secretary and slaving housewife, she provided the perfect support for Jack's blossoming career.

Within weeks of their marriage, a New York book publisher, S.S. McClure, wrote offering to publish virtually anything Jack produced:

> We are greatly interested in you and want you to feel that you have the warmest kind of friends right here in New York. I wish you would look upon us as your literary sponsors hereafter. If you will send us everything you write we will use what we can, and what we cannot we will endeavour to dispose of to the best possible advantage.

The offer was accompanied by a monthly retainer of $100 which would fund Jack while he worked on what McClure hoped would be his first best-seller, a book to be called *A Daughter of the Snows.* Following McLure's offer – a blessing for any young writer – Jack learned that Bess was pregnant. An heir was also now promised. Never had his career, finances and biological destiny looked so healthy. At long last, he had joined the bourgeoisie.

Howling at the Moon

His personality invested his every movement and every detail of his life with alluring charm. One took his genius for granted, even in those early years when he was struggling with all his unequalled energies to impress himself upon the world . . . He was a captive of beauty – the beauty of bird and flower, of sea and sky and the icy vastness of the Arctic world.

ANNA STRUNSKY, 'Memoirs of Jack London'

JACK HAD MARRIED the wrong woman. It was another he actually loved – Anna Strunsky, a young Russian Jewess with long, lustrous black hair. The first great love of his life was, as one contemporary described her, 'a pretty little ingenue who played the part of a Stanford University intellectual to perfection. She had soft brown eyes, a kindly smile and a throaty little voice that did things to your spine.'

Anna was from a Russian Jewish family that had escaped the pogroms in Russia and took pride in its connections with the notorious anarchist Emma Goldman and other radicals. Though she was just seventeen when she met Jack in autumn 1899 at a left-wing lecture, she was already called 'the girl socialist of San Francisco'. At Stanford University she had been suspended for 'receiving a male visitor in her room instead of the parlour'.

In Anna's eyes, Jack was 'a young man with large blue eyes fringed with dark lashes, and a beautiful mouth which, opening in its ready laugh, revealed an absence of front teeth. The brow, the nose, the contour of the cheeks, the massive throat were Greek. His body gave the impression of grace and athletic strength. He was dressed in grey and was wearing a soft white shirt with collar attached, and black neck tie.'

Jack was immediately infatuated with the romantic and spiritual Anna, even though he had developed an image of himself as a hard man who lived by the rule of cold logic. 'He systematised his life,' Anna later wrote. 'Such colossal energy, and yet he could not trust himself! He lived by rule. Law, Order, and Restraint was the creed of this vital, passionate youth.'

'I too was a dreamer,' Jack confided to Anna shortly after his marriage to Bess: 'But early, at only nine, the hard hand of the world was laid upon me. It was never relaxed. It has left me sentiment, but destroyed sentimentalism. It has made me practical, so that I am known as harsh, stern, uncompromising. It has taught me that reason is mightier than imagination; that the scientific man is superior to the emotional man.'

As with many of his friends, the more Anna got to know Jack, the more concerned she became about his philosophy of life. Theirs would be a relationship of opposing minds. Time and again, as their friendship blossomed, Anna would combat his Spencerian belief that 'all is law'.

'Our friendship can be described as a struggle – constantly I strained to reach that in him which I felt he was "born to be",' Anna later recalled. 'I looked for the Social Democrat, the Revolutionist, the moral and romantic idealist; I sought the Poet. Exploring his personality was like exploring mountains and the valleys which stretched between troubled my heart . . . He was a Socialist, but he wanted to beat the Capitalist at his own game. To succeed in doing this, he thought, was in itself a service to the Cause; to show them that Socialists were not derelicts and failures had certain propaganda value.'

Anna warned Jack that to 'pile up wealth, or personal success' was to play by the capitalists' rules. Such a game could only end one way – in the defeat of non-material ideals. She never doubted 'the beauty and the warmth and the purity of his own nature'. But she was afraid where his philosophy might lead him. 'These ideas were not worthy of him,' she thought. 'They belittled him and eventually they might eat away his strength and grandeur.'

Despite Anna's warnings and mockery of his contradictions, Jack was soon head over heels in love with her. He had married Bess only after Anna had failed to respond to his advances, and still pursued his infatuation. In the early summer of 1902 he openly declared his passion in a letter which he would sign 'The Sahib'.

This love letter was not included in *The Kempton–Wace Letters* (1903), a collaboration between Jack and Anna. As early as 1900, Jack had asked her to work on a book of correspondence between a young economics professor who believed in 'logic and evolution', played by Jack, and an older friend who believed in 'romantic idealism', played by Anna.

'A young Jewess of 'Frisco and myself,' Jack told Cloudesley Johns at the outset of the project, 'have often quarrelled over our conceptions of love. She happens to be a genius. She is also a materialist by philosophy, and an idealist by innate preference, and is constantly being forced to twist all the facts of the universe in order to reconcile herself with herself. So, finally, we decided that the only way to argue the question would be by letter. Then we wondered if a collection of such letters should happen to be worth publishing. Then we assumed characters, threw in a real objective love element, and started to work.'

In the first of the letters, Kempton (Anna) congratulates Wace (Jack) on his engagement. 'No, I am not in love,' Wace responds. 'I am very thankful that I am not . . . I am arranging my life so that I can get the most out of it, while the one thing to disorder it, worse than flood and fire and the public enemy, is love.' Wace believes 'love is a disorder of mind and body . . . a means for the perpetuation and development of the human type' that can be 'improved and controlled by the intellect'.

Kempton concludes that Wace is in 'the toils of an idea, the idea of selection, and that he exploits it like a drudge' – just like Jack's revered Herbert Spencer, who had considered the pros and cons of marriage and, unlike Jack, opted to remain a bachelor.

Given the attitudes he expressed in *The Kempton–Wace Letters*, and his infatuation with Anna, it was surprising that Jack's marriage to Bess Maddern lasted longer than the three-day honeymoon. 'It's all right for a man sometimes to marry philosophically,' he would later concede, 'but remember, it's damned hard on the woman.'

*　　*　　*

Throughout his platonic affair with Anna, Jack socialised with a growing circle of similarly artistic friends, 'the Crowd', a Bohemian group that often spent its Sunday afternoons picnicking, reading each other's latest compositions, gossiping about each other's infidelities and frolicking beneath the cherry boughs in the hills of Piedmont, near Oakland.

Its central characters were Joaquin Miller, a bearded poet and accomplished novelist who liked to think of himself as a spiritual guru; James Hopper, Jack's old college friend and now a magazine writer; Jim Whitaker, who had, with Jack's encouragement, begun to make a literary name for himself; and Xavier Martinez, a flamboyant painter with handlebar moustache and long, flowing black hair who had married a teenage girl half his age. One member other than Jack would achieve lasting fame: Arnold Genthe, an itinerant young German who would one day become the most celebrated portrait photographer of his age. 'Jack London,' Genthe later recalled, 'had a poignantly sensitive face. His eyes were those of a dreamer . . . Yet at the same time he gave the feeling of a terrific and unconquerable physical force.'

Shortly after Jack's marriage to Bess, the Crowd had begun to drop by his home every Wednesday night for dinner, conversation and raucous card games. After charades and singalongs, Jack would sometimes read his latest fiction. Those who attended these evenings would remember them with nostalgia for the rest of their lives. Many who met Jack in the first flush of success thought him an 'artist-genius', even if he had not yet shown it beyond doubt in his prose. The sculptor Finn Frolich recalled: 'I never saw a man in all my life with more magnetism, beautiful magnetism. If a preacher could have the love in his make up, and the life, God, this whole world would go religious. When he talked, he was marvellous. His hair was bushy, and he wore an eyeshade, and his eyes were big, and his mouth was just as sensitive and full of expression, and his words came out of him just rippling. It was something inside of him, his brain just ran sixty miles a minute, you couldn't follow him. He talked better than he wrote.'

One of the many women to fall under his spell, Mira Maclay, a young artist, would remember Jack sitting on a chair on a late November afternoon, his tousled hair seemingly bathed in a halo of light. Others were not so impressed. Carrie Sterling, the wife of a San Francisco poet, believed Jack was a bad influence and not to be trusted. Before long she would be joined in this belief by Bess. She, of all people, knew the real Jack, the man he was when not surrounded by admirers.

Bess was soon irritated by Jack's weekly *soirées*. She perhaps sensed they were his opportunity to show off, to flirt with other women and flatter his ego, and to remind her how little her qualities now appealed to him. Gradually, Bess came to resent playing hostess at parties which consumed her housekeeping and whose guests she regarded as husband-hunting sycophants.

Among them was Charmian Kittredge, the secretary who had been working at the *Overland Monthly* when Jack burst into the office demanding payment for 'The White Silence'. An orphan who had been brought up by her aunt Ninetta Eames, Charmian was a fierce advocate of women's suffrage. Unlike Bess, she could discuss censored books, and had little time for conventional attitudes to sex and marriage. One of the first women in the Bay area to ride a horse astride, not sidesaddle, she was the spitting image of the ideal 'Mate Woman' Jack described in *The Kempton–Wace Letters*: 'wonderful and unmoral and filled with life to the brim'.

Charmian's kind, first identified as the 'New Woman' by the novelist Sarah Grand in the *North American Review* in 1894, was beginning to make an impact in America. Although they did not yet have the right to vote (they would have to wait until 1920 to do so), women had started to enjoy a freedom of which their mothers could only have dreamed. It was still possible for a woman to be arrested for smoking a cigarette while riding in an open car in Manhattan, but opportunities for employment had grown considerably. Many women had started to wear shorter skirts, revealing their ankles, some played tennis, smoked cigarettes, and even had sex outside marriage. Women such as Charmian, outspoken and daring, would inspire many of Jack's heroines, including that of his first novel, *A Daughter of the Snows*.

While writing that book, Jack continued his correspondence with Cloudesley Johns. In one letter he conceded that he had perhaps taken on more than he could manage in attempting a novel. By the time he reached the last chapters, he admitted to Johns the book was a failure. He had ignored the advice he had given to Johns, who was also writing a book, *The Philosophy of the Road*:

> You are handling stirring life, romance, things of human life and death, humour and pathos, but God, man, handle them as they should be. Don't you tell the reader the philosophy of The Road. HAVE YOUR CHARACTERS TELL IT BY THEIR DEEDS, ACTION, TALK. Study Stevenson and Kipling and see how they eliminate themselves and create things that live, and breathe, and grip men, and cause reading lamps to burn overtime. Atmosphere stands always for the elimination of the artist. Get your good strong phrases, fresh and vivid: write intensively, not exhaustively or lengthily; don't narrate – paint! draw! build! CREATE! Better one thousand words that are builded than a whole book of mediocre, spun-out, dashed-off stuff. Damn you! Forget you! And then the world will remember you!

Success was beginning to go to Jack's head. He was becoming impatient with those who did not share his dreams, his Calvinist work ethic, his Spencerian world view. 'If I see a man with a good brain who simply won't get down and dig,' he told Cloudesley Johns, 'who won't master fundamentals, I cannot help but pity him. So it is with you. You refuse to systematise yourself; refuse to lay a foundation for your life's work; say that such is not your temperament, etc.; and in short are cowardly.'

For all his belief in 'dig', however, Jack had not yet mastered the fundamentals of the novel. *A Daughter of the Snows* was a badly executed jumble of his current intellectual confusions. Its disorganised melodrama and unconvincing characters failed to impress his publisher, who rejected it for publication in *McClure's* magazine. The book-publishing subsidiary also turned it down, and in 1902 McClure sold it on to J.B. Lippincott in Philadelphia, who paid an advance of $750.

A Daughter of the Snows' heroine, Frona Welse, has a 'prize-fighter's biceps' and a 'philosopher's brains', and nothing but contempt for middle-class women: 'the hot-house breeds – pretty, helpless, well-rounded, stall-fatted things'. She seduces Vance Corliss, a Yale-educated mining specialist, and encourages him to forget the city and adopt 'the faith of the trail and mining camp'.

The most perceptive critique of Jack's first novel came from Julian Hawthorne, the son of Nathaniel Hawthorne, in *Wilshire's* magazine. 'In spite of all that her creator can do,' Hawthorne wrote, 'the young lady [Frona Welse] betrays at every step the most wearisome self-consciousness and affectation; I cannot recall a single act or word of hers that has a genuine ring to it. She is, indeed, as much a monster – a thing contrary to nature – as the phenomenon constructed by the philosopher Frankenstein.'

Some critics have, however, since argued that Jack's depiction of women such as Frona was far ahead of its time, and that he was a groundbreaking writer in terms of gender issues. In fact, he would always struggle to create authentic female characters. Even his best fiction would suffer because of his unwillingness to fully explore the female psyche, despite his having been surrounded as a child by strong women.

Hawthorne concluded his review: 'He [Jack] knows his scenery well, and can draw it vigorously; he understands his frontiersmen, and can make them credible ... Upon the whole, this writer is to be welcomed; for it is much better to fail in doing a difficult thing than to succeed in doing a trifle. There is bone, fibre and sinew in Mr London. If his good angels screen him from popular success, during the next few formative years of his career, he may do something well worth the doing, and do it well. But if he is satisfied with his present level of performance, there is little hope for him.'

The most disagreeable aspect of the novel, although Hawthorne and most other contemporary critics seem scarcely to have noticed it, is Frona Welse's tendency to spout claptrap about Anglo-Saxon superiority. 'The sharp-beaked fighting galleys,' she swoons at one point, 'and the sea-flung Northmen, great muscled, deep-chested, sprung from the elements, men of sword and sweep ... the dominant races come down out of the North ... a great race, half the earth its heritage and all the sea! In three score generations it rules the world!'

Jack's belief in Anglo-Saxon superiority would be severely tested later in life, but in his twenties it was so deep-seated that it invaded far more than his fiction. In 1899 he had told Cloudesley Johns: 'I do not believe in the universal brotherhood of man . . . I believe my race is the salt of the earth,' and in June that year had added: 'Socialism is not an ideal system devised for the happiness of all men; it is devised for the happiness of certain kindred races. It is devised so as to give more strength to these certain kindred favoured races so that they may survive and inherit the earth to the extinction of the lesser, weaker races.'

As with any man who adopts a fixed philosophy of life, Jack's world view was constantly punctured by actual events. In the early hours of 15 January 1901, Bess gave birth not to a strapping Anglo-Saxon son, the first of the seven he had allegedly set his heart on, but to a screaming baby girl. Just nine days before the birth, Jack had told Anna Strunsky: 'And, O Anna, it must be make or break. No whining, puny breed. It must be great and strong. Or – the penalty must be paid. By it, or by me; one or the other.'

When Bess had gone into labour she had called a doctor, who arrived in such haste that he forgot to bring any pain-killer. Jack was dispatched to buy a bottle of chloroform. On the way home he fell off his bicycle, broke the bottle and cut his hand.

During the birth, the doctor decided to use medical instruments to 'save the mother, if not the child'. When the baby finally emerged, she showed no signs of breathing. After placing the bloodied infant in Jack's mother-in-law's outstretched arms, the doctor and nurse turned their attention to Bess. Suddenly, 'a thin wail transfixed everyone'. The baby was alive.

Though overjoyed that his daughter, whom he named Joan, had survived, Jack felt increasingly frustrated with her mother. During Bess's pregnancy he had told Anna: 'just when freedom seems opening up for me I feel the bands tightening and the riveting of the gyves. I remember now when I was free, when there was no restraint and I did as the heart willed.' Jack told male friends Bess was a gossip, mean-spirited, as cold as the Klondike.

In notes he later made, he planned 'a great novel' whose subject was to be his marriage with Bess. 'His faith and tolerance,' he jotted,

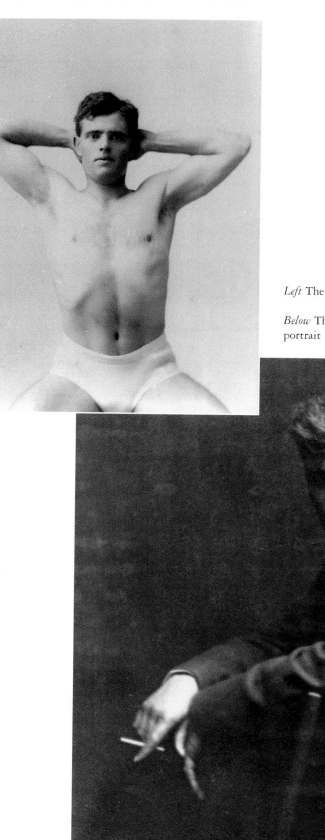

Left The Nietzschean superman.

Below The 'Napoleon of the pen', portrait by Arnold Genthe.

Left Anna Strunsky, 'a pretty little ingenue'.

Below Jack and Charmian pose in oilskins before the launch of the *Snark*. Portrait by Annie Brigman.

Right 'San Francisco is gone.' Street scene after the 1906 earthquake.

Captain Jack and his Mate aboard the *Snark* in Oakland, 1907.

'lack of nagging, never a scene. He early discovered how microscopic she was . . . She was an egomaniac; her mother was, and so was his. So the three could not get along together. Her peasant mind. The band across her brows. In her talk, it was always herself – what she had done, what she was doing, her sacrifices; how she had slaved for her husband; how he lacked consideration . . . His horror, later, when he learns there was nothing too sacred for her to gossip about, and that she lied about those things as well . . . How he loved elsewhere before he knew she lied, how he looked on her sleeping face, and the child's, and cursed himself for a cur.'

Jack had a willing accomplice on his forays to find love elsewhere – Carrie Sterling's husband George: 'the ideal poet in appearance, tall, gracefully built, with a mop of dark hair that fell over his forehead (but properly cut), large grey eyes that had an eternally burning softness, a beautifully curved mouth, which was generally smiling'. Sterling 'observed none of the sartorial vagaries of the traditional poet. In fact he wore black broadcloth, well cut, well fitted, well pressed.' He paid the rent by working as the secretary of his uncle, Frank Havens, a speculator – the worst kind of capitalist – who was making a fortune investing in Oakland real estate. Jack had once shovelled coal, all those years ago, for one of Havens' companies.

Joseph Noel, who worked for the *Oakland Herald*, joined Jack and George on several visits, early in their relationship, to the wild and wanton Barbary Coast. In his memoirs, *Footloose in Arcadia*, Noel would supply a picaresque account of Jack's antics there. While many of Noel's anecdotes were prejudiced by a bitter dispute with Jack in later years, they provide a vivid, if perhaps unreliable, picture of Jack at his most hedonistic: 'Our first dinner together was the poet's choice. We went to Marchand's . . . There were vintage wines and truffles for the Sterling–London feast, and much verbal footwork to get in an occasional intellectual blow between drinks, with George nebulous and at times incoherent and Jack cool, factual and, I thought, a trifle patronising.'

George had introduced Jack to gourmet cooking. Before long, Jack had conducted George on several increasingly debauched adventures in San Francisco's underworld. One night they went to a prize fight between Walcott, 'a Barbados Negro who stood five feet one', and a man called 'Gunboat Smith'. As the boxers bludgeoned each other, Jack shouted and raged, his eyes blazing. 'The urge in him to do or die betrayed itself with every smashing blow on the raw flesh,' Noel observed. 'Sterling, on the other hand, sat grey-faced, quiet.'

After the fight, the two men rushed to a food counter where Jack wolfed down a 'cannibal sandwich . . . washed down with strong coffee'. Further forays to the Barbary Coast cemented their friendship. Jack loved the seedy atmosphere of the burlesque clubs, and would sit in rapture and watch the dancing like a small boy visiting the circus for the first time. He could listen all night to the life stories of the performers he met, and would ply them with resin-tinted beer to keep them talking. Jack was never more at home than when he was knocking back shots of whiskey at the Barbary Coast's long mahogany bars. But his favourite establishment was a casino on Market Street where gamblers used gold coins rather than chips, betting their life savings on one spin of the roulette wheel.

One evening early in their relationship, Jack took George and Noel to another dubious establishment. As they crossed Chinatown, they passed shop-windows which mesmerised George. 'The smells alone pay for the trip,' he said. 'Far Shanghai and Samarkand, Tokyo, the Islands of Spice, Canton, all are here.' Jack turned into an alley and rapped on a door. A Chinese man, dressed in black, ushered them down a dimly-lit hallway to a room where a bamboo cage hung from the ceiling. It contained a white-faced Chinese girl dressed in a flowered yellow kimono.

Some Chinese men entered, nodded approvingly and poked the girl gently in the ribs.

'Don't let them think you're afraid,' Jack said. He, George and Noel also examined the girl, then returned to the street. George looked relieved to be outside. Jack pointed to two more girls sitting at barred windows nearby.

'Two bitty for thisa,' they chirped. 'Four bitty for thata.'

'The Oriental is a callous beast,' said George.

'He sure is,' Jack agreed. 'Callous and indifferent where women are involved.'

They carried on until they came across a church with a blazing cross made from lightbulbs above its entrance. A few yards away was a cul-de-sac lined with cubicles, each containing a young white prostitute.

'What about Oriental callousness?' Jack asked, pointing to the cross. 'This narrow little street, thoroughly Christian and superior, pays more than its fair share of taxes. Every dollar comes from commercialised love, which is segregated here under the law to increase the profits.'

'Let's have a drink,' George replied.

Jack led the way to Stockton Street, where he stopped in front of another door. An overweight woman ushered them into a cosy room decorated with expensive furniture and an Oriental rug. In one corner, a stunning redhead began to play a waltz on a piano. The madam poured drinks and a gorgeous blonde served them. Soon three other young women smelling of patchouli joined the men. Jack began to reminisce about the exotic dancers he had known in the Klondike, where the overweight madam had also run a brothel.

George couldn't hide his disdain. When the madam left them to attend to another client, he described her as 'a procuress'. Detecting a sneering tone in George's voice, Jack exploded: 'You think that woman is a pariah because she satisfies one of the great fundamental needs of man. Is the grocer a pariah? The manufacturer? Human needs are satisfied by them and for exactly the same reason. Profit.'

The women giggled and served more drinks.

'Here is a reasonable, responsible, intelligently ordered clearing house of the passions,' Jack said. 'Here a man may resolve his defeats, forget his limitations, gather spiritual strength to reach for the stars again.'

As Jack and George reached for the stars together, they became increasingly intimate. Soon George was calling Jack 'Wolf' and beginning letters to him with 'My Darling Wolf'. Jack began signing his intimate letters 'Wolf', as if warning lovers of his primitive nature. He later kept a husky he called Brown Wolf, and as the years passed he would associate himself more and more with the shadowy beast who had symbolised both destruction and the source of life since the ancient Romans. Jack, surely, was a lone wolf – the lonely writer fighting for truth. And also, at times, the leader of the pack, the King of the Crowd.

'The Greek', as Sterling was nicknamed because of his aquiline nose and classical features, and the Wolf shared a love all of things physical. As prototypical Californians, they rejoiced in the release that came through rigorous exercise. They admired each other's well-toned bodies and delighted in showing off their attributes. In seaside Carmel, an artists' community near San Francisco, George loved to be photographed in the nude, his penis folded between his thighs as he crouched in the foetal position on the beach. Jack himself took some of the pictures.

Whether their deep affection for each other ever became sexual is doubtful. Both would have furiously denied any inference of even latent homosexuality. In their style of dress and their sensibilities they were artists who mocked the starchy prudery of American society at the turn of the century. They were, in fact, pioneers of a casual Bohemianism which would later be adopted by the Beat Generation of the 1950s. Jack's relationship with George was, he would have blustered, a mutual fascination with the games of his lost youth and with the adult pastimes of the Barbary Coast. Above all, George offered the companionship he had been denied in boyhood.

George's descent into hedonism would ultimately exact a terrible price. Not long after he met Jack, he rented a room in San Francisco explicitly for carrying on his affair with the flesh, and he was to contract several venereal diseases. But it was not syphilis that would finally kill the Greek, but cyanide. Even before he met Jack in 1901, Sterling, like several other members of the Crowd, carried a vial of the poison in the lower left-hand pocket of his waistcoat, claiming that when the time was right he would take it. This he did in 1926, by which time, a pathetic wretch, he had worked his way, with increasing desperation, through almost every woman who expressed the faintest interest in his poetry.

Even in death, Sterling was forced to play second fiddle. Eight years before, his wife, traumatised by his debauches which she blamed partly on Jack's influence, had swallowed her own fatal capsule and drifted off with Chopin playing in the background.

Jack financed his descent into the realm of the senses with the regular flow of cheques he received as an increasingly successful magazine writer. But by the time he received a cheque, it would invariably have been spent supporting his family and lavishly entertaining friends. Other than a brief period in 1904 when he would have $4000 to his name, Jack would never be free of debt. Eventually, he would become as adept at deficit management as he would be at spending his royalty cheques before they had even been issued. It was as if he needed the constant threat of bankruptcy to spur him on. In his youth, he had never got what he wanted. Now he could afford it, he impulsively bought only the best. Be it a shotgun or a pair of boxing gloves, Jack was fixated with quality, with the material trappings which reminded him, however tight his finances became, that he was still a success.

In 1901, rather than rein in his expenses and concentrate his energies on writing another novel, Jack maintained his income by dashing off articles for the *San Francisco Examiner*, a paper owned by the arch-capitalist William Randolph Hearst. His first piece was a jingoistic description of the SS *Oregon* as it returned from the Spanish–American war through the Golden Gate. He also wrote features such as 'Washoe Indians Resolve to be White Men' and 'Girl who Crossed Swords with a Burglar' for the newspaper's Sunday supplement.

Jack argued that knocking out such 'yellow journalism' was no worse than writing a short story to suit a particular magazine – it was all about giving the editors what they wanted. The exposure also brought him a wider audience for his short stories, many of which during this period were of outstanding quality.

The three volumes of his Yukon stories that appeared between 1900 and 1902 – *The Son of the Wolf*, *The God of his Fathers* and *Children of the Frost* – sold only moderately well, but they did establish Jack's reputation. His first story about a dog, 'Bâtard' (June 1902), showed Jack at his best at this time. Bâtard is the son of a grey timber-wolf bitch. He has been bought by a sadist, Black Lêclère, who tortures him in scene after scene of gruesome brutality. As a result, Bâtard becomes a dog from hell – 'Hell's Spawn', as he is soon called. One night he leaps at Lêclère's throat while he sleeps, nearly killing him. Lêclère refuses to have him put down, having become perversely bound to him through their mutual violence. When he is falsely accused of killing a fellow prospector, Lêclère is tied up and left by a group of sourdoughs. They return to find that Bâtard has finally killed his tormentor.

The climax of 'Bâtard' was perhaps the most masterful description of savagery that had ever appeared in American fiction. And while the violence throughout the story may have been a touch gratuitous, it was riveting *and* convincing. Above all, 'Bâtard', as with so much of Jack's early fiction, pulsed with an irresistible energy, like that which made him himself such a dynamic personality in the eyes of his friends.

Unlike those who accused him of selling out by writing the hack articles which bought him time to complete his serious fiction, Jack knew how cold and dispiriting the artist's garret really was. He was a professional writer, he could proudly declare, a man who lived by his words. It was a reasonable defence, yet friends such as Anna Strunsky still disapproved of his work for Hearst, and privately agreed with the sentiments expressed in a lampoon of Jack which appeared in a local magazine, *Town Talk*, in November 1901:

> Dear London: Do I hear aright,
> Or has some grey witch of the night
> Her evil spell upon me cast
> And to a nightmare chained me fast?
> You writing stuff for Willie Hearst?
> . . . Alas, for this degen'rate day
> When Genius grovels to its pay!
> When such a mind of sterling worth
> As gave 'An Odyssey of the North'
> Shall stultify its brilliant thought
> Just that the nimble pence be caught . . .

Jack soldiered on regardless. If the money was good enough, his pen was always ready for hire. He had, he rationalised, discovered the paradox of the writing game: 'that what the world prizes most it demands least, and that what it clamours the loudest after it does not prize at all . . . The deepest values of life are today expressed in terms of cash. That which is most significant of an age must be the speech of that age. That which is most significant today is the making of money . . . it is only fair that literature be expressed in terms of cash.'

From the start, he had been painfully honest about his reasons for becoming a writer. 'It's money I want,' he had told Johns, 'or rather the things money will buy; and I can never possibly have too much.

As to living on practically nothing, I propose to do as little of that as I possibly can. It's feed not the breed that makes the man. More money means more life to me. The habit of spending money, ah God! I shall always be its victim . . . If cash comes with fame, come fame; if cash comes without fame, then come cash.'

Jack sounded bullish when he talked about his motivation for writing, but when he sat at his desk and began to work he was sometimes overcome by bouts of depression. Even to his close friends he presented himself as carefree, ever hopeful and uncomplicated, but he could not hide his feelings from himself. The other Jack London, the solitary comrade, was still haunted by the fears of his childhood – of being alone, unwanted, worthless. He had been hungry all his life, it seemed, for affection and love. When Jack was most depressed, he would binge on barely cooked duck washed down with bottles of wine, as if by gorging himself he could make up the deficit. So began a pattern that would last a lifetime: when he lacked confidence and felt maudlin, he allowed his appetites full rein. When the depression passed, he would abstain, often for months on end, from heavy drinking and overindulgence. But whatever his mood, he rarely failed to write his daily quota of a thousand words.

In early 1902, Jack admitted that he still lived in the shadow of his brutalising youth. 'I dined yesterday on canvasback and terrapin,' he told Anna Strunsky, 'with sparkling champagne and all manner of wonderful drinks I had never tasted before warming my heart and brain, and I remembered the sordid orgies of my youth. We were ill-clad, ill-mannered beasts, and the drink was cheap and poor and nauseating. And then I dreamed dreams, and pulled myself up out of the slime to canvasback and terrapin and champagne, and learned that it was solely a difference of degree which art introduced into the fermenting.'

Only days before Jack wrote this, he had received news which should have heartened him for months. On 27 December 1901, one of the most influential and respected publishers in the English-speaking world, George P. Brett, president of the Macmillan Company in New York, had written to him. Brett said he believed Jack's fiction represented 'the very best kind of work' being done in America, and he wanted to publish all his future writing, starting with the short-story collection *Children of the Frost*, which he promptly scheduled for October 1902.

Brett was one of a rare breed – a gentleman publisher who was admired for his generosity and loyalty as well as his editorial judgement. Winston Churchill, no less, revered him. 'Mr Brett,' Churchill had observed, 'has an undoubted genius for publishing, but he possesses likewise the higher genius for friendship.'

A few weeks later, Jack decided to move his family to the country after George Sterling showed him a bungalow near his own in the Piedmont hills, thirty minutes from the Oakland estuary. As soon as he had a spare minute, Jack wrote to Cloudesley Johns:

> Piedmont, California
> February 23, 1902
> Dear Cloudesley
> Behold! I have moved! Therefore my long silence. I have been very busy. Also, I went to see a man hanged yesterday. It was one of the most scientific things I have ever seen. From the time he came through the door which leads from the death-chamber to the gallows-room, to the time he was dangling at the end of the rope, but twenty-one seconds elapsed.
> And in those twenty-one seconds all the following things occurred: He walked from the door to the gallows, ascended a flight of thirteen stairs to the top of the gallows, walked across the top of the gallows to the trap, took his position upon the trap, his legs were strapped, the noose slipped over his head and drawn tight and the knot adjusted, the black cap pulled down over face, the trap sprung, his neck broken, and the spinal cord severed – all in twenty-one seconds, so simple a thing is life and so easy it is to kill a man.
> Why, he made never the slightest twitch. It took fourteen and one-half minutes for the heart to run down, but he was not aware of it. One fifth of a second elapsed between the springing of the trap and the breaking of his neck and severing of his spinal cord. So far as he was concerned, he was dead at the end of that one-fifth of a second . . .
> Lord, what [a] stack of hack I'm·turning out! Five mouths

and ten feet, and sometimes more, so one hustles. I wonder
if ever I'll get clear of debt.

Am beautifully located in new house. We have a big living
room, every inch of it, floor and ceiling, finished in redwood.
We could put the floor space of almost four cottages (of the
size of the one you can remember) into this one living room
alone ... We also have the cutest, snuggest little cottage right
on the same ground with us, in which live my mother and
my nephew ... A most famous porch, broad and long and
cool, a big clump of magnificent pines, flowers and flowers
and flowers galore ... our view commands all of San Francisco
Bay for a sweep of thirty or forty miles, and all the opposing
shores such as San Francisco, Marin County and Mount Tam-
alpais (to say nothing of the Golden Gate and the Pacific
Ocean) – and all for $35.00 per month.

Now removed from the distractions of city life in Oakland, Jack
was able to step up his output. Aside from short stories and journalism
for Hearst's newspapers, he was still working on *The Kempton–Wace
Letters*. He was as besotted as ever – as only 'god's own mad lover'
could be – with his co-author. A month after moving to Piedmont,
with fifty thousand words written, Jack invited Anna to stay in his
new country home to complete the book.

For a few days, Bess was 'cordial and manifested great interest' in
their work, but then Anna became convinced that she was not welcome. 'She [Bess] did nothing of any importance to make me feel out
of place,' Anna later recalled, 'but judging from several little occur-
rences I decided it was best for me to leave.'

Bess had a different story. She later said she had come across Anna
sitting on Jack's knee in his study. Their heads were glued together
over a manuscript. What, she implied, was a loyal wife supposed to
think? Jack, of course, protested his innocence. 'It was her intellect
that fascinated me, not her womanhood,' he would later claim. 'Primarily she was intellect and genius. I love to seek and delve in human
souls, and she was an exhaustless mine to me. Protean, I called her.
My term for her of intimacy and endearment was what? a term that
was intellectual, that described her mind.'

One letter to Anna during this period gave a different impression altogether:

> Dear, Dear You,
>   I shall be over Friday afternoon. I am doing 2000 words a day now, and every day, and my head is in such a whirl I can hardly think. But I feel. I am sick with love for you and need of you.

Anna Strunksy would always harbour deep affection for Jack, if not love. Had she not been so committed to the Jewish faith, and had Jack been single, their relationship would probably have developed beyond close friendship. But it was not to be. In the late summer of 1902, Anna told Jack that she was moving to New York. She had learnt that he was still having sex with Bess, and accused him of lying about his feelings for her. Jack, in a rage, denied that he had lied, and accused Anna of being 'the cruellest woman I have ever known . . . who can wound others in degree equal only to her own capacity to be wounded . . . You beg my pardon for your impetuousness worming that "I love you" from me. Then I do not love you, and I have spent months building up a wonderful tissue of lies. Wasted months, and years, for, not loving you, the thing is purposeless.'

Anna's move to New York came as a heavy blow to Jack. He had relied on her support and advice throughout his fraught marriage to Bess. In her, Jack had met for the first time a woman who was powerfully attracted to him and yet shrewd enough not to get too close to a man for whom love was, he stressed, an irrational foible. Would he ever understand the opposite sex as people, rather than as romantic illusions or sex objects? Domesticity would always grate against his core belief in his right to go wherever and do whatever he pleased. Would he ever see women as more than pleasure attached to chains? If a woman did not play the role he assigned her, would he ever be able to react with anything other than the bitter resentment he felt towards his mother?

Jack's correspondence with Anna continued, but without the intimacy that had characterised the first, heady years of their friendship. In New York, Anna would fall in love with and marry a very different kind of socialist to Jack: William English Walling, a millionaire philanthropist and major stockholder in *Wilshire's* magazine, who would help found the National Woman's Trade Union League and the National Association for the Advancement of Colored People.

The Abyss

Society grows, while political machines rack to pieces
and become scrap. For the English, so far as manhood
and womanhood and health and happiness go, I see a
broad and smiling future. But for a great deal of the
political machinery, which at present mismanages for
them, I see nothing else than the scrap heap.

JACK LONDON, *The People of the Abyss* (1903)

BY JULY 1902, aged just twenty-five, Jack was burnt-out: $3000 in
debt and contemptuous of his work. If something did not come along
soon, he told Cloudesley Johns, he would return to drink. Bess had
announced that she was pregnant again, and the woman he really
loved – Anna Strunsky – had not responded to his advances.

Nor was his career matching his aspirations. Try as he might, he
had not yet managed to dig himself out of the lucrative Klondike
genre. He had even resorted to reading books by other veterans of
the gold rush for inspiration.

'A man does one thing in a passable manner,' he told Johns, 'and
the dear public insists on his continuing to do it to the end of his
days.'

There seemed no way out of the hole he had dug for himself.
'Concerning myself,' he wrote on 12 July, 'I am moving along very
slowly . . . Some day I shall begin to do things, until then I merely
scratch a living. Between you and me, I wish I had never opened the
books. That's where I was the fool.'

Less than a fortnight later, a way to flee his failing marriage came
out of the blue. On 21 July he received a telegram from the American
Press Association (APA). The Boer War had just ended, and the APA

wanted to know if America's best young adventure writer would be willing to report on the postwar situation in South Africa.

It had been four years since Jack had returned from the Yukon. Desperate to free himself of the responsibilities that now suffocated him, he immediately wired his acceptance, packed a bag the same night, and the following morning left for the East Coast. On arriving in New York, however, he discovered that his assignment in South Africa had been cancelled, as the officials he was to interview had already left Capetown for Europe.

Jack conferred with the APA about a new project. As he had already bought his ticket to England, he proposed to go to London, where his work was already winning admirers such as H. Perry Robinson, managing director of the publisher Ibister & Co, who had enthusiastically published his second collection of Klondike-set short stories, *The God of His Fathers*, in 1902. Jack planned to write an exposé of London's notorious East End slums. He would spend several weeks among the city's underclass, again becoming a tramp so as to hide his true identity.

On 30 July Jack boarded the *Majestic*, a trans-Atlantic steamer. 'A week from to-day I shall be in London,' he wrote to Anna Strunsky during the crossing. 'I shall then have two days in which to make my arrangements and sink down out of sight in order to view the Coronation from the standpoint of the London beasts. That's all they are – beasts – if they are anything like the slum people of New York – beasts, shot through with starry flashes of divinity.'

He arrived in England on 6 August and immediately plunged into the 'social abyss', disguising himself as an American sailor down on his luck, just off the boat. Members of the Social Democratic Federation, with whom Anna had put him in touch, found him a room in the Whitechapel area, where fourteen years before Jack the Ripper had stalked prostitutes. The Federation also provided official reports which Jack would quote at length in documenting social conditions.

Having checked in with the American consul-general and told him about his project, Jack headed straight for the East End.

'Drive me down to the East End,' he ordered a cab-driver.

'Where, sir?'

'To the East End, anywhere. Go on.'

Several minutes later, the driver pulled up.

'Wot plyce yer wanter go?' he asked.

The driver had never been instructed to take a 'gentleman' to the heart of the East End. After being dropped off in Stepney, Jack soon saw why. The streets were 'filled with a new and different race of people, short of stature, and of wretched or beer-sodden appearance ... the air was obscene with sounds of jangling and squabbling ... little children clustered like flies around a festering mass of fruit'.

'The London Abyss is a vast shambles; no more dreary spectacle can be found,' he wrote. 'The colour of life is grey and drab, everything is hopeless, unrelieved, and dirty. Bathtubs are a thing totally unknown; any attempts at cleanliness become howling farce. Strange, vagrant odours come drifting along the greasy wind; the Abyss exudes a stupefying atmosphere of torpor which wraps about the people and deadens them. Year by year rural England pours in a flood of vigorous young life that perishes by the third generation.'

There was more than a little hyperbole to Jack's prose, but he was genuinely outraged by what he saw in the backstreets of the centre of the greatest empire the world had ever known. Shocked by the degradation and poverty, he wrote to Anna Strunsky: 'I am worn out and exhausted, and my nerves are blunted with what I have seen and the suffering it has cost me. I am made sick by this human hell-hole called the East End.'

Within days of submerging into the abyss, Jack could not but agree with the British journalist Theodore Parker: England was 'the paradise of the rich, the purgatory of the wise, and the hell of the poor'. He himself was not completely at the mercy of the streets. He had a sanctuary, a rented room in the home of a detective which he used to change clothes and write his book. He had risen too far from the 'submerged tenth' truly to return to the ghetto.

Three of them walked down the Mile End Road, and one was a hero: a slender lad of nineteen, so frail that a gust of wind could have blown him over. He was already a veteran of political demonstrations and had led protests against the Boer War. His companions were Jack and a twenty-eight-year-old workman who had promised to show them what a sweatshop looked like. The workman had a grey complexion.

His body was gnarled, his shoulders bent. The young firebrand told Jack about fights and broken glass and 'giddy battles on stairways . . . wrecked lecture halls, and broken heads and bones'.

'How I envy you big, strong men,' he said, looking at Jack. 'I'm such a little mite I can't do much when it comes to fighting.'

Jack smiled at the memory of the fist-fights of his own youth. The young man beside him, he thought, was the kind to show the world that men had not forgotten how to die.

'I'm a 'earty man, I am,' the workman said. 'Not like the other chaps at my shop, I ain't. They consider me a fine specimen of manhood. Why, d'ye know, I weigh 140 pounds!'

Passing down Leman Street, they cut through into Spitalfields and then into a backstreet called Frying-Pan Alley. A group of dirty children cluttered the 'slimy pavement'. A woman was seated in a doorway suckling a baby. Jack wrote that her breasts were 'grossly naked and libelling all the sacredness of motherhood'. He stepped over her and through another group of dirty, screaming children, and climbed three flights of stairs. Each landing was heaped with filth and refuse.

The house contained seven rooms, each one home to a family of several people. In one room, Jack learned, a widow lived with her only son of sixteen, who was dying of tuberculosis. 'The way he coughs is something terrible,' the worker told Jack. 'We hear him in here while we're working and it's terrible.' When times were good, the worker said, when there was work to be had, he could earn as much as 'thirty bob a week', far less than Jack made from one morning's hack.

'But it's only the best of us can do it,' he added. 'An' then we work twelve, thirteen, and fourteen hours a day, just as fast as we can. An' you should see us sweat! Just running from us! If you could see us, it'd dazzle your eyes – tacks flyin' out of mouth like from a machine. Look at my mouth.' His teeth were worn down to coal-black stumps. 'I clean my teeth,' he insisted, 'else they'd be worse.'

They left the house and made their way down a narrow gravel path, past benches on which a dozen women, ranging from twenty years to seventy, were trying to sleep. A raw wind was blowing and the women were huddling together for warmth. The scene was 'a welter of rags and filth, of all manner of loathsome skin diseases, open sores, bruises, grossness, indecency, leering monstrosities, and bestial faces'.

'Oh, why did you bring me here?' the nineteen-year-old cried out, his face ashen.

'Those women there,' said the worker, 'will sell themselves for thru'pence, or tu'pence, or a loaf of stale bread.'

'For heaven's sake,' the boy shouted, 'let's get out of this.'

The rain slanted down, drenching the huge crowd waiting for their new monarch to arrive. Jack stood with them, on Coronation Day, 9 August 1902, in Trafalgar Square, 'the most splendid site in Europe, and the very uttermost heart of the empire'. In awe, he watched the procession that heralded the crowning of King Edward VII, the first coronation in England in sixty-four years, and one of the greatest shows of pomp and circumstance in royal history. 'There were many thousands of us,' he later recalled, 'all checked and held in order by a superb display of armed power.'

He was enthralled by the show of imperial might. The base of Nelson's Column was surrounded by blue-jackets. There were Lancers and Hussars around the statue of George III. Before him marched the 1st Life Guards, 'heroes' mounted on chargers with steel breast-plates. 'And further, throughout the crowd, were flung long lines of the Metropolitan Constabulary, while in the rear were the reserves – tall, well-fed men, with weapons and muscles to wield them in case of need.'

Soon, Jack was even deeper amongst the people of the abyss. 'Out all night with homeless ones, walking the streets in bitter rain, drenched to the skin, wondering when dawn would come,' he wrote in exhaustion when he returned to his dingy room. 'Sunday I spent with the homeless ones in fierce struggle for something to eat. I returned to my rooms Sunday evening, after thirty-six hours continuous work and one short night's sleep.'

On 22 August he wrote to George and Carrie Sterling:

How often I think of you, over there on the other side of the world! I have heard of God's country, but this country is the country God has forgotten he forgot.

I've read of misery, and seen a bit; but this beats anything I could even have imagined. Actually, I have seen things and looked the second time in order to convince myself that it really is so. This I know, the stuff I'm turning out will have to be expurgated or it will never see magazine publication . . . You will read some of my feeble efforts to describe it some day.

I have my book over one-quarter done and am bowling along in a rush to finish it and get out of here. I think I should die if I had to live two years in the East End of London . . .

Each dawn brought fresh horrors. In a cheap hotel for migrant workers, he went from bed to bed and looked at the sleepers. They were young men, aged between twenty and forty. Old men could not afford a bed there. In a workhouse Jack looked at the young men, scores of them, and thought them 'not bad-looking fellows': 'Their faces were made for women's kisses, their necks for women's arms. They were lovable, as men are lovable. They were capable of love. A woman's touch redeems and softens, and they needed such redemption and softening instead of each day growing harsh and harsher.'

Jack wondered where these women were, and then he heard a whore's 'ginny laugh'. Now he knew. They were selling themselves on Leman Street, Waterloo Road, Piccadilly and the Strand.

In late September, just seven weeks after arriving in England, Jack finished *The People of the Abyss* (H.G. Wells's term for the urban poor). It was a triumph of impassioned reporting. Outrage underscored every one of its sixty-three thousand words. 'Of all my books,' he would later write, 'I love most *The People of the Abyss*. No other book of mine took so much of my young heart and tears as that study of the economic degradation of the poor.'

He was exhausted and emotionally drained. He had studied pamphlets, books and government reports on poverty, interviewed scores of men and women, taken hundreds of photographs, tramped miles of streets, stood in breadlines, slept in parks. What he had seen had seared his soul. London was more brutal in its unrelenting misery than the Klondike. 'If this is the best that civilisation can do for the human,' he wrote bitterly, 'then give us howling and naked savagery. Far better to be a people of the wilderness and desert, of the cave and the squatting place, than to be a people of the machine and the Abyss.'

The People of the Abyss was published by Macmillan in 1903. It was a surprise success, selling over twenty thousand copies in America. But when Macmillan brought out the book in England, many critics could barely conceal their anger that an American had pointed out what was so widely denied. They smelt prejudice and artifice, rather than detachment and cool analysis. The tone of the London *Daily News* was typical: '[Jack London] has written of the East End of London as he wrote of the Klondike, with the same tortured phrase, vehemence of denunciation, splashes of colour, and ferocity of epithet. He has studied it "earnestly and dispassionately" – in two months! It is all very pleasant, very American, and very young.'

In New York, the *Bookman* accused Jack of 'snobbishness because of his profound consciousness of the gulf fixed between the poor denizens of the Abyss and the favoured class of which he is the proud representative . . . he needs must assure the reader that in his own home he is accustomed to carefully prepared food and good clothes and daily tub – a fact that he might safely have left to be taken for granted'.

What made Jack such an effective but controversial reporter was his personal involvement. His greatest strength was his passionate bias in favour of capitalism's victims. He knew their suffering because he had felt it himself. His critics had not. Throughout his stay in London, memories of his youth had returned. Only by reassuring himself that he had escaped the conditions of his childhood could he control his fear that he might one day return to them.

He left England in October 1902, his most affecting non-fiction work already behind him. 'Henceforth,' he wrote to Anna Strunsky, 'I shall dream romances for other people, and transmute them into bread and butter.' In his notes, he later scribbled his final disillusionment with the centre of the Anglo-Saxon world: 'Anyway, if I were God one hour, I'd blot out all London and its 6,000,000 people, as Sodom and Gomorrah were blotted out, and look upon my work and call it good.'

*   *   *

Jack did not return to America immediately after leaving the 'hell-hole' of the East End. Instead, he travelled by train for three weeks through Germany, France and Italy. Remarkably little is known about his grand tour. In a later letter, however, he did recall his arrival in Italy:

> On the train I met a Frenchman who spoke a little Italian and less English. We grew chummy. At Spezzio we were delayed by a train-wreck. We went sailing in the harbour, & on an Italian man-of-war became acquainted with a boatswain. The latter got shore liberty and proceeded to show us the town. Both he and the Frenchman were revolutionists. Birds of a feather, you know – and by three in the morning there were a dozen of us, singing the Marseillaize (spl?) and clashing with the police. Now I wouldn't write such an adventure for the Woman's Home Companion, but you can bet I saw more in one night of the real human life of Spezzio than could a whole generation of tourists.

'Oh, it was glorious,' he wrote to Anna Strunsky. 'The Revolution looms large and the bourgeoisie will not see it. How I curse them sometimes these days when I see all this worse than useless misery. I think I understand anarchy better by far than I did before.'

But these glorious days were soon at an end. Jack was duty-bound to return to California and resume his responsibilities. On 20 October Bess had given birth to a second daughter, and Jack arrived back in New York on 4 November with the final draft of *The People of the Abyss* in his suitcase. A friend who met him at the dock recalled that he wore 'a wrinkled sack coat, the pockets of which bulged with papers and letters. His trousers bagged at the knees. He was minus a vest, and his outer shirt was far from immaculate. A leather belt around his waist took the place of suspenders. On his head he wore a dinky little cap.'

After a brief visit to George Brett at Macmillan, who gladly loaned him $150 for his train-fare, Jack headed for home. From Piedmont, a few weeks later, he wrote to Brett expressing his hopes for the future. 'I want to get away from the Klondike,' he stressed. He had served his apprenticeship writing about Alaska. Now he felt 'better fitted to attempt a larger and more generally interesting field. I have half a

dozen books, fiction all, that I want to write. I have done a great deal
of thinking and studying in the last two years, since I wrote my
first novel, and I am confident that I can today write something
worthwhile.'

Within weeks, Brett offered him $150 a month for two years in
return for the right to publish six books, including *The People of the
Abyss* and *The Kempton–Wace Letters*. But, canny operator that he
was, Brett included a proviso: 'I hope that your work from this time
on will show the marks of advancement which I found so strong in
your earlier books. But which is not so marked in the last volume or
so, these showing signs of haste. There is no real place in the world
of literature for anything but the best a man can do.'

Jack explained that the reason he had written so much was that he
had worked 'day in and day out, without taking a rest'. 'Once I am
in a position where I do not have to depend upon each day's work
to keep the pot boiling the next day,' he promised, 'where I do not
have to dissipate my energy on all kinds of hack, where I can slowly
and deliberately ponder and shape the best that is in me, then, at that
time, I am confident that I shall do big work.'

Although Jack had told Brett that he wanted to escape the Klondike,
the story he began on 1 December 1902 – as soon as he had settled
back into his life in Piedmont – was again set in the Northland. From
the first pages, the story of Buck, half St Bernard, half Scotch shepherd,
took on a life of its own. The creative frenzy that gripped him was
greater than any he had experienced.

Buck is a placid mongrel living on a ranch in northern California.
When gold is discovered in the Klondike he is kidnapped by a servant
and sold to a sadist who supplies sourdoughs with sled dogs. After a
vicious beating, Buck is taken by boat to Alaska where he is suddenly
'jerked from the heart of civilisation and flung into the heart of things
primordial. No lazy, sunkissed life was this, with nothing to do but
loaf and be bored. Here was neither peace, nor rest, nor a moment's
safety. All was confusion and action.'

To survive in this new environment, Buck adapts to the law of
'club and fang', the brutal rules that determine survival in the Klondike
and which Jack had experienced in Erie County Penitentiary. Buck
discovers his primal instincts, learning how to burrow a hole in the

snow at night, how to kill, and how to devour raw meat before another predator arrives on the scene. 'His muscles became hard as iron . . . Sight and scent became remarkably keen, while his hearing developed such acuteness that in his sleep he heard the faintest sound and knew whether it heralded peace or peril.'

After savaging another dog, Spitz, in a Darwinian battle for supremacy, Buck assumes his position as leader of a sled team. But soon he is sold to a new owner, a Scottish half-breed who works and starves him almost to death. Salvation arrives in the form of John Thornton, a kindly sourdough who nurses him back to health, and in so doing earns his undying loyalty. When Thornton visits a small settlement to pick up supplies, a miner attacks him. Buck kills the man, and later saves Thornton's life again when he is swept away by rapids. But Buck has changed. He is no longer a tamed animal. Memories of his long-dead ancestors haunt him as he sits beside Thornton deep in the forest at night, especially when he hears the howls of roving wolves.

With the money Thornton wins from a bet that Buck can pull a sled laden with a thousand pounds for a hundred yards, he hires labourers and ventures deep into the wilderness in search of a long-lost goldmine. While the men are panning for gold, Buck steals away to stalk prey and run with the wolves. After four days spent tracking a huge bull moose, Buck discovers that in his absence Indians have killed Thornton. He fearlessly attacks the tribe, killing several, then rejoins a wolf pack. Before long he has again proved his superiority, becoming the pack's leader.

For three weeks Jack did nothing but follow Buck through the white silence, scratching out word after word in thick pencil. There was no time for Bess or his new baby, let alone his debts and the Crowd, many of whom he had not seen in several months. On 13 March 1903 he told Anna Strunsky that he had finished, that it had simply got out of hand and ended up as a thirty-two-thousand-word novella. For once he had not paused to lecture his readers about Anglo-Saxon supremacy, but had concentrated instead on telling a story.

At a Wednesday-night open house a few weeks later, Jack sat in an easy chair beside a fire in the large redwood-panelled room he used for entertaining. A distant view of San Francisco, of schooners passing through the Golden Gate, was framed by a window behind him. His guests made themselves comfortable on cushions spread across the floor. As Irving Stone later described the scene, there were no raucous card games that night, only a silence that grew deeper with every turn of the page.

'There is an ecstasy that marks the summit of life, and beyond which life cannot rise,' Jack read, his soft voice reaching every corner of the room. 'And such is the paradox of living, this ecstasy comes when one is most alive, and it comes as a complete forgetfulness that one is alive. This ecstasy, this forgetfulness of living, comes to the artist, caught up and out of himself in a sheet of flame ... and it came to Buck, leading the pack, sounding the old wolf-cry, straining after the food that was alive and that fled swiftly before him through the moonlight.'

Jack's guests were stunned into silence by the lyrical force of his prose and his vivid depiction of the frozen north. There were not even any murmurs of approval. From the look on their faces, Jack knew he had produced his most powerful fiction yet.

The Call of the Wild was published by Macmillan in July 1903. George Brett had asked Jack to 'remove [the] few instances of profanity in the story, because, in addition to the grown-up audience for the book, there is undoubtedly a very considerable school audience'. Jack had made the cuts; as a result, 'By Gar' was the book's strongest oath. Brett had also expressed reservations about the title, and had urged Jack to find a better one: 'I hope something else will occur to you, as I like the story very well indeed, although I am afraid it is too true to nature and too good work to be really popular with the sentimentalist public.'

He was spectacularly wrong. Jack had struck as lucky as George Carmack, judging by the praise lavished on *The Call of the Wild* from the moment it left the presses. It was instantly hailed as a 'classic enriching American literature', 'a spellbinding animal story', 'a brilliant dramatisation of the laws of nature'. It was, indisputably, the best study ever of the 'beastly manners of civilised men and the civilised manners of beasts'. Almost a century later, it is the most widely read American classic, having sold millions of copies.

'The most virile, freshly conceived, dramatically told, and firmly sustained book of the season is unquestionably Jack London's *Call of the Wild*,' announced a New York literary magazine, the *Criterion*. 'Such books as these clarify the literary atmosphere and give a new, clean vibrant breath in a depression of romances and problems; they act like an invigorating wind from the open sea upon the dullness of a sultry day.'

As Richard O'Connor has noted, some reviewers paid Jack what he considered the ultimate compliment by saying *The Call of the Wild* was as good as anything Rudyard Kipling had written. He had finally 'struck the chord that awakened the fullest response' in American readers. He had discovered for them a 'dreamland of heroic opportunity'. 'Except for the similar sensation caused by the appearance of Mark Twain's mining-camp humour in the midst of Victorian America, nothing more disturbing to the forces of gentility had ever happened in our literature,' the critic Kenneth Lynn would later write, 'and it decisively changed the course of American fiction.'

The Call of the Wild took naturalism into uncharted territory: the region of the 'dominant primordial beast', as Jack put it. Like Jack, Buck had answered the call to adventure, had begun his transformation in harsh conditions, descending into an icy Hades before achieving apotheosis.

Jack's most convincing character, a dog, had allowed him to say 'more than would otherwise have been possible about mankind'. 'In describing Buck's progress from tameness to wildness,' the critic Roderick Nash would later write, 'the author passed judgement on his contemporaries. They, too, he implied, suffered from overcivilisation, and in the early 1900s the idea struck a sympathetic chord.'

Yet Jack insisted he wrote his masterpiece without intending it to be a human allegory: 'I was unconscious of it at the time. I did not mean to do it.' Jack was aware that mankind's terror has always been its most basic emotion. As he wrote in an article, 'The Terrible and Tragic in Fiction', published in *The Critic* in February 1903, it has far deeper roots than love, tracing back to the days before history, when man was just another wild, frightened savage. Fear had made Jack escape the ghetto and achieve success. It had inspired his most brilliant prose.

Through Buck, Jack had also expressed his desire to be free to prowl, to satisfy every want. In Erie County Penitentiary he had resolved never to become trapped by either fate or circumstance. Only by rising above the pack, only by becoming a better man than his fellows, stronger and more powerful, could he truly escape the poverty of his past.

The last sentence of *The Call of the Wild* was the most revealing Jack ever wrote:

> When the long winter nights come on and the wolves follow their meat into the lower valleys, he may be seen running at the head of the pack through the pale moonlight or glimmering borealis, leaping gigantic above his fellows, his great throat a-bellow as he sings a song of the younger world, which is the song of the pack.

At just twenty-seven, Jack had reached the literary summit of America. All he had to do from now on was to reawaken the demons that had made Buck flesh and blood, and a lifetime of riches, artistic as much as material, would be his.

He would soon be making huge sums from his fiction. But nothing would come so close to genius as *The Call of the Wild*. In that lonely month in 1903, when he had sung the song of the pack, he had become the artist of his most precious dreams.

2

Behind Enemy Lines

Live dangerously. Build your cities on the slopes of Vesuvius.

FRIEDRICH NIETZSCHE, *The Gay Science*

EVEN THE SKYLARKS were singing his praises. Jack pulled down his cap to protect his eyes from the sun. In the distance, across the choppy waters of the bay, he could see the mansions of San Francisco. In the other direction, the slums of his youth. He listened again to the sound of birdsong.

From New York to San Francisco, the literati were astounded. How could he have risen so quickly, written so much, and captivated America in less time than it takes others to complete a first draft? Did he not despise the bourgeoisie with the same ferocity with which the timber wolves in his stories ripped each other apart? Who was this young pretender, this twenty-seven-year-old sensation?

Jack smiled and tugged again on the string. His kite fluttered and then rose steadily in the cloudless California sky. From coast to coast, he was being lionised by jaded men in threadbare suits who dreamed of writing their own books while reviewing his. *The Call of the Wild* was causing a sensation, selling faster than any novel in living memory. He was settled in a home with spectacular views over America's most beautiful city, and he had two healthy daughters.

In the fields behind his cottage in the Piedmont hills, he spent the summer afternoons of 1903 blowing bubbles, picnicking under the cherry trees with George Sterling and other friends, and flying kites. On this particular afternoon 'an enchanted little girl', his daughter

Joan, watched him. The golden poppies around him seemed to glow in the sun.

That evening, determined to relish his overnight fame, he would hold a party. He wanted to surround himself with admirers, to revel in his success.

But later that night, when he had drunk a drop too much, and listened to too many toasts to his brilliant prose, he could not beat down a surging feeling of emptiness. Many of the newcomers to his Wednesday-night parties were 'sycophants, well dressed, well mannered and glib', who clung to him as the name of the moment. For ten years he had worked towards recognition, mostly in isolation and without encouragement. If success now felt hollow, he would not show it – even if inside he had begun to panic.

Jack had thought his passions would subside when he achieved fame, but now his hunger was greater than ever. He had made the impersonal editorial machine in the east respond to his command. He had smashed his way into polite society. But he was still not satisfied.

With the publication of *The Call of the Wild*, Jack's struggle for recognition had ended in spectacular acclaim. Yet he was no nearer achieving his other great ambition – financial security. Although *The Call of the Wild* sold out its entire first edition of ten thousand copies within twenty-four hours, Jack did not profit from its rapid climb up the bestseller list. Instead of royalties, Brett had offered to buy the book for a flat fee of $2000, promising to give it extensive promotion. Desperate for cash, Jack had accepted what appeared a reasonable offer – $2000 was a generous sum for a 32,000-word novella in 1903. He would later say that he never regretted his decision, even though, by Joseph Noel's estimate, he lost 'upward of a hundred thousand dollars' by giving up royalties.

With the money he did receive from Brett, Jack decided to buy a yacht, the *Spray*, named after the boat in which Joshua Slocum had sailed around the world between 1895 and 1898. From now on, Jack vowed, he would return to the water whenever possible. He wanted to recapture its feel, having decided to set his next book at sea. Its provisional title was *The Mercy of the Sea*. If it was as well received as

The Call of the Wild, his financial problems would be over, provided he was paid royalties.

One of Jack's associates from this period, an architect/poet named Herman Scheffauer, later recalled a sail on the *Spray* with some of the Crowd. It had been a perfect summer day on the water until late in the afternoon when fog suddenly swirled in from the Pacific and blanketed the yacht. All that pierced the murk was the call of foghorns; then, suddenly, came the clatter of fast-approaching paddle wheels.

Some of the women in the party began to scream. Jack remained calm, Scheffauer recalled, holding 'a rusty foghorn in the bow of the boat, lustily blowing his warning note against the white wall of the unknown from behind which Destruction was approaching. The next moment – white, spectral, gigantic – the ferry-boat shot past us a mere boat's length away. We heard shouts from the horrified passengers, and the next moment it vanished again as we were flung to the side by the wash.'

The *Spray* provided other opportunities for excitement. Its comfortable cabin was ideally suited to bolstering Jack's reputation as the stallion of the Piedmont hills. The fruits of celebrity included women, who were drawn to him 'as moths to a flame', and the *Spray* was the perfect place to enjoy the pleasures of a mistress.

Success only increased Jack's frustration with Bess. She seemed unable or unwilling to live up to her new role as the wife of California's most glamorous young writer. When Jack asked her to dress in the latest fashions, she stuck to her starched blouses and plain skirts. At a banquet held in his honour at the Bohemian Club in San Francisco, she looked like a nun compared to the other women with their elegant ballgowns and coiffed hair.

'She's devoted to purity,' Jack complained to George Sterling late one night aboard a ferry as they crossed San Francisco Bay. 'When I tell her morality is only evidence of low blood pressure, she hates me. She'd sell me and the children out for her damned purity. Every time I come back after being away from home for a night, she won't let me be in the same room with her if she can help it. I can see the horror in her eyes when I go near the children. She wants to make me a house animal that won't go anywhere without her approval. And worse than anything else, she's converting that bungalow into a prison.'

Who, among the throngs of women throwing themselves at him, should he elect as his lover? He drew up a shortlist of candidates from the Crowd, including Charmian Kittredge, but before he could pounce, fate intervened. After injuring his knee in a buggy accident, Jack was forced to recuperate in bed for several days. Bess was on holiday with the girls at Wake Robin, a small village fifty miles northeast of San Francisco, so he found himself alone in the Piedmont bungalow. Over the next few weeks Charmian became a frequent visitor to his bedside. When she made to leave after one of her first visits, Jack surprised her by kissing her. She responded in kind.

Five years older than Jack, Charmain was a free-spirited woman, the only one in the bay area to support herself in the traditionally male occupation of stenographer. She was no gold-digger, unlike the adventurous beauties Jack had met in the Klondike, but neither was she naive when it came to attracting the interest of eligible men. In a diary she kept during her twenties, she reported that men fell for her after a single smile. But she also admitted a mounting loss of self-confidence as lover after lover, married or single, failed to commit himself to her.

In a biography of Jack written in the 1930s, twenty years after his death, his daughter Joan claimed that several of Jack's friends found Charmian's 'laughter a little loud, her horsemanship too spectacular, her eagerness to play and sing at the piano distasteful ... They did not fully appreciate that behind much of this exhibitionism lay a woman's very natural desire to attract a husband before it was too late.'

Certainly, Charmian was looking for love. But she was involved with another man when she first visited Jack in Piedmont, and it was Jack who initiated their affair – contrary to the claims of members of the Crowd. Jack was in any case deaf to their gossip. For all he knew, these same friends also belittled him behind his back. 'Ask people who know me today, what I am,' he wrote to Charmian in the summer of 1903, shortly after their affair began. 'A rough, savage fellow, they will say, who likes prize-fights and brutalities, who has a clever turn of pen, a charlatan's smattering of art, and the inevitable deficiencies of the untrained, unrefined, self-made man which he strives with a fair measure of success to hide beneath an attitude of roughness and unconventionality. Do I endeavour to unconvince them? It's so much easier to leave their convictions alone.'

The Crowd were simply jealous. They did not understand – Jack had found the perfect companion, even if she was a vegetarian whose mouth was a little too wide and whose nose turned up a little too much. Her charm derived from her readiness to accept any kind of challenge. Whether it was cribbage, fencing or boxing, she never tired of playing whatever game or role Jack assigned to her, including that of sparring partner. Though she tried to give as good as she got, Jack more often than not won their bouts with clinical efficiency.

'Yes, I have been hurt – one does not box for cool relaxation,' Charmian later wrote, 'but for the zest of rousing the good red blood and setting it free to race through sluggish veins to clear lungs and brain and give one a new lease of life. To Jack, who loved gameness above all virtues, it was his proudest boast that on two or three occasions gore had been drawn from one or the other of our respective features; but it was of his own undoing he was vainest, because "the Kid-woman squared her valiant little shoulders and stood up with her eyes wide open and unafraid and delivered and took a straight left".'

At last, here was a woman who adored fornication, expected Jack to make her climax, and to do so frequently, and who didn't burst into tears when the sadist in him punched her in the mouth. 'Yes, we must have been planned for each other from the beginning – at least you for me,' he told her. 'You meet me on every side of me. I have met so many ones, who had this side, or that side, or the other side; but none had every side. Here they missed, and there they missed, just where you hit and hit.'

Known to her aunt, Ninetta Eames, by the nickname 'Childie', Charmian could prattle like an overexcited, overindulged small girl, but there was nothing coy about her approach to sex. In the bedroom she lacked all inhibition, having been influenced by a foster mother who followed the teachings of Victoria Woodhull, the first woman in America to advocate free love. Above all, as Jack admitted to Cloudesley Johns, it was Charmian's prowess between the sheets that first hooked him. For the first time he was enjoying an intensely adventurous and fulfilling sex life. Yet still he could not bring himself to leave Bess, for all her fustiness and narrow view of life. Although she could

not make him happy, he was torn between his responsibilities to his
family and his desperation to escape a dead marriage.

According to Bess's later account, when Jack joined her and their
daughters at Wake Robin after he had recovered from the buggy accident, he appeared to be the perfect father and husband. In the mornings,
he sat in a leafy knoll and worked on *The Sea Wolf*. After lunch, he taught
his girls to swim, and after sunset, he barbecued over an open fire. His
every gesture suggested that he intended to stay at Bess's side.

A way to avoid the breakdown of his marriage had occurred to
him. Why not move to southern California and settle on a desert
ranch, far from the distractions of the Crowd? As so often before,
Jack could only resist temptation by fleeing it. As Bess told it, one
afternoon in late July, as they walked along a stream that ran through
Wake Robin, he broached the idea. She said she was willing to make
the move, and they agreed to leave later that autumn. Bess then took
their daughters back to their cabin for an afternoon nap. Four hours
later, Jack found Bess watching over them as they slept.

'I'm leaving you,' he said.

'You mean you're going back to Piedmont?' Bess asked.

'No, I'm leaving you . . . separating.'

'Why? What do you mean? You've just been talking about southern
California.'

He repeated that he was leaving her, and would say no more.

'What's happened to you?' she cried.

Jack returned to the Piedmont bungalow on 24 July and packed
his belongings before moving in with his old school friend Frank
Atherton in a six-room apartment in Oakland. He rented a house
nearby for Flora and Johnny Miller, his eternal liabilities. Meanwhile,
Jack tried to keep his affair with Charmian secret, rarely seeing her
more than twice a week, usually on the *Spray*.

Throughout the remainder of the summer and the autumn of 1903,
Jack and Charmian wrote to each other daily, exchanging ever more
passionate and florid love letters. In *The Kempton–Wace Letters*, Jack
had written that romantic love was 'pre-nuptial madness . . . an artifice,
blunderingly and unwittingly introduced by man into the natural
order'. Now he had changed his mind. His letters to Charmian showed
no sign of the cold hand of logic. 'When I say I am your slave,' he

declared in one, 'I say it as a *reasonable* man – which goes to show how really and completely mad I am.'

Charmian matched his every sentiment, and then some. 'Ah, my love, you ARE such a man. And I love you, every bit of you, as I have never loved, and shall never love again!' Responding to her passionate affirmation of his masculinity, Jack confessed in a letter written aboard the *Spray* to subconscious fears that he might lose her:

> I had all sorts of horrible nightmares last night about you – Seemed you were in Paris, another man's wife, but that you loved me. That we spent a terrible, endless night trying to meet each other, & trying vainly. And then, at grey dawn, we met, in a park or garden. But we had just met, & our arms were about each other in the first embrace, when your maid gave the signal of warning and you had to fly. And while the day was yet young I had the pleasure(?) of being run down by your husband and a dozen friends, before your eyes, & of being killed before your eyes. At least, at the moment I was killed, I woke up, and was very glad to know you were my wife and not another man's.

These lines . . . seem to tell me all of our Greater Intimacy:

> I drank your flesh, & when the soul brimmed up
> In that sufficing cup,
> Then slowly, steadfastly, I drank your soul;
> Thus I possessed you whole.

Although Jack had not given Bess a reason for leaving, she guessed he had found another woman. Searching through his waste-paper basket, she had pieced together a typed, unsigned letter from Charmian. Who was it from? What woman could entice him into sacrificing his family? Knowing how intimate Anna Strunsky and Jack had become while writing *The Kempton–Wace Letters*, Bess began to suspect Anna. She still regarded Charmian as a confidante, and on Jack's advice, in order to avoid suspicion, Charmian paid Bess and the children a consoling visit. It was a callous act, for which she would never be forgiven, and she left feeling guilty. 'Sometimes,' she confessed to Jack, 'I have to fight off a feeling of actual WICKEDNESS.'

Several years would pass before Bess exacted her revenge on Jack for his desertion. Punishment from the press was more immediate. So far he had been the local golden boy, the prodigy who never failed to provide lively copy. But what the press could make they could also break. For the first time, Jack began to suffer serious bruising from insatiable reporters. Several newspapers even suggested his separation from Bess was a desperate attempt to promote the *Kempton–Wace Letters*, which had failed to take off as Jack had promised Brett, and which was receiving decidedly mixed reviews. 'Mr Jack London, the author,' the *Chicago Record Herald* declared, 'has found a new method of advertising that will undoubtedly prove a great help to him and his publishers.'

Even though every article coupled him with Anna Strunsky, Jack offered no comment. He would not tell the truth – he had to protect Charmian even if Anna's reputation was sullied in the process. 'It will soon die away, I believe,' he apologised to Anna. 'And so it goes. I wander through life delivering hurts to all that know me . . . it is the woman who always pays.'

Jack insisted he had acted bravely in ending his stale marriage; he had performed what he considered 'the very highest of right acts'. In fact, guilt consumed him. When he heard in October that his eldest daughter Joan was seriously ill with typhoid fever, he dropped everything and rushed to her. Reunited with Bess at his daughter's bedside, according to press reports, he considered returning to his family.

As soon as Joan recovered, however, Jack resumed his affair with Charmian. 'Remember,' he told her, 'each moment I am robbed of you, each night and all nights I am turned away from you, turned out by you, give me pangs the exquisiteness of which must be measured by the knowledge that they are moments and nights lost, lost, lost forever.'

New Year's Day, 1904. Two weeks earlier the Wright brothers had made the first successful flight in history. The entrepreneur Henry Ford was making the final preparations which would lead to him setting a new world speed record of 91.37 miles per hour on frozen Lake St Clair in Michigan. In San Francisco, the renowned young author Jack London was working on the final pages of *The Sea Wolf*, and taking stock of the last couple of years.

He would soon be twenty-eight years old. He was involved in a bitter separation. He and his mother were estranged, even though he still supported her. Jack's finances were equally beleaguered (he had just $20.02 in his bank account), and he had run out of ideas for new novels, having exhausted the rich source he had found in the Klondike.

The newspaper headlines predicted the imminent outbreak of war between Russia and Japan over the possession of Manchuria. For over a decade the two countries had disputed each other's presence in the region, and in the first days of 1904 Jack was asked by five major news organisations to report on the situation. He decided to accept the highest offer – from William Randolph Hearst – to cover the impending war for the *San Francisco Examiner*, the *New York Journal* and other Hearst papers.

Hearst, on whom Orson Welles would later base his film *Citizen Kane*, was already well on his way to establishing the most influential media conglomerate in America, and could afford to hire the very best. Stephen Crane, the young author of the classic *The Red Badge of Courage*, Mark Twain and even the high-minded Henry James had all been seduced into working for Hearst's sensationalist publications.

Before leaving for Korea, Jack tied up several loose ends: he rushed to complete the second half of *The Sea Wolf*; asked Brett to send his monthly checks to Bess; told his stepsister Eliza to provide for Charmian if necessary; and arranged for Charmian and George Sterling to edit and proofread his work in his absence. On 7 January 1904, wearing a dark suit, with a cap covering his tousled hair, Jack passed through the Golden Gate Strait aboard the SS *Siberia*. Japan's modern army, the sleeping giant of Asia, had already mobilised. Foreign observers in St Petersburg were predicting that it was a matter of days, if not hours, before Russia and Japan would be at war.

From almost the moment Jack left San Francisco, his stint as a war reporter went badly. He came down with 'flu, then tripped over while larking about on deck with some other reporters, badly spraining his left ankle. After spending the next sixty-five hours lying on his back, he was still barely able to walk when he arrived at Yokohama on 25 January.

Jack and his fellow American reporters were escorted to Tokyo, where they were wined and dined by their Japanese hosts. Among his colleagues were Frederick Palmer, a veteran war correspondent, and Robert Dunn, a photographer for *Collier's Weekly*. At the head of the correspondents' table sat Richard Harding Davis, 'the most admired and envied man in America at the turn of the century', who 'cast an aura of romance and respectability around the newspaper business . . . He was braver and handsomer than any general, more romantic than any actor, more publicised than any politician . . . His books [*The Pride of Jennico* and *Soldiers of Fortune*], glorifying men much like himself, or as he saw himself, were best-sellers.'

Jack was determined to outshine even Davis. But how? He had no experience as a correspondent, and had never covered a war. He had heard of one Hearst reporter who, prevented from reaching the front lines by official red tape, had covered a battle without moving from his bar stool. There was no way, Jack vowed, that he would do the same.

Within hours of his arrival in Tokyo, Jack sensed that the Japanese had no intention of allowing correspondents to report from the front. He decided to strike out on his own. He would sail across the Yellow Sea to Korea and from there find his way north to Manchuria. If his plan worked, he would be in the thick of the fighting while the rest of the press pack were chasing geisha girls around Tokyo.

In the port city of Moji, a few miles from Nagasaki, Jack found a steamer bound for Korea. He then roamed the streets taking photographs of local Japanese. Almost immediately, he was arrested and frogmarched to the nearest jail. Moji, he soon discovered, was also a naval base, and he had been arrested on suspicion of being a Russian spy.

Questioned for eight hours, then moved to another police station for further interrogation, Jack was finally released when it was realised that he was a foolhardy American reporter rather than an agent of the Czar. He managed to book a passage on another boat, the *Keigo Maru*, but two days before he was due to sail, the military commandeered the boat, converting it into a troopship. In a last-ditch effort, Jack chartered a junk. Two days later he was cowering in its stern, praying for the most vicious storm he had ever seen to pass.

When the storm started to abate, Jack pulled out a notepad and pencil.

> Saturday, Feb. 13/04
> Dear Charmian
>   . . . Well, concerning tides. Yesterday morning found us on a lee shore all rocks, with a gale pounding the whole Yellow Sea down upon us. Our only chance for refuge, dead to leeward, a small bay, and high and dry. Had to wait on the 40ft tide and we waited, anchored under a small reef across which the breakers broke, until, tide rising, they submerge it. Never thought a sampan (an open crazy boat) could live through what ours did. A gale of wind, with driving snow – you can imagine how cold it was.

At last, the Yellow Sea relented. Jack and the crew of five Japanese sailors managed to direct the broken junk to the port of Kunsan, on the northern peninsula of Korea. Once ashore, Jack left instructions for emergency repairs and headed for the nearest place to soothe his aching body. It wasn't long before five young women were helping him undress and admiring his white Anglo-Saxon skin as they showed him how to make use of a Japanese bath-house.

He set out to sea again the following day, more determined than ever to reach the front lines before any other American reporter. For six more nights, in temperatures that reminded him of the Klondike, Jack and his crew battled gale-force winds. There was nothing to eat but rice and raw fish; the only source of heat was a charcoal stove that gave off 'clouds of poisonous fumes'.

The winds were now so fierce that Jack and the crew were forced to seek shelter behind a natural breakwater. When waves pounded over the barrier, they crawled out from under a tarpaulin, ran up a sail and steered the boat into a calmer stretch of water in a sheltered bay.

Finally, on 16 February, Jack arrived in Chemulpo, where, to his surprise, he was greeted by Robert Dunn, who had made a similar, though less hazardous, journey from Japan. Dunn barely recognised

Jack, even though it had been just two weeks since they had seen each other in Tokyo. In Dunn's eyes, Jack was a 'physical wreck. His ears were frozen; his fingers were frozen; his feet were frozen. He said that he didn't mind his condition so long as he got to the front.'

After a few days spent regaining his strength, Jack joined Dunn in mustering together some horses and recruiting a group of Korean porters. The pair then set out for Seoul, which they reached on 24 February. Now all that lay between them and the Manchurian border to the north were two hundred miles of frozen ice fields and precipitous gorges. Jack made slow progress – the first few days were spent learning how to ride.

'The combination of a slippery man and a slipping horse,' he wrote in one despatch while hiding from the sleet and ice-rain in his tent, 'is not a happy one . . . I shall not forget such an ice-slope we climbed at the rear of a column of infantry. The men were sprawling right and left. Slipping became contagious . . . But my poor Belle, my horse, had four feet sliding in many simultaneous directions . . . She was pawing and scrambling wildly . . . When we gained the summit – and there was no stopping till we did – all her shoes were loose and two could be pulled off by hand.'

For the next two months, Jack subsisted on cold rice and barely cooked vegetables, interviewed shivering soldiers and tried to assess the strength of the Japanese army. His despatches almost all made the front pages, and further spread his name across America. The hundreds of photographs he took were to earn him a prominent place in the early history of war photography.

Meanwhile, the rest of the pack were still knocking back highballs, rewriting official press releases and seething with frustration in Seoul. When they heard that Jack had scooped them, several grumbled that the Hearst man and his companion Dunn had received special preference, or how else would he have got so close to the front?

Within days, Jack and Dunn were arrested, and then recalled to Seoul. Now he would miss the action after all. 'I am profoundly irritated by the futility of my position,' he wrote to Charmian from the headquarters of the First Japanese Army. 'Whatever I have done I am ashamed of. The only compensation for these months of irritation is a better comprehension of Asiatic geography and Asiatic character. Only in another war, with a white man's army, may I hope to redeem myself. It can never be done here by any possibility.'

Jack joined his colleagues in drowning his frustration at Martin's Bar in downtown Seoul. Because of the reporting restrictions imposed by the Japanese, they could do little but drink and wait, and many an evening was washed away. Robert Dunn recalled one occasion when, 'after a good deal of vodka', he and Jack went hunting tigers in the caves outside Seoul. 'He turned up for lunch [at Martin's Bar] next day,' Dunn wrote, 'shyly worried because he hadn't been asked'. Jack stayed for lunch, afternoon cocktails and dinner. As he was about to sign for his drinks tab, a 'slick stranger with prison pallor' caught his eye.

'I've been in jail myself,' Jack said to Dunn.

'Who hasn't been?' Dunn replied. 'Where were you pinched?'

'Niagara Falls, New York, the first time. I was fifteen. Got thirty days as a vagrant. The injustice helped make me a socialist . . . I'm a socialist because it's got to come some day. Anyway, I like a fight. Now then, what are all you bourgeois drinking?'

There were other scenes which colleagues would vividly recall. When the locals pressed in too closely as he ate lunch, Jack would use a bizarre weapon to fend them off. 'Jack's front false teeth were attached to a plate,' Frederick Palmer wrote. 'When the staring sheep faces pressed too close, Jack stuck his tooth plate on the edge of his tongue, and the Koreans fell back in disorder for four or five yards. Cautiously and curiously they would draw near again; and again Jack would repulse them.'

According to Palmer, Jack was 'the most inherently individualistic' and 'unsocialistic of all the Socialists I have ever met . . . He preferred to walk alone in aristocratic aloofness, and always in the direction he chose no matter where anybody else was going. He had his own separate mess and tent; general and private of his army of one, he rode in front of his two pack-donkeys, which jingled with bells, the leader bearing an American flag.'

Jack's army actually comprised a Japanese interpreter, Mr Yamada, a cook who would accompany him back to America and remain a loyal servant for several years – a Korean youth called Manyoungi whom he had employed for $17.50 a month – and two Mapus (Korean grooms). '[Manyoungi] dressed in European clothes,' Jack had written in his first war report, 'with a white shirt, standup collar, tie, studs, and all complete, and he talked English better, far better, than my provisional interpreter . . . Not only did he know how to work himself and achieve results, but he possessed the miraculous faculty of getting work out of other Koreans.'

By May, Jack was praying for an honourable discharge. He now despised the Japanese bureaucracy, and there seemed little point in pretending to be reporting a war when most of his time was spent at a hotel bar. 'Perfect rot I am turning out,' he complained bitterly. 'It's not war correspondence at all.'

When Jack saw a group of Russian prisoners of war, he found himself sympathising with their plight. 'These men were my kind,' he wrote, adding that he would rather join the Russians behind bars than 'remain in freedom amongst aliens'.

Ever the opportunist, Jack decided to switch sides. He wrote to his employers asking if he could report the war from behind Russian lines – at least the Cossacks knew how to drink. Before he received a reply, however, his war came to an abrupt end. Told that a Japanese groom was stealing fodder meant for his horses, Jack threw a punch at the alleged thief, knocked him over and in so doing sparked 'an international incident', as Robert Dunn later described it.

Wild man London had finally overstepped the mark. Again he found himself behind bars, this time in Seoul, after his third arrest in four months. But now he was facing the serious charge of assaulting a Japanese citizen. There was even talk among the Japanese high command of a court-martial.

Richard Harding Davis saved his skin by sending an urgent telegram to President Theodore Roosevelt, a personal friend, which explained the situation. Roosevelt promptly wired the Japanese government and demanded Jack's instant release. The Japanese chief of staff agreed, but only after Jack had sworn to leave on the next boat. In late June 1904, Jack once again found himself contemplating the grey waves of the Yellow Sea as he headed back to San Francisco.

His fellow reporters were sad to see him go. Even those who were envious of his scoops grudgingly admired his courage and resilience.

'I want to say that Jack London is one of the grittiest men it has been my good fortune to meet,' Robert Dunn would write. 'He is just as heroic as any of the characters in his novels.'

Ever after, Jack would harbour a deep contempt for the Japanese. In print, he had complimented their infantrymen on their supreme organisation. To fellow correspondent Frederick Palmer, he expressed his true feelings: 'They may be brave, but so are the South American peccary pigs in their herd charges.' In an essay written shortly after leaving Asia for good, 'The Yellow Peril', Jack warned that the 'yellow' Chinese and the 'brown' Japanese might one day join forces. 'The menace to the western world,' he wrote, 'lies, not in the little brown man, but in the four hundred millions of yellow men should the little brown man undertake their management.'

The Russo–Japanese war continued for another year before ending in total humiliation for the Czar on 27 May 1905, after the crushing defeat of the Russian fleet in just under an hour off Tsushima Island. It was not only the extent of Japanese naval power which took the Czar and the watching world by surprise. The Japanese army had also shown in a series of brilliant tactical moves that careful planning and a well-supplied force could bring even the mighty Russian bear to its knees.

But however advanced the Orientals were, Jack believed, however spectacularly they had awoken from their slumber, they were still a long way behind the white man. He later stressed this point at a meeting of the Oakland chapter of the Socialist Party. According to one bystander, he also 'cursed the entire yellow race in the most outrageous terms'.

One comrade pointed out that an exploited proletariat also existed in Japan. Another called Jack's attention to the slogan above the portrait of Karl Marx that hung on a nearby wall: 'Workers of all countries, unite!'

Jack started to pound his fist on the table. 'What the devil!' he shouted. 'I am first of all a white man and only then a socialist!'

Before leaving Japan aboard the SS *Korea* in mid-June 1904, Jack had told Richard Harding Davis that he was overjoyed to be on his way – it had been a lousy God-damned war. Had he known what awaited him back in America, aside from 'yellow' comrades in Oakland, he might not have been in such a hurry to leave the land of the rising sun. Even a Japanese prison would seem more welcoming than the reception he was about to receive at home.

Yours for the Revolution

I think of all the assassins in Russia as comrades.
Remember that when the embattled farmers of Lexington fired upon British soldiers, their acts were no worse
than what assassins and revolutionaries are doing today.

JACK LONDON, *Revolution and Other Essays* (1910)

JACK HAD NOT HOPED FOR brass bands and cheering crowds on
his return to America. Nor had he expected a man to clamber aboard
the SS *Korea* before it had even docked in San Francisco and thrust
divorce papers into his hands. When he read them, he gasped with
shock. Bess had not only alleged that he had given her gonorrhoea (a
claim which was never substantiated), she had also named Anna Strunsky in the divorce proceedings.

Jack scanned the docks of the Embarcadero. There was no sign of
Charmian, but a letter was waiting for him in which she explained
that she had gone to Newton, Iowa, to stay with an aunt until the
scandal of Jack's divorce, which was front-page news across America,
had blown over:

> I fear you will be disappointed that I am not in California.
> The terror of all my dear ones, the scandal, makes me sicker
> every time I think of the possible happenings during the next
> few months. I am not writing coldly, dear; indeed there never
> was a moment since we loved each other that I was madder
> for you than right now, but I am forced for the sake of others,
> as well as my own, to be level-headed.

There was no escape for Anna. When the press discovered that Bess
had named her as the 'other woman', they laid siege to her home in

New York. Had she actually made love to Mr London while staying in the same house as his wife, as Bess claimed? Was this the kind of behaviour Mr London had in mind when he proselytised about free love?

'Absurd is hardly a word strong enough to be used in regard to the silly stories about the love-making that went on before Mrs London's eyes,' Anna snapped back. 'Mr London and I were very good friends, and we treated one another as such – no more. Besides, Jack London is hardly the man to make love to another woman in his own house, invited there on another errand altogether. His behaviour was most circumspect toward me, and always has been.'

It was crucial, for the sake of Anna's reputation, that Bess withdraw her name from the divorce petition. When Jack asked her to do so, she listened to him quietly, too proud to show her true feelings. When he admitted that Charmian, not Anna, was the other woman, she could barely choke back her anger. How could Charmian have stolen her 'Daddy Boy' and then have had the gall to act as her confidante? It was with Charmian, of all people, that she had tearfully shared her hopes that Jack might one day return to her.

Bess nevertheless agreed to Jack's request: she would file suit for divorce instead of separation, and would change her complaint from adultery to desertion, thus sparing Anna further shame. In return, Jack agreed to provide a home in Piedmont and maintenance for Bess and his daughters, as long as she did not remarry.

Ever after, Bess would view Charmian as 'a figment of evil, mystery and menace'. 'The foremost rule of my mother's life was loyalty,' her eldest daughter would later say, 'and what she could never forgive was, not Charmian's stealing her husband, but pretending to be her sympathetic friend . . . such two-facedness was utterly reprehensible. Thus, in later years, my sister Bess and I were never permitted to see our father in Charmian's presence. She felt such a treacherous woman couldn't be trusted for a moment with her daughters.'

Although Jack had sacrificed his family for her, he did not welcome Charmian with open arms when she finally returned to Oakland in late July. He was still hurt by her failure to be there for him when he had returned from Korea. He had sent her a train ticket and repeatedly asked her to join him, but still she had stayed away. Had he left his family for a woman who fled at the first sign of danger and then ignored his commands?

When she returned to the bay area, Charmian realised that her absence had possibly been a costly mistake. It looked as if Jack had fallen for another woman. 'I saw you watch for her in the audience when you were through speaking,' Charmian told Jack after hearing him lecture in late November in Oakland. 'I saw you wave to her; I saw her backing and filling and fluttering after her manner. I saw you come together in the light of your cigarette, and I knew that you had been together the evening before.'

The woman in the audience was Blanche Partington, a beguiling drama critic whose affair with Jack had been encouraged by the Crowd. Charmian began to fear the worst: Jack was fast slipping away, as so many of her lovers had before. 'I realise Mate's sad condition, and try to get him out of it,' she noted in her diary. 'My growing sorrow and hopelessness over him.'

Just as Charmian began to give up all hope, Jack suddenly grew closer. In the spring of 1905 he ended his affair with Blanche and visited Charmian in Wake Robin, where she was staying with her aunt, Ninetta Eames. The more he had heard her slandered by the Crowd, the more Jack had come to value the freedom she allowed him. Unlike Bess, she seemed prepared to forgive him even when he slept with other women.

'I am not trying to belittle the feeling Jack had for you,' Charmian later wrote to Blanche. 'He loved you well, while he loved you. But all the trouble and slander wrought havoc with his emotions and madness, and made him see more clearly than ever that the wonders he found in our mateship at first were real and good. Blanche, I have never seen a woman who loved Jack that ever got over it. I am loathe to believe that you have got over it, or that you ever will.'

When Jack finally stepped out with Charmian in public, the unrequited passion and frustrated love of her twenties were finally behind her. On her arm was America's most dashing young writer. 'So good to be going about publicly together – Jack and I,' she wrote in her diary in July 1905. 'I've waited so long, so long.'

Despite their attempts to drive a wedge between him and Charmian, Jack still tried to win the Crowd over to her, writing two long letters to Carrie Sterling, Charmian's principal detractor. Charmian had not broken up his marriage, he insisted, and she should not therefore be shunned by those who sided with Bess.

Neither Carrie nor her husband was convinced by Jack's arguments. As the Greek saw it, Charmian had muzzled the Crowd's top dog and lured him away from the pack. The Wolf had, after all, promised to love him forever and always to stand close by.

'No, I am afraid that the dream was too bright to last,' Jack soothed in a letter to George dated 1 June 1905, '– our being near each other. If you don't understand now, some day sooner or later you may come to understand. It's not through any fault of yours, nor through any fault of mine. The world and people just happen to be so made.'

Charmian had won her man, even though they were forced to live apart until Jack's divorce became final in November 1905. Now she had to keep him. Unlike Bess she would have to be tomboy and vulnerable girl, secretary and housewife, sparring partner and ethereal muse. By late 1905 she had learned to sail, box, decipher Jack's handwriting, proofread and follow his moods.

Just as his life was based on immutable laws, so now would hers. But they were not the laws of Darwin or Karl Marx. They were the London code: she could not have a separate bank account, or even a monthly allowance; she could not question him in public; she could not wear what she liked. From now on he wanted her to dress in flowing silks and puffed-up satin robes.

Jack London, she would later concede, was not an easy man to live with. Yet she enjoyed a freedom which was both exhilarating and almost unique in turn-of-the-century America. Jack would eventually become a staunch ally of women's suffrage. From the outset he encouraged Charmian's independent spirit and artistic nature, urging her to write fiction, some of which would find a publisher, and asking for her judgements on his own work. When, four years earlier, she had read *The Son of the Wolf*, she had been captivated by Jack's imagery, but had noted 'certain inadvertencies – false syntax and flagrant misuse of an occasional word – which are the result of inexperience or carelessness'.

In the summer of 1904 Charmian provided constructive criticism as Jack wrote *The Game*, his first and most successful boxing story.

Described by the *Atlantic Monthly* as an 'excellent novelette', and praised by the American lightweight boxing champion Jimmy Britt for its realism, *The Game* was a gripping, tautly plotted romance which demonstrated Jack's peerless gift for suspense. The shop assistant heroine, Genevieve, is in love with Joe, a boyish boxer whose skin is almost as white as her own. Joe is pitted against John Ponta, 'a beast with a streak for a forehead' whose upper torso is covered in a thick mat of hair. In a blood-curdling finale, Ponta strikes Joe with such force that he crushes his skull and kills him. In the boxing ring, as in life, Jack implied none too subtly, brute strength usually wins out.

Jack would constantly push on Charmian the most recent novel he had read, and would expect her to be able to debate the latest political events. Above all, he wanted her to accompany him on the adventure path – to travel as often as possible and share his experiences. She needed little encouragement.

Charmian's effect on another work in progress did not at first bode well. Their affair had begun when Jack was midway through writing *The Sea Wolf*. He had completed the book during their most passionate encounters, and their highly charged romance had found its way into the second half of the novel, published by Macmillan in November 1904.

The Sea Wolf begins with the collision of two vessels in San Francisco Bay. Among those thrown overboard is the narrator, Humphrey van Weyden, an effete writer. He is saved from drowning by Wolf Larsen, the psychotic captain of a seal schooner, the *Ghost*. Larsen rules his crew with a fist of iron, savagely beating them on the slightest pretext. Van Weyden, reduced to a cabin-boy, is summoned to his cabin where he must endure long philosophical rants in the course of which Larsen rages that there is only one law in life: might is right. He realises that he will have to become strong if he is to survive on this death-ship, where Larsen's sickening violence has brutalised every man on board.

Larsen's sadism was unprecedented in American literature. When one of his crew answers him back, he and his mate 'struck him with their fists, kicked him with their heavy shoes, knocked him down, and dragged him to his feet to knock him down again'.

In another scene, Larsen throws the ship's cook overboard with a rope tied around his waist. Unfortunately, a ravenous shark happens to be passing by: '[The cook] came in like a fresh-caught fish on a line ... But a fountain of blood was gushing forth. The right foot was missing, amputated neatly at the ankle.'

Modelled on Alexander McLean, the sealing captain Jack had heard about while on board the *Sophie Sutherland*, Larsen is Jack's most 'memorable human character', a self-educated savage who embodies Jack's ideal of virility and espouses Herbert Spencer's philosophy. Larsen believes 'life is a mess. It is like yeast, a ferment, a thing that moves and may move for a minute, an hour, a year, a hundred years, but that in the end will cease to move. The big eat the little that they may continue to move, the strong eat the weak that they may retain their strength. The lucky eat the most and move the longest, that's all.'

Through Larsen, Jack gave unforgettable expression to his dark side: the pessimist who despised bourgeois sissies such as van Weyden – a weak man and a dilettante writer. 'Underneath we are as savage and elemental and barbarous as primitive man,' blusters Larsen, echoing Jack's own view. 'More than ever today is the race to the swift, the battle to the strong. Nor have the meek and lowly yet come to inherit the earth. In the struggle for food and shelter, for place and power, the weak and less efficient are crowded back and trampled under, as they always have been.'

It was not just Larsen's metaphysical ranting which suggested autobiography; even his Christian name, 'Wolf', gives the game away. Through van Weyden Jack also expressed homoerotic yearnings, for although van Weyden fears Larsen, he rapturously admires his physique: 'I had never before seen him stripped, and the sight of his body quite took my breath away ... His great muscles leaped and moved under the satiny skin ... I stood motionless, a roll of antiseptic cotton in my hand unwinding and spilling itself down to the floor.'

Several critics have seized on such passages as evidence of Jack's repressed homosexuality. Early in their relationship, he told Charmian he had always looked for 'a great Man-Comrade', 'delicate and tender, brave and game'. Did van Weyden's admiration of Larsen's physique resemble Jack's feelings for George Sterling? Did Jack's tales of derring-do in *John Barleycorn* mask a long-standing shame at suffering abuse on board the *Sophie Sutherland*, from his older 'pal' in Erie Penitentiary and from others while on the road?

Larsen's body, says van Weyden, 'was as the fairest woman's. I remember his putting his hand up to feel of the wound on his head, and my watching the biceps move like a living thing under its white sheath. It was the biceps that had nearly crushed out my life once ... I could not take my eyes from him.' Just as the struggle between the two men is building to a climax, Larsen rescues a poet, Maud Brewster, from the sea. Maud is Charmian in a younger body, 'a delicate, ethereal creature, swaying and willowy, light and graceful of movement'. Did Jack introduce a woman midway through the book because he dared not consummate the sado-masochistic relationship between van Weyden and Larsen?

Despite Larsen's efforts to seduce Maud, she falls for van Weyden instead. The couple escape the *Ghost* and row to an island, on which they manage to survive despite the harsh conditions. Van Weyden marvels at Maud's resilience: 'Truly she was my woman, my mate-woman, fighting with me and for me as the mate of a caveman would have fought, all the primitive in her aroused, forgetful of her culture, hard under the softening civilisation of the only life she had ever known.'

Then the *Ghost* runs aground on the island, abandoned by all its crew except Larsen. *The Sea Wolf* ends with Larsen's sudden death from a brain haemorrhage, which Jack intended as conclusive proof of the novel's moral: love and co-operation redeem, whereas unbridled individualism leads only to despair and self-destruction. Few among Jack's readers would, however, acknowledge his warning about untamed egotism. For many, Larsen was the book's true hero.

In the final scene Maud and van Weyden passionately embrace as a ship steams over the horizon to their rescue. What might have been a gripping *tour de force* collapses into sentimental romance. Had Maud been a more plausible character, *The Sea Wolf* might have been a better book. 'The "love" element, with its absurd suppressions and impossible proprieties, is awful,' wrote one critic. 'I confess to an overwhelming contempt for both the sexless lovers.'

Blood and gore could drip from Jack's pages, but 'lolly' – as

Charmian called sex – was never made explicit. Though Jack claimed he was a realist, he, like other writers of the time, did not write about sexual intimacy for fear of alienating his readers. Yet still he protested: 'The critics had expected to have my hero make love with a club and drag my heroine by the hair of her head and into a tree. Because I didn't they branded my love as sentimental bosh and nonsense – and yet I flatter myself I can make love as well as the next fellow, and not quite as ridiculously as the average critic.'

On beginning his affair with Charmian, Jack had abandoned the forceful style which had made his name, and had thereby squandered the gritty promise of the first half of *The Sea Wolf.* Yet even Ambrose Bierce, a notoriously scathing critic, had to concede that the book was 'a rattling good story'. 'The great thing – and it is among the greatest of things – is that tremendous creation Wolf Larsen,' Bierce told George Sterling. 'If that is not a permanent addition to literature, it is at least a permanent figure in the memory of the reader. You "can't lose" Wolf Larsen. He will be with you to the end.'

Readers agreed with William Randolph Hearst's favourite critic, and were enthralled by the book's ground-breaking violence and primitive credo: eat or be eaten. *The Sea Wolf* was a great popular success, selling forty thousand advance copies and over half a million more in Jack's lifetime. Readers, well-to-do and working-class, old and young, could not put it down.

As a gothic thriller, *The Sea Wolf* remains American literature's most brutal seafaring epic. It has been filmed more times than any other American novel, and it revived the proud tradition of Poe's *The Narrative of Arthur Gordon Pym* (1838), R.H. Dana's *Two Years Before the Mast* (1840), and Melville's *Typee* (1846) and *Moby-Dick* (1851).

According to one newspaper report, 'Jack London 1905', the author of *The Sea Wolf* was a 'complex of contrasts'. He was 'handsome, much admired by friends of both sexes, a popular writer who had won a smashing success with an early book ... followed by *The Sea Wolf,* living a self-indulgent life attended by an obsequious Korean valet'. But he was also beset by problems. 'He had fallen in love with a woman somewhat older than himself, had separated from his wife and two small daughters, was constantly worried by financial demands of three households, his own, his mother's, and that of his first wife. On top of all this, he was a zealot thoroughly convinced of the over-riding rights of the common man, an active socialist and an ardent revolutionist.'

The character sketch, by journalist Lois Rather, did not mention that the pessimism Jack had articulated through Captain Larsen was not exorcised through writing. He was in fact so dispirited by spring 1905, even after *The Sea Wolf* had climbed to third place in the national best-seller list, that he kept 'a loaded revolver in his desk ready to use against himself at any time'. 'I meditated suicide coolly, as a Greek philosopher might,' he later confessed. 'So obsessed was I with the desire to die, that I feared I might [shoot myself] in my sleep, and I was compelled to give my revolver away.'

There was a reason for such feelings at a time when Jack should have been enjoying the popular acclaim that came with *The Sea Wolf* – the book that confirmed his status as the most successful and dynamic writer of his generation. He had not considered what he would do once he realised his dream of success. Naively, he had assumed that the reward would be total fulfilment. He would have shown the capitalists a thing or two, and won the game. But now, in the spring of 1905, he found himself standing at the summit, two best-sellers to his credit, gazing at the promised land, and he realised that the view wasn't worth the climb. So began what he called his 'long sickness': a feeling that, despite all he had achieved, it had meant nothing. His battle for recognition had resulted in crippling disillusionment with the ephemeral rewards it bestowed.

'The things I had fought for and burned my midnight oil for had failed me,' he later wrote. 'Success – I despised it. Recognition – it was dead ashes. Society, men and women above the ruck and muck of the waterfront and forecastle – I was appalled by their unlovely mental mediocrity. Love of woman – it was like all the rest. Money – I could sleep in only one bed at a time, and of what worth was an income of a hundred porterhouses a day when I could eat only one? Art, culture – in the face of the iron facts of biology such things were ridiculous, the exponents of such things only the more ridiculous.'

Jack's disgust was aggravated by ill-health. Though not yet thirty, his body was beginning to betray him. Perhaps, he feared, he had driven himself too hard and permanently weakened it. That spring he developed a skin complaint, and a non-malignant tumour was removed from his rectum in late March.

As therapy, Jack plunged into the works of Nietzsche. He began reading *Thus Spake Zarathustra*, with its central message that 'the world belongs to the strong who are noble'. But Jack garbled Nietzsche, confusing 'blond gods' with supermen, whereas in fact by 'blond gods' Nietzsche meant men who could not transcend their animal instincts, and thus became destructive. Nietzsche, like Jack, believed that different races inherited different traits, although he condemned racism. Jack overlooked this key distinction, or perhaps chose to ignore it. Anglo-Saxons, he believed, were the only true supermen. Lesser breeds – racial weaklings – should make way for the Anglo-Saxons, who alone would determine the destiny of the human race.

Jack made this point in an essay, 'The Salt of the Earth', published in the *Anglo-American* magazine in August 1902: 'The history of civilisation is a history of wandering – a wandering, sword in hand, of strong breeds, clearing away and hewing down the weak and less fit. In the misty younger world, peoples, nobody knows whence or whither, rise up in blood-red splendour, conquering and slaying, and, like phantoms, conquered and slain pass away.'

Such sentiments have an echo in the writings of another self-educated man who mangled Nietzsche – Adolf Hitler. In *Mein Kampf*, Hitler would also use social Darwinism to underpin his ideology. He too would translate the struggle to survive from the world of animals to that of mankind. For Hitler and his followers, the struggle to survive would, as it had with Jack, become confused with racial theories. Hitler would adopt Nietzsche's blond, blue-eyed beast as the most likely animal to survive. In Hitler's eyes, these supermen were Aryan. As Jack saw them, they were simply his mirror image, 'Anglo-Saxon through and through'.

Though Nietzsche inspired Jack, he could not make him happy. Only Charmian managed to lift him for short periods from his despair. He should try to enjoy the small things in life, she stressed, and activities that did not bear a price-tag: fresh air, open fields, the Sierras, the Golden State itself. With $350 he received from a *Black Cat* story, 'A Nose for the King', she bought him a thoroughbred gelding, Washoe Ban, and persuaded him to spend afternoons riding with her around Glen Ellen.

One spring morning in 1905, Jack and Charmian had dismounted to admire a superb view of hilly country covered with redwood trees, conifers and manzanita. Jack learned later that year that part of the land was for sale, and at Charmian's urging he agreed to buy it. They began to fantasise. They would hire farm-workers, try their hand at raising cattle and pigs, and build their own home. 'I am really going to throw out an anchor so big,' he told George Sterling, 'and so heavy that all hell could not get it up again.'

The 130 acres cost $7000, and Jack agreed to buy horses, cows and farm machinery from the owner for another $600. Yet again he asked Brett to pay for it, through a $10,000 advance on royalties. Brett agreed, but warned of the problems that might result from the venture 'no matter how beautiful and productive'. The money disappeared within weeks. Again facing insolvency, Jack came up with a brilliant solution: a companion to *The Call of the Wild*, which he would entitle *White Fang*.

'I'm going to give the evolution, the civilisation of a dog – development of domesticity, faithfulness, love, morality,' he told Brett. Unlike Buck, White Fang would hear 'the call of fire and of man – the call which it has been given alone among all animals to the wolf to answer'. Taking the opposite path to Buck, White Fang would be born in the wilds of Alaska, but would end up on a Santa Clara Valley ranch where he would be called 'Blessed Wolf' – George Sterling's term for Jack.

White Fang begins with several descriptions of Alaska which are as evocative as anything in *The Call of the Wild*. Two men, Henry and Bill, weighed down by the corpse of a dead man, are trying to reach safety. Pursued by a pack of hungry wolves, they are running low on ammunition and hope. Their sled-dogs are disappearing, lured away by a magnificent she-wolf. Bill resolves to shoot the she-wolf, but before he can do so he is killed by the wolf pack.

The narrative then switches to the she-wolf, who gives birth to a grey cub. They wander into an Indian camp, and White Fang, as the cub is named, quickly learns to obey humans, and gains a reputation for a savage ability to kill other dogs. A gruesome-looking man, Beauty Smith, tricks White Fang's Indian owner into selling the killer dog to him. White Fang suffers abuse and cruelty until, during a fight with a bulldog, he is saved by the noble Weedon Scott, who takes him back to California. White Fang saves Scott from being murdered by a 'primordial' human, and earns the undying love of the Scott family through his courage and intelligence.

On 22 October 1906, Brett wrote to congratulate Jack on *White Fang*: 'I have been re-reading it and like the contents of it more and more. It seems to me to be a much better knitted piece of work than any other long story that you have written, and to show a clear advance in your art, especially in being much stronger than *The Sea Wolf*, a book which seemed to me to have enormous interest through two-thirds and then in some way to let a little of the interest escape in the conclusion.'

White Fang was twice as long as *The Call of the Wild*, but not half as well executed. While much of Brett's praise for the book was justified, it suffered from too much authorial intrusion, out of Jack's desire to preach evolutionary theory and to show how human kindness can redeem savage instincts. Though it proved popular among young adults, and sold a very healthy thirty-five thousand advance copies, *White Fang* lacked the artistry of *The Call of the Wild*, reading at times like a zoology lecture. Jack had described Buck's experiences, by contrast, in prose that read like an epic poem.

Of the critics, the *New York Independent*'s was among the most generous: 'There are in the story touches of the brutality which Mr London never quite escapes; but from beginning to end the experience of White Fang is dramatised with striking effectiveness.'

Others were less complimentary, notably the President of the United States, Theodore Roosevelt, who considered himself an out-doorsman first and a politician second. After reading *White Fang*, Roosevelt accused Jack of being 'a nature faker' and, worse still, of knowing next to nothing about wolves: 'I am certain he knows nothing about their fighting, or as a realist he would not tell this tale.'

'President Roosevelt,' Jack replied, 'does not think a bull-dog can lick a wolf-dog. I think a bull-dog can lick a wolf-dog. And there we are . . . what gets me is how difference of opinion regarding the relative merits of a bull-dog makes me a nature-faker and President Roosevelt a vindicated and triumphant scientist.'

Roosevelt was not alone in his accusations of 'nature-faking'. The gold rush veteran Thomas Williamson was to write that Jack knowingly described 'a non-existent Alaska', and the naturalist Arthur Stringer also questioned Jack's depiction of the north: 'The sin that lies darkest at Mr London's door . . . is not one of mere local colour and detail . . . It is, rather, that general and persistent tendency to "foreigneer" things, to translate everything northern into the lurid. The map of the north must be all red or nothing. Everything above the forty-ninth parallel must be written down as blood and raw beef.'

Yet many gold rush veterans, looking back on their own harsh winters, agreed with Jack's impressions. As the *Critic* pointed out: '[The Klondike is] a horrible land and its stern savagery is unspeakable. You have only to watch the faces of men who have come back from the Klondike to see what havoc it makes of ordinary human nature.'

Nevertheless, Jack was guilty of demonising the region's wildlife. Perhaps more than any other writer, he was responsible for turning wolves into the man-eating monsters of popular imagination. As Barry Lopez, the author of *Of Wolves and Men*, has written: 'London's novels show a preoccupation with "the brute nature" in men, which he symbolised in the wolf . . . But it is, ultimately, a neurotic fixation with machismo that has as little to do with wolves as the drinking, whoring, and fighting side of man's brute nature.'

'In all his writings Jack London is changing dogs into wolves and wolves into dogs,' wrote the English critic Stephen Graham. 'In the course of it all London himself became a civilised dog, reconciled to kennel and master. But he constantly bays at men and the moon to assure them that he is wolf at heart.'

The accusations of nature-faking, which his old ally Richard Harding Davis would later repeat, stung Jack badly, and not just because the most vociferous criticism had come from the White House. He had begun to call himself a rancher as well as a writer. The country, not the city, was now his home.

In moving to Glen Ellen, he had begun what would become a

retreat from mankind. White Fang's mythic journey had ended with integration into civilised society. Jack's sense of estrangement from bourgeois values, combined with his continued yearning for a place where he could belong, would eventually lead him in the opposite direction, towards alienation. One day, he had already resolved, he would create his very own Eden, a spread in the hills where he could separate himself from the demons of his past by ploughing them into the ground.

On a hot July afternoon in 1905 at the Wake Robin camp, the sun blazed overhead as Jack read to Charmian. Suddenly he put down the book he was reading, Joshua Slocum's *Sailing Alone Around the World*, the story of a circumnavigation of the globe in a boat built for a few hundred dollars. Charmian later recorded the conversation that followed.

'If Slocum could do it alone in a thirty-foot sloop,' Jack said, 'with an old tin clock for a chronometer, why couldn't we do it in a ten-foot longer boat with better equipment and more company? What do you say? Suppose five years from now, after we're married and have built our house somewhere, we start a voyage around the world in a forty-five-foot yacht? It'll take a good while to build her, and we've got a lot of other things to do besides.'

'I'm with you every foot of the way,' Charmian replied. 'But why wait five years? Why not begin construction in the spring and let the house wait? . . . We'll never be any younger, nor want to go any more keenly than right now. You know, you're always reminding me that we are dying, cell by cell, every minute of our lives.'

Jack could already picture the boat. It would have three staterooms, a powerful engine, copper sheathing, and all the latest navigational devices. And, of course, his dream vessel would be unsinkable, with an iron keel and only the best Puget Sound planking on deck.

'Oh, by the way,' Jack was to tell an astonished Brett, 'I've got another big project in view. After I've settled down and enjoyed my mountain ranch for about five years, it is my intention to build a boat 40 feet long, and go off on a several years' cruise round the world. Now, don't think I'm joking. I mean it. I have never more ardently desired anything in my life. I don't care very much for ordinary travel anyway, and this certainly would be everything but ordinary . . . Lord! Lord!' he added for good measure. 'Think of the chance to write without interruption when I'm between ports.'

But how would he pay for it? A possible solution soon presented itself in the form of an enquiry from the Slayton Lyceum Lecture Bureau in Chicago. Would Jack be interested in undertaking a cross-country lecture tour? He accepted immediately. It made perfect sense. He could promote his books and socialism at the same time, being paid $600 a week plus expenses in the process.

The tour could not have been better timed. Across the nation, socialism was being hotly discussed in the aftermath of the Russian uprising of January 1905 and the Socialist Party's gains at the November 1904 presidential election. Eugene V. Debs had polled 402,460 votes, far less than the victor, Theodore Roosevelt's 7,628,834, but still a remarkable performance for a party formed just three years earlier.

On 7 July 1905, as a reaction against the more conservative American Federation of Labor, the Industrial Workers of the World (later known as 'the Wobblies') was founded, and rapidly became the most radical labour union in American history. It was against this background that Jack's first collection of non-fiction pieces, *The War of the Classes*, was published on the eve of his lecture tour. It included lectures he had given previously: 'The Class Struggle', 'The Scab', 'The Tramp' and 'How I Became a Socialist', and it provides fascinating glimpses of his often primitive political beliefs. Perhaps the most powerful passage is his own highly romantic definition of socialism:

> Socialism deals with what is, not with what ought to be . . . the material with which it deals is the 'clay of the common road', the warm human, fallible and frail, sordid and petty, absurd and contradictory, even grotesque, and yet, withal, shot through with flashes and glimmerings of something finer and Godlike, with here and there the sweetness of service and unselfishness, desires for goodness, for renunciation and sacrifice, and with conscience, stern and awful, at times blazingly imperious, demanding the right – the right, nothing more nor less than the right.

Less than impressed, the magazine *Charities'* review of *The War of the Classes* concluded that 'except that socialism stands for discontent with the present industrial order, the reader gains no clear idea of what the movement really is'. Jack was a social Darwinist first, and only then a socialist – of sorts. But he sincerely believed that it was only through open revolt, by following the example of their Russian comrades who had shed blood in St Petersburg on Bloody Sunday, that American socialists would gain the promised land. During his lecture tour he would make this point over and over again. In so doing, he would earn more for each week he stood at the podium than the average labourer made in a year.

Jack had a profound reason for wanting to plant the seeds of revolution in the American heartland, as he later explained:

> I was a born fighter. The things I had fought for had proved not worth the fight. Remained the PEOPLE. My fight was finished, yet something was left still to fight for – the PEOPLE ... By the people was I handcuffed to life ... I threw all precaution to the winds, threw myself with fiercer zeal into the fight for socialism, laughed at the editors and publishers who warned me and who were the sources of my hundred porterhouses a day, and was brutally careless of whose feelings I hurt and of how savagely I hurt them.
>
> As the 'well-balanced radicals' charged at the time, my efforts were so strenuous, so unsafe and unsane, so ultra-revolutionary, that I retarded the socialist development in the United States by five years. In passing, I wish to remark, at this late date, that it is my fond belief that I accelerated the socialist development in the United States by at least five minutes.

'I'm not a lecturer,' Jack admitted before one of his first engagements in the midwest. 'I shall tell them experiences tonight ... I can make more money at home, and be at home with my swimming and boxing and fencing ... As I understand it my stunt is to get up there and let people see me. My talk is to give me something to do when I'm there.'

At every opportunity, the 'socialist sensation-monger' added to his own mythology, seducing audiences with anecdotes from his days as a tramp, his adventures in the Klondike and his spectacular rise to literary fame. He was no dilettante writer, but a true proletarian hero. When a reporter from the left-wing newspaper *Common Sense* interviewed him, he couldn't resist taking a swipe at the other so-called 'artists' in the movement – the middle-class *poseurs*.

'You must not attach too much importance to these artists and literary people in the Socialist movement,' he said. 'Many of them – most of them in fact – are Socialists, but they are not the Socialist movement and never will be. The Socialist movement is made up of people to whom grocery and rent bills are as ghosts that haunt forever. These artists and literary people are parasites. They can afford a fad ... they are not pressed by the terrible realities that the exploited wealth producers are.'

Jack showed the reporter his callused hands, recalling when he sold papers on the San Francisco streets and sweated his heart out for a measly buck a day.

'I have become a parasite,' he then conceded. 'But I was not always one.'

In his lectures, the man who ended his letters with 'Yours for the revolution' reserved his most heartfelt contempt for those who had cursed his childhood, the capitalist bosses and their bourgeois lackeys. He spat bitter recriminations at his audience. 'You are drones that cluster around the capitalist honey-vats,' he ranted at one group of captains of industry. 'You are ignoramuses. Your fatuous self-sufficiency blinds you to the revolution that is surely, surely, coming, and which will as surely wipe you and your silk-lined, puffed-up leisure off the face of the map. You are parasites on the back of labour.'

'Do you know what will be the result of your revolution?' one millionaire shouted back.

'It is not MY revolution,' Jack interrupted. 'It is YOURS. Yes, yours and your kind's. You are the cause of it!'

'Anarchy! Civil war! Death and crime! These will be the results of the revolution that you are prophesying. National upheaval,' the millionaire predicted.

'I know it,' Jack shot back. 'But what are you going to do about it? How are you going to stop it?'

As the lecture tour took him east towards that 'man-trap', New York, Jack drew larger and more volatile crowds. Audiences gaped as if the New Messiah had appeared before them, rather than a soft-spoken chain-smoker with a Korean manservant waiting in the wings. At Yale University, he lambasted the students for their lack of revolutionary fervour. At Harvard, he was greeted by the legendary activist Mother Jones, who marched up to the rostrum and kissed him on both cheeks.

When not thumping his fist on a podium, Jack was planning a novel which would win him the enduring respect of socialists the world over. To his dismay, he had discovered during his lecture tour that most socialist leaders in America believed that capitalism would be democratically eliminated. He didn't hesitate to call them deluded. An apocalyptic vision of the future, *The Iron Heel* is the story of an oligarchy of American capitalists who seize power at the very moment when a socialist victory seems inevitable at the polls. The book describes, in heavily footnoted detail, the crushing of labour by this oligarchy between 1912 and 1932.

The Iron Heel is narrated by Avis, the wife of Ernest Everhard, 'a natural aristocrat . . . a superman, a blond beast such as Nietzsche has described and in addition he was aflame with democracy'. He was also Jack. As Earle Labor has written: 'Psychologically speaking, *The Iron Heel* is one of London's most revealing books; it is the fictional articulation of his private dreams of revolutionary glory. The novel's hero, earnest and "ever-hard", is a fantasy figure of Jack London purged of his obsession to win the good life of the American Dream.'

The tone of *The Iron Heel* is set early on when Ernest says to Avis: 'The gown you wear is stained with blood. The food you eat is bloody stew. The blood of little children and of strong men is dripping from your very roof-beams. I can hear it drip, drop, drip, drop, all about me.'

Everhard is invited to speak before 'The Philomaths', a group of wealthy businessmen. He preaches about the coming revolution, ending, as Jack had ended many of his speeches, with the defiant words: 'This is the revolution, my masters. Stop it if you can.' The audience is incensed. One businessman stands up and warns him: 'When you reach out your vaunted strong hands for our palaces and purpled ease, we will show you what strength is. In roar of shell and shrapnel and in whine of machine-guns will our answer be couched. We will grind you revolutionists down under our heel, and we shall walk upon your faces.'

Everhard makes further speeches warning – again as Jack had done – that if the middle classes do not unite with the workers, the entire population will be crushed under the 'iron heel' of the oligarchy. This prediction is soon proved correct, as the police break up strikes and thousands of workers are sent to concentration camps. Yet most socialists and trade union members remain unaware of the true evil of the oligarchy, and its intention: the setting up of a dictatorship. Unlike Everhard, they believe that the ballot box will be the ultimate decider.

When war between the plutocracies of America and Germany seems imminent, the press – run by the ruling class – whips up war fever so as to distract the proletariat in both countries from the true struggle against capitalism. The organised left still cling to their belief in democracy, but when fifty socialists are elected to Congress, the oligarchy starts to assert its power. The labour movement is split and weakened by in-fighting, and its leaders jailed or executed. Finally the people rise up in Chicago, where a commune has formed.

But it is all to no avail, and Jack vents his true feelings towards those among the 'mongrelised' masses who are too stupid to save themselves, portraying them not as heroes in the class struggle but as beasts in an urban jungle, 'dim, ferocious intelligences with all the godlike blotted from their features and all the fiend-like stamped in apes and tigers, anaemic consumptives and great hairy beasts of burden, wan faces from which vampire society had sucked the juice of life ... the refuse and scum of life ... a raging, screaming, screeching, demoniacal horde'. When Chicago is left a ruin, the few surviving socialists, led by Everhard, go underground and resort to terrorism. The novel ends with Everhard's execution.

The Iron Heel was a brave book. Jack wrote it in the full knowledge that it would damage his career by alienating some of his readers, and that it would also undermine his standing among fellow socialists. He was right. But Jack did not care. He had to get this book 'out of his system'. It would be his final warning that making friends with the bosses would not get exploited workers any nearer the promised land.

Brett, who was no revolutionary, was equally courageous in deciding to publish *The Iron Heel*. As Philip Foner has noted, Brett's only request was that Jack delete a libellous footnote which could have sent both his star author and himself to jail. 'If they find me guilty of contempt,' Jack replied, 'I'd be only too glad to do six months in jail, during which time I could write a couple of books and do no end of reading.'

When it was published in 1908, *The Iron Heel* failed to impress any but the most dogmatically Marxist critics. *Outlook* echoed many others: 'as a work of fiction it has little to commend it, and as a socialist tract it is distinctly unconvincing'. According to Foner, Jack's comrades were divided in their reaction. The most radical figures on the left, such as Eugene Debs, Bill Haywood and Mary Marcy, applauded its central message: accommodating the rich and powerful will only ever end in defeat for the working classes. The middle-class leaders of the Socialist Party, however, were as scathing as the literary critics. At the very moment when the party was making exciting progress, along came Jack London, predicting ultimate failure for the movement if it continued on its present course. Jack in action was a much better spectacle, they sneered, than in print.

Though it was slammed by middle-class critics, *The Iron Heel* would sell over fifty thousand copies in hardback. Within weeks of publication it was being passed along production lines throughout the nation, and was quickly devoured by many in the IWW who were inspired by Jack's uncompromising stance. Its impact abroad was even more forceful. In Europe, revolutionary socialism had a longer and more ideological tradition than in America. Class-consciousness was well developed in many of Europe's manufacturing cities, particularly in Britain and the newly industrialised Russia. Aneurin Bevan, later the architect of Britain's National Health Service, read the book as a young miner in Wales in the 1920s and was converted to socialism because of it, as were, he later wrote, 'thousands of young men and women of the working class in Britain'.

Anatole France wrote an introduction to the French edition in 1923, praising Jack for 'that particular genius which perceives what is hidden from the common herd' and for possessing 'a special knowledge enabling him to anticipate the future'. Lenin and Trotsky both praised the novel, and it is the only American book in Bukharin's bibliography of Communism.

The Iron Heel's enduring power comes from its prophecy rather than its prose. As a prediction of how organised labour would be crushed by those whose interests it endangered, it was chillingly accurate. It was not to be an oligarchy of capitalist bosses, however, against whom the European left would be pitted in the coming decades, but the forces of fascism. Thirty years after the book's publication Trotsky would write: 'The fact is incontestable: in 1907 Jack London already foresaw and described the fascist regime as the inevitable result of the defeat of the proletarian revolution. Whatever may be the "errors" of the novel – and they exist – we cannot help inclining before the powerful intuition of the revolutionary artist.' George Orwell was to write: 'London could foresee fascism because he had a fascist streak in himself: or at any rate a marked strain of brutality and an almost unconquerable preference for the strong man as against the weak man.'

Jack had also predicted substantial gains for the left in the 1912 Presidential election which would accomplish nothing. Again, he was right. The Socialist Party would reach the peak of its power in that year, with Eugene Debs polling almost 900,000 votes, 6 per cent of the total. And Jack's description of the Iron Heel's repression would be mirrored in the thwarting of the IWW in the coming years, and in the imprisonment of leading American radicals during the Red Scare of 1918–19.

The crowd in New York's Grand Central Palace was growing restless. Their hero had been scheduled to appear before them over an hour ago, and still there was no sign of him. Among the thousands packed into the smoke-filled hall on 19 January 1906 was a *New York Times* reporter. There were twice as many women as men in the audience, he noted, and most wore red dresses and hats covered in red ribbons. As they shuffled about impatiently, hawkers noisily plied their trade. 'Genuine blood-red Jack London souvenirs of a great and momentous occasion!' they cried.

A ripple of expectation passed through the crowd. Countless red flags, costing 10 cents each, began to flutter in the air. Finally, the tanned author of *The Call of the Wild* made his entry. As he 'strode down the aisle and up to the platform, his chunky figure clad in a black suit, white flannel shirt and white tie, the assemblage exploded with enthusiasm'.

Jack took a sip of water from a glass which his Korean valet, Manyoungi, had placed on the podium, then lit a cigarette. To his working-class readers, Jack embodied the promise of socialism. They had arrived in the New World only to languish in the ghetto. But here was a man to show them a new way to the promised land.

'Consider the United States,' Jack began, 'the most prosperous and most enlightened country in the world. In the United States, there are ten million people living in poverty . . . This means that these ten million people are perishing, are dying, body and soul, slowly, because they have not enough to eat . . . The revolution is a fact. It is here now. Seven million revolutionists, organised, working day and night, are preaching the revolution – that passionate gospel, the Brotherhood of Man. Not only is it a cold-blooded economic propaganda, but it is a religious propaganda with a fervour in it of Paul and Christ.

'The capitalist class has been indicted,' Jack shouted to a roar of approval and euphoric waving of red banners. 'It has failed in its management and its management is to be taken away from it. Seven million men of the working class say they are going to get the rest of the working class to join with them and take the management away. The revolution is here, now. Stop it who can.'

The day after his headline-grabbing lecture in New York, Jack lunched at Mouquin's restaurant with the editor of *Wilshire's* magazine and a talented young writer called Upton Sinclair. Jack's eyelids, Sinclair later recalled, 'were inflamed, and there were in his face and speech all the signs of alcoholism I had learned to recognise. He ordered drinks throughout the meal and during hours of talk which followed.' Jack also regaled Sinclair with 'tales of incredible debauches; tales of opium and hashish, and I know not what other strange ingredients; tales of whiskey bouts lasting for weeks'.

Jack waxed nostalgic well into the afternoon, recalling his days on the waterfront, and how he once 'never drew a sober breath' for three weeks. When he worked in a laundry he had taken up 'industrial drinking' and got blind drunk every Saturday night. 'I, the long-time intimate of John Barleycorn,' he reminisced, 'knew just what he promised me – maggots of fancy, dreams of power, forgetfulness, anything and everything save whirling washers, revolving mangles, humming centrifugal wringers, and fancy starch, and interminable processions of Dutch trousers moving in steam under my flying iron.'

There was a good reason for Jack's increased alcohol consumption. He was under enormous stress. The press was reporting his every move, and each day, it seemed, another part of his body began to buckle under the strain. He may have looked like a superman, with his broad, muscular chest, but his constitution was far from strong. His hands and feet were small for his stature, his joints were weak, and because of his bad teeth, hardly a day passed when he was not in pain.

On 18 November 1905, several weeks before meeting Sinclair at Mouquin's, Jack had received a telegram from California informing him that his divorce from Bess had been granted. Immediately he had wired Charmian, telling her that he would pass through Chicago the next day. Without fail, she must meet him there. They would then get married, as he had always promised.

It was a cold Saturday evening when Charmian's train pulled into Chicago station, three hours later than scheduled. Dressed in a dark gabardine travelling suit, she found Jack chain-smoking nervously, wearing his trademark dark suit and soft flannel shirt. He had bad news: he did not have a marriage licence. Worse still, the press had got wind of their plans.

Later that night, after shrugging off the reporters, Jack managed to persuade a junior clerk to open his office and make out a licence. A justice of the peace, J.J. Grant, married him and Charmian at 10 p.m. in his home. When they then arrived at their honeymoon hotel, the Victoria, Charmian took the stairs to their suite. Jack wrote 'Mrs Jack London' below his name in the register. As he waited for his key, three reporters accosted him with questions about the lecture tour. A fourth sneaked a glance at the register. In an instant, Jack turned tail and joined Charmian. He found her wearing silk undergarments, specially embroidered for the occasion. She wrote in her diary: 'Grant married us, with my mother's wedding ring. Back to the Hotel Victoria – night made hideous by reporters! – Jack adorable – my perfect bridegroom and lover, at last.'

The newlyweds were on a train from Geneva Falls, Wisconsin, two days later when Jack casually picked up a paper. To his horror he read the headline JACK LONDON MARRIAGE INVALID. The state of Illinois had, apparently, just passed a law preventing divorcees from remarrying less than a year after their final decree. 'I'll get married in every state of the Union just as fast as I can get from one to another,' Jack blustered. A few days later, he discovered that the marriage was in fact valid.

'Fame depends more on the amount of printer's ink you spill in the headlines than on what you put into your story,' Jack had once told a friend. That ink now looked like blood. Newspapers condemned the 'indecent haste' of the marriage and attacked him and Charmian with disturbing vitriol. It had been assumed that Jack and Bess were divorcing because they could not live together. Now the truth was out: Jack, 'the Socialist apostle of immorality', had left his wife and children for an 'ugly-faced girl from California'.

When Jack and Charmian returned from a four-day honeymoon in Jamaica, they found that their 'immorality' had become the subject of national debate. In the midwest, Jack's lectures were cancelled, women's associations condemned him – along with college football – as the most depraving influence on the nation's young men, and many libraries removed his books from their shelves. When Jack fell ill with tonsillitis in late February 1906 in the wilds of North Dakota, he decided to cancel the remaining dates on his lecture tour. Chased by the media, shocked by the violent reaction to their wedding, he and Charmian returned to California in a first-class Pullman car.

At three o'clock one morning, as their train crossed the Sierra Nevada mountain range, a hollow-cheeked Jack woke his new wife. 'Throw on your kimono and come out on the platform with me,' he said. 'I want to show you something.'

A few minutes later, they stood on a rattling platform at the rear of the train and watched in awe the 'great Shasta, upthrust fourteen thousand feet, snow-crowned, into the moonlit, night-blue dome of the sky; and the Lassen Buttes, stark and flat in the beams of the setting moon, like peaks cut from heavy dull-gold cardboard'.

On his return home, Jack declined commissions to write an exposé of child labour in the Southern cottonfields and to cover a trial of IWW activists in Idaho. Some day soon, he had vowed, he would escape America and live life on his own terms, free of the constant attention of the press. His days as an active revolutionary would soon be over.

The Voyage of the *Snark*

I'd rather win a water-fight in the swimming-pool, or remain astride a horse that is trying to get out from under me, than write the great American novel . . . The ultimate word is I LIKE. It is I LIKE that makes the drunkard drink and the martyr wear a hair shirt; that makes one man a reveller and another man an anchorite; that makes one man pursue fame, another gold, another love, and another God. Philosophy is very often a man's way of explaining his own I LIKE.

JACK LONDON, *The Cruise of the* Snark (1911)

5 A.M., 18 APRIL 1906. San Francisco was calm and peaceful. From the terrace of his villa, Bailey Millard, the editor of *Cosmopolitan* magazine, could hear the bells of Old St Mary's Church at the edge of Chinatown. For several days, seated before his easel trying to recreate on canvas the city skyline at first light, Millard had listened to them announce the dawn. Below him, San Francisco stretched over the hills and down to the great bay.

5.16 a.m. Bailey Millard lay in shock, 'his canvas ripped, easel smashed and paints scattered' across the undulating pavement. Below him, the entire city seemed to be 'rocking and rolling under the most fantastic motion'. From where he was sprawled, he now had a 'panoramic view' of the most destructive earthquake in American history, measuring 8.25 on the Richter scale.

Across the bay, fifty miles to the north in Glen Ellen, the force of the quake shook Jack – one of Millard's contributors – out of bed. Within minutes, he and Charmian had saddled horses and galloped to the crest of nearby Sonoma Mountain. Gazing towards San Francisco, all they saw was a 'pillar of fire and smoke'. 'I wouldn't be surprised if San Francisco has sunk,' said Jack in shock. 'The Atlantic could be washing at the feet of the Rockies.'

His first thought was of his family, and he rushed to Oakland and confirmed that his mother, ex-wife and daughters were unharmed. He and Charmian then crossed over to San Francisco on the last ferry permitted to land in the city. Already it was starting to burn to the ground. Bailey Millard and thousands of others were trying to stem the advance of flames from over fifty fires that had broken out with the rupturing of cable-car wires and gas pipes.

As darkness fell, the extent of the blaze became apparent. Not a corner of the city was safe from fires which seemed to engulf entire blocks in seconds. In some spots, the temperature reached over 2700 degrees Fahrenheit. Iron and steel were becoming putty; the marble entrances to offices melted. 'That night,' Charmian would later recall, 'proved our closest to realising a dream that came now and again to Jack in sleep, that he and I were in at the finish of all things – standing or moving hand in hand through chaos to its brink, looking upon the rest of mankind in the process of dissolution.'

All night they wandered through the scorched streets. 'At nine o'clock Wednesday evening [18 April],' Jack would write, 'I walked down the very heart of the city. I walked through miles and miles of magnificent buildings and towering skyscrapers. Here was no fire. All was in perfect order. The police patrolled the streets. Every building had its watchman at the door. And yet it was doomed, all of it. There was no water. The dynamite was giving out. And at right angles two conflagrations were sweeping down upon it.'

At every street corner they had to avoid explosions set off by dyna-miters hoping to stop the fire before it reached San Francisco's most prestigious areas. Downtown, the *San Francisco Examiner* building, owned by William Randolph Hearst, had collapsed, along with count-less others. As Jack and Charmian trudged up Nob Hill, a south wind began to propel the flames towards the mansions built by the city's robber-barons. The capitalists' homes, it seemed, were as doomed as the hovels in the Italian and Chinese shanty towns below. It was as if the inferno was God-sent to remind the rich and immoral of their past sins. For the city itself, however, there would be no salvation.

Near the crest of Nob Hill, Jack sat down on the top steps of a house not far from the celebrated Fairmont Hotel, which had already begun to smoulder. The owner of the house, a man named Perine, came out and began to lock his door. Then he decided to invite Jack and Charmian inside.

'Yesterday morning,' the old man said, 'I was worth six hundred thousand. This morning this house is all I have left. It will go in fifteen minutes.'

Midway through a tour of his home, Perine asked Charmian to try out his grand piano. Hesitating, she glanced at Jack.

'Do it for him,' he whispered. 'It's the last time he'll ever hear it.'

She played a couple of chords, but then Perine grimaced with painful memories and motioned for her to stop. A few minutes later, they hurried out of the house and back down Nob Hill towards Union Square, at the heart of the city. A man was willing to pay $1000 if someone could provide horses to pull a truck which he had loaded with trunks. Everywhere, they could hear the 'strangled cries and sobs of people trapped in rubble'.

Charmian would never forget the face of a man she saw carried into a doorway. 'His back had been broken, and as the stretcher bore him past, out of a handsome, ashen young face, the dreadful darkening eyes looked right into mine. All the world was crashing about him and he, a broken thing, with death awaiting him inside the granite portals, gazed upon the last woman of his race that he was ever to see. Jack, with tender hand, drew me away.'

When the flames finally died down, Nob Hill, Chinatown and several other districts lay in ruins. 514 city blocks no longer existed. Over three thousand people had lost their lives – far more than the official estimate of seven hundred. Seven people had been shot for looting, which had spread almost as rapidly as the fire. Two hundred would die of plague spread by the rats which soon overran the charred city.

Jack was so disturbed by the razing of his native city that he vowed not to write about it. But when he arrived back in Glen Ellen he found a telegram from *Collier's* magazine begging him to send 2500 words straight away. According to Richard O'Connor, they were offering twenty-five cents a word, the most he had ever been paid by a

magazine. He sat down and reluctantly dashed off the piece. Its opening lines are still famous: 'San Francisco is gone. Nothing remains of
it but memories and a fringe of dwelling-houses on its outskirts . . . Not
in history has a modern imperial city been so completely destroyed.'

The earthquake could not have come at a worse time for Jack. It had
spread its carnage on the very morning that he was due to lay the
keel to his dream vessel, the *Snark*, whose construction he had begun
in earnest after pulling out of the lecture tour and finishing *The Iron
Heel*. After the fires had been extinguished, the cost of raw materials
soared as rebuilding efforts consumed every spare piece of timber and
every worker. Because of the earthquake, Jack's original budget of
$7000 doubled in one night. Most men would have postponed con-
struction. But not Jack. It was as if the disaster only increased his
determination to get away. He stepped up the pace and ordered
materials from New York, at enormous cost. The boat, named in
honour of Lewis Carroll's mock-epic poem 'The Hunting of the
Snark', had become an all-consuming obsession.

'Spare no expense,' he told Roscoe Eames, Charmian's grey-bearded
uncle, whom he had placed in charge of construction. 'Let everything
on the *Snark* be of the best. And never mind decoration. Plain pine
boards is good enough finishing for me. But put the money into
construction. Let the *Snark* be as staunch and strong as any boat
afloat.' Jack boasted that the *Snark* would be the finest yacht ever
constructed in San Francisco. But as the weeks became months, and
the deadline for completion passed and new ones were not met, it
seemed that the *Snark* would never leave dry-dock.

Jack could scarcely have found a worse building supervisor than
Eames, a lazy incompetent who had never sailed beyond the Golden
Gate Strait. Paid $60 a month to supervise construction, Eames 'failed
to examine materials and ignored shoddy work'. To Jack's outrage,
he even insisted on being addressed as 'captain' of the *Snark*. More
serious were the results of his negligence: the *Snark*'s oak beams were
in fact pine, her planking warped and knotted, 'parts wore out faster
than they could be replaced'. Instead of sailing on 1 October 1906,
Jack was forced to push the date back to April 1907. Local sailors
laughed. The press poked fun.

While Eames botched even the simplest of tasks, Jack tried to forget his frustrations for at least a few days by socialising with the Crowd. By 1906, many of its key figures had moved south of San Francisco and built cottages in the coastal village of Carmel. The once sleepy settlement was now a bohemian colony of artists who became inveterate hedonists after dark: Nora May French, a death-obsessed poet who would take cyanide within a year; Mary Austin, a novelist who wore flowing Indian robes; Joaquin Miller, a veteran poet, and many others, including the Crowd's stalwarts, George Sterling, Jimmy Hopper, Arnold Genthe and Xavier Martinez. So aware were Carmel's artists-in-residence of their inclination towards dissolution, it was ordained that no social contact should take place before midday. With Jack and Charmian's arrival for a vacation in February 1907, however, the rule was forgotten for several days.

Mary Austin later described Jack as 'sagging a little with the surfeit of success, obtained through idleness, making him prefer the lounging pitchwood fire or the blazing hearth' to hikes along the thousand-foot cliffs of Big Sur with George Sterling and Jimmy Hopper. The Jack of old, before his split from Bess, had always been first to put on the gloves or reach for the foils. Now he seemed content to gorge on abalone and to strike poses.

Yet Jack had lost none of his magnetism, nor his attractiveness to women, among them Austin herself. As she recalled in her memoirs, *Earth Horizon* (1932): 'Women flung themselves at Jack, lay in wait for him . . . Jack thought – and Jack had material enough, God wot, on which to base a conclusion – that the assault that men of genius yielded to, or withstood according to their capacities, was the biological necessity of women to mate up, ascendingly, preferring, he thought, the tenth share in a man of distinction to the whole of an average man.'

Arnold Genthe provided a vivid picture of one picnic at Carmel: 'George Sterling, who was proud of his classic contours, had climbed to the top of the cliff in his bathing trunks. Somewhere or other he had procured a trident and he was standing silhouetted against the sky while Jimmy Hopper was taking his picture. This was too frivolous for Mary [Austin] (dressed in the beaded leather costume and long braids of an Indian princess) who was gazing at the setting sun.

Standing on the beach with outspread arms, she began something which sounded like a quotation from Browning.

' "'Tis a Cyclopean blacksmith," she chanted, "striking frenzied sparks from the anvil of the horizon."

'Jack was standing with a fork in hand, having just wolfed down an abalone steak. Looking in Mary's direction, then at the horizon, he shouted: "Hell! I say this sunset has guts!" '

In Carmel, Jack seemed bullish. But as soon as he returned to his desk in Glen Ellen he sank into depression. He was, as never before, 'handcuffed' to his editors. To pay for the *Snark*, he was churning out fiction for Macmillan and magazines at a prodigious rate. Aside from *The Iron Heel*, which he finished late in 1906, he had also knocked off *Before Adam* (1907), the story of a 'boy's dreams of being born in prehistoric times', which won a rave review from the normally reticent *New York Times*: 'Jack London . . . has builded a romance of the unknown ages, of the creatures that may have been, and endowed it all with poignant reality.' He also completed several short stories, including 'The Apostate', a semi-autobiographical account of his days working in the jute mill.

He found time to write a round-robin letter to the editors of half a dozen magazines, offering them the chance to sponsor his jaunt around the world. He would first visit the Hawaiian islands, then cross the South Seas to Tasmania, New Zealand, the east coast of Australia, New Guinea, and then by way of the Philippines to Japan. 'There isn't a European country in which I shall not spend from one to several months,' he wrote. 'This leisurely fashion will obtain throughout the whole trip. I shall not be in a rush; in fact, I calculate seven (7) years at least will be taken up by the trip . . . When I strike a country, say Egypt or France, I'll go up the Nile or Seine by having the mast taken out, and under power of the engine . . . There is no reason at all why I shouldn't in this fashion come up to Paris, and moor alongside the Latin Quarter, with a bowline out to Notre Dame and a stern line fast to the Morgue.'

He did not tell prospective sponsors that he had already mortgaged everything he owned, as well as his mother's house in Oakland. Nor that the *Snark* was still only half-built. Nor that of the hundred suppliers he had contracted, not one had delivered on time. By New

Year's Day 1907 he had spent $20,000 on what the press gleefully called 'London's folly'. 'I won't be happy until I get away,' he told one potential sponsor, the editor of *Woman's Home Companion*. 'And I'm going to get away as fast as God, earthquakes, and organised labour will let me.'

Jack assured his fellow-socialists: 'Don't get the idea that when I cruise around the South Seas I'm letting up on Socialism. Not a bit.' Many of his comrades, though, begged to differ. One of them, Algie Simons, wrote to Jack that he resented the trip. At a crucial period in the class struggle, one of its leading icons planned to be absent for seven years. Jack was hardly setting a good example.

Before he had even put to sea, Captain Jack was faced with mutiny. Having faithfully obeyed his every command for over two years, Manyoungi, his Korean valet, now began to call him 'Mr London' rather than 'Master'. According to Charmian, Manyoungi's 'bold black eyes and studiedly nonchalant tongue advertised bid upon bid for discharge'.

At first Jack tolerated his demotion because Manyoungi had the 'perfect spirit of service', and could make both Charmian and himself 'ready in half an hour for Timbucktoo'. But he finally lost his patience one evening when the Korean asked what he wanted for his nightcap: 'Will God have some beer?'

Manyoungi was sent packing the next day, and was eventually replaced by a Japanese youth called Tochigi. Many others, though, could not wait to sign on for the voyage. A millionaire's son offered $500 for a berth. A college professor was prepared to pay $1000 to do anything. Doctors, dentists, lawyers, reporters, students, teachers, engineers, retired sea captains, electricians and bored housewives also volunteered their services.

The one crew member Jack needed was a cook. A famous chef, earning $200 a week, was among the applicants, but after sorting through piles of correspondence, Jack found a letter from a young man in Topeka, Kansas, named Martin Johnson. Jack wired Johnson, who had never prepared a salad, let alone worked in a swaying galley at sea, and asked him whether he could cook. 'Just try me,' Johnson volunteered.

'When it comes to doing the trick at the wheel,' Jack replied, 'I want to explain that this will not be arduous as it may appear at first.

It is our intention, by sail-trimming, to make the boat largely sail herself, without steering. Next, in bad weather, there will be no steering, for then we will hove to ... Incidentally, if you like boxing, I may tell you that all of us box, and we'll have the gloves along. You'll have the advantage of us on reach. Also, I may say that we should all of us have lots of good times together, swimming, fishing, adventuring, doing a thousand and one things.'

Formal qualifications were not a condition of employment on the *Snark*. Jack, aware that sponsors would not be so keen to back a world cruise made up of professional seamen, assembled possibly the most amateurish crew ever to attempt a Pacific crossing. Rather than sack Roscoe Eames, Jack actually recruited him as navigator, though there is little evidence that he even knew how to use a sextant. Martin Johnson, who could not cook, would be the cook, and another inexperienced young man, Herbert Stoltz, would be the ship's engineer. The only one of them with any real sailing experience was Jack, and even he did not know how to navigate.

It was surely tempting fate, Jack and Charmian's friends argued, to set out for Hawaii, two thousand miles away, in a jinxed boat with a crew that had never been to sea. Did Jack have to make the odds of survival so slim that editors would think they were buying his last work? Jack was paying his crew more than the going rate for experienced sailors, yet they had never lowered a lifeboat or dropped anchor in their lives.

Complex motives lay behind Jack's decision to leave California for what he hoped would be seven years of uninterrupted adventure. He had already grown weary of life as a literary celebrity, even though it was less than four years since the publication of *The Call of the Wild*. By distancing himself from California, he hoped to leave behind the pressures of success. At sea, by testing himself to the limit of his physical endurance, he could reinvent himself as a legendary traveller, a man who could face any challenge and still conquer.

During a storm one night in April 1907, two boats collided with the moored *Snark*, badly damaging her hull. Yet still Jack insisted on leaving as soon as possible, and completing the outfitting in Hawaii. At any cost, he had to depart, before the stress overwhelmed him. He was again eating compulsively: at one sitting he would consume several 'excessively rare' ducks accompanied by mountains of potato *au gratin* and washed down with imported bottle after ice-cold bottle of his favourite Liebfraumilch.

It was during the final weeks of preparation for the voyage that Frank Pease and several other University of California students met Jack at a 'beer bust'. As Pease saw him, Jack was 'the type of man to have commanded other men', and he had the ability to 'inflame youth, inspire men, madden women'. His most impressive feature was his eyes, 'all steel and dew, all sweetness and hidden ferocity . . . eyes common enough, maybe, when the world was young . . . [they] changed with the changing colour of his soul, and often seemed filled with the anguish of sins impossible to commit'.

Finally, the *Snark* was declared seaworthy. Jack had one last task – to say goodbye to his daughters, Joan and Bess. 'He was excited and happy and eager to be off, and at the same time he was sad, reluctant to leave us,' his daughter Joan later recalled, 'and curiously worried about our safety during the long years he expected to be away.'

Jack asked his daughters to write to him and Bess to send pictures of them every few months.

'I'll send you curios from all the places I visit,' he promised.

'What are curios, Daddy?' asked Joan.

He looked towards a brass-studded chest which he had brought back from Korea.

'That's a curio, made in Korea by Koreans, and different from all the other chests in the world, except other chests made by Koreans . . . You'll explain it to them later, Bess?'

'Of course,' she agreed. 'And we'll get books from the public library about the various countries so they'll know something about the far-away places your letters will come from . . . And I've thought of something else, Jack: when they're available, why not get little dolls dressed in the native costumes? The girls would love them.'

'Fine! Good idea. I'll remember that.'

Through 'a mist of tears' his daughter Joan watched him 'stride out into the lovely April twilight, stopping, as always, before the high fence next door shut him from view to turn and wave and blow kisses, and then he was gone'.

The following morning, Jack boarded the *Snark* with a 'chequebook, fountain pen, blotter', and nearly $2000 in cash, and waited for a line of his creditors to form on the quayside. Instead, a US marshal arrived and tacked a notice on the boat's main mast. The *Snark*, it declared, was being impounded because of unpaid bills – or, as Jack put it, because of the 'bourgeois panic' of his creditors.

Two days later, after their captain had settled the debt, the *Snark*'s crew finally walked up the gangway on 23 April 1907. With hundreds of people lining the dockside, Jack moved to the bow of his $30,000 vessel (Slocum's *Spray* had cost just $553.62). Among the well-wishers were George Sterling and Jimmy Hopper, Jack's old college friend. Jack hoisted Jimmy Hopper's football sweater to the top of the *Snark*'s mast and raised the anchor himself by hand. Slowly, as if hesitating every yard of the way, the *Snark* crossed Oakland Estuary and finally sailed through the Golden Gate Strait.

It was heavy going from the start. After serving dinner that evening, Tochigi – the only member of the crew qualified for his role, as cabin boy – brought out his flute and 'played the most mournful piece . . . as the last note died away [he] rushed precipitately up on the deck and relieved his deathly sickness at the rail. Mrs London speedily joined him.'

As the charred ruins of San Francisco receded in the distance, Jack managed his first smile of genuine pleasure in months. He had been robbed, ridiculed and written off as a deluded fantasist. As he now felt the swell of the ocean, the months of frustration and public humiliation began to ebb away. In a matter of weeks, he would be 'in the South Seas, building his grass house, trading for pearls and copra, jumping reefs in frail outriggers, catching sharks and bonitas, hunting wild goats among the cliffs of the valley that lay next to the valley of Taiohae'.

Jack had fantasised about a voyage to the South Seas ever since reading Herman Melville's *Typee* as a small boy. Before leaving Oakland, he had stowed over five hundred books aboard the *Snark*, enough to last seven years. Among this floating library were the works of Joseph Conrad and, of course, Melville himself. 'Consider them both,' Melville had written in *Typee*, 'the sea and the land; and do you not find a strange analogy to something in yourself? For as this appalling ocean surrounds the verdant land, so in the soul of man there lies one insular Tahiti, full of peace and joy, but encompassed by all the horrors of the half-known life.'

Peace and joy seemed a long way off during the first weeks of the voyage. Within hours of leaving San Francisco Bay, the *Snark*'s supposedly watertight compartments had begun to leak, as had the gasoline tanks. The luxury appliances in the state bathroom broke off in Jack's hands. Even his lifeboat, supposedly the best available, was unseaworthy. 'More trust could be placed in a wooden toothpick,' he later seethed, 'than in the most massive piece of iron to be found aboard.'

The sensible course of action was to turn back and at least give the *Snark* and her crew a fighting chance of survival. But Jack could barely bring himself to turn his head eastward, let alone contemplate the humiliation of facing his friends and the press if he returned so soon. To make matters worse, Charmian had decided that he should give up smoking, and had cajoled one of the crew into throwing all his tobacco overboard.

When a sudden squall swept away the staysail on the third day out, Jack tried to make the *Snark* heave to so that the crew could retire below decks and wait for the storm to pass. To his astonishment, the *Snark* refused to perform even this most basic manoeuvre. When he tried his costly sea anchor, it failed immediately. A makeshift wooden one simply dragged behind. 'It's enough to make a man turn to wine and actresses and race horses,' he told Charmian bitterly.

Because the *Snark* was unable to heave to, within days her entire crew were bruised from head to toe from being thrown about in the high seas. 'I have seen many acrobatic feats,' Martin Johnson later wrote, 'but nothing resembling in mad abandon the double handspring Mrs London turned one day when her hand missed its hold and she landed down the companionway in the middle of the table, on top of a dinner which I had just cooked, and which Tochigi was serving.'

It was Johnson who first expressed reservations about the voyage. Did Jack know where the nearest land was?

'We're not more than two miles from land now,' Jack reassured him.

'Which way?'

'Straight down, Martin, straight down.'

Exactly how far the *Snark* was from land was a very good question. Roscoe Eames, who had sworn to Jack that he could navigate, did not have a clue. For all any of the others knew, they could have been off the coast of China.

Fear not, their captain assured them. He would teach himself to navigate on the spot.

'One whole afternoon I sat in the cockpit, steering with one hand and studying logarithms with the other,' he later recalled. 'Two afternoons, two hours each, I studied the general theory of navigation and the particular process of taking a meridian altitude. Then I took the sextant, worked out the index error, and shot the sun. The figuring from the data of this observation was child's play.'

While Jack shot the sun, Charmian stayed steady at the wheel. Already she had become an essential member of the crew, crucial to their survival, and she relished every instant in her new role as the loyal first mate facing calamity at her husband's side. The Pacific brought out the best in her.

Except when the seas pitched the *Snark* like a cork, Jack continued his habit of writing a thousand words a day. 'He would get up in the morning,' Martin Johnson recalled, 'take his trick at the wheel, have breakfast, and then shut himself in his stateroom for just two hours and write. He always laughed at what he called the tomfoolery of waiting for inspiration to come. He doesn't believe there is any such thing as inspiration – he himself can write just as well at one time as at another. It is plain work, he says, and the only way he can do it is to go ahead and do it.'

The two hours Jack spent with a fountain pen were devoted to what would be his most autobiographical novel, the story of an uncouth sailor who becomes a successful writer. In his cabin on the *Snark*, Jack began to recreate his own struggle for recognition, one just as arduous as his continuing battle against the Pacific. Jack began to reflect on his unprecedented rise to fame and success. What had he gained from his fight for recognition? Was he any happier now that he had achieved what others his age could only dream of? At first he thought of giving the book an ironic title, 'Success', but then he changed it to *Martin Eden*, borrowing the name from a woodcutter he remembered from Wake Robin.

The book opens with its eponymous hero saving the life of Arthur Morse, a respectable member of the Oakland bourgeoisie. Martin visits Morse's home, where he meets his sister Ruth, an 'ethereal creature with wide spiritual blue eyes and a wealth of golden hair'. Ruth feels a strong attraction to Martin despite his rough ways.

Martin vows to become cultured, and devours Darwin, Spencer and Marx. But for all his striving, he fails to fully integrate with Ruth and her kind. Unable to overcome his sense of social inferiority, he rails against academics, critics, the well-read and the well-to-do. His relationship with Ruth becomes strained when she fails to encourage his attempts at writing. One of his friends, a poet named Brissenden – based on George Sterling – does recognise his talent, and persuades him to join the Socialist Party. He also predicts crippling disappointment for Martin if he succeeds as a writer by turning his back on the people.

When a controversial essay brings Martin overnight acclaim, he is inundated with requests for new material. As Jack had done, he sends out dozens of previously rejected manuscripts. He soon becomes wealthy, the toast of polite society; yet he laughs at his success. He has written nothing new or meaningful. He has simply become the name of the moment, a literary celebrity. Before long he grows to despise the very people who have brought him success: 'They were numskulls, ninnies, superficial, dogmatic, and ignorant . . . What was the matter with them? What had they done with their educations? They had had access to the same books he had. How did it happen that they had drawn nothing from them?'

When the *Snark* was becalmed, Jack would work on deck, the sound of opera floating from a large horn across the glassy water as he wrote. He had brought along a gramophone, as well as an Edison 'language machine' with cylindrical recordings in Italian, German, Spanish, and French, so that the crew would have a selection of languages with which to greet welcoming parties.

In a fit of disgust, Martin finally turns his back on society and sets sail for the South Pacific, hoping to discover a more meaningful existence. But it is too late. Before he can reach paradise, his disillusionment defeats him. He crawls out of a porthole and plunges into the ice-cold water of the Pacific.

Down, down, he swam until his arms and legs grew tired and hardly moved. He knew that he was deep. The pressure on his ear-drums was a pain, and there was a buzzing in his head ... Colours and radiances surrounded and bathed him and pervaded him. What was that? It seemed a lighthouse; but it was inside his brain – a flashing, bright white light. It flashed swifter and swifter. There was a long rumble of sound, and it seemed to him that he was falling down a vast and interminable stairway.

The porpoises bobbing in their wake were the first clue. Then they spotted thirty to forty whales snorting fountains of water in the near distance. Finally, twenty-seven days after leaving San Francisco, the crew of the *Snark* stood in silence, gaping at the horizon. They had made their first landfall. Looming ahead they could make out a crest of snow – the summit of Haleakala, the House of the Sun, a ten-thousand-foot volcanic crater on the Hawaiian island of Maui.

Jack had first glimpsed the volcanic peaks of Hawaii from the decks of the *Sophie Sutherland* in 1893, and he had spent a day swimming at Waikiki in January 1904 on his way to report the Russo–Japanese War. But it was not until now that he began fully to appreciate the jagged volcanoes towering above him. His navigation had been masterful. They were bang in the middle of the main sea lane leading to Honolulu. Yet they were still far from safe. Within sight of land, the *Snark* actually began to sink. Bert Stolz, the young student from Stanford, had left a tap running in the engine room, and soon the *Snark* was flooding with water. Jack knew that his expensive lifeboat was useless. When Bert finally managed to close the cock, the entire crew sighed with relief.

A launch from the Hawaiian Yacht Club came out to meet them, its delegation carrying newspapers and telegrams from well-wishers around the world, including Bailey Millard, who had commissioned Jack to write a series of articles about the voyage for *Cosmopolitan* magazine. One newspaper had reported that the *Snark* and all hands had gone down at sea. Jack laughed. What did he care? He had arrived in paradise. At first sight, he and his crew fell in love with the gentle islanders who threw fragrant garlands around their necks. Every moment seemed to bring a new pleasure.

In 1907 the Hawaiian islands had been part of the United States for less than a decade. A bloodless coup, organised by American residents who wanted Hawaii to become an annexe of the United States, had deposed the ruling Queen Liliuokalani in 1893. Despite a royalist counter-revolution in 1895, the Republic of Hawaii lasted until 1898, when Hawaii was incorporated as a self-governing territory within the United States.

Jack and Charmian were swept off their feet by Hawaii's ruling class. They dined with Charles L. Rhodes, editor of the *Star*, toured plantations and ranches with their owners, and befriended the Portuguese consul. Hawaiian royalty even honoured them when Jack was invited to fish by torchlight with Prince David Kawananakoa.

Jack discovered that he felt quite comfortable among Hawaii's successful ranchers and businessmen, especially those who had made their own fortunes. Power was what these men craved, not necessarily money. As in the waterfront bars of his youth, Jack found that when he drank fruit cocktails on breezy verandas in Hawaii with such men, they did not make him feel inadequate. Among the expatriate rich, the colonial elite, he felt relatively at ease.

Yet he still presented himself as a man of the people, keeping a straight face while delivering his 'Revolution' lecture to an audience of bemused Hawaiian industrialists. 'Jack London created quite a sensation here in an address on "*Revolution*" before the Research Club,' reported the *San Francisco Chronicle*, 'in which he declared that under present economic conditions, the laboring-classes had a harder time than they did in the stone age. He said that, barring a few degenerates, who always appeared on such occasions, the man who threw a brickbat at a strikebreaker was actuated by as good motives and was doing as noble a thing as the colonists who, from behind fences and stone walls, shot at the British redcoats at Lexington.'

Distracted by the pleasures of Hawaii, Jack had neglected the *Snark*. He was soon cursing himself for the oversight. Two weeks after arriving, when he went to inspect the boat, he found a beached wreck. Roscoe and Bert Stoltz had left it to rot under the tropical sun, and the costly sails had 'mildewed beneath their damp canvas covers'. This negligence was to cost hundreds of dollars.

Jack immediately replaced both men. A chastened Eames returned to San Francisco, and Herbert Stolz went back to his studies at Stanford University. 'So utterly, agedly helpless was he,' Jack wrote of Eames, 'that he was unable to order a sailor to throw a few buckets of salt water on the *Snark*'s decks.' When the press back in America discovered the men's fate, they couldn't resist drawing parallels between the *Snark* and the *Ghost*, between Captain Jack and Wolf Larsen. 'When I discharged an incompetent captain, they said I had beaten him to a pulp,' Jack later protested. 'When one young man returned home to continue at college, it was reported that I was a regular Wolf Larsen, and that my whole crew had deserted because I had beaten it to a pulp.'

A month after arriving in Hawaii, Jack received a sack of mail from the mainland. To his dismay, he discovered that his novel *The Iron Heel* had been rejected for serialisation by every notable magazine in the US. 'I thought it would be timely, that book,' he told Charmian, 'but they're all afraid of it. See, the socialists, even my own crowd, have thrown me down – they decry it as a lugubrious prophecy, and the other camp, of course, revile it as they revile everything of mine.'

Casting the rejections aside, he sat on a veranda overlooking Pearl Harbor in a blue kimono and began to write. Mynah birds called, and the Pacific lapped against palm-fringed beaches, yet he was oblivious to it all; his thoughts were in the frozen Arctic tundra. The story was 'To Build a Fire', possibly the most widely read short story in all American fiction, a work of dazzling power.

A lone man, accompanied by a large husky, is walking through a frozen wilderness when he slips through ice and wets his feet. As quickly as possible, he must build a fire and dry out or die of frostbite. Again and again he tries unsuccessfully to kindle a flame. Finally, he faces inevitable death with dignity. 'It was like taking an anaesthetic,' Jack wrote, sipping on a cocktail, his eyes shaded from the tropical sun by a green visor. 'Freezing was not so bad as people thought. There were lots worse ways to die.'

As Jack dashed off one of his best short stories, again without a single rewrite, in the distance he could see bronzed figures risking their lives in conditions just as extreme as those in the Northland. Suddenly a young Polynesian rose from the water and rode a wave to the shore by balancing on the edge of a board. Jack gazed in disbelief. This young man, riding murderous waves with complete abandon, was surely a superman?

Introducing the sport to American readers, Jack described the awesome surfing hero in 'A Royal Sport: Surfing at Waikiki', an article first published in *Cosmopolitan* and later included in *The Cruise of the Snark*, Jack's account of the voyage:

> He is impassive, motionless as a statue carved suddenly by some miracle out of the sea's depth from which he rose. And straight on toward shore he flies on his winged heels and the white crest of the breaker. There is a wild burst of foam, a long tumultuous rushing sound as the breaker falls futile and spent on the beach at your feet; and there, at your feet steps calmly ashore a Kanaka – and more, he is a man, a member of the kingly species that has mastered matter and the brutes and lorded it over creation.

Whatever the dark-skinned races could do, an Anglo-Saxon superman could surely do better. Jack snatched a board and joined some Hawaiian boys in the shallows. While he flailed in the water, they caught wave after wave. Just as he was about to admit defeat, above the crash of the surf a white man called out. His name was Alexander Ford, an American globetrotter, headed for Australia, who had picked up the basics after a month of imitating the natives. 'Get off that board,' Ford ordered. 'Chuck it away at once. Look at the way you're trying to ride it. If the nose hits bottom, you'll be disembowelled. Here, take my board. It's a man's size.'

Jack took it and, lying flat, paddled out to the breakers.

'Imagine your legs are a rudder,' Ford advised. 'Hold them close together, and steer with them.'

Jack managed to steer, but could not mount the board. But he refused to be beaten by the pounding waves that could snap a man's neck if he was caught at the wrong angle. 'The *Snark* shall not sail from Honolulu,' he vowed, 'until I, too, wing my heels with the swiftness of the sea, and become a sunburned, skin-peeling Mercury.'

After several bone-jarring days in the surf, Jack finally managed to ride a wave. But the momentary victory came at a heavy price. He had taken no precaution against the tropical sun. His lips were now swollen, his eyes puffed shut, his joints so burnt he could not bend them. For almost a week, all he could do was crawl around naked on his palms and heels.

'Don't let me laugh!' he begged Charmian through flaking lips. 'It hurts too much.'

Excruciating as it was, Jack was about to see afflictions which would make his sunburn seem mild by comparison. On their approach to Hawaii they had sailed past Molokai – 'the pit of hell, the most cursed place on earth', Jack had commented, as the island's distinctive cliffs (the tallest in the world) had come into view. Molokai was home to several hundred sufferers of leprosy, then the most dreaded disease known to man.

Fascinated by Molokai, Jack and Charmian decided to join a group of islanders who had been diagnosed as suffering from leprosy. At 4 a.m. on 2 July 1907, as the moon was setting, they landed on the island along with twenty-five new patients. The lepers were 'greeted in low tones' while Jack and Charmian were led to a small cottage for a few hours of fitful sleep.

The scene they woke to was not the nightmare of gruesome dis-figurement they had expected. Their cottage looked out onto a village green where attractive young women smiled as they strolled by. The colony of eight hundred was a self-sufficient collective, in fact a model community – the very opposite of the hell they had imagined. It had six churches, a Young Men's Christian Association building, a bandstand, baseball diamonds, a racetrack, two brass bands and even a firing range. An ace shot with pistol or rifle, Charmian was asked to join a group for target practice. Normally she would have had no problem in hitting the bullseye, but now she missed, and later partly blamed 'the audience of curious men whose personal characteristics were far from quieting to *malahini wahini* [white women's] nerves'.

Jack and Charmian tried not to show their reactions to the extent of the disease's ravages, even when they watched minor operations being carried out on some of the islanders. Deeply impressed by the community's resilience and the humanity they saw exhibited at every turn, they could not help but be disturbed by the suffering they witnessed. Particularly upsetting to Charmian was the way the disease appeared to affect women far more than men. One day a group of young girls were brought to entertain her. 'Clustered around a piano, one played with hands that were not hands – for where were the fingers? But play she did, and weep I did, in a corner, in sheer uncontrol of heartache at the girlish voices gone shrill and sexless and tinny like the old French piano.'

On the morning of 4 July, Independence Day, Jack and Charmian were woken by noises so strange that they wondered whether they were not 'struggling in nightmare'. They quickly grabbed their kimonos and sandals and rushed outside. What they saw left them speechless.

> In the eery whispering dawn there gambolled a score or so 'horribles', men and women already horrible enough . . . and but thinly disguised in all manner of extravagant costumings. They wore masks of home manufacture, in which the makers had unwittingly imitated the lamentable grotesqueries of the accustomed features of their companions – the lopping mouth; knobby or effaced noses, flapping ears; while equally correct in similitude, the hue of these false-true visages was invariably unpleasant, pestilent yellow.

During their five-day stay on Molokai, one of the islanders begged Jack to 'write us up straight'. In his non-fiction, he did not disappoint. Leprosy, he wrote, had to be segregated, but it was far from the 'horrible nightmare' of popular perception. 'I would by far prefer to spend the rest of my days on Molokai than in any tuberculosis sanitarium.'

While the views Jack expressed in his journalism were sober and humane, his treatment of the disease in his fiction would lead to a vicious attack three years later from the publisher of the *Honolulu Advertiser*, Lorrin A. Thurston, who had befriended Jack and Charmian during their first days on Hawaii. He would call Jack 'a sneak of the first water, a thoroughly untrustworthy man and an ungrateful and untruthful bounder . . . he has made the worst out of the leprosy situation here, distorted facts, invented others where the truth was not enough to suit his purpose and thoroughly misrepresented conditions'. Thurston was referring to two of Jack's stories, 'The Sheriff of Kona' and 'Koolau the Leper'.

In the former, a leper's face is described as 'a living ravage, noseless, lipless, with one ear swollen and distorted, hanging down from the shoulder'. In the latter, lepers are portrayed as 'monsters – in face and form grotesque caricatures of everything human ... Their faces were the misfits and slips, crushed and bruised by some mad god at play in the machinery of life.'

Robert Louis Stevenson, who had stayed on Molokai in 1888, had also been viciously attacked for daring to mention leprosy and Hawaii in the same sentence. In Stevenson's day, conditions on Molokai had been far less civilised than those Jack found. There were no shops, community services or adequate medical facilities. Stevenson had heard the story of a saintly Catholic priest, Father Damien, who many years before had volunteered to spend his life caring for the lepers, and who had died alongside them after contracting the disease. To Stevenson, Damien was a hero. To many Protestants on Hawaii, however, he was the opposite. In a famous open letter, published in 1890, Stevenson had denounced Damien's critics, among them several missionaries whom he believed had corrupted the South Seas while hiding beneath a veil of Christianity.

During Jack's visit to Hawaii, almost two decades later, attitudes towards leprosy had barely changed. The last thing the nascent tourist industry wanted was to be associated with the disease, however remote Molokai was from the golden sands of Waikiki. Even in the middle of the Pacific, Jack could not escape the censure of America.

12

The Heart of Darkness

'The horror! The horror!'
JOSEPH CONRAD, *Heart of Darkness*

THEY WERE SITTING in a shaded part of the boat. The only sounds were the occasional creaking of the rigging and the steady slap of waves against the hull. Their captain begged them to be patient. It would rain any day now. He was certain of it. In any case, they could survive on what water they had left. If they got back on course. If they escaped the doldrums. If they found even the faintest hint of breeze to fill the *Snark*'s slack canvas.

Jack went to his cabin. For the next few hours he scratched away with his fountain pen, working on a tale about a castaway sailor who dies of thirst while drifting in an open boat. When he had finished, Jack came back on deck looking 'gaunt and haggard, but with eyes burning with enthusiasm'.

'Boys!' he cried. 'That yarn's one of the best I ever did!'

They were too tired to congratulate him. For several days, their thoughts had only been of water. At night they tossed and turned in their bunks, dreaming of mountain springs, of diving into lakes of ice-melt. Every morning when they saw the cloudless sky they cursed and then prayed for rain.

On 7 October 1907 they had left Hawaii in excellent spirits and health. After five months of refitting, the *Snark* had finally been made seaworthy. To replace Eames and Stolz, Jack had hired a deckhand called Hermann de Visser, a Japanese chef, Wada, and a new cabin boy, Yoshiatsu Nakata, an eighteen-year-old whose only word of English was 'yes', and who agreed to join the ship in the mistaken belief that it was bound for Japan. As sailing-master, Jack had recruited James Langhorne Warren, a paroled murderer who had been pardoned by the governor of Oregon.

After two weeks at sea, Jack had begun to leaf through a book on sailing in the Pacific. He read that the crossing to the Marquesas Islands, his next port of call and over a thousand miles away, was impossible without a motor. To his horror, when he then tested the *Snark*'s expensive engine, it did not work. From now on, the *Snark* would be at the mercy of the trade winds. But there were no winds.

For days which stretched into weeks they were becalmed in the remotest of Pacific solitudes, adrift in a barren sea. A sudden squall would carry them miles off course, then the wind would die and they would find themselves looking anxiously for a breeze to fill the sails. On they drifted, further into the lonely expanses of the South Seas, 'wedged between the trades and the doldrums'.

During his winter in the Klondike, Jack had learned how to keep his nerve while waiting for the weather to change. Pitted against the most brutal master – the ocean – he was at his best. 'Fallible and frail,' he would later explain, 'a bit of pulsating, jelly-like life – it is all I am. About me are the great natural forces – colossal menaces, Titans of destruction, unsentimental monsters that have less concern for me than I have for the grain of sand I crush under my foot . . . these insensate monsters do not know that tiny sensitive creature, all nerves and weaknesses, whom men call Jack London, and who himself thinks he is all right and quite a superior being.'

On 20 November, disaster struck. During a sudden squall, the tap on one of the water tanks was left turned on. By the next morning half the water supplies had vanished. As if this wasn't enough, the boat was also running low on fuel. The crew stopped cooking, resorting instead to spooning 'cold rations straight from the tin'.

Whenever his crew began to lose faith, Jack energised and distracted them. As Charmian noted in her journal, he had 'the delightful characteristic of always wanting to share everything in which he is interested – his amusements, his books, or the thing he is studying . . . he wants me to feel the tug of the fish on the line; and he draws all of us together to reread, aloud, some book he knows will give pleasure'.

With his hook baited with a whole flying fish, Jack would wait patiently for hours until, with a split-second flash, a dolphin would strike. There would then be a high-pitched hiss as the fishing line unreeled and the dolphin leapt into the air. Soon, six hundred feet of line separated Jack and the hooked beast. Like Lord Byron before him, he was captivated by the changing colours of the animal as it passed from shades of green or blue in the water, to yellow-gold when hooked, and then, as it writhed on deck, through hues of blues, greens, and yellows. Finally, it turned a deathly white, speckled with blue spots. When it wriggled no more, it returned through the colour spectrum, ending in a mother-of-pearl grey.

By 23 November, despite Jack's attempts to boost their morale, every one of his crew was preparing for the worst. Then, miraculously, a cloud crossed the sun. A few hours later the sky darkened and, to cheers of joy, salvation arrived. The tropical raindrops were huge, it seemed, sweeter tasting than any nectar. Instantly the crew rigged an awning to collect the water and then stood, sunburned necks craning towards the heavens. The rain streamed down their faces, soaking them to the bone. In two hours they managed to collect 120 gallons. Two weeks later they made landfall. They had arrived at Nuka Hiva, one of the islands of the Marquesas chain. They had survived 'the impossible traverse'.

It was 10 p.m. on 6 December 1907 when the *Snark*'s expensive anchor plunged through eleven fathoms to the coral seabed below. From the cliffs above came the faint bleating of wild goats. When the crew woke the next morning, they found themselves in 'a placid harbour that nestled in a vast amphitheatre, the towering, vine-clad walls of which seemed to rise directly above the water'. They had arrived at an island steeped in literary tradition; both Herman Melville and Robert Louis Stevenson had spent time there.

For Jack, the cruise of the *Snark* was as much a literary pilgrimage as an escape from the pressures of fame. As a teenager he had been tempted to sign on for a voyage to the South Seas solely because he wanted to follow in the wake of the author of *Moby-Dick*. From the day they had left San Francisco, Jack had read Conrad and Melville to his crew, as if by intoning the greats he could absorb some of their magic. Now he had arrived at Mecca: Melville's paradise garden – the valley of Typee.

To his delight, Jack was able to rent the very cottage where Stevenson had stayed for six weeks in 1888 during his voyage in the yacht *Casco*. A Mrs Fisher, who had cooked for the Stevensons, agreed to do the same for Jack and Charmian. Leading from the cottage, a trail meandered up a steep cliff and then to the valley which Melville had described so graphically in his 1846 debut novel *Typee*, the story of two Yankee sailors, Tommo and Toby, who flee from a whaling ship and take refuge on Nuka Hiva.

Midway up the steep climb, Jack and Charmian reached a lookout point. Below, they could see the *Snark* moored in a bay of cobalt blue. In the other direction, dropping off a thousand feet, lay the valley itself. Through the heat haze they could make out a waterfall which Melville had described. Every step Jack now took brought him closer to the lake where Fayaway, Tommo's Polynesian lover, had joined him in a canoe, and stood in the prow with her shawl spread to catch the wind.

At the edge of the lake Jack stopped at a small thatched hut for a drink of water. An old-looking, yellowing woman offered him her gourd. In the background shuffled her husband, dragging one of his legs, bloated to twice its size with elephantiasis. Nearby, the couple's young children played in tall grass – they also showed signs of leprosy.

Jack and Charmian had not stumbled into paradise. Judging by the suffering they soon witnessed, they had arrived in killing fields fertilised by the devil. Colonisation had decimated the indigenous people; in two decades of French rule, because of imported illnesses such as tuberculosis and asthma, the population had plummeted from fifty thousand to just five thousand. 'All this strength and beauty has departed,' Jack mourned. 'Life has rotted away in this wonderful garden spot.'

Though physically ravaged, the natives still had spiritual strength, and still showed the naive generosity that had made them such rapid victims of French imperialism. One evening, Jack and his crew feasted as chanting hula dancers performed in the flicker of flames while others carried stuffed boars that looked, in the dancing shadows, uncannily like human bodies skewered on long bamboo poles. When the feast ended, the *Snark*'s crew watched the moon rise over the mountain behind them.

'The air was like balm,' Jack wrote, 'faintly scented with the breath of flowers. It was a magic night, deathly still, without the slightest breeze to stir the foliage; and one caught one's breath and felt the pang that is almost hurt, so exquisite was the beauty of it. Faint and far could be heard the thin thunder of the surf upon the beach. There were no beds; and we drowsed and slept wherever we thought the floor softest. Near by, a woman panted and moaned in her sleep, and all about us the dying islanders coughed in the night.'

Deeply moved by the natives' plight, Jack repaid their hospitality. As coughing islanders gathered around the following evening, he played them Chopin on his portable gramophone. The natives danced long into the still night, and then Jack finally played the 'Marseillaise'. As its last chords drifted across the still air and the impromptu concert came to an end, under 'scudding black clouds' the entire village lay down for the night.

It was now twelve weeks since they had received word from home. Time to leave Melville's island. Her decks laden with fresh fruit and vegetables, the *Snark* set sail on 18 December 1907 for Tahiti. On Christmas Eve, a gale blew her off course. Certain they had hit a reef, Charmian rushed on deck where she was greeted by sheets of lightning. Back in her cabin, she noted in her journal, which would eventually form the basis of a book about the voyage, *The Log of the* Snark, published by Macmillan in 1915: 'The heavens roll above me; and the sea swallows and licks its wet lips over me.'

Two days later, the *Snark* arrived in Papeete, 'the Paris of the Pacific', and capital of Tahiti. Three months of mail, most of it containing bad news, greeted them: Jack had just $66 left in his bank account; an Oakland bank had threatened to repossess Flora's home in Oakland because of unpaid debts; $800 worth of cheques had bounced in Hawaii; America had again plunged into recession, and as a result magazine rates had tumbled. Since the publication of *The Call of the Wild* in 1903, Jack had earned more than $100,000, but, even though his earlier work was still selling, he discovered that he was now destitute. Why?

In his absence he had left Charmian's aunt, Ninetta Eames, in charge of his literary affairs. She was just as inept as her husband Roscoe. Not only had she changed banks without Jack's knowledge (hence the bounced cheques), she had also sold his stories at bargain-basement prices. Without consulting him, she had spent thousands of dollars on the Glen Ellen ranch, and had even had the gall to try to censor his work. She had complained to George Brett that Chapter 23 of *Martin Eden* was 'a covert attack on *The Overland Monthly*', where she had once worked. 'Our Jack,' she had added, 'has obviously made a free and, I fear, ill-considered use of the licence of fiction in this case.' Brett had tactfully pointed out that he could not amend Jack's manuscripts without his approval.

The woman whom Jack affectionately called 'Mother Mine' also widened the rift between him and his real mother. 'There is one thing at least, upon which you and I agree – namely the character of my mother,' he had replied after receiving a letter of 11 July 1907 in which Ninetta had written:

> . . . that woman is a horror in flesh and blood. She is in fact, unforgivably vile, and she isn't your mother, dear Jack. The very idea is preposterous . . . That ungrateful old hag!!! . . . Sometimes I feel like choking off the allowance you make just to see her wriggle awhile . . . She is horrible, horrible – full of mean innuendoes about the ones she depends upon for her living, and she would do you an injury as quick as the chance came. I never saw so utterly hopeless a woman – no redeeming trait in her. I should sicken and die outright if I had to live with her. And she is fattening on the good things you provide for her – swelling hideously in hips and paunch like a gorged swine. Jack, Jack – you darling, darling – don't you ever think you were born of anything so repulsive.

Ninetta's one achievement had been to secure $7000 for the serial rights to *Martin Eden*, which would eventually appear in the *Pacific Monthly* between September 1908 and September 1909. Brett at Macmillan was also delighted with the first chapters of what some critics argue is Jack's best book.

After asking Brett to wire him money to pay for their passage, Jack and Charmian boarded a steamer, the *Mariposa*, and returned to San

Francisco, leaving the rest of the crew to enjoy the pleasures of Tahitian hospitality. Ostensibly, Jack was returning to straighten out his finances. But there was another reason which he did not mention to the reporters waiting on the dockside in California, who grilled him mercilessly, insinuating that the *Snark* had all along been a publicity stunt.

Jack had heard that Bess was considering remarrying. Now he began to feel possessive of the children he had not seen in over ten months. After several days of frantic dealings with creditors and local banks, and a tense meeting with Ninetta Eames, he went to see his daughters, and told Bess that he would continue to provide for them, but not for her if she remarried. In 1909 she would call off her engagement to a local man, Charles Milner, an employee of the Southern Pacific Railroad whom she had known all her life.

On the return journey to Tahiti, again aboard the *Mariposa*, Jack spent most of his time at the poker table and fighting off a bad bout of 'flu. His visit to California, although it had lasted just eight days, had resurrected the misanthrope in him. Now he mooched about the ship and began to drink heavily. So far in the voyage, their setbacks had forged an ever more intimate bond between Jack and Charmian. She had risen to every challenge and become an indispensable member of the crew, so hardy and adaptable that she had fast become a first-rate sailor. But now, as the *Mariposa* cruised at full steam back to Tahiti, she sensed a growing distance between her and Jack. His 'long sickness' had returned. They argued about his drinking and she burst into tears several times. 'I think Jack is sick sometimes, mentally, or he wouldn't do as he does,' she noted in her journal.

All was forgiven when they reached Tahiti. Jack apologised to Charmian, telling her one morning that he would rather have her than all the money of J.P. Morgan and J.D. Rockefeller put together, and cut back on his alcohol intake. He also rushed to finish *Martin Eden*, dashing off in just three days the final chapters, which end with Eden crawling through a porthole of a ship called the *Mariposa* to commit suicide by drowning. The dark ending reflected the agony Jack often felt during the six weeks of his stay in Tahiti. Throughout March 1908 he spent most of his time either at the dentist or fighting the pain of his rotten teeth.

When not writhing in agony while Charmian held his hand as he sat in the dentist's chair, Jack visited an American expatriate, Ernest Darling, a self-styled 'Nature Man' who had left California for an even more balmy climate, and who flew a red flag from his hut.

'What does this red flag mean?' Jack asked him.

'Socialism, of course.'

'Yes, yes, I know that,' said Jack, 'but what does it mean in your hands?'

'Why, that I've found my message.'

'And that you are delivering it to Tahiti?'

'Sure.'

Even at the end of the world, Jack discovered, socialism was alive and well. While critics at home accused him of turning his back on the class struggle by escaping to the South Seas, he remained politically active. Other than Ernest Darling, however, he met few willing converts to the cause. Although he gave his 'Revolution' lecture again, this time at a club called *Aux Folies Bergère* in Papeete, his performance had little impact on the bemused colonials.

'So you write books,' Darling commented one morning when Jack, tired and sweaty, had just finished his statutory thousand words. 'I, too, write books.'

Jack had not come all this way to be pestered by a white man wearing a grass skirt who thought he could write.

'This is the book I write,' Darling smiled, and began to pound his chest. 'The gorilla in the African jungle pounds his chest till the noise of it can be heard half a mile away.'

'A pretty good chest,' Jack joked. 'It would even make a gorilla envious.'

On leaving the island on 4 April 1908, Jack and Charmian were surprised to see a small outrigger canoe following in the *Snark*'s wake. In the stern sat the 'Nature Man', waving goodbye with his red flag.

On they sailed, Jack now growing more excitable by the hour. They were just days from the island of Apia in Western Samoa where Robert Louis Stevenson had spent his last years before dying there in 1894. Determined to see the Scotsman's grave – *Treasure Island* was his favourite book – as soon as he had found his land legs Jack led Charmian along a path which cut through a jungle of bamboo and palm trees and then wound its way up the side of Mount Vaea. Rocks and creepers blocked their path, as well as drifts of pink petals from blossoming trees which rained down on them as they clambered higher. Late in the afternoon, they paused to rest.

'How did they manage to carry his body up here?' Charmian wondered.

Jack explained that when the islanders heard that this was where Stevenson wished to be buried, five hundred of them had taken out their machetes and worked their way through the jungle one long night. In the morning, their chiefs had lifted Stevenson's corpse onto their shoulders and carried it to the mountaintop.

Finally, Jack and Charmian rounded a large boulder and found themselves before the tomb. They clasped hands.

'I wouldn't have gone out of my way to visit the grave of any other man in the world,' said Jack.

A fresh hibiscus grew at the base of the monument. On the western side, inscribed in the Samoan language, were the lines 'Thy people shall be my people, and thy God my God: where thou diest, will I die.' On another side, Jack read Stevenson's epitaph:

> Here he lies where he longed to be;
> Home is the sailor, home from the sea,
> And the hunter home from the hill.

Jack had been mesmerised when he first read Joseph Conrad's *Heart of Darkness*, the tale of a riverboat captain who goes upriver in search of Kurtz, a white trader gone insane. Now, as he headed for the 'cannibal' islands of the South Pacific, it seemed as if the cruise of the *Snark* was also a quest. But Jack was not searching for a man who had escaped sanity's grasp. He was seeking to become the master mariner who could sail the world and write best-sellers at the same time.

One night, as they sailed through the New Hebrides, they passed a 'score of active volcanoes', molten lava flowing into the flaming ocean lapping at their bows. They were visited by plagues of insects. Day and night, cockroaches crawled over them.

When they arrived at the heart of the Solomon Islands, they began to lose their nerve. The Solomon chain ran for almost a thousand miles at the northern edge of Melanesia, and comprised German and British protectorates. It was 'copra-plantation and slave-trading' territory, where white heads hanging above a chieftain's throne were much-prized status symbols. To his shock, Jack heard a rumour that the entire crew of his old sealing ship, the *Sophie Sutherland*, had met their deaths in the Solomons some years earlier. Apparently they had ventured into the high interior of one island and were poisoned by 'scratch-scratch', a severe skin irritation which, unless quickly treated, results in agonising death.

At every opportunity, Jack and his crew practised with the *Snark*'s arsenal of Mausers, Colt pistols and Smith & Wesson revolvers. Jack kicked himself for not fitting the *Snark* with a machine gun as he had originally planned. Whenever Charmian found herself among the rougher plantation owners, she would casually fire a few rounds at a difficult target. A couple of bullseyes in rapid succession usually brought instant respect.

One morning, as Jack and Charmian idled about the island of Pendruffyn, they met a Captain Jansen of a British ship, the *Minota*, a 'teak-hulled converted yacht which cruised the coast of Malaita picking up plantation labour'.

'Why not come along?' asked Jansen.

Charmian and Jack looked at each other and debated silently 'for half a minute'. Then they nodded in unison.

'You'd better bring your revolvers along, and a couple of rifles,' warned Jansen. 'I've got five rifles aboard, though the one Mauser is without ammunition. Have you got a few rounds to spare?'

As they were about to board the *Minota*, Jack heard another story just as unnerving as the one about his old sealing ship: six months previously, a band of natives had raided the boat and killed its former captain. It had been all too easy for the raiders to get on board; the slave ship's rail was only six inches high. Even when brass stanchions were screwed into the rail and a double row of barbed wire stretched around the *Minota* 'from stem to stern', Jack was far from reassured: '[the wire] was all very well as a protection from savages, but it was mighty uncomfortable to those on board when the *Minota* took to jumping and plunging in a sea way.'

One night, Jansen invited them to go dynamite-fishing. 'Bristling with rifles, every man of us(!) with a pistol in his belt,' Charmian later recalled, 'we approached to within less than thirty feet of a fallen tree outjutting from that soundless, moveless wall of mangroves, reversed the boat, and the charge was tossed into the water. And simultaneously with the explosion, like screen pictures on a prepared scene, there appeared a score of stark naked cannibals, armed to the eyebrows with every fighting device known to savage man.'

Thankfully, the cannibals were not hungry enough to launch their canoes. Sobered by this encounter, Jack began to study the 'mangrove-studded coastline' more closely. What would happen, he asked, if the *Minota* were to run aground?

'She's not going to,' Jansen said curtly.

'But just in case she did?'

'We'd get in the whale-boat,' Jansen almost whispered, 'and get out of here as fast as God would let us.'

The *Minota*'s first stop was the island of Malu, one of the Solomon chain. To their relief, Jack and Charmian were greeted not by head-hunters but by the island's sole missionary, an Englishman named Caulfield. He wished them luck. On 19 August, as the *Minota* was heading back out to sea through a gap in the reef, the wind suddenly changed direction and she was blown off course. Seconds later, she struck the reef. A large breaker smashed her further onto the rocks. Then her anchor chain broke.

The 'savages' were upon them in minutes. 'Like vultures circling down out of the blue, canoes began to arrive from every quarter. The crew, with rifles at the ready, kept them lined up a hundred feet away with a promise of death if they ventured nearer. And there they clung, a hundred feet away, black and ominous, crowded with men, holding their canoes with their paddles on the perilous edge of the breaking surf. In the meantime the bushmen were flocking down from the hills, armed with spears, Sniders [rifles], arrows, and clubs, until the beach was massed with them.'

While some of the *Minota*'s crew struggled to keep her from ripping open on the reef, Jack rowed off in the whale-boat with an SOS for the captain of another 'blackbirder', the *Eugenie*, anchored five miles away. While he was gone, Caulfield did his best to buy the stricken *Minota* some extra time.

'I know what you think,' he shouted at the massed savages as they waited to pounce. 'You have plenty tobacco on the boat and you're going to get it. I tell you plenty rifles on the boat. You get no tobacco, you get bullets.'

Three hours later, Captain Keller of the *Eugenie* arrived with a crew of armed men. 'The white man,' Jack later wrote, 'the inevitable white man, coming to the white man's rescue.'

While the *Eugenie*'s men stood guard, the *Minota*'s crew tried to release her from the reef. Meanwhile, Caulfield knelt and prayed, his bushy-haired converts standing around him, 'leaning on their rifles and mumbling amens. The cabin walls reeled about them. The vessel lifted and smashed upon the coral with every sea. From on deck came the shouts of men heaving and toiling, praying, in another fashion, with purposeful will and strength of arm.' For three more days and two nights the *Minota* pounded the reef; but she held together, and the 'shell of her was pulled off at last and anchored in smooth water'.

Not all of Jack and Charmian's stay in the Solomons was as alarming as this. They were so delighted at their reception by the British plantation owners of Pendruffyn that they stayed three weeks. The colonials knew how to exploit the natives *and* how to enjoy themselves when new guests arrived. For seemingly endless nights they drank, sang and even donned fancy dress. Jack's costume was that of a South Seas pirate, fitting attire for a man who frequently confessed to Charmian that he loved nothing more than a night out 'pirooting'.

After dinner one evening, a trader named Bernays brought out some hashish. Each night, the revellers decided, one of them should take a large dose. The first night they took their supplier's drugged body, laid it out on a platform and held a mock funeral ceremony. When it was Jack's turn, he became violently ill and had to be put to bed. The next day he was 'dull and crusty from hasheesh', but several days later he compensated by way of 'an orgy of love on embroidered rug on the floor'. 'Aren't you ashamed of yourself?' he teased Charmian afterwards.

Eager to explore other islands, Jack and his crew headed deeper into the tropics, towards the Fiji islands, a few hundred miles to the south-west. In late September, among the atolls marked 'Ringgold Islands' on their chart, they lost their way. Eight days later the *Snark* found herself in the Koro Sea, a bizarre seascape dotted with bamboo rafts carrying Fijians with great masses of fuzzy hair. At last they had arrived at the heart of Melanesia, otherwise known as 'the death islands'. Here the bushmen were apparently so brutal that even veteran missionaries were afraid to venture among them. Jack eventually found a burly Scots trader who could move freely inland because he sold the natives rusty Springfield rifles. But at the last minute even the Scotsman backed out, and sent his assistant, a young Englishman, his body ravaged by malaria, to act as their guide instead.

The sun was high overhead when they emerged into a clearing circled by grass houses. At the centre squatted fifty or so cannibals, most of whom ran into the jungle at the sight of Charmian – they had never seen a white woman before. Brandishing spears, they peered back at her while those brave enough to remain stared with 'dead eyes', their bodies, 'worse than naked', covered with a matted fur. Others were smeared with the juice of berries. Most wore belts and anklets of coconut shell. All were pierced. Even the babies had holes in their earlobes, plugged with hairpins, bone rings and shells.

Every scene Jack and Charmian now came across, it seemed, was more disturbing than the last. Their contact with indigenous cultures had long since lost its charm. What had started out as an exciting and pagan Pacific of coconut-milk cocktails and tattooed chiefs had become a dark archipelago of death and horrifying disease.

Among the remote islands, as in Alaska, Jack's belief in Anglo-Saxon superiority was tested to the limit. He was disturbed by what he saw of colonialism up close, but he did not analyse it in Marxist terms. His socialism extended only to oppressed whites. He would not even concede, despite his own horrendous sunburn, that darker-skinned breeds were better suited to the tropics.

Throughout his time in the Pacific, Jack kept up his routine of a thousand words a day, eventually completing three books apart from *Martin Eden*: a collection of short stories, *South Seas Tales*; *The Cruise of the* Snark; and a novel set amongst the plantation owners of Pendruffyn, *Adventure*. Despite the haste and discomfort in which he had to write during the voyage, several of his short stories showed that in the Pacific he had found territory as fertile in its human drama as the Klondike.

'The Chinago', set in Papeete, tells the story of a servant who is executed because a gendarme confuses his name with that of a local murderer. In 'Samuel', Jack created one of his few convincing female characters, Margaret Henan, who is over seventy years old and has borne twelve children. Ironically, when Jack wrote about women from outside the Anglo-Saxon middle classes, whether from Polynesia or Alaska, he often did so with sympathy and subtlety. Perhaps the finest story completed during the voyage was the semi-autobiographical 'The Sea-Farmer', about an old sea-captain who has grown weary of journeying across the oceans and longs to settle down on a farm.

More often, Jack's Pacific was a malarial Hades, crawling with improbably huge and grotesque insects; a region as brutal and extreme as his fictional Alaska, and like it a testing ground for the superiority of white men. Jack's attitudes to the wilderness had, however, changed. Whereas the Northland had been revivifying, a last Eden for the frontiersman, the South Seas were Paradise lost, and in some of the stories worse than hell.

In one particularly blood-soaked tale, 'Mauki', the eponymous islander is tortured by a white sadist, Bunster, who burns him with a cigar, rips open his pierced nose and then half-skins him alive: 'Bunster had a mitten made of ray-fish skin. The first time he tried it on Mauki, with one sweep of the hand it fetched the skin off his back from neck to armpit.' Mauki manages to survive, and when Bunster is laid low by blackwater fever, he takes his revenge.

The house deserted, he entered the sleeping-room, where the trader lay in a doze. Mauki first removed the revolvers, then placed the ray-fish mitten on his hand. Bunster's first warning was a stroke of the mitten that removed the skin the full length of his nose . . . a hideous, skinless thing came out of the house and ran screaming down the beach till it fell in the sand . . . and gibbered under the scorching sun. Mauki looked toward it and hesitated. Then he went over and removed the head, which he wrapped in a mat and stowed in the stern-locker of the cutter.

Was Jack being ironic, poking fun at the white man, in such stories as 'The Inevitable White Man'? 'The black will never understand the white, nor the white the black, as long as black is black and white is white,' says Captain Woodward in the story, whose hero, Saxtorph, saves Woodward with his sharpshooting: 'Bang, bang, bang, bang, went his rifle, and thud, thud, thud, thud, went the niggers to the deck.'

Some biographers have pointed to another short story, 'The Terrible Solomons', as evidence that Jack's racial views began to change in the tropics. In order to survive in this part of the world, Jack wrote, the Anglo-Saxon 'must have a certain grand carelessness of odds, a certain colossal self-satisfaction, and a racial egotism that convinces him that one white is better than a thousand niggers every day of the week . . . He must not understand too well the instincts, customs, and mental processes of the blacks, the yellows, and the browns; for it is not in such a fashion that the white race has tramped its royal way around the world.'

Was Jack indicting colonialism in such passages, or praising the white man for his 'colossal self-satisfaction'? Unlike Robert Louis Stevenson, who spent six years living among them, Jack did not 'understand too well' the native peoples of the South Seas. In *The Cruise of the* Snark he described the disease and suffering imported by the white man, but would not condemn his own race. The indigenous cultures he brushed up against were doomed because they were inferior:

When one considers the situation, one is almost driven to the conclusion that the white race flourishes on impurity and corruption. Natural selection, however, gives the explanation. We of the white race are the survivors and the descendants of the thousands of generations of survivors in the war with the micro-organisms. Whenever one of us was born with a constitution peculiarly receptive to these minute enemies, such a one promptly died. Only these of us survived who could withstand them. We who are alive are the immune, the fit – the ones best constituted to live in a world of hostile micro-organisms.

In one sense, Jack agreed with Stevenson: the Anglo-Saxon's behaviour in conquering the tropics had been far from exemplary. Unlike Stevenson, however, he believed that the white man should show himself superior to the 'nigger' and not stoop to his savage level. Colonialists had let the side down.

By September 1908, apart from Jack, only Charmian and Martin Johnson of the *Snark*'s original crew remained. For over a year, they had pushed their bodies to the limit of physical endurance. They had not taken adequate precautions against the sun's rays, and were now weak with tropical diseases. That they were still alive was testament to their stamina and the strengthening powers of adrenaline.

Just as he had taught himself to navigate, Jack was forced to learn the basics of tropical medicine. His first and most serious patient was himself. He had already limped about the *Snark*'s rotting deck for several months because of five deep sores around his ankles – infections from scratching Samoan mosquito bites. Somehow, he had managed to close these holes in his flesh with 'corrosive sublimate', a mercury-based potion which he had found at the bottom of his medicine chest. Such self-medication was extremely risky, and would continue well beyond the voyage. Charmian was the first to warn against it, and when Jack wasn't watching, the first to throw her daily ration of 'medicine' overboard.

Soon, the whole crew was suffering from malaria. Finally the cook Wada broke down, fearing that he would be eaten by cannibals, and jumped ship while the *Snark* was anchored in Meringe Lagoon off the island of Santa Isabel. He would later rejoin the crew after being captured and brought back to Pendruffyn on Captain Jansen's *Minota*.

Jack fought hard against the illnesses that rampaged through the *Snark*. He had joked earlier that the next book he was going to write would be called *Around the World in the Hospital Ship* Snark. By mid-September, it was no joke. Had there been a doctor on board, he would have been busy night and day tending to the sick. Other than toothache, stomachache and headache, the crew suffered malaria, diarrhoea, boils, ulcers, burns, cuts, infections, sores and dysentery.

On 19 September, during a cruise to the island of Ontong Java, Jack noticed that his hands had begun to swell. He suspected he might have leprosy, but could find no mention of his symptoms in his medical books. Soon his hands were twice their normal size; his body was decaying before his very eyes. 'The skin peels off in patches, with other skins readily forming and peeling underneath,' Charmian noted. 'I do not believe his nervous system was ever made to thrive in the tropics.'

Finally, in early October, Jack conceded defeat. Concerned that his mysterious illness would spread to the other members of the crew, he ordered that the *Snark* should head back to Pendruffyn, from where they would take the next steamer to Australia, where they could receive medical treatment.

From Pendruffyn, Jack found time to write to his second daughter Bess, now six years old, back in America:

Pendruffryn, Guadalcanal
Solomon Islands
October 28th, 1908
Dear Bess

I am sending you in this letter two ear-rings which the savages wear here. Joan tells me in her letter that you have a new tooth. Well, well, I am different from you. I get old teeth – from the savages. I pull them out. I pulled out one to-day for a big black cannibal. He groaned very much.

Tell mama that I say that the pearls and rings and all the things I send you and Joan, are for you to have and use now. Never mind waiting until you are older. When I was a little boy I liked candy. I never got any candy. By and by, they told me, when I was older I would eat all the candy I wanted. But when I was older my teeth were aching and I could not each much candy.

Tell Joan I am writing a novel and that I have named the girl in it Joan. When you are older I shall name a girl in one of my books after you. With a whole armful of love.

Daddy.

On 4 November, Jack, Charmian, Nakata and Martin Johnson boarded the *Makambo*, bound for Sydney. They arrived there on 14

November and immediately checked into a private hospital. Charmian's malaria was treated effectively, but doctors were baffled by Jack's skin condition. His hands grew worse, and his toenails became infected, grossly thickened. Months later, reading a book about the effects of the sun in the tropics, Jack discovered the cause of his mystery illness. He had actually come down with pellagra, a fairly common condition resulting from lack of vitamins and proteins.

After five weeks spent recuperating, Jack announced that he would not go on with the voyage. Charmian was heartbroken. She pleaded with him, but he would not relent. For several months she would feel such a sense of defeat that she could scarcely speak of the *Snark*. The most intensely vital months of her life were over. She had done things which she could not have imagined before meeting Jack. Now, she feared, she would never do them again.

Johnson returned to Pendruffyn and sailed the *Snark* back to Sydney, where she was sold to a group of Englishmen for $3000, a tenth of what she had cost. Ironically, the boat that Jack built would end her days as a slave ship like the *Minota*. Wada signed on as chef aboard a steamer bound for Honolulu. Martin Johnson decided to continue around the globe with money borrowed from Jack. After reaching Paris, where he worked as an electrician, he crossed the Atlantic from Liverpool to Boston on a cattle boat. He and his wife Osa, whom he married in 1910, became world-renowned wildlife photographers and film-makers. He died in an aircrash near Los Angeles in 1937. As for Nakata, he remained in the service of the Londons for six more years before studying dentistry and then running a successful practice in Honolulu.

Jack and Charmian remained in Australia for five months, slowly regaining their strength and spending January 1909 in Tasmania. Jack somehow summoned up enough energy to report on a world championship boxing match in Sydney – Charmian was the only woman in the crowd of twenty thousand – and to give several lectures and exhaustive interviews. While the cruise of the *Snark* had wrecked his illusion of a Pacific paradise, it had not altered his political convictions. In an article for the *Sydney Star*, which contrasted strike methods in the United States and Australia, he reasserted his belief in the class struggle and predicted that 'the future belongs to labour'.

Such statements did not impress the left-wing journalist Andrew M. Anderson, who wrote a scathing attack, 'Jack London – A Criticism', in the Australian magazine the *Socialist*. Anderson felt that fame had made Jack a snob, and that he had not furthered the socialist movement while in Australia. Jack had put his own career above socialism, and in his fiction he was 'too willing to honour the exalted; i.e., those who are standing on the backs of their fellows'.

Jack was wounded by the article, and wrote an angry reply to the editor of the *Socialist*: 'God knows we are all made differently, but that is no warrant for you to bash me just because God didn't see fit to make me in your image, and give me your conception of the function of literary art.'

On 8 April 1909 Jack and Charmian boarded an English tramp steamer, the *Tymeric*, bound for central America. Their last link with the South Seas came on 2 May as they watched a rainbow arc above the sheer cliffs of Pitcairn Island, famous as the final refuge of the *Bounty* mutineers.

Later that afternoon, Jack wrote to George and Carrie Sterling:

Onboard S.S. *Tymeric*,
between Australia and Ecuador
and on this day, May 2, 1909 off Pitcairn Island
. . . Am boxing every day now – with the first, second and third mates – all husky young Englishmen. The First has a couple of beautiful black eyes I gave him. My straight left to the Second precipitated a gumboil that raised his face four inches and kept him from boxing for a week. And the straight lefts I presented to the Third, yesterday, have swollen his nose to twice its normal size.

O, I'm doing nicely, thank you. I've got two game thumbs, and my face has divers discolorations, and I get cramps in my legs while fighting – but I'm getting into condition. Haven't had a drink for a month. But I think they know how to make dry Martinis in Guayaquil.

Love to Carrie. Tell her I've some splendid Samoan tapa for her when I get back and unpack it – and a war-club and spears for you – to say nothing of a clitoris, dried with appurtenances attached and strung on a string for an ear ornament – procured in Solomon Islands.

Charmian joins in love to both of you. Remember us to the rest.

Wolf

The sighting of Pitcairn was the most poignant moment in their entire South Seas adventure. For just as the dream of a Pacific paradise had ended in disease and disillusion for the *Bounty*'s crew, it had also ended in bitter disappointment for those aboard the *Snark*. There was no denying it. On arriving in San Francisco, Jack told gloating reporters he was 'unutterably weary'. He was, in fact, so depressed he could barely hide his sense of defeat. His 'ineradicable smile', one reporter noted, seemed to have been lost at sea.

13

King of the Castle

Why should we clutter the landscape and sweet-growing ground with our mouldy memories? Besides, we have the testimony of all history that all such sad egoistic efforts have been failures. The best the Pharaohs could do with their pyramids was to preserve a few shrivelled relics of themselves for our museums.

JACK LONDON, Letter to Hugh Erichsen, 16 October 1916

JACK HAD BEEN in no hurry to return to California after leaving Australia. Stopping off in Ecuador, he had visited ancient ruins, hunted alligators and attended his first and only bullfight. He then headed for New Orleans via Panama, where he watched construction of the new canal. Reluctant to admit defeat, even when he crossed the American border Jack decided to linger, making for the Grand Canyon instead of home.

It was a ravaged mariner who finally arrived in Glen Ellen on 23 July 1909. Again, it was a bitter homecoming. He found his financial affairs in chaos, and relieved Ninetta Eames of her duties. In his absence, it seemed, the men in threadbare suits had moved in for the kill. His twenty-five months at sea had cost more than his health.

Worse was to come. The publication of *Martin Eden* by Macmillan in September was greeted by mostly negative reviews. For once, the reviewers agreed: *Martin Eden* – the thinly disguised story of Jack's own ascent to dizzying heights – was disappointing. The *Bookman* declared that Jack was 'out of his element' when he tried to write about 'that ordinary society which is variously described as decent, as respectable, as cultured, or as good, and, in his language, as bourgeois'.

Jack was bewildered by the reaction of the critics. Above all he was dismayed that most of them, including those on the left, regarded the book as proof that he had abandoned his belief in socialism. To the end of his life, according to Philip Foner, he would repeat that *Martin Eden* was the most misunderstood of all his works. In the flyleaf of one copy, on 4 April 1910, he wrote:

> This is a book that missed fire with the majority of the critics. Written as an indictment of individualism, it was accepted as an indictment of socialism; written to show that man cannot live for himself alone, it was accepted as a demonstration that individualism made for death. Had Martin Eden been a socialist he would not have died.

Martin Eden was Nietzsche's *Ubermensch*, a man who in the process of turning his back on bourgeois society and fleeing to the South Seas also fatally cut his ties with his own class. Martin's fate was Jack's: by rising from the working class through writing – an essentially bourgeois occupation – Jack had also found himself adrift in a world of superficiality and cynicism. His success had made him a role model, a hero to millions. Yet it had brought him only unhappiness and despair. Unlike Martin, however, Jack had found the motivation to go on, thanks to socialism and Charmian, what he called his 'bribes for living'. The 'people' and a fulfilling marriage had saved him – so far.

In describing Martin Eden's spiritual demise, Jack had written America's first existential novel, a story of modern man's alienation from society, from his roots, from himself. *Martin Eden* was far ahead of its time, predating Camus and Sartre's quest to make sense of existence in a godless world. Not until F. Scott Fitzgerald's *The Great Gatsby* in 1925 would there be another novel which cut so mercilessly to the heart of the American Dream, especially from one of its most blessed sons. As the critic Jonathan Harold Spinner has written: '*Martin Eden* is a rude shock to a literature overwhelmed with the Horatio Alger-Gospel of Wealth myth . . . no other American novel of the era is so hopeless, so empty, so awful in its view of man . . . one sees in this novel a terrible vision of self-knowledge, of self-awareness for America in the twentieth century.'

Although *Martin Eden* didn't please the reviewers, it eventually sold a quarter of a million copies in its hardcover American edition alone.

As Andrew Sinclair has noted, it proved particularly popular among young writers, who empathised strongly with Martin's struggle to achieve success. Indeed, while the novel failed to indict individualism, it succeeded as autobiography. Over the years, *Martin Eden*'s powerful symbolism and stark message have become if anything more resonant, and it remains one of Jack's best novels.

Martin Eden's unfavourable reception depressed Jack but did not interfere with his production schedule. In three short stories published in 1909–10, he demonstrated that he had lost none of his talent for combining drama with a powerful political message.

'The Dream of Debs', published in the *International Socialist Review* in January–February 1909, told of a nationwide strike, as viewed by the rich in San Francisco, in which the workers starve their bosses into submission. 'South of the Slot', published in the *Saturday Evening Post* of 22 May 1909, was another story of class struggle set in San Francisco. 'The slot' is an iron dividing line running along Market Street separating the rich from the poor, and the scene of a climactic street fight between protesting workers and the police. 'The Strength of the Strong', published in *Hampton's* magazine in May 1910, tells of a rebellion in prehistoric times in which an oppressed tribe is destroyed, because it lacks unity, by another tribe, the Meat-Eaters.

As the California sunshine accelerated his recovery from his South Seas ailments, Jack was soon churning out so much fiction that it would bring in an average annual income of $75,000 (over $1 million today) for the rest of his life. When his imagination failed, he resorted to his old tricks of the trade. But even these were sometimes not enough to sustain his thousand words a day. 'I'm darned if any stories just came to me,' Jack had admitted when talking of his earlier work. 'I had to work like the devil for the themes. Then, of course, it was easy to just write them down. Expression, you see – with me – is far easier than invention.'

Jack began to buy plots from a struggling writer, Sinclair Lewis, paying between $5 and $7 per story. A decade later, Lewis would become an overnight sensation with *Main Street* (1920), an exposé of small-town America. This would be followed by four other major novels: *Babbitt* (1922), *Arrowsmith* (1925), *Elmer Gantry* (1927) and

Dodsworth (1929). In 1930 he became the first American to win the Nobel Prize for Literature.

One of Lewis's plots provided Jack with the basis of *The Abysmal Brute* (1913), the second of his novels about boxers, 'the gladiators of the Machine Age'. Uniquely in the annals of boxing, Pat Glendon, the hero of *The Abysmal Brute*, carries a prayerbook into the ring, and reads Browning's sonnets when not running his forty miles a day. Then he falls for Maud Sangster, daughter of a fabulously wealthy industrialist and yet another of Jack's superwomen: a poet, reporter and tennis champion who has dived to the bottom of the Golden Gate and yet retains an exquisite femininity. She convinces Pat to leave the ring for good, but not before he has given bemused ringside spectators a ten-page speech about the evils of capitalism. The *Boston Evening Transcript* would deride *The Abysmal Brute* as 'trivial in plot, weak in execution and scarcely worthy as a whole of the reportorial capacities of a skilful penny-a-liner'.

Jack also ransacked magazines and newspapers for ideas, a practice which brought several charges of plagiarism. As early as 1903, he had been attacked for alleged similarities between sections of *The Call of the Wild* and Egerton R. Young's *My Dogs in Northland*. Jack did not deny that he had used Young's book as one of his sources, and was even more frank after it was pointed out that a speech in *The Iron Heel* had been lifted from a British magazine, *Candid Friend*: 'I, in the course of making my living by turning journalism into literature, used material from various sources, which had been collected and narrated by men who made their living by turning the facts of life into journalism.'

But what did Jack care if critics accused him of stealing other writers' work? What he now wanted most was to be a successful landowner. His adventure in the Pacific had destroyed his fantasy of physical supremacy. He would now return to his roots, to the parched soil which his fellow Californians had farmed into exhaustion.

Like the naturalist John Muir, for whom the rugged beauty of the Sierra Nevada had provided moments of epiphany, Jack began to bemoan the destruction left behind by the first settlers. Humanity's greatest social experiment – America – had once been 'a new country, bounded by the oceans, situated just right in latitude, with the richest land and vastest natural resources of any country in the world'. Yet its settlers had despoiled the new Eden. 'They had moved over the face of the land like so many locusts, destroying everything – the Indians, the soil, the forests, just as they destroyed the buffalo and the passenger pigeon ... So they gobbled and gambled from the Atlantic to the Pacific, until they'd swined a whole continent.'

Jack's new mission was to salvage at least one corner of California from the swine: the thousand acres near Glen Ellen which he now called his 'Beauty Ranch'. Over the coming years, he would plough most of his energy into the Beauty Ranch, continually extending it and eventually buying pedigree pigs, Jersey cows, thoroughbred shorthorn bulls, a $2500 shire horse – Neuadd Hillside – which had been foaled in England, white leghorn fowl, and thirty horses that devoured $40-worth of barley a day.

By 1910, like the *Snark*, the Beauty Ranch had become a major undertaking which consumed every cent of Jack's considerable income. It would, he hoped, be both an environmental marvel and one of the most profitable ranches in the area. He wanted to imitate the Chinese, he would tell one editor, by 'grading the land, making it over into rolling contours and abrupt terraces. It's the only way that such land should be cultivated anyway, as it gives a chance for good, long furrows along the hillside.'

Jack did not have in mind a smallholding carefully nurtured to the point of viability. He began instead to develop a model of scientific farming: he was determined to test the Darwinian theories of evolution which had fascinated him all his adult life. He intended to establish a breeding laboratory on the Beauty Ranch which would introduce advanced breeds. It was not only the techniques for producing better animals which interested him. In a letter to Frederick H. Robinson of the *Medical Review of Reviews*, he would write:

> I believe that the future human world belongs to eugenics, and will be determined by the practice of eugenics. At the present moment I am operating a stock farm. If one of my registered Jersey heifers gets through a hole in the fence to an ornery scrub-grade bull, I am shocked. I know that the result of said breeding will be bad and not good; will be worse

rather than better. The stolid, practical-headed judgement of a stock-breeder should apply with equal force to the breeding of humans. Humans breed in ways very and quite similar to those of animals; and if humans misbreed, the results are misbreds.

In Jack's day, eugenics was in its infancy. American eugenicists believed, as Jack did, that the white race was superior to others, and that the Anglo-Saxon was superior to other whites. They also assumed that hereditary qualities explained the class system, an argument Jack would eventually echo, and campaigned to prevent the 'lower elements' from producing so many children. Lesser breeds, the more fanatical eugenicists believed, should actually be eliminated.

For Jack, the Beauty Ranch represented far more than an opportunity to test eugenic theories on animals. It also provided him with an excuse for turning his back on political activism. He could wait for the Revolution no longer. He would begin one in his own backyard. On the ranch, by marrying science and nature, he hoped to create his own utopia, an autarky which would support a small community over which he would preside as a benevolent squire.

The Beauty Ranch would be an expression of his contempt for industrialisation and for the compromising stance of the urban intellectuals in the American Socialist Party. Jack had heard that the party was considering affiliating with the moderate American Federation of Labor. Believing such a union would be an act of 'suicide', on 30 November 1909 he wrote to Anna Strunsky's husband, William English Walling: 'Depend upon me for one thing. I am a hopelessly non-compromising revolutionist, and I shall stand always for keeping the Socialist Party rigidly revolutionary . . . If the socialist movement in the United States goes in for opportunism, then it's Hurray for the oligarchy and the Iron Heel.'

If Jack could succeed as a farmer, as his stepfather John London had, briefly, during his childhood, he would also finally be able to stop churning out his thousand words a day. Aware of the paradox he faced – that to establish a successful farm would entail considerable investment, which could only come through the proceeds of his writing – Jack decided, nevertheless, to take the biggest gamble of his life. 'I have pledged myself,' he announced, 'my manhood, my fortune, my books and all I possess to this undertaking.'

In January 1910, six months after arriving back in California, Jack rolled the dice and purchased sixteen thousand eucalyptus trees, having consulted experts such as Luther Burbank and the University of California at Davis as to their viability for land unsuited to more traditional crops. 'I have been trying hard to get out of the writing game for many years,' he explained. 'I have never liked to write and only took up the profession as a third and last choice of life. It has been a miserable occupation, but I did it to make money and I made it. I think my eucalyptus trees will help me make my getaway in the near future and it will be a relief for me to get out of the scorching focus of the public eye.'

Jack's next bet was equally bullish. In May 1910, he contracted to purchase the nearby Kohler and Frohling Ranch for $26,000. He had not even begun to recover from the financial disaster of the *Snark*. Now he was adding seven hundred acres he could not afford to buy, let alone cultivate. It was as if a limitless appetite for land had supplanted his hunger for fame. 'I am trying to master this soil and the crops and animals that spring from it,' he would later write, 'as I strove to master the sea, and men, and women, and the books, and all the face of life that I could stamp with my "will to do".'

These early days of the Beauty Ranch were perhaps Jack's happiest. Always at his best when setting himself seemingly impossible tasks, he threw himself body and soul at this new challenge. When he surveyed his plans for the ranch, his 'ineradicable smile' reappeared. At last, he had found a role he felt ideally suited to: as a pioneer of organic farming, bravely subverting conventional wisdom and rejuvenating the earth beneath his feet.

As the ranch expanded, Jack began to gather around him a surrogate family. Wisely, he invited his stepsister Eliza to manage the mushrooming estate – she would later prove a godsend, her diligent management saving him from bankruptcy. In 1914 he would also employ his stepsister Ida's husband, Jack Byrne, as his personal assistant, thereby releasing Charmian from her daily chores of typing up his work and answering his correspondence.

His own flesh and blood, however, grew more distant by the day.

His mother had started a home bakery and sold loaves to her neighbours in Oakland, claiming that Jack refused to support her. In fact
he provided her with an allowance of $55 a month, and paid for the
house in which she, Johnny Miller and Aunt Jennie lived. Eventually
Jack persuaded Flora to give up the loss-making bakery. He was less
successful in attempts to influence other members of his family.

Since his move to the country in 1905, Jack had become convinced
that Bess was trying to turn his daughters against him. Why else would
she forbid them from setting foot on the Beauty Ranch? Repeatedly,
he had beseeched her to allow them to visit, but still she refused.

Exasperated, he decided to build a house for Joan, Bess and their
mother in Glen Ellen. He could then visit his daughters every day.
When he explained his plan to a neighbour, Adela Rogers St John,
who was also his god-daughter, she asked what effect this might have
on Charmian and Bess.

'Oh – they won't need to see much of each other . . . It seems to
me this would benefit everybody.'

'What does Joan say about it?'

'She won't answer my letters,' he replied bitterly.

Surely Jack could see how his daughter might feel? He had deserted
her mother for another woman. He had sailed off around the world
at a crucial period in her childhood.

'How can a child know what a man feels?' he blustered. 'What he
needs, the measures of his temptations, the obligations to his work –
how he must venture into the unknown because he is afraid of it?'

When Jack put his plan to Bess, she rejected it out of hand. Old
wounds had not healed. As his daughter Joan, who understandably
sided with her mother, would later write, Bess still 'despised and
mistrusted Charmian'. Never would she allow her daughters to live
in proximity to 'the other woman'. According to Joan, Jack responded
to the rejection by 'declaring war, a fatal, self-defeating course that
would . . . lead irrevocably to failure and alienation'. His opening
salvo was mild by comparison with later attacks:

Dear Bessie
     In reply to yours of January 4. First of all, let me tell you
that I am in the thick of hard times. I have mortgages of over

$30,000.00 upon which I am paying interest. In addition to this I have something like $10,000 in debts . . . Please don't think for a moment that you're the only person who loves Joan and Bess. And don't forget this danger: The less I am acquainted with my children, the less I shall know my children, the less I shall be interested in my children . . .

Your narrowness is the narrowness of the narrowest cell in all hell . . . Remember, that when I asked you to marry me, and you accepted me, that it was there and then stated explicitly by me that I did not love you. You accepted me on that basis. Long afterwards I found somebody whom I could love.

Do you think Charmian wants to alienate my children from you? Please don't forget that no woman is particularly enthusiastic about taking any hand in raising another woman's children. Yet Charmian is noble, Charmian has no peasant-mind, and Charmian is willing to meet me and go any distance with me in this matter at issue.

And another thing that you must not forget, is: That over half of my work is done by Charmian. That for every dollar you receive from me, Charmian has earned over 50 cents of it; that every piece of bread and butter or chunk of meat you put in your mouth, Charmian has paid for more than half of the same. And yet, you are willing to eat this bread and butter and meat, and ask for more, and yet at the same time deny me any acquaintance with my children, because you are a sexually-offended, jealous female creature.

Are you a woman? Or are you a mere sexual beast, filled with such sex-jealousy and hatred that you will sacrifice your children and your children's father to your own morbid hatred? Wild Indians, headhunters and cannibals, have some-times in their deepest depths of degradation, been like this: Are you willing so to classify yourself?

I've watched you, and waited for you to show your better self. It's high time you did, if you've any lingering shreds of it in you . . .

Such letters served only to make Bess more stubborn in her refusal to allow her daughters to spend time with their father. Had Jack been more conciliatory, he might have succeeded in establishing a more intimate relationship with them.

Charmian, meanwhile, hoped that she might be able to provide Jack with a child of their own. In late 1909, she announced that she was pregnant for the first time. Although she was now thirty-eight, Jack was convinced her pregnancy would be a mere formality. He began to exude affection, she noted, and to talk about 'we three'.

Now his legacy would be one of flesh and blood, not just dusty books and a revitalised earth. When he mounted his horse and cantered across the Beauty Ranch at dusk, he could at last puff out his chest, slap his horse's neck, and dream of his long-hoped-for heir. But there was something lacking as he surveyed the rolling hills that were his and his alone. He could remember the long, dusty afternoons of his boyhood when he had built a model of a magical palace which matched the description he had read in Washington Irving's novel *Alhambra*. From 'fallen chimney bricks and beads and plaster' he had built his own dream palace. He could still remember crying all the way home from school when, after handing back his tattered copy of *Alhambra* to a teacher, he was not given another to replace it.

Jack needed a home to suit his nature – a castle fit for a London dynasty. There was no time to lose. He would begin construction immediately, and commissioned a local architect, Albert Farr, to draw up plans. Materials for his new home would be indigenous to the nearby Valley of the Moon: great red volcanic stones and timber from ancient redwood trees. It would be U-shaped around a reflecting pool (fifteen by thirty feet) 'filled with mountain stream water and stocked with black bass'. There would be a dozen rooms for guests, an entire wing for Charmian to call her own, servants' quarters, and a lounge for men only, where he could drink, puff on Havanas, and play billiards late into the night. And when he felt the need to retreat, he would climb a spiral staircase connecting his library of fifty thousand volumes to a womb high in the sky which would double as his study. At George Sterling's suggestion he would name the stone mansion 'Wolf House'.

There would be other monuments. To house his pedigree hogs, which he would eventually treat as if they were his own children, he built a revolutionary pen which local papers soon dubbed his 'Pig Palace'. Increasingly worried about hygiene, he had his visitors sterilise their feet before entering it. He also developed the first mechanical manure-spreader and installed the first concrete silo in California, forty-three feet high and eleven feet in diameter.

While Wolf House was being built, he and Charmian lived in a bungalow overlooking a vineyard on the newly acquired Kohler ranch. Its six rooms were divided by a passage, with Jack's study and sleeping-porch on one side and Charmian's boudoir on the other. The bungalow was linked to an adjoining stone winery by a covered porch. Jack converted it into a thirty-eight-foot dining hall, and decorated the walls with South Sea souvenirs, photographs from Korea and original illustrations to his books.

Wanting to show off his latest extension to the ranch or break-through in breeding the perfect pig, Jack again began to entertain lavishly. On his 'ranch of good intentions', as he called it, there would always be a spare bed and a place at the dinner-table. 'Sometime, when you're out in California,' he told one critic in 1911, 'run up and visit my wife and me on our ranch, and we'll show you what comrade-ship, mateship, and connubial happiness are.'

James Hopper and Cloudesley Johns – surviving friends of his youth – made regular visits. Jack even managed to coax his old flame Mabel Applegarth into staying. But it was a different woman he greeted from the ethereal goddess he had once worshipped. Mabel was now so weak from tuberculosis that she did not even have the strength to join Jack at his baronial dinner-table. Perhaps the most remarkable and entertaining guest was the world-famous escapologist Harry Houdini, who visited with his wife Bess, later spending Thanks-giving Day 1915 with the Londons.

The flow of guests was soon so heavy, and their stays so prolonged, that Jack had a schedule printed so visitors knew what to expect. Charmian later recalled that 'he was always buying blankets; never so happy as when all the beds were full. His heart was soft, and all were treated alike – friend, stranger, of whatsoever estate.' His hospitality came with only one condition: guests must never disturb his unerring daily work schedule.

*   *   *

Most days began the same way. Jack woke, 'mouth parched and dry, with a slight heaviness of head, and with a mild nervous palpitation in the stomach'. In his own words, he was 'suffering from the morning sickness of the steady, heavy drinker' – otherwise known as an alcoholic. What he needed was a 'pick-me-up, a bracer. Trust John Barleycorn once he has broken down a man's defences!'

Around 5 a.m., Jack's Japanese servant Nakata would bring the Master piping hot coffee. Jack would then lie in bed, large pillows at his back, and begin work on a story.

A poem was pinned on the wall nearby:

> Now I get me up to work,
> I pray the Lord I may not shirk;
> If I should die before the night,
> I pray the Lord my work's all right.

Writing had become just a job, a process as mechanical as filling cans with sardines in a factory. He had built his own system for manufacturing the day's ration of copy, a system as rudimentary as the plots supplied by Sinclair Lewis. Across his bed dangled a string, hung with notes scribbled anywhere and at any time. As he moved from scene to scene, so the stuff of fiction passed before him along a literary washing-line. Jack wrote as he often talked – in staccato bursts, shooting from the hip and never retracting a word. To rewrite was to waste precious time.

By 11 a.m. he had usually finished his daily quota. He then turned to the stacks of mail he had to answer. By 1911 he was receiving an average of ten thousand letters a year. He always replied to his most ardent fans. Some days he dictated replies to a hundred letters or more. Charmian typed them all.

'This is what I like,' Jack told her one morning midway through the day's dictation. 'While we are together, carrying on our work, the guests can do what they like. Look,' he said, gesturing towards the window. 'I love the rail out there under the oak, with our horses tied, saddled and waiting . . . Mate, do you really know how I love it all?'

Around one o'clock, his work done, he would wander onto his back porch, his hair dishevelled, his soft cotton shirt open, his green eyeshade tilted across his forehead, chain-smoking and clutching a stack of papers. Korean wind chimes tinkled in the trees nearby. Then the gong for luncheon sounded.

Though Jack's taste in decor was ultra-modern in its simple utility – he hated gaudy nineteenth-century flourishes – there was nothing ascetic about his palate. Wine from the best local grapes flowed into crystal glasses. In his childhood, he claimed, he went hungry, and stole meat from other children's sandwiches. Now he and his guests could gorge to their hearts' content.

During the autumn duck season, plate after plate of barely-cooked mallard was brought to the table, along with his favourite side-dish, stuffed celery. Jack's Korean cook Yamamoto never failed to serve up the Master's most beloved main course, roast wild duck, to his exact specification: 'The plucked bird should be stuffed with a tight handful of plain raw celery, and, in a piping oven, roasted variously eight, nine, ten, or eleven minutes, according to size of bird and heat of oven. The blood-rare breast is carved with the leg, and the carcass then thoroughly squeezed in a press. The resultant liquid is seasoned with salt, pepper, lemon, and paprika, and poured hot over the meat.'

Near the end of the meal, Nakata would place a notepad and pencil before Charmian, who would 'figure the horses, saddles, bridles, and riding costumes of transient guests from two to a dozen – and, in season, as many swimming-suits besides'.

After luncheon, Jack cleared up any outstanding business of the day. Sometimes this included an interview with the left-wing press, although this was growing increasingly rare. One afternoon he gave one of his most revealing interviews to Emanuel Haldeman-Julius, associate editor of the *Western Comrade*, a socialist publication based in Los Angeles, a city Jack and Charmian loathed.

What are your dreams, Haldeman-Julius asked, *now that you are away from it all, here on what you call the Beauty Ranch?*

'I dream of beautiful horses and fine soil,' said Jack. 'I write a book for no other reason than to add three or four hundred acres to my magnificent estate. I write a story with no other purpose than to buy a stallion. Here I have the most precious thing in the world – the love of a woman. I have beautiful children; I have lots and lots of money; I have fame as a writer; I have a beautiful ranch.'

So why do you seem so pessimistic?

'I look at things dispassionately, scientifically, and everything appears almost hopeless. After long years of labour and development, the people are as bad off as ever. There is a mighty ruling class that intends to hold fast to its possessions. I see years and years of bloodshed. I see the master class hiring armies of murderers to keep the workers in subjection, to beat them back should they attempt to dispossess the capitalists. That's why I am a pessimist. I see things in the light of history and the laws of nature.'

Do you still consider yourself a socialist? You are a landowner now, after all. Surely you no longer view the possession of property as theft?

'I became a socialist when I was seventeen years old. I'm still a socialist, but not of the refined school of socialism. The socialists, the ghetto socialists of the east, no longer believe in the strong, firm socialism of the early days. Mention confiscation in the ghetto of New York and the leaders will throw up their hands in holy terror.'

What do you intend to do, Mr London?

'I've done my part. Socialism has cost me hundreds of thousands of dollars. When the time comes I'm going to stay right on my ranch and let the revolution go to blazes.'

You mean that?

'Well, that's how I feel right now. I suppose when the time comes, I'll let my emotions get the best of my intellect and I'll come down from the mountain top and join the fray.'

Would that be all? He had guests to amuse, and the day was no longer young. But what should he do? Mischievous thoughts crossed his mind. Did any of his guests have toothache? They knew how he loved to pull teeth. Had he not shown them his portable dental kit? He took it everywhere. What about bringing out the glasses with small holes bored into them? Or should he send for the rope? (His favourite trick was to attach a rope to a guest's bed, then, as they took an afternoon nap, to tug on it and scream 'Earthquake!')

He saw the sun high above. No time for schoolboy pranks today. He must show his visitors the Beauty Ranch. Saddled horses were brought into the yard between the cottage and a nearby barn. Jack led a small group of friends and admirers to the peak of Sonoma

Mountain, then along a range of hills which overlooked San Francisco Bay and the scenes of his youth.

When the sun blazed especially hot, bleaching the hills golden brown, he would gallop a mile to a swimming pond he had created by damming a stream. In changing-rooms made from fresh-cut redwood logs that still smelled of sap, his guests would don woollen costumes and go boating in 'warrior canoes' which Jack had brought back from the South Seas. Sometimes he read to them as they sunbathed.

His most recent novel, published in 1910 and panned by the serious critics, was a hymn to the pastoral life. *Burning Daylight*, Jack explained for the benefit of those guests who had not read it, was the story of a Klondike superman, Elam Harnish, who leaves Alaska to make his fortune on Wall Street. In amassing his millions he also sacrifices his soul. He falls in love with his secretary, the beautiful Dede Mason, but she will only marry him if he renounces his materialism and moves to the country.

Harnish was the first in a long line of post-*Snark* heroes who would articulate Jack's neuroses. Like Jack, he was concerned about his physical condition. Jack boasted that his body had 'survived where weaklings died like flies'. Elam Harnish's concerns told a different story.

In Alaska, Harnish had been 'a supreme organic excellence residing in the stuff of the muscles themselves'. But in balmy California he worries that he is no longer the same man. Defeated in an arm-wrestling bout, he decides to follow the example of an 'anaemic, alcoholic degenerate' who had turned himself into a superman by adopting the life of an outdoorsman in northern California. He buys a small ranch in the Valley of the Moon, not dissimilar to Jack's, and wins a rematch of the arm-wrestling contest.

The heroine of the novel, Dede Mason, is Charmian projected as Jack's fantasy California woman, a mannish bluestocking who carries a copy of Browning to her work as Harnish's secretary (ownership of any of Browning's works is a recurring indication of intellectual accomplishment in Jack's fiction). Like Charmian, Dede sits 'man-like' in her saddle, and she decorates her apartment, as Charmian adorned her boudoir, with coyote skins, books, fresh flowers, and the pelt of a mountain lion.

The novel's climax is inevitable: Superwoman Dede and the reinvigorated Harnish fall in love as passionately as Jack and Charmian had. The book ends with them making love in a farmhouse in Sonoma as Harnish's Alaskan husky – the most credible character in the novel – looks on.

Hastily written, *Burning Daylight* nevertheless marked a return to form for Jack in terms of sales: 163,698 copies in hardback alone, a quarter of the total for *The Sea Wolf*, but still a respectable performance. Jack had learned an important lesson from *Martin Eden*: his readers preferred optimism to nihilism. The editors of popular magazines, to which Jack sold serial rights to almost all his fiction, were also hungry for upbeat narratives: the *New York Herald* paid $8000 for serial rights to *Burning Daylight*.

When the shadows began to lengthen, Jack would lead his sunburned party through the redwood and manzanita groves, the air heavy with the scent of sticky pine resin. Often they began to shiver at the bottom of the Valley of the Moon, where cool air collected in pockets. Sometimes the fog from the ocean piled up so high that by late afternoon it spilled into the canyons of the Beauty Ranch.

As Jack led the way back to the bungalow, they passed through a clearing littered with building materials and dominated by a spider's web of scaffolding. His face would crease in a broad grin and he would dismount clumsily – ever the sailor on horseback – and gesture to his guests to follow him on a guided tour of Wolf House.

In vivid detail, he described the stone fireplaces that would warm his guests on foggy autumn mornings, the redwood balconies and wine cellar. The red-tiled roof would cost $3500, but would be worth every cent. The dining-room would seat fifty guests, and there would be an ultra-modern refrigeration plant. What they saw before them would soon be the most practical and comfortable home in America.

Later, back at the cottage, the guests would prepare for dinner and make small talk with new arrivals. On a typical evening Jack's guests might include Fred Lockley, editor of *Pacific Monthly*; his neighbour Earl Rogers, the best criminal lawyer in the west; the ravishing Ula Humphrey, who would play Maud Brewster in a dramatisation by Joseph Noel of *The Sea Wolf*; Finn Frolich, an accomplished sculptor who was working on a bust of Jack; and Luther Burbank, an expert in horticulture and passionate booster of spineless cacti, which Jack had begun to cultivate on the Beauty Ranch.

While his guests became better acquainted with each other, Jack usually asked one of them to join him for an aperitif in his study. One evening, Fred Lockley was the chosen one. There was 'a ghostly semi-twilight' in the room. As he stood in the doorway and waited for Jack to turn on the light, Lockley could just make him out in the gloom; he appeared to be taking something from an upper shelf, a dark, round object about the size of a coconut. Jack handed the object to Lockley. Its 'peculiar touch' gave him the shivers. When Jack turned on the light, Lockley gasped in horror. In his trembling hands he held a human head. The hair was coarse and black, the lips sewn together. There was an ugly scar on the neck.

Mercifully, Nakata sounded the dinner-gong – an ancient concave disc of Korean brass. Lockley and his fellow guests had exactly fifteen minutes to seat themselves at Jack's banquet table. Only when everyone was in their place would the host make his entrance and sit in his throne, a red koa chair at the head of the table.

Over dinner, the discussion would range from world politics to the most arcane avenues of philosophy. Sometimes Jack became carried away. It would be impossible to follow his logic as he reverted, in his excitement, to the slang of his youth.

'Oh, it's only my shorthand,' he would say sadly when he saw the blank faces.

Regular guests soon learned to sip their soup in silence as he gesticulated and waved his arms aggressively to hammer home a point.

'I'm afraid I was always an extremist,' Jack would finally apologise. 'So don't mind my violence.'

Jack liked to keep his guests – especially the more radical among them – on their toes. When anarchists such as Emma Goldman visited, he left a book entitled *A Loud Noise* on their dinner plate. Sure enough, when the unsuspecting syndicalist opened it, it exploded like a fire-cracker.

Goldman later recalled how Charmian would 'sew on the outfit for the baby while we argued, joked, and drank into the wee hours of the morning', and how exuberant Jack was at the prospect of becoming a father. 'Here was youth,' she wrote, 'exuberance, throbbing life. Here was the good comrade, all concern and affection. He exerted himself to make our visit a glorious holiday. We argued about our political differences, of course, but there was in Jack nothing of the rancour I had so often found in socialists I debated with.'

Although Jack had once been attracted to anarchism, he now believed Goldman and her kind were naive. 'The anarchists I know are dear, big souls whom I like and admire immensely,' he told Charmian. 'But they are dreamers, idealists. I believe in law . . . you can see it in my books – all down in black and white.'

When the talk turned to San Francisco, Jack would sigh heavily. It was not the same city. Too modern. The reason he lived in rural isolation was to escape the twentieth century and industrialisation. Look at what they'd done to the old town. Its silhouette was scarred by skyscrapers. The Barbary Coast? A pale imitation of what it was in the glory days. Jack called the city of his memories, before his retreat from mankind, 'Frisco'.

A young female guest rebuked him politely: 'Oh, don't say Frisco! Say San Francisco!'

'Let Frisco alone, you!' he replied. 'We love the western tang of it, we oldsters who knew her by name before you were dry behind the ears! Frisco . . . Frisco . . .'

At times he regretted that he never learned the 'soft, pretty ways of social intercourse'. Before long, the conversation would turn again to politics. His regular guests would smile sweetly at him, some nodding emphatically in the hope that Marx and Engels and Darwin and Nietzsche might be replaced by a more digestible subject. Finally, the Beauty Ranch became the topic of discussion.

'A man finds a rut that interests him, it can still be a rut,' said Earl Rogers, Jack's outspoken neighbour – a man who didn't mince his words. 'A rover, a seeker, an adventurer of the body or the spirit, for him it's the same as a grave, only the man is buried alive. Line it with plush, put gold handles on, for the rebel, the revolutionist, it's a coffin!'

'Can't you see?' Jack shouted back. 'I'm leading a revolution right here!'

He had already planted some of his fields with Canadian peas, rye and other crops which he would plough under for three years to increase the humus content and enrich the over-farmed soil. 'In a few years,' Jack swore, 'this valley will prove what I have said. Men will learn that by modern methods more reward can be brought from ten acres of land than in the old days could be obtained from two or three hundred.'

After dinner, the Master retired to his sleeping-porch. But the day was far from over. Nakata had been busy all evening preparing his bedside table. As with his Master's twice-daily visit to the toilet, preparations for his long night ahead were holy rites, never to be disturbed. Everything must be in its exact place. On his night-table the photographs of his two great loves – Charmian and his shire horse Neuadd Hillside – were positioned just so. His sharpened pencils were arranged like bullets in a magazine, and his notepads stacked in perfect piles beside a tower of cigarette packets and his brass ashtray from Korea.

And the red velvet pincushion beside his polished Colt 44 – surely that couldn't be his? Indeed it was. He took it everywhere, and insisted it must be left with the pins driven in to their heads each evening. Next was an array of innocent-looking thermos flasks and glasses, standing beside bowls of dried fish and other titbits which the Master would snack on during the midnight hour. Because his kidneys had difficulty processing alcohol when he drank heavily, he had to sweat the impurities out. To help him breathe through his skin, as he put it, he sipped fruit juice or buttermilk or whatever his current tipple happened to be.

If he had been drinking at dinner, often the pleasant feeling of being 'jingled', of loving his fellow man, passed with the last course. He sometimes became maudlin alone in his room, and if he couldn't sleep he made notes and planned extensions to the ranch. One night he pulled a book from his bookcase, sociologist Josiah Flynt's autobiography, *My Life*, and on the book's endpapers he noted:

Why should I be sad? land, money, children, wife, health of body, brain, recognition from the world – everything . . . I pore over deeds from days of old Spanish grants, the men who toiled and cleared and planted and gazed with labour-stiffened bodies in these same sunsets and sunrises, the autumn red of grape, the fogs over Sonoma Mountain. These men are gone.

I, too, ride and gaze on all this. And will some day, too be gone. This dreary agitation of the dust . . .

World-sickness – my disintegrating body has been dying since I was born. I am aware that I carry a skeleton inside this flesh, a grinning noseless one, I am not afraid of you. My smashed knees and ankles – ruptured tendons of my thumbs, scars, and marks, arsenic slough on cheek from Australia hospital, broken bone, never set in hand from hitting my horse – my missing teeth . . .

I return across the ranch. Twilight the hunting animals. No mortality in nature, only in man and man has created it.

Another night, Jack fell asleep at his desk, a cigarette still dangling from his lips. His celluloid eyeshade caught fire and exploded. His hair, which he told his barber to cut 'not fancy, you know, but rough', was badly singed.

At last, on 19 June 1910, around 1.30 a.m., Jack got what he wanted most. More than untold wealth. More even than the power of William Randolph Hearst, and certainly more than literary prestige. When Charmian went into labour he lay on the bed beside her, grasped her hand and breathed with her until she could stand the pain no more. The doctors then administered ether and took a baby girl from her. 'Boy or girl, it doesn't matter – so long as it's Charmian's,' he said. He described the infant's fair skin and grey eyes to Charmian: 'Anglo-Saxon through and through!'

Two days later, Charmian awoke to find Jack and Eliza at her bedside. Jack looked grey-faced and distraught. Their daughter had been delivered a seemingly healthy baby, Jack explained, but a doctor had botched the birth. In fact, he had broken the baby's spinal cord. The child, whom they had named Joy, had lived for just thirty-eight hours.

In her grief, Charmian did not realise how seriously ill she was herself. She insisted that Jack go and report on the build-up to the world title fight in Reno between Jim Jeffries and Jack Johnson, on whose outcome he had bet $4,000 (which he would lose when the white Jeffries was knocked out by the black Johnson). When Jack had left, Charmian found a mirror. The haggard face that stared back at her looked close to death.

It would be several weeks before she could leave hospital. 'More babies are being born,' she wrote one day in her diary. 'I learn their voices – some loud and strident, others soft and cooing, conciliatory, caressing – I love to hear them and still must not think.'

A month after the delivery, she had recovered sufficiently to walk to her locker for a robe. There, along with her own clothes, she found a small dress. Joy had worn it for only a few hours.

'How many patients are in the Maternity Cottage?' she asked her nurse one morning.

'Nine mothers and eight babies,' the nurse replied.

'I am the ninth mother,' Charmian wrote. 'But how much better that my arms never nested her, seeing she was to go so soon. She is more a child of the imagination, and must always remain so; but, more tangible than this, are the sweet months of carrying her, when I was so well and happy among the hills, during long trips with Jack, days upon days, and dreaming of the nursery to be. I am a mother – I bore a child – but there is not a child.'

A few hours after Joy's death, Jack went to meet his journalist friend Joseph Noel at the Tavern Café, run by Timothy Muldowney, at the heart of Oakland's Tenderloin area. On the way he bought four copies of Jim Jeffries' autobiography as research for the forthcoming fight.

In an article that appeared two days later in the *San Francisco Examiner*, Jack described what happened next: 'I had the books under my arm when I entered Muldowney's place. He suspected me of being a quack doctor bent on posting some placards. He saw the pasteboard-covered books and believed them to be a package of posters [warning against venereal disease].'

Muldowney and Jack got into an argument which ended in fisticuffs and Jack being ejected from the bar. He then had Muldowney arrested on a charge of battery. Muldowney responded by charging Jack with the same offence. When the case came to trial on 8 July, the presiding judge, George Samuels, dismissed the case.

Jack was furious. For weeks he raged that Muldowney should have been prosecuted. When he discovered that Samuels owned the bar,

Charmian, Jack, Martin Johnson (third from right) and others in Pendruffyn, Solomon Islands, 1908.

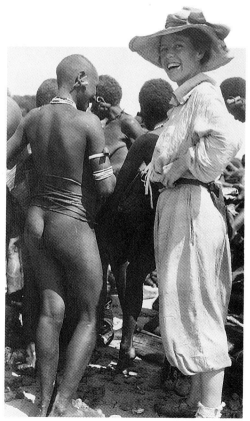

Above Jack and friend in fancy dress, Pendruffyn, 1908.

Right Mate Woman among the 'savages'.

Top Jack and Charmian return from the South Seas aboard the *Tymeric*, 1909.

Above Jack with daughters, Bess and Joan.

The Master looking over his Valley of the Moon.

Right Jack, Charmian and Laurie Smith aboard the *Roamer*.

Below Jack amongst the *Roamer*'s sails.

Above Jack with hs old adversary, French Frank. December 1914.

Right Jack sculling a boat, with Possum aboard, past Petaluma bridge.

Left The 'nature-faker' at rest.

Below Jack aboard the *Roamer*, photographed by Charmian in 1914.

Jack with old colleagues in Mexico, 1914.

Above Jack hunting duck with a Winchester .22 rifle.

Left Jack bandaged because of chronic toothache, aboard the *Roamer*.

Right Jack in furs, Sierra Nevada, 1915.

Below The Ranch of Broken Dreams. Note the terracing in the background.

Jack and his Mate Woman, Honolulu, 1915.

Left Jack in Honolulu, 1915.

Above The Londons six days before Jack's death.

he lost his senses. In a letter to Samuels which was reprinted in newspapers across America, Jack swore: 'someday, somehow, somewhere, I am going to get you . . . get you I will, somewhere, someday, somehow, and I shall get you to the full hilt of the law and the legal procedure that obtains among allegedly civilised men'.

Samuels was quoted in the *San Francisco Chronicle* as saying: 'This young man has long been known as an obstreperous youth . . . It is clear that the letter comes from one who has gained little in the way of judgement by experience in the ways of the world which he claims to have had. He is an Oakland boy, and he is still a boy – a foolish boy, at that.'

Jack had the last laugh, writing a short story, 'The Benefit of the Doubt', which was bought by the *Saturday Evening Post* for $750. It featured Carter Wilson, a professor and author of books on 'Christ and cavemen'. After being beaten up in a bar and suffering the same fate in court as Jack, Wilson finds the judge on his country estate, pulverises him and is then acquitted.

While Charmian recuperated, Jack locked horns with another adversary, the acerbic Hearst journalist Ambrose Bierce. Bierce had tried to persuade George Sterling to give up his friendship with Jack, claiming that Jack's commercial instincts would inevitably corrupt Sterling's artistic aspirations. And during the cruise of the *Snark*, Sterling had written to Bierce expressing concern for Jack's safety. Bierce had replied that Jack was in no danger, because if the *Snark* was wrecked, 'the ocean will refuse to swallow him'. Bierce had also slammed Jack's fiction in several vitriolic letters to Sterling.

When Jack learned that Bierce would be present at the Bohemian Club's annual 'High Jinks', a week-long male-only gathering beside the Russian River in northern California, he wrote to Charmian: 'Damn Ambrose Bierce. I won't look for trouble but, if he jumps me, I'll go him a few at his own game. If we meet, and he's introduced I shall wait for his hand to go out first. If he doesn't hostilities begin right there.'

J.B. Cassell, an associate editor of the *San Francisco Bulletin*, was in earshot when Bierce and Jack met several days later. Jack did not lunge for Bierce. Instead, he offered him a drink.

'Here you are, Bierce, if you don't mind taking a drink from the wildcat of literature.'

'Thank you, London,' said Bierce. 'But why drag in literature?'

'Because,' Jack shot back, 'you're a good judge of verbal tatting, having indulged in it all your life. Have another drink.'

'Here's good health, London, and I'm sorry I wasted even an impoverished pattern on one who thinks civilisation is a slum.'

'Here's how, Bierce, and I think civilisation's a slum only when it's cluttered up with critics. Then it smells bad. Have another drink.'

'Thank you, London. This is good liquor. Very good. If I were sure it would have the improving effect on your manners that it obviously has on your repartee, I should recommend it. By proper indulgence you might in time become a gentleman.'

'Even if you should patronise the same bar all your life, you'd never become that.'

Bierce then turned to George Sterling, who was standing close by. 'Call him off, Sterling. I'll kill him if you don't.'

'I'll tie your breastbone in knots if you start anything,' Jack snapped. 'Have another drink.'

The drinking duel continued late into the night, George Sterling recalled, as Bierce and Jack consumed 'a bottle each of three-star Martell. God knows of what they talked. I was to awaken at seven with the worst headache of my life. Truly they were made of the stuff of heroes.'

When Jack had recovered from his hangover, he took Charmian on a month-long cruise of the local coast and rivers aboard a new yacht, the *Roamer*, which he had purchased after returning from the South Seas. It was mid-October as they sailed from Oakland across the bay of San Francisco and then passed through the creeks and rivers of Benicia, Suisun Bay, the Sacramento and San Joaquin. 'Jack looked much like his piratical self in blue dungarees, his time-honoured "tam" (sailor's cap) pulled down, with a handful of curls, over his sailor-blue eyes,' Charmian wrote.

As his wife slowly regained her strength, Jack reminisced about his days with the Fish Patrol and as an oyster pirate. To his delight, he came across his old adversary French Frank, now a broken seventy-year-old living in a squalid duck-hunter's shack.

While the loss of Joy depressed Jack and Charmian, it also brought them closer together, as they shared their grief and resolved to try for another child. Aboard the *Roamer*, Jack and his 'Mate-Woman' would be at their most intimate over the coming years. As sailors, constantly searching out new adventures on the choppy waters of San Francisco Bay, they were perfectly compatible. Nor did their wanderlust dull once they were on dry land. Seeking to retrace the trails of the pioneers, in autumn 1911 Jack and Charmian would take a three-month, 1500-mile trip through northern California and Oregon in a Studebaker wagon pulled by four of Jack's best horses. The man at the reins still lived as if every day might be his last, as if he would one day 'burn his life out by his enjoyment of it', as Ford Madox Ford put it.

When Jack returned to the Beauty Ranch, however, he often found that problems there had mounted up in his absence. On 16 November 1910 he had made a quick assessment of his financial situation. He had $1200 in his bank account, and three outstanding bills: $900 for life insurance; $500 for taxes; $1000 for his mortgage.

'I'm riding for a fall, financially,' he told Charmian, 'but I'm not worrying – you've never seen me stay down long. I'll work harder than ever.'

Desperate for funds, Jack began to wonder whether he could improve on the deal he had struck with his publishers. While he was receiving a royalty of 20 per cent on every book sold above five thousand copies, he had heard that some star authors had cut better deals. After having published twenty-four books with Macmillan, he began to look elsewhere.

Jack had already fallen out with the company over the loss of his illustrations to *The Cruise of the* Snark, and he believed Brett was not doing enough to promote his new fiction, relying too heavily on Jack's name. Why, for example, had Macmillan not brought out a uniform edition of his works, when men who 'weren't dry behind the ears' when he had started writing were having their 'measly seven and eight and ten volumes out in uniform editions'?

Although *Burning Daylight* had sold well, his most recent books – *South Seas Tales*, *Adventure* and *The Cruise of the* Snark – had failed to take off, and had received mostly negative reviews. Jack was no longer a sure thing, and Brett was not inclined to fight 'tooth and claw' to keep the author of *The Call of the Wild*, which had made Macmillan hundreds of thousands of dollars.

In a letter of 13 June 1911, Brett suggested that Jack negotiate separate contracts for each of his forthcoming books. He also expressed his concern that Jack was turning out too many volumes of short stories and not enough novels. He may have read an interview in which his star author admitted: 'I have no unfinished stories. Invariably I complete every one I start. If it's good, I sign it and send it out. If it isn't good, I sign it and send it out.'

On 20 September, Jack wrote to the publishers Doubleday, Page & Company, asking whether they would be interested in publishing a collection of short stories: 'I am on the eve of severing my iron-bound connection with The Macmillan Company – this of course confidential.'

Jack's disaffection with Macmillan was fuelled by his plot supplier, Sinclair Lewis, who was now working as publicity director at the New York publishers Frederick A. Stokes Company. In a letter dated 1 December 1911, Lewis mischievously detailed how he had asked Charles Hanson Towne, the editor of the *Delineator*, a woman's magazine, and William Morrow, the editor-in-chief at Stokes, how much other famous authors were being paid for their work.

According to Lewis, Sir Arthur Conan Doyle was making fifty cents a word from *Collier's* for his Sherlock Holmes stories; the former President Theodore Roosevelt an incredible dollar a word from *Scribner's* magazine for his African travel pieces; Kipling, fifty cents a word; Jack's old ally Richard Harding Davis $1000 a short story; and the same for Edith Wharton.

For all Lewis's manoeuvring, Stokes did not land their man. Instead, Jack signed with the Century Company. Within months, he regretted the move from Macmillan. Although Century would publish a collection of unremarkable Klondike stories, *Smoke Bellew*, and *The Abysmal Brute*, his short prize-fight novel, as well as *John Barleycorn*, they would do so without the enthusiastic support of their author. Century demanded two books a year, not three or four, and refused to increase the advance for each new book. Jack claimed that the company was slow to pay him. It did not understand that his primary concern was for cash. He needed large, regular sums in order to avert bankruptcy.

By 1913 he would be trying everything possible to wriggle out of the Century contract. Late that year, with relief, he would return to Macmillan, where he would stay until his death. Not only had Century refused to indulge him with large and regular advances of money, they had also wanted more editorial control over his work than he was prepared to accept. George Brett, by contrast, had always understood the severity of Jack's cash-flow problems. And although he was increasingly concerned that Jack was turning out too much too quickly, Brett granted his star author total creative control of his work.

It was in order to finalise his deal with Century that Jack had planned to visit New York early in 1912. He had promised Charmian that they would not stay too long. As soon as it could be arranged, they would go on to Baltimore and sign on as crew – Charmian as steward, Jack as third mate, although their duties would be minimal – aboard a three-master bound for Seattle, via Cape Horn. The voyage would, Jack hoped, provide excellent background material for an adventure novel for young adults, *The Mutiny of the* Elsinore. It would also, he swore to Charmian, be a chance for him to dry out.

'Almost any passage in our companionship I contemplate with more pleasure than that 1912 winter in "Gotham",' Charmian recalled. 'The trip had been one of our happiest; but, once off the train, and his enthusiasm expressed over the new Pennsylvania Station, it was the old story. The City reached into him and plucked to light the least admirable qualities.'

14

Whiskey and Rye

> I prefer living to writing.
>
> JACK LONDON, letter to Alice Lyndon, 29 July 1909

MANHATTAN HAD A WAY of bringing out the worst in Jack. Whenever he arrived there, it was as if he was determined to play the carousing provincial, one eye on every young woman who crossed his path, the other on the lookout for a new late-night bar. He had promised himself one last fling before throwing John Barleycorn overboard as he sailed round Cape Horn. Within days he had left Charmian in an apartment on Morningside Heights while he went to boxing matches, frolicked with long-legged chorus girls and trawled Broadway's fashionable bars before ending the night at Dunstan's restaurant for a dawn breakfast of Irish bacon and eggs.

Charmian sometimes read about these late-night exploits in the morning papers. It was not only the gossip columns which increased Jack's notoriety. He was also plagued by doubles, men who gave his name instead of their own when caught bouncing cheques, in a bar fight or in another woman's bed. 'I have been pestered for a long time with a double,' he complained, 'who cashes bad paper on banks, in my name; in my name makes love to married women, spinsters, virgins, and widows with large families; and does a few-score other things that are embarrassing.'

Aside from meeting editors at Century, Jack socialised with old friends such as Arnold Genthe, Anna Strunsky and Emma Goldman, and writers such as Mary Austin and Rex Beach, who enjoyed enormous success with his tales about the Klondike. He spent several hours arguing politics with the famed anarchist Alexander Berkman, and agreed to write an introduction to Berkman's now-classic *Prison Memoirs of an Anarchist*. Berkman was to reject it because Jack refused to endorse anarchism.

Several of Jack's interviews in New York were with Sophie Irene Loeb, a thirty-five-year-old divorcee who was making a name for herself as a campaigning journalist for the *Evening World*. According to Clarice Statz, Charmian knew that Jack often visited Sophie's apartment and frequently spoke with her on the phone. Bitter that he was spending so much of his time with others, she consoled herself that once they were at sea, bound for the South Atlantic, she would be able to welcome back 'the sane and lovable boy'. But when Jack did not return one night, her anguish finally overwhelmed her.

Joseph Noel, whose account of Jack's antics in New York is supported by Charmian's own diaries, describes one morning when Charmian lost her composure in public. In a crowded subway train, she told Jack to keep his 'house in order'. Jack glared at her. She knew the rules. He had laid them down clearly enough, hadn't he? Very early in their marriage, he had warned her: 'Don't forget what I have been and been through. There may, mark, I say only may, come times when the temptation to "drift" – for an hour, or a day, will stick up its head; and I may follow. I have drifted all my life – curiosity, that burning desire to know.'

With 'unmistakable emphasis', Jack now told Charmian that he would do whatever he pleased.

Her face turned grey. If only she could pull him away from New York.

'I'm hungry for a tall ship,' she muttered.

One evening, while out drinking with Joseph Noel and an editor, Jack passed the Flatiron Building, which was where New York's male prostitutes congregated. Jack's attention was drawn to a small group of them, 'with little dabs of rouge on their cheeks and mascara on their eyelashes'.

'Arthur Rimbaud, the French poet, fell into the hands of homosexuals,' the editor lamented. 'The soul of a great artist was done to death by just such scoundrels as these. I'd hang them all.'

'They were soldiers that perverted Rimbaud?' Jack asked.

'Yes.'

'Sailors are that way too. Prisoners in cells are also that way. Whenever you herd men together and deny them women their latent sex perversions come to the surface.'

Jack told his companions about the 'fo'castle lovers' he had encountered aboard the *Sophie Sutherland*. His description was, in Noel's words, 'frank, brutal, disgusting'.

'A man should love women, and plenty of them,' said Jack. He refused to walk another step, so they climbed into a taxi-cab. 'I won't walk in the country where the earth is soft to the feet,' he smiled. 'Why should I do it on these hard pavements?'

After eating 'excessively thick steaks' in the Liberty Chop House on Cedar Street, they continued to a nearby graveyard. A frosty wind blew but Jack was oblivious to the bone-numbing gusts, for they were now in the 'great dark canyons of the money changers' – Wall Street.

'Oh, this is where it's done,' said Jack. 'This little spot has set the standard for all the rest of the country. What they do here becomes right. They have the power to make it right. I've seen it before, but always in the daytime. It's more sinister at night.'

A few days later, Jack and Noel again hit the town. This time they spent the night at a gambling club along with a group of burlesque-club managers whose language would have made even Captain Wolf Larsen blush. After several drinks, Jack and his new friends sat down to play poker for 'stakes that would make an amateur's eyes bulge'. As usual, with a few whiskey chasers warming his belly, Jack began to talk lyrically about the Beauty Ranch and Wolf House. One of the club owners asked him what he was going to do when he had built his stone mansion.

'Live in it,' Jack replied curtly. 'I'll be away from everybody I don't want around.'

From now on, people would have to come to him, perched on his mountaintop. He would not seek out companionship. Never again would he waste his time on cities such as New York and the crowded humanity that mired them. When a reporter later asked if he thought the city was 'the best place for his observations', Jack vented his true feelings.

'Great Scott, no, no! I must have the open, the big open. No big city for me, and above all not New York. I think it is the cocksure feeling of superiority which the people of the metropolis feel over the rest of the country that makes me rage.'

Jack had no interest in painting, opera or the *avant garde*. New York reminded him of how alienated he felt from 'bourgeois' culture, and of the rejection he had suffered at the hands of editors when he had first tried to write.

In her 1907 novel *Ancestors*, Gertrude Atherton had described how San Francisco's temptations and easy living often proved fatal to artistic ambition: 'Never was such a high percentage of brains in one city. But they must get out. And if they don't go young they don't go at all. San Francisco is a disease.' By 1912 many of Jack's peers, including several members of the Crowd, had moved from California to the more competitive New York, often to salvage their careers: Atherton, Anna Strunsky, Mary Austin, Joseph Noel, Arnold Genthe and Frank Norris. George Sterling would follow in 1914 after divorcing Carrie, preferring Greenwich Village to seaside bohemia in Carmel.

Jack remained in California. Yet he could not perhaps help wondering whether he might have risen to greater heights if he had moved to New York. 'London's failure to exorcise New York's hold upon his imagination,' Kevin Starr has noted, 'dramatised a larger California dilemma. London, after all, so uniquely a son of California, remained committed to regional living while the others fled east – and yet even he could not be at peace with his decision.'

Not a second too soon, on 1 March 1912, the hour arrived for Jack and Charmian's departure from Baltimore aboard the *Dirigo*, a three-thousand ton, four-masted barque, bound for Seattle via Cape Horn. While waiting for Jack to return from the barber, Charmian sat in their hotel room writing farewell letters. Suddenly, the door cracked open. She heard Jack giggling with Nakata.

'Wait until Mrs London sees me!'

Jack's head was 'as naked as a billiard ball'. As if to atone for the suffering he had caused her in New York, he had had it shaved. When he saw Charmian's shocked expression, he began to laugh.

'But it isn't funny,' she said, beginning to cry.

'Oh, now don't feel badly,' he reassured her. 'It's such a good rest for my head – I often did it in the old days.'

That afternoon, just before embarking, Charmian and Jack visited Edgar Allan Poe's grave. Despite the presence of a photographer, Charmian could not hide her red eyes. Surrounded by local dignitaries, she shivered in new fox furs. Beside her, Jack peeped furtively from below a wide-brimmed hat. It was a poignant photograph, capturing for posterity a moment when a short-story writer, whom the critics were increasingly dismissing as a hack, stood in homage to a master, long dead, who had also been written off during his lifetime and whose immortality was, more than sixty years after his death, yet to be assured.

Jack London and Edgar Allan Poe had a great deal in common. Both would have their literary reputations revived after their deaths. The two men's pathologies and addictions were also almost identical, and both understood that 'deep down in the roots of the race is fear'. As the critic Earle Labor has written, they were both 'moody, often lonely, individuals who yearned for the securities of home, companion-ship, and love – and whose basic insecurities were concealed under the cloak of reckless egotism only to be manifest in a weakness for alcohol'.

That evening, under a 'cold but sparkling sky', Charmian began a diary of the five-month voyage ahead of them. 'Jack's shaved head,' she wrote. 'Try not to look at him at all! AWFUL! – Jack's last drink day for duration of voyage . . . An unpromising crew, mostly landlubbers to the eye. We ask for chanteys (shanties), and Mr Fred Mortimer, first mate, obligingly gets them to sing, the few who know chanteys, and leads off to hearten the weaklings, few of them sober.'

On one of the first nights at sea, drinking became the subject of conversation at dinner. 'I never drink on duty,' Mortimer said. 'I drink very little anyway, just a glass now and again on shore with the fellows.'

'That is what I am working toward,' Jack replied. 'I have, by putting myself, for the first time in my life where I am absolutely free for months of alcohol, with alcohol purged from my system . . . learned, to my absolute satisfaction, that I am not an alcoholic in any sense of the word.'

For the rest of the voyage, not a drop of alcohol passed Jack's lips. Each day he went without a drink, he became even more sure that he would be able to put his days of binge drinking behind him for good. So much so, in fact, that he was considering writing a confession of his debauches with John Barleycorn. On 16 April Charmian noted in her diary:

> Jack is swinging along steadily (his habit!) on *Valley of the Moon*; but I think he has in mind his 'alcoholic memoirs', *John Barleycorn*, for an early opus. Anyway, he has been copying out all his scribbled notes of years past, for J.B. And I am finding them very interesting indeed. He is all for youth being deprived of the chance to learn a taste for alcohol. The object of this book, more or less autobiographical (with the artist touch of exaggeration of his own case in order to point his moral) is to make the world a better place for YOUTH.

One afternoon, as Jack walked the *Dirigo*'s decks, Charmian called to him. She had already put on her boxing gloves, and handed him his. The bemused crew gathered around, 'grinning the tops of their heads nearly off'. For some minutes, Charmian fended off Jack's blows. Then he landed a few punches to her stomach and head, dazing her slightly. At least he hadn't drawn blood, like the time he gave her mild concussion on their second wedding anniversary.

Beaten in the ring, Charmian dared Jack to climb high into the rigging and sit in the crow's nest. A few minutes later he was scrambling ahead of her, a safety rope tied around his waist. Every few seconds he looked back and smiled at her through his gritted false teeth, his heart pounding. The South Atlantic, ice-cold and grey, was soon ninety feet below. Jack clambered onto the small platform; his breathless wife, grinning from ear to ear, followed. After catching her breath, she pulled out a piece of embroidery and set to work with her needle. Jack opened a book and began to read to her.

All afternoon they sat in the swaying crow's nest. Jack talked of his boyhood, and about the adventure books that had made him long to see the world. High above the lurching deck of the *Dirigo*, with the lethal waters around Cape Horn getting nearer by the hour, Jack reminisced about his youth – 'lawless, wild and free'. It was as much to seek adventure as to escape John Barleycorn, he explained, that he first went to sea.

'Cape Horn on the starboard bow!'

'Gee – you folks are lucky!' Mortimer cried out.

At 8.30 a.m. on 10 May 1912, Jack and Charmian could make out in the murky distance the rugged coastline of Cape Horn, the southernmost tip of America.

'I tell you,' Mortimer said, 'I've made this passage more times than I can remember, and I haven't laid eyes on that there island since 1882. The fog has never raised.'

As they rounded the Horn, Jack stared at the rotting hulks of wrecked ships. This black coast had once greeted Vasco da Gama, Charles Darwin and Captain Cook. How they must have shivered and cursed the place as an outcrop of hell.

Jack could remember the first time he had gone to sea aboard the *Sophie Sutherland*. His young lungs had filled with the fresh breeze as he left a wasted youth in his wake. Now, twenty years later, he was again filling his lungs with the ocean air. Aboard the *Dirigo* he had stashed more than fifty books, including Richard Henry Dana's classic *Two Years Before the Mast* and *The Letters of Robert Louis Stevenson*, and he would lose himself in the pages of other perennial favourites: Herman Melville's *Moby-Dick* and *Typee*. He could still sense the swell of the Pacific and taste its salty spray when he dipped into them. But the book he now prized most was *Signa*, by Louise de la Ramée, the tale of a ragged boy living in rural poverty in Italy. In New York he had found a battered copy in a second-hand bookstore, and had stowed it with his other favourites.

For several days he read sections to Charmian, who would later recall: 'I listened, not always with dry eyes, to the rhythmic, caressing voice, as Jack reread the loved romance which had opened to his groping intelligence the gates to unsurmised beauty.' When Jack had read *Signa* as a boy, forty pages at the end of his copy were missing. Now, thirty years later, he discovered the ending. The small boy grew up to be a world-famous artist.

While he continued to dry out, Jack played deck games and bagged trophies for his woman – at Charmian's request he caught a huge albatross in a net. Nakata, whose shipboard duties included taxidermy, stuffed the bird which had proved the Ancient Mariner's downfall. Before they turned in for the night they admired spectacular sunsets, sat awestruck beneath sparkling night skies and read each other their favourite poetry. A powerful intimacy recharged their sex life. As they had done throughout their marriage when they were happiest, they spent many afternoons making love. Several weeks after leaving Baltimore, Charmian felt unwell.

'What's the matter with you, Mate?' Jack asked.

'I don't quite know, unless it's what we both hope,' she replied.

'Think,' he said softly, 'a baby of yours, of ours . . .'

The good news was, however, overshadowed by Charmian's continuing grief over Joy's death. 'And here is Joy-Baby's second birthday,' she wrote in her diary. 'What is it all about, when there was a baby, and there is no Baby. Never even seen by me. Oh, well, I was not put on earth to repine. And I am not lonely; there are two to be sorry, and, now, hopeful. Oh, yes, HOPEFUL. We are fairly certain our dreams will come about.'

It was almost five months before they received word from an 'almost forgotten world'. While they had read Tennyson and rekindled their love for each other, 1517 people had drowned at the opposite end of the Atlantic, aboard a supposedly unsinkable ship called the *Titanic*. Another piece of news was equally dismaying. Their 'old acquaintance, President Alfaro of Ecuador, and his son (a West Point man) had been murdered in Quito and their headless bodies dragged through the streets'.

Finally, on Friday 26 July 1912, the *Dirigo* docked in Seattle. Sensing that she would not have Jack to herself again for some time, Charmian could barely bring herself to leave the ship. Tears welled in her eyes at the thought of the distractions that would soon, inevitably, crowd her out of his life again.

A fortnight later, she miscarried. With the spots of blood that first alerted her to the loss went all hope of having a child. Jack, she noted, was 'sadly cast down, though he said little'. As a means of extending the London line, the 'Kid Woman' had failed yet again.

*   *   *

'In the working-class world, disasters do not come singly,' Jack had written in his powerful review of Upton Sinclair's best-selling exposé of the Chicago stockyards, *The Jungle*, published in 1906. High in the redwood-clad hills above the wineries of Glen Ellen, he soon discovered that, even for men who build castles in the sky, calamities can arrive in multitudes. 'My face changed forever in that year of 1913,' he would later tell Charmian. 'It has never been the same since.'

The year began disastrously, and grew steadily worse. One of his prized mares, in foal, was found in a field with a bullet through her brain, possibly shot by a disgruntled farm-hand or a jealous neighbour. The spring brought not rain but a plague of grasshoppers which gorged themselves on his eucalyptus trees. The mounting cost of Wolf House, now nearing completion, had forced him to remortgage everything he owned. As if this were not enough, Jack also had to contend with an unfaithful wife, or so it appeared.

Charmian had become intimate with one of the most frequent guests to the Beauty Ranch: Allan Dunn, a handsome, English-born aspiring writer in his twenties, who had first met her and Jack when he interviewed them for *Sunset* magazine just before they had left for the South Seas. He and Charmian shared a love of riding and landscape painting, and had spent several days together, painting and taking long walks through the Beauty Ranch. On 3 March Charmian noted: 'Allan and I ride to Sonoma Mountain and have a glorious time watching the fog clear and crowd in again. Lovely, rainless weather – booful, but bad for ranch. Trees blossoming and flowers. Having a lovely experience.'

Was the relationship between Charmian and Dunn purely platonic? Was Charmian simply using Dunn to make Jack more aware of her needs? Jack had become so preoccupied with the ranch and his guests that he had neglected her.

Like Bess before her, Charmian had grown tired of the hangers-on, as she saw them, who left little time for her to share with Jack. In particular she complained about Frank Strawn-Hamilton, a pseudo-philosopher whom Jack treated as a guru; James H. Seymour, a homeless poet; Spiro Orfans, a carpenter and former socialist; and 'Lone Wolf', another of the self-educated tramps who had pitched permanent camp on the Beauty Ranch. While Jack had lost touch with many of his socialist friends from Oakland, he remained loyal to his dear 'bums', with whom he felt a bond that stretched back to his own tramping days. All his life he had supported others because he felt duty-bound, and he reacted angrily when Charmian questioned his generosity. On 19 November 1912 he had written to her:

> As for Hamilton, I get more sheer pleasure out of an hour's talk with him than all my inefficient Italian labourers have ever given me. He pays his way. My God, the labourers never [underlined three times] have. The Ranch has never lost very much money on . . . the fellows who've had a few meals & beds out of me. The Ranch has lost a hell of a lot of money on the weak sticks of $1.75 cash per day labourers who've fattened off me & on me . . . And I give these paltry things of paltry value out of my heart. I've not much heart-throb left for my fellow beings. Shall I cut this wee bit thing out too?

On 10 March 1913, Charmian drove Allan Dunn to the station in Glen Ellen and found Jack waiting when she returned to the Beauty Ranch. They began to discuss her intimacy with Dunn. Suddenly, Jack realised how alone and helpless he would be without her. If she deserted him, he would lose a mother and a lover, a secretary and a friend.

'I am the proudest man in the world,' he told her. 'I have found that I have a heart.'

Charmian's intimacy with Dunn had succeeded, it appeared, in making Jack aware of how much he needed her. A powerful intensity returned to their sex life, and they spent hours 'making love to death' on the living-room floor. On 14 March Jack wrote to an editor at *Cosmopolitan*, Roland Phillips, with a 'splendid motif for a novel': 'Three characters only – a mighty trio in a mighty situation, in a magnificently beautiful environment. Each of the three is good; each of the three is big. It will be a winner. It is all sex from start to finish – in which no sexual adventure is actually achieved, and in which, nevertheless, is all the guts of sex, coupled with strength.'

The novel, *The Little Lady of the Big House*, was to be his weakest – as its title alone suggests. It would differ markedly in tone from the

also highly autobiographical *The Valley of the Moon*, which he completed aboard the *Dirigo*, before Charmian's involvement with Dunn.

The Valley of the Moon celebrated the California good life. Again,
it was a love story set in the redeeming countryside, that happy place
in the sun which Jack believed he had finally found on the Beauty
Ranch. The novel's heroine, Saxon Brown, a laundress, meets and
falls in love with Billy Roberts, a union activist. But theirs is far
from a conventional courtship. Billy's methods of seduction confirm
Herbert Wace's belief in *The Kempton–Wace Letters*: 'the natural
expression of the love instinct is bestial and brutal and violent'.

In an early scene, Billy punches Saxon on the chin: '[her brain]
snapped with a white flash of light, while her whole body relaxed,
numb and weak, and her vision reeled and blurred'. Next, he beats
her to the point of 'paralysis, accompanied by a stoppage of breath'.
They finally make love, but only after Billy grasps her in a half-Nelson
until 'she felt that her arm was a pipe-stem about to break'.

Despite Billy's violence, the couple marry. Descended from California pioneers, they scrub for a living among the proletariat, forced
to compete with Italian and Chinese immigrants for crumbs from the
capitalists' table. Billy believes that his union activities will eventually
improve their lot, but he is arrested during a strike and thrown in
jail. On his release, fellow strikers mistake him for a scab and break
his arms. As if this were not enough, Saxon suffers a miscarriage when
strikers and police fight a pitched battle near her home.

The couple decide to forsake the city, and set out on a year-long
quest for a plot of land on which to settle and become farmers. Finally
they buy a small ranch in the Valley of the Moon and live happily ever
after, distanced from industrial warfare and their working-class roots.

Through Billy, Jack expressed his growing disaffection with American socialism: 'Look at the socialists themselves. They're always dis-
agreeing, splitting up, an' firin' each other out of the party. The whole
thing's bughouse, that's what, an' I almost get dippy myself thinkin'
about it. The point I can't get out of my mind is that we want things
now.'

The Valley of the Moon received mixed reviews. 'London has written
a man's size book, containing a man's size idea,' declared the *New
York Times*. 'The land is still the ancient Mother, from whom we

come, and to whom we go. On her breath is healing and in her lap is peace ... If only Mr London would not write (to use one of his own locutions) so much like a Mr Man-in-a-Hurry!'

The magazine *Current Opinion* also accused Jack of rushing his work: 'Jack London has recently informed a listening world that he would do much more work if only he did not sleep so much. We are sometimes tempted to wish that Mr London would not sleep a little longer but would not work quite so hard when he is awake; in other words that he would stop and think a little more. Then he might really become a great American storyteller (for he has the gift), and not merely a popular romancer.'

The Little Lady of The Big House was further evidence, as Carolyn Johnston has argued, that 'from 1910 onwards, the distinction between [Jack's] fictional and actual worlds blurred, as he seemed to be enacting his own fictions.' Unlike *The Valley of the Moon*, the novel reflected a growing ambivalence towards 'the healing power of the wilderness'. Planned during 1913 – Jack's *annus horribilis* – it is, as Kevin Starr has written, 'a story about death, the last in a long line of apocalyptic fictions by London, in which life battles against death, desire against satiety, civilisation against chaos'.

The novel's protagonist, Dick Forrest, leaves home to become a sailor, then attends a crammer and the University of California before going to the Klondike and Mexico. A superb farmer who breeds prize-winning hogs, Forrest identifies with a magnificent stallion, Mountain Lad, a symbol of masculine potency throughout the novel. Forrest even looks like Jack, his mouth 'girlish and sweet to a degree that did not hide the firmness to which the lips could set on due provocation'. His wife Paula is barren, suffers insomnia and 'plays the piano like a man'. Forrest calls her his 'boy girl, the child that never grew up'. To a remarkable degree, she resembles Charmian.

Benevolent critics have argued that Jack intended *The Little Lady of the Big House* as an apology to Charmian for ignoring her needs, and as a critique of himself, a 'rational' man, cut off from his feelings and feminine side. A success as a scientific farmer, Forrest is a failure as husband and lover, having applied the scientific management principles of 'Taylorism' to every area of his life. His marriage, outwardly blissful, is in fact a sham.

When Evan Graham, 'good stuff, old American stock, a Yale man', arrives on the ranch, Paula falls for him, as Charmian had for Allan Dunn. But she is still attached to Dick who, after contemplating suicide, insists that she choose between him and his rival. The dilemma is finally too much for Paula, who shoots herself. 'She beat me to it,' thinks Dick.

Does this climax reveal a subconscious wish to harm Charmian after her dalliance with Dunn? Perhaps. As Andrew Sinclair has perceptively noted, far more revealing are Paula's last moments, which hint at Jack's use of pain-killers such as morphine, belladona and heroin, all legal at the time. He had first taken them in the Solomon Islands to ease the pain of his skin condition, and in 1913 he had spent many afternoons receiving dental treatment for agonising gum disease.

Paula is brought back to life by a doctor who administers a strong stimulant, but then injects her with a giant overdose of morphine to put her out of her misery:

> 'Sleepy, sleepy,' she twittered in mimicry of drowsy birds. 'I am ready, doctor. Stretch the skin tight, first. You know I don't like to be hurt – Hold me tight, Dick.'
>
> . . . 'Sleepy, sleepy, boo'ful sleepy,' she murmured drowsily, after a time.
>
> Semi-consciously she half-turned on her side, curved her free arm on the pillow and nestled her head on it, and drew her body up in nestling curves in the way Dick knew she loved to sleep.
>
> After a long time, she sighed faintly, and began so easily to go that she was gone before they guessed. From without, the twittering of the canaries bathing in the fountain pene-trated the silence of the room, and from afar came the trumpet-ing of Mountain Lad and the silver whinny of the Fotherington Princess.

The Little Lady of the Big House, whose ending made Jack and Charmian weep in each other's arms, reflected other dashed hopes.

For several years, Jack had kept an eye on the nascent motion-picture industry. In 1903 he had read about *The Great Train Robbery*, a 'flicker' created by Edwin S. Porter. The film established modern-day film technique through its pioneering use of cuts. By 1908 eight thousand nickelodeons across America were pulling in twenty-five million viewers a week, providing distributors with unimagined profits.

Jack hoped that motion pictures would one day make him as wealthy as Dick Forrest. 'There is a pot of money we shall get hold of yet,' he told Eliza, 'if the lawyers don't eat it all up.' According to the *Los Angeles Express*, he was so taken with the possibilities of the new medium that he wanted to star in film versions of his best-sellers. 'I shall appear as the leading actor in all my own short stories and novels dramatised into motion pictures,' he told a reporter. 'Will it mean a fortune to me? Well, I'll buy two or three Jersey cows for my Valley of the Moon ranch with the proceeds.'

In February 1913, Jack signed a deal with the Balboa Amusement Producing Company, granting exclusive motion picture rights to all his stories in return for a share of future profits. Just four months later, he backed out of the deal on the grounds that the company had failed to produce four films by 1 July, as stipulated in the contract. Several weeks later Hobart Bosworth, an actor, director and producer in Hollywood, visited Glen Ellen to propose another deal. He wanted to film *The Sea Wolf*, he told Jack, and swore that his version would have 'real artistic merit'.

Bosworth himself would play Wolf Larsen, and direct and produce the film. Because he was operating on a shoestring, as did most early Hollywood producers, he couldn't offer Jack any money up front, but promised him 50 per cent of net profits. 'Gruff and businesslike', Jack agreed, and just weeks later the first scenes of *The Sea Wolf* were shot aboard a rented yacht in San Francisco Bay. 'Jack and Charmian were aboard with us,' Bosworth recalled, 'watching all the scenes of the panic among the passengers, and the lifeboats, like a pair of children.' Within a month, as was usual in early Hollywood, the film was finished. Jack was delighted when he saw a rough cut: Bosworth had played Wolf Larsen to perfection. 'Great Scott, man, I'm amazed that you've stuck to my story,' Jack told him. 'I thought the movies always changed everything.'

Due to lack of copyright protection, Bosworth was not the only showman to put *The Sea Wolf* on the silver screen in 1913. Two other producers, Jack discovered, had made their own pirate versions.

Immediately he decided to sue for compensation, and in the process hopefully establish an important precedent on the control of motion picture rights. There was, he convinced himself, far more at stake than intellectual property rights in this new battle. 'If they get me,' he told Charmian, 'you might as well know that we'll lose everything we have – the ranch even; everything.' In which case, he added, they would escape for good. With what little they would have left, they would 'buy a big ship outright . . . And we'll put in a fireplace . . . and take your grand piano, and be quit forever of a country where a man's life work can be cheated out of him by a lot of theatrical sharks.'

One of these sharks was none other than his journalist friend Joseph Noel. Although Jack had granted Noel dramatic rights to *The Sea Wolf* in 1905, he now wanted them back, and threatened to fight him 'in every court in the country'. The dispute between the two would rumble on until the end of Jack's life. In the process, Noel would become one of his most malicious detractors, responsible for many rumours which exaggerated the extent of Jack's drinking and womanising.

Jack's activities in New York, which he was forced to visit several times during his battle over copyright, often appeared to lend credence to Noel's gossip. One night he and a burlesque club acquaintance were taking a singer and a chorus girl home in a taxi when it was involved in a collision.

'When we turned over,' he wrote to Charmian, 'our taxi flew to pieces as if it had been exploded by a bomb. As usual, I was under the whole pile. Four other persons were mixed with me, mostly on top of me – And broken glass! I lay and spat it out of my mouth for a very long time . . . Both my arms are black and blue, skin off knuckles of my right hand, forehead cut with glass, nose sore, left cheek bruised, right cheek so bruised it looks as if somebody had really kicked me there.'

If Charmian did not already suspect it, she must have begun to doubt Jack's fidelity when she received a telegram from a woman who signed herself 'Amy'. According to Amy, Jack was spending most of his time in New York with a woman who lived at the Van Cortland Hotel on West Forty-Eighth Street, just off Times Square. Jack denied the allegation, protesting that he often visited the hotel for late-night drinks with his burlesque-club friends. In any case, Charmian was far superior, he insisted, to any of the women he met in that great 'man-trap' New York.

'Oh, I know, your thoroughbredness that is the one time irk and the highest joy to me,' he assured her. 'No man may ride a thorough-bred mare without tenseness and irritation along with the correspond-ing joy that is aroused by the very tenseness and irritation. You've never seen me infatuated with cows. Ergo – my arms are around you, as they shall always have to be around you for love of you and appreciation of you – you damned thoroughbred!'

While in New York, Jack also helped set up the Authors' League of America. Along with Rex Beach, Booth Tarkington, Ida Tarbell, Ellen Glasgow, President Theodore Roosevelt and other concerned authors, he tried to change the law so that he would never again have to see two unauthorised versions of *The Sea Wolf* appearing in theatres in one Los Angeles street, as happened in 1913. When Congress passed tougher copyright laws, the Authors' League held a banquet to cele-brate the victory. President Woodrow Wilson had been invited to make the after-dinner speech, but instead sent his Secretary of State, the notoriously pompous William Jennings Bryan.

'Young writing men and women of America, do you realise your responsibility?' Bryan began, pausing to let his words reach the furthest corners of the hushed banquet hall. From one of them came a voice which 'sounded thin and slight in contrast with Bryan's organ tones, but which carried'.

'Bunk!' the heckler shouted, shrugging off attempts by others to keep him quiet.

The audience looked in the direction of the voice. There sat Jack, according to one report, with a half-bottle of gin and a packet of cigarettes before him, grinning from ear to ear.

'Blah, blah.'

Bryan started to point out the writers' duty to their 'country and our Creator' and then to lecture them about 'impurity' and 'alcoholism'.

'Hokum!'

Finally, to drown out Jack's heckling, several writers began to clap during Bryan's pauses.

That Jack could make such a spectacle of himself was not, perhaps, surprising, given his past record. But in 1913 an outburst like this was astonishing. It was if he wanted the entire nation to call him a hypocrite. He had, after all, just written *John Barleycorn*, a book which would significantly influence the growth of the Prohibition movement in America.

A brave and groundbreaking book, *John Barleycorn* detailed one binge after another, and described Jack's years of heavy drinking in terms that every alcoholic would recognise. Particularly effective were passages describing the maudlin feelings induced by alcohol which Jack dubbed 'the white logic': 'the messenger of truth beyond truth, the antithesis of life, cruel and bleak as interstellar space, pulseless and frozen as absolute zero, dazzling with the frost of irrefragable logic and unforgettable fact'.

The academic John Sutherland has called the book 'a classic of American autobiography': 'In terms of London's remarkable life, the early chapters are among the most self-revealing things the author wrote. The later chapters are among the most thoughtful things he ever wrote . . . Too often London's supporters have neglected the book out of existence, downgrading it as mere fiction so as to protect their man's reputation.'

John Barleycorn was both bully pulpit and confession box. The book's enduring power, however, results from its relentless drama and often crystalline prose. When writing honestly about himself, Jack became a different writer to the man whose name was emblazoned on the covers of dime romances.

'I achieved a condition in which my body was never free from alcohol,' he admitted. 'Nor did I permit myself to be away from alcohol. If I travelled to out-of-the-way places, I declined to run the risk of finding them dry. I took a quart, or several quarts, along in my grip . . . I was carrying a beautiful alcoholic conflagration around with me. The thing fed on its own heat and flamed the fiercer. There was no time in all my waking time, that I didn't want a drink.'

Upton Sinclair, the son of an alcoholic, would chronicle the alcoholism of his contemporaries in *The Cup of Fury*. Among them were some of America's finest writers: Scott Fitzgerald, Theodore Dreiser,

Sinclair Lewis, Jack's old opponent Ambrose Bierce, George Sterling and Jack himself:

> Jack had hurtled upwards on the basis of his own unbounded talent, overflowing good spirits, and persevering courage. Think of him as he takes stock of himself: he has everything in the world to make him happy. He has a wife who is devoted to him, an estate which is his dream of loveliness, horses to ride, and a host of friends riding at his side . . . He has fame – his name is known and honoured all over the world. But the only thing that's important now is a bottle. Not even a bottle – just a drink!

Jack had fooled himself before that he was too strong-willed and self-aware to commit the sins of the characters he created: the ghosts such as Dick Forrest, Martin Eden and Wolf Larsen who haunted his subconscious. Although the protagonist in *John Barleycorn* was himself, he still clung to the belief that he was someone else, not the dipsomaniac who heard the white logic screaming inside his head. He insisted that alcoholism was an extremely rare, congenital condition, and denied that alcohol was addictive, mistakenly describing it as a stimulant rather than a depressant.

When the *Saturday Evening Post* serialised *John Barleycorn* and Century published it in August, Jack struck paydirt. The book became an instant best-seller, the most widely discussed book of 1913. When a film version appeared the following year, it played to packed audiences across America, becoming one of the most successful of all early Hollywood films.

Not since the publication of *The Call of the Wild*, a decade before, had Jack been so universally acclaimed. In October 1913 the *San Francisco Examiner* declared *John Barleycorn* a 'vivid and palpitating human document', by 'this big brother of our own with his prizefighter's jaw and philosopher's forehead, with his instincts of a caveman and aspirations of a poet'. The *New York Times* offered rare praise: 'perhaps the most vivid and compelling narrative he has ever written . . . A distinguished achievement, a book surely destined to a high place in the world's esteem.'

The Prohibition Party, the Young Christian Temperance Union

and the Women's Christian Temperance Union all pushed the book on their members. Jack was not slow to see other promotional opportunities, and even served as vice president of a National Defense Association which drafted a 'No Drunkard Bill' proposing that every citizen be permitted only two binges a year. 'I am absolutely convinced that the no drunkard plan is the finest thing that has yet been presented,' Jack declared.

Some reviewers, while praising the book, pointed to a glaring inconsistency, and questioned whether Jack really had stopped drinking. 'As a tract against the saloon, and a professed argument for woman suffrage in order that the saloon be done away with,' cautioned the *Nation*, 'it will please the prohibitionists and suffragists. As a record of glorious sprees and multifarious good-fellowship, it is capable of exciting thirst in the thirst-minded. As a tract, it suffers from this drawback that the author does not pretend to have "sworn off", or even express a wish to swear off.' Upton Sinclair, an over-zealous teetotaller, later commented: 'That the work of a drinker who had no intention of stopping drinking should become a major propaganda piece in the campaign for Prohibition is surely one of the choice ironies in the history of alcohol.'

'*John Barleycorn* is frankly and truthfully autobiographical,' Jack insisted. 'There is no poetic licence in it. It is a straight, true narrative of my personal experiences, and is toned *down*, not up.' But his frankness only stretched so far. He described how the white logic had left him feeling suicidal, with 'but one freedom, namely the anticipating of the day of his death'. But he would go no further, leaving the question of his mental state ominously uncertain in light of the book's conclusion, a classic example of alcoholic denial:

> No, I decided; I shall take my drink on occasion. With all the books on my shelves, with all the thoughts of the thinkers shaded by my particular temperament, I decided coolly and deliberately that I should continue to do what I had been trained to want to do. I would drink – but, oh, more skilfully, more discreetly, than ever before.

Nowhere in *John Barleycorn* did Jack mention his use of opiates as a substitute for alcohol, which could numb his mind but not physical pain. One morning in July, Charmian found him bent double in agony. After an emergency operation he was informed that his kidneys were badly diseased, told to stop drinking and given a prescription for painkillers such as heroin and morphine.

Jack was still recovering from his operation in late August. Only his excitement at the imminent completion of Wolf House distracted him from his health problems. Having lavished $65,000 on his castle in the sky, he was at last seeing the final touches put to it. Only the interior woodwork and a few minor jobs needed to be completed. According to one celebrated architect, Harrison Fisher, Jack's new home was 'the most beautiful in the west'.

The left-wing press, however, regarded it as all the evidence they needed to hang Jack as a hypocrite and traitor to the Cause. At a time when the local Socialist Labor Party was desperately short of funds, campaigners resented the thousands Jack had frittered away on a baronial pile. He employed servants, they also pointed out, and yet the more bourgeois his lifestyle grew, the more uncompromising his rhetoric became. 'It would serve this man London right,' said Mark Twain, 'to have the working class get control of things. He would have to call out the militia to collect his royalties.'

Jack retorted that having wealth did not make him a capitalist; he had made his money without exploiting a single comrade. Except perhaps Charmian. But even she had a wardrobe crammed full of flouncy silk and lace ensembles, and a jewellery box brimming with Australian opals and other precious stones. And if she wanted further evidence of his love, she need only survey the ultimate symbol of their union, Wolf House.

15

Twilight of the Idol

Love, let us wander, you and I,
Where but charred embers and pale ashes lie;
Here where my dreams and fancies took still shape,
In all their glory, laid in wood and stone.

Here, blow thy kisses, many, for a stair,
That we may rise where thy line of rooms –
Rooms for thyself alone – we had them thus,
Where none might enter but the moon and I.

Dear love, the smoke is yet about my heart,
The crackle of the fire yet sears my brain.
– You will be kind, and dream and care no more,
Nor sorrow for what was my house of dreams.

MARGARET COBB SMITH, quoted in
The Book of Jack London

THE CRACKLE OF FLAMES filled the isolated redwood grove. Within minutes, the fire was raging out of control. An hour later, at midnight on 21 August 1913, Eliza knocked on Jack's sleeping-porch. 'Come quick!' she cried. Wolf House was ablaze.

Jack woke Charmian. Only the day before, he had presented her with a copy of *John Barleycorn* with the inscription: 'You know. You have helped me bury the Long Sickness and the White Logic.' They had talked excitedly about moving into Wolf House.

'What's the use of hurrying?' Jack said as they neared the fire. 'If that is the Big House burning, nothing can stop it now.'

'Promise me,' Charmian begged, 'that you won't forget yourself, and overdo.'

When they arrived at the construction site, over a mile away, it was already too late. Every room in Wolf House roared with flame. Due to a summer-long drought, there was no water to hand, and all Jack could do was stand and watch, tears streaming down his face, as his uninsured dream burnt to the ground.

'I would rather be the man whose house was burned,' he mumbled, 'than the man who burned it.'

By dawn, Wolf House was no more. Jack lay sobbing and shaking 'like a child' in Charmian's arms. The fire had killed something in him, she later recalled, and he 'never ceased to feel the tragic loss'. Again, as over the death of Joy, Jack suppressed his grief. Several times he vowed to rebuild the house, but would never do so.

Could someone have deliberately started the fire? Jack suspected local socialists, and even his own workers. The more likely culprit, however, was a mass of turpentine-saturated rags which had been left on the site. (Over eighty years after the blaze, scientific testing suggested that these rags, with which the woodwork had been rubbed down, may have burst spontaneously into flame.)

In stricken silence, Jack wandered around the charred stone shell. What had he done to deserve this? Had he really committed such terrible crimes? His wife was unable to provide him with a child. He was tens of thousands of dollars in debt. The Beauty Ranch was eating up more than he could earn, well over $50,000 a year. He was no nearer escaping the writing game.

The loss of two children, his ill-health and then finally the disaster at Wolf House had damaged beyond repair his public image as the action hero of American letters. All his life he had condemned the spiritualism of his parents as charlatanism. Now he embraced it.

The novel he began to work on in the weeks following the fire, *The Star Rover*, is still a cult classic. When it was published in 1915, it received little attention and sold poorly. It is, however, among Jack's better books, crisply written and skilfully plotted. Based on the recollections of Ed Morrell, who had served five years in solitary confinement, *The Star Rover* was intended as an exposé of the Californian penal system, and to show man's resilience to suffering. One of

Jack's most personal books, it reveals the extent of his introspection following the disasters of 1913. For the first time in his fiction, Jack – the professed 'material monist' – looked beyond science for answers. As a result, *The Star Rover* is his most soulful work. 'The key-note of the book is: THE SPIRIT TRIUMPHANT,' he wrote.

The Star Rover's hero is Darrell Standing, a professor of 'agronomics' at the University of California who has been sentenced to death for killing a fellow academic. Falsely accused of smuggling dynamite into prison, he is strapped into a straitjacket by a sadistic warden. He survives the ensuing torture by transcending it – by transporting himself back through time, via 'astral projection'. He becomes a French count; a wagon boy who is killed by Indians; a Robinson Crusoe figure cast away on a remote desert island; a sixteenth-century Englishman fighting in the Far East; and a Roman legionary at the time of Christ's crucifixion.

For all his newfound spirituality, Jack still struggled to escape the shadow of Nietzsche. As the *Bookman* pointed out: 'Jack London's evolution is more an outer evolution than an inner one. It is still in his mind the blond superman who is supreme, who is a master of men.' It would be a few more years before Jack finally outgrew the influence of his earliest philosophical mentors.

If only his own life would imitate his art. If only astral projection could work for him too. But there was no escaping the disappointments that crowded his life. He had always viewed life as a game. Now, recognising its cruel absurdities, he began to act as if it was indeed, as he put it, a 'pretty picayune world'.

Money meant nothing to him, he insisted, and he gave away what little he could spare. Virtually anyone smart enough to write a semi-literate begging letter received a cheque from him. He sent cash to unknowns struggling to finish books. He contributed to strike funds. An Australian woman who had lost both her sons received $50 a month from him until he died. When he feared the cheques would bounce, he asked Brett to send the money and dock it from future earnings.

Jack's generosity to strangers knew no bounds. When it came to his own family, however, he was more circumspect. For years his daughters had written to him asking for necessities such as a new winter coat, or money for schoolbooks. If several weeks passed and he did not receive a letter, he often mistook their silence for rejection.

Shortly after losing Wolf House, he wrote to Joan:

> What do you feel for me? Am I a fool who gives much and receives nothing? ... My home – one of my dreams – is destroyed. You have no word to say ... Joan, my daughter, please know that the world ... does not belong to the ones who remain silent, who, by their very silence lie and cheat and make a mock of love and a meal-ticket of their father. Don't you think it is time I heard from you? Or do you want me to cease forever from caring to hear from you?

One Sunday afternoon in October 1913, Jack went to see Joan in the hope of persuading her to visit him more often, and maybe one day even live with him at Glen Ellen. 'Daddy was deadly serious,' she later recalled, 'unsmiling, visibly controlling his anger each time it was roused; Mother was tense and mostly silent, although outrage compelled her to bitter protest from time to time.'

Jack began to quote the Bible: 'To everything there is a season, and a time to every purpose under heaven, a time to get, and a time to lose; a time to keep, and a time to cast away ...'

Joan looked bewildered. She was being asked to choose between her mother and father, and it was tearing her apart. She reiterated her love for both. She defended her mother. Then she pleaded for time 'to grow up a little more'. She opted to stay with Bess.

For four months, Jack brooded. 'Everything he had accomplished thus far had been won by fighting for it,' Joan recalled, 'and he was not yet ready to yield, to acquiesce, to wait patiently. Grief over what he surely persuaded himself was my rejection of him gave way to wounded pride – for I think he had been confident of victory – and then to anger.'

She was just thirteen when she received four closely typed pages from 'Daddy'. To the end of her life she would be appalled by their 'relentless, calculating cruelty'. It was a heartbreaking letter from a man desperate to share the lives of his daughters:

Glen Ellen, Calif.

February 24th 1914

Dear Joan

In reply to yours of February 10, 1914. I have just got back from the East, and am taking hold of my business. Please find herewith check for $4.50, according to account presented by you. When I tell you that this leaves me a balance in the bank of $3.46, you will understand how thin the ice is upon which I am skating . . .

Now I have what most persons would deem a difficult letter to write: but I have always found that by being frank and true, no thing is difficult to say . . . Let me tell you a little something about myself: All my life has been marked by what, in lack of any other term, I must call 'disgust'. When I grow tired or disinterested in anything, I experience a disgust which settles for me that thing forever. I turn the page down there and then.

When a colt on the ranch, early in its training, shows that it is a kicker or a bucker or a bolter or a balker, I try patiently and for a long time to remove, by my training, such deleterious traits; and then at the end of a long time if I find that these vicious traits continue, suddenly there comes to me a disgust, and I say Let the colt go. Kill it, sell it, give it away.

So far as I am concerned I am finished with the colt. So it has been with all things in my whole life from the very first time that I can remember anything of myself. I have been infatuated with many things, have become disgusted with those many things, and have turned down the pages forever and irrevocably on those many things. Please believe me – I am not stating to you my strength, but my weakness. These colossal disgusts that compel me to turn down pages are weaknesses of mine, and I know them; but they are there. They are part of me. I am so made.

Years ago I warned your mother that if I were denied the opportunity of forming you, sooner or later I would grow disinterested in you, I would develop a disgust, and that I would turn down the page. Of course, your mother, who is deaf to all things spiritual, and appreciative, and understanding, smiled to herself and discounted what I told her. Your mother today understands me no more than has she ever understood me – which is no understanding at all.

Now, do not make the mistake of thinking that I am now running away from all filial duties and responsibilities. I am not. I shall take care of you; I shall take care of Baby B., I shall take care of your mother. I shall take care of the three of you. You shall have food and shelter always. But, unfortunately, I have turned the page down, and I shall be no longer interested in the three of you.

I do not imagine that I shall ever care to send you to the University of California, unless you should develop some tremendous desire to do specific things in the world that only a course in the University of California will fit you for. I certainly shall never send you to the University of California merely in recognition of the bourgeois valuation put upon the University pigskin.

I should like to see you marry for love when you grow up. That way lies the best and sweetest of human happiness. On the other hand, if you want career instead, I'll help you to pursue whatever career you elect. When you were small, I fought for a year the idea of your going on the stage. I now withdraw my opposition. If you desire the stage with its consequent (from my point of view) falseness, artificiality, sterility and unhappiness, why go ahead, and I will do what I can to help you to it.

But please, please remember that in whatever you do from now on, I am uninterested. I desire to know neither your failures nor your successes; wherefore please no more tell me of your markings in High School, and no longer send me your compositions.

When you want money, within reason, I shall send it to you if I have it. Under any circumstances, so long as I live, you shall receive from me food in your stomach, a roof that does not leak, warm blankets, and clothing to cover you.

A year from now I expect to have a little money. At the

present moment, if I died, I should die one hundred thousand dollars in debt. Therefore, a year from now I may be more easy with you in money matters than I am capable of being now.

I should like to say a few words further about the pages I turn down because of the disgusts that come upon me. I was ever a lover of fatherhood. I loved fatherhood over love of woman. I have been jealous of my seed, and I have never wantonly scattered my seed. I gave you, well (we'll say my share at least) a good body and a good brain. I had a father's fondest love and hope for you . . . But when the time came for you to decide (not absolutely between your mother and me) – to decide whether or not I might have a little hand in showing and training you to your paces in the big world, you were already so ruined by your trainer, that you declined . . .

Unless I should accidentally meet you on the street, I doubt if I shall ever see you again. If you should be dying, and should ask for me at your bedside, I should surely come; on the other hand, if I were dying I should not care to have you at my bedside. A ruined colt is a ruined colt, and I do not like ruined colts.

Please let me know that you have read this letter in its entirety. You will not understand it entirely. Not for years, and perhaps never, will you understand. But, being a colt breaker, I realise that a colt is ruined by poor training, even though the colt never so realises.

Whenever you want money, within reason, for clothes, books, spending, etc. write me for it, and if I have it at the time, I shall send it to you.

Jack London.

Joan's father had always told her not to cry when she was hurt. Only sissies and weaklings showed their true emotions. Now she sobbed her heart out. Although she would continue to see Jack, she now sided totally with her mother.

*   *   *

Jack's letter to Joan was written during a period of severe stress. By spring 1914 he was further than ever from being able to throw away his portable Remington typewriter. The strain of turning out his thousand words a day was overwhelming him. His financial situation was worse than ever. He dared not total his debts for fear that the figure might be ten times, twenty times, what he had partially accounted for. He began to gamble on several get-rich-quick schemes, just as his mother had done throughout her life.

Like Mark Twain, however, Jack was an unlucky businessman. He lost $10,000 on a Mexican land deal. A scheme to sell his grapes ended with a company he had incorporated under his name going bust, and with its shareholders suing him for $41,000. On Joseph Noel's advice he invested heavily in a new 'wonder' printing press, the 'Millergraph'. Yet again, he lost thousands.

In increasingly rare moments, Jack could still sound like the young man who had overcome every obstacle. But he was fast losing his stamina. The destruction of Wolf House had crushed his optimism and to an extent forced a loss of faith in his fellow man – how could someone, as Jack believed, have so callously burnt down his dream home? Neither socialism nor Charmian could save him any longer from encroaching despair. More and more he began to resemble Martin Eden as his 'long sickness' returned with a vengeance.

Jack's 1914 novel *The Mutiny of the* Elsinore revealed the full extent of his despondency. The book's hero, John Pathurst, echoes Wolf Larsen and Jack at his most pessimistic, believing that the 'chemical ferment', as Jack described existence, is a struggle which ends in nothing more than death. *Outlook* magazine summed up *The Mutiny of the* Elsinore as an 'exciting, excessively brutal tale of a sea voyage in a sailing sloop, in which happens nearly every conceivable sensational thing made possible by a crew of cripples, incompetents, scoundrels and maniacs'.

In reply to a reader who complained that his writing had lost its punch, Jack wrote: 'You are right. I am all in ... The one last adventure remains to me – the making of my will.'

It would not be his last adventure, but his will would represent the final expression of his bitterness at not knowing his daughters. His mother would receive $45 a month and housing; Virginia Prentiss, his wet-nurse, $15 a month and housing. To his stepsister Eliza he would leave $2500 in cash and $35 a month. She had staked him in the Klondike, bought his first bicycle, paid for his false teeth. To his two daughters, he left just $25 a month each. Their mother would get a paltry $5 a month. Charmian would have complete control of his estate. If his own flesh and blood ever had need of more, they would have to ask 'the other woman' for it.

By 1914, the ranch from which he effectively disinherited his daughters was one of the largest in northern California, totalling more than 1400 acres. He had withdrawn from active politics but he would not give up his agrarian dream, even though the Beauty Ranch, he admitted, was really just six bankrupt ranches rolled into one. According to Charmian he was still 'far more interested in introducing better farming into Sonoma County and the country at large than he was in leaving behind masterpieces of literature'.

'The soil is our one indestructible asset,' Jack insisted, 'and by green manures, nitrogen-gathering cover crops, animal manure, rotation of crops, proper tillage and draining, I am getting results which the Chinese have demonstrated for forty centuries.' Indeed, his first crops of hay won awards, and his use of terracing, which he had discovered in Korea, revitalised much of the over-farmed soil.

Yet for all the energy he expended on it, Jack's 'ranch of good intentions' was still a long way from turning a profit. As with all his other grand schemes, Jack's plans for the Beauty Ranch were blighted by cruel misfortunes. His prize shorthorn bull slipped and broke its neck. His Pig Palace turned out to be an expensive slaughterhouse when most of his pedigree pigs died of pneumonia. Nevertheless, Jack was not deterred, and continued, to his last days, to introduce modern techniques of farming, convinced that one day his investment would pay off. Charmian later wrote that because of his 'disheartenment with human beings, both in the mass and as individuals in the main, he turned to the soil to save himself'.

Anna Strunsky described Jack as a 'Napoleon of the pen'. Like Bonaparte, Jack had the qualities and flaws of a larger-than-life character, and the Beauty Ranch was fast becoming his St Helena, an exile from happiness and health where the agony of his physical decline prompted momentary delusions of grandeur.

Whenever the disappointments became too much, Jack returned to the water, leaving behind for months on end the idyll he had chosen as his final retreat. One morning in late 1913, as he sailed aboard the *Roamer* with Charmian on San Francisco Bay, with the snow-capped Sierras visible in the distance, he burst out: 'I'm going to live a hundred years.'

'Yes? Why?' asked Charmian.

'Because I want to.'

He would only manage forty. A long way short of his hoped-for century, but time enough for one last adventure.

For some years Mexico had been torn apart by a bloody struggle for power amongst warring groups. A moderate president, Francisco Madero, had been replaced by the brutal General Victoriano Huerta, but for all his repression he could not stem peasant revolts, the most serious of which was led by Pancho Villa, a legendary outlaw who travelled in an armoured train and kept northern Mexico and American border towns in a constant state of anxiety.

In early 1914, fearing that its oil interests in Mexico were at risk, the United States began to look for a convenient excuse to stamp its authority on its unruly neighbour. The perfect opportunity arrived in March 1914. While buying supplies, a junior paymaster with the American fleet was arrested in Vera Cruz on Mexico's Atlantic coast by General Huerta's men. Washington instantly demanded his release, and that the garrison apologise by way of a thirteen-gun salute to the stars and stripes. When Huerta refused, President Woodrow Wilson authorised the seizure of the customs house in Vera Cruz. After four Americans were killed in the process, it looked as if there might be war.

In America itself, labour unrest was threatening to plunge the nation into a far greater crisis than that developing across the border in Mexico. Anxious politicians urgently needed a foreign adventure to distract attention from the increasingly bloody repression of the IWW. On 20 April 1914, National Guardsmen and hoodlums hired by the Rockefeller-owned Colorado Fuel & Iron Company set fire to tents occupied by striking mineworkers. Those fleeing the flames were shot. Three men, two women and thirteen children were murdered in what became known as the 'Ludlow Massacre'.

As the tragedy at Ludlow unfolded, *Collier's* offered Jack $1100 a week plus expenses to report on the deteriorating situation in Mexico. 'Now,' he told Charmian, 'I may be able to redeem myself as a war correspondent, after what I was held back from doing by the Japanese Army.'

Jack was the only correspondent to be accompanied by his wife. Fearing for his health and safety, Charmian insisted on going with him to Galveston, Texas, where they would pick up the documents which would allow them to travel on to Vera Cruz. To Jack's amazement, he was denied credentials. Richard Harding Davis, who had saved Jack's skin back in Korea and who was now reporting for the World Syndicate, again came to the rescue. The authorities had turned him down, Davis revealed, because of a pamphlet, 'The Good Soldier', which bore his name.

'Young Men,' the pamphlet began, 'The lowest aim in your life is to become a soldier. The good soldier never tries to distinguish right from wrong. He never thinks; never reasons; he only obeys. If he is ordered to fire on his fellow citizens, on his friends, on his neighbours, on his relatives, he obeys without hesitation ... "The Good Soldier" is a blind, heartless, soulless, murderous machine. He is not a man. He is not a brute, for brutes only kill in self defence ...'

After several hours of heated wrangling, Davis and other colleagues managed to convince the officials that Jack was not the author of the pamphlet; when Jack also gave his word of honour that this was the case, they backed down and issued the necessary papers. Many of Jack's socialist comrades would soon wish the American military had stuck to their guns.

In February 1911, Jack had written an open letter to the 'dear, brave comrades of the Mexican Revolution':

> We socialists, anarchists, hobos, chicken thieves, outlaws and undesirable citizens of the United States are with you heart and soul in your efforts to overthrow slavery and autocracy in Mexico. You will notice we are not respectable in these days of the reign of property. All the names you are being called, we have been called. And when graft and greed get up and begin to call names, honest men, brave men, patriotic

men and martyrs can expect nothing less than to be called chicken thieves and outlaws . . . I subscribe myself a chicken thief and revolutionist,
    Jack London.

Jack had also expressed his support for the revolution in a short story, 'The Mexican', published in the *Saturday Evening Post* on 12 August 1913, which ranks among the best of his sporting fiction and offers resounding proof that he had lost none of his talent for crafting powerful drama. While much of his fiction now suffered from the financial necessity of giving magazine editors the formulaic material they desired, 'The Mexican' showed that he was continually experimenting with new subject matter, still toying with new ideas.

When right-wing thugs slaughter his family, Felipe Rivera decides to become a prize-fighter, and vows to buy guns for the Mexican revolution with his winnings. Pitted against a Gringo fighter, he knocks his opponent out, to the consternation of the white crowd:

> There were no congratulations for Rivera. He walked to his corner unattended, where his seconds had not yet placed his stool. He leaned backward on the ropes and looked his hatred at them . . . till the whole ten thousand Gringos were included. His knees trembled under him, and he was sobbing from exhaustion. Before his eyes the hated faces swayed back and forth in the giddiness of nausea. Then he remembered they were guns. The guns were his. The revolution could go on.

By 1914 the 'chicken thief' was a reformed man. Jack not only failed to toe the Socialist Party line by supporting the insurgents, but actually assaulted them in print, writing them off as 'stupid anarchs'. He reported the situation as he saw it, arguing that the revolution was merely an excuse to 'shake down' the American oil interests 'who had found and developed the oil-fields'.

'The exotic civilisation introduced by America and Europe is being destroyed by a handful of rulers who do not know how to rule,' Jack wrote, 'who have never successfully ruled, and whose orgies at ruling have been and are similar to those indulged in by drunken miners sowing the floors of barrooms with the unfortunate gold dust . . . The policeman stops a man from beating his wife. The humane officer stops a man from beating his horse. May not a powerful and self-enlightened nation stop a handful of inefficient and incapable rulers from making a shambles and desert of a fair land wherein are all the natural resources for a high and happy civilisation?'

He reserved his strongest bile for the Mexicans of mixed race, the 'mestizos' who made up a fifth of the population. They were the class that 'foments all the trouble, plays childishly with the tools of giants, and makes a shambles and a chaos of the land. These "breeds" represent neither the great working class, not the property-owning class, not the picked men of the United States and Europe who have given Mexico what measure of exotic civilisation it possesses. These "breeds" are the predatory class. They produce nothing. They create nothing. They aim to possess a shirt, ride a horse, and "shake down" the people who work and the people who develop.'

By the time Jack arrived in Mexico, there was very little action to report. After marines had occupied Vera Cruz, the Huerta regime had made its apologies to the United States, including the salute to the flag. In contrast to the radical journalist John Reed (later to become famous as the author of *Ten Days that Shook the World*), who had spent several months with Pancho Villa's army, Jack did not venture far from Vera Cruz, and was content to write colour pieces which flattered the Americans and insulted the 'half-breed' Mexicans.

The English writer Ford Madox Ford tagged along with him on one rare foray aboard an oil-tanker bound for the port of Tampico. 'Let's go and see what oil smells like,' Jack had said. In Ford's eyes, Jack seemed to embody every dreamy Celtic quality: 'small, dark, full of movement, with eyes that could glow like topazes when something exciting was happening'. Ford, who collaborated on several works with Joseph Conrad, would always think of Jack as 'the most lovable child' he had ever met: 'Like Peter Pan, he never grew up, and he lived his own stories with such intensity that he ended by believing them himself.'

After docking in Tampico, Jack and Ford made for the nearest bar. Almost as soon as they had sat down, two drunken oilmen drew their revolvers. For a few seconds, it looked as if there would be a gunfight. Jack sat with a look of 'childish glee' on his face – this kind of action was priceless. When Ford made to intervene, Jack pushed him back into his seat. Two shots rang out. Fortunately, both missed. Drinking resumed. 'Now,' Jack grinned, 'what do you think about that?'

At the bar in the Diligencias Hotel in Vera Cruz, Jack bumped into Robert Dunn, his old drinking buddy from Korea, who was now representing the *New York Post*. They talked about old times, and Dunn noticed that Jack looked 'peaked, yellow'. Finally, the conversation turned to Jack's writing. What was he working on?

'Too much,' Jack said wearily. 'An idea every day . . . Fancy a drink, Bob?'

Dunn toasted the White Horse bar in Korea where they had got jingled so many times before. But Jack couldn't hear him. The White Logic was screaming too loud in his ear. 'In ten seconds I'll feel 'em crawling,' he mumbled. 'The worms, Dunn.'

'Is that in *John Barleycorn*?' asked Dunn.

'The white worm, tunnelling through our brains!' Jack cried.

'Not mine,' Dunn replied. 'Jesus, liquor never takes me that way.'

They ordered another round. Jack insisted that booze made white worms crawl through any brain, not just his. Dunn said it affected everybody differently, 'like love or war, mountains or the sea'.

'His lack of early schooling was an advantage offset by easy enthusiasms against which he had no reserves of resistance,' Dunn later recalled. 'He oddly paralleled another of my best companions, Jack Reed – each a revolutionary to socialists, a romantic to me. Beginning with humour, both had most of the weaknesses tagged bourgeois, a word I never heard either use.'

Jack found amusements to kill the time. In a marathon craps game, he 'cleaned out all the newspaper correspondents plus the ambassadors of Spain and France'. He also planned to take his first trip in an aeroplane, but on the day of the flight he came down with acute dysentery and was forced to take to his bed instead. Charmian, Nakata and two doctors tended to him in a bullet-riddled hotel room for several days, fighting a 'desperate, cautious campaign against death, but as usual, the patient managed by his uncommon recuperative powers to make a spectacular recovery'. Having survived dysentery, Jack next struggled to shake off a serious case of pleurisy. His body a wreck, he made it back to Glen Ellen and 'white man's climate and grub' on 17 June.

Jack's dispatches from Mexico had strained to breaking point his relations with the left in America. Yet again, it appeared, he had failed to apply a Marxist analysis to the situation, social Darwinism and his belief in Anglo-Saxon supremacy blinding him to the true nature of American imperialism. The liberal *Nation* was astonished: 'That an eminent apostle of red revolution should audibly be licking his chops over millions of gold dollars wrested from its rightful owner, the Mexican peon, by the predatory ministers of international capital, is somewhat disconcerting.' John Kenneth Turner, a prominent socialist figure, claimed that Jack had been bribed by the 'flattering good fellow-ship' of the oil companies to produce 'a brief for the oil man, a brief for intervention, a brief for what Mexicans call "Yankee Imperialism" '.

Even to his own daughter, writing two decades later, Jack's reports represented 'a tragic sellout, for he had been subsidised, bought body and soul, by the kind of life he had thought he wanted, and it was destroying him . . . The several articles he wrote for *Collier's* during his stay in Mexico reveal such a complete *volte face* in his attitude toward the Mexican revolution and America's role in it that one is almost tempted to believe that they were written under his name by an entirely different person.'

But Jack's views deserve to be seen in a different light – in the context of what would soon happen in Mexico. By 1916 the various warring groups would have German, American and Japanese backing, and the 'Mexican Revolution' would no longer be a popular rising, but a contest between imperial powers to dominate the region. Jack's reports may have read like 'Hearst editorials' to George Sterling and others, but they did at least acknowledge the complexity of the unfolding situation.

The change in Jack's opinions may also have reflected his present way of life and his status as a land-owner. He was no longer one of the downtrodden, exposed to their concerns and the conditions they suffered. Now he was weary and disillusioned. Back at the Beauty Ranch he discovered that many of his workers loafed when his back was turned, and that local suppliers had overcharged him. He had always naïvely ascribed to other men his own qualities of hard work and self-discipline. Now humanity succeeded mostly in disappointing him.

Jack was still recuperating in late August 1914 when he heard that war had broken out in Europe. The assassination of the Archduke Franz Ferdinand in Sarajevo marked the beginning of the bloodiest war in human history, one which would eventually claim over twenty million lives. It was also the end of innocence for countless idealists and romantics across the globe. 'I can only tell you,' Jack wrote to one of his readers, 'that in all my life no experience has affected me so profoundly, so vitally as this present great war. It is with me waking and sleeping, in fact in my sleep it is a positive nightmare.'

Jack could not bear the idea of the British and Germans tearing each other apart. It was a tragic waste of damned precious Anglo-Saxon blood. Unlike his socialist comrades in America, however, he would not sit on the sidelines, urging neutrality. He had supported the British in the Boer War against the 'lesser breed' Boers. He had always boasted of his English heritage. There was no question which side he was on. 'God help them when the British turn savage!' he cried one morning. 'Germany has no honour, no chivalry, no mercy. Germany is a bad sportsman. Germans fight like wolves in a pack, and without initiative or resource if compelled to fight singly.'

Following the German invasion of Belgium, Thomas Hall Caine, a Christian Socialist, wrote to Jack from England asking him to contribute to *King Albert's Book*, a collection of propaganda pieces by well-known writers which he was compiling. The proceeds from the book would go to a relief fund for Belgian refugees. Jack's contribution would have satisfied the most hysterical jingoist. 'Belgium is rare. Belgium is unique. Among men arises on rare occasions a great man, a man of cosmic import. Among nations on rare occasions arises a great nation, a nation of cosmic import.'

In the Kaiser and his country – 'the Mad Dog of Europe' – Jack had found targets worthy of his surging bitterness at his own body's failure. When Jack learned of the death at the hands of the 'Krauts' of the English nurse Edith Cavell, something 'snapped' in him. 'Eyes and soul full of . . . the mad slaughter,' Charmian later recalled, 'he became more and more furious with the brutal stupidity of the Hun.

He lingered in almost speechless wonder over the monstrous bestiality of German cartoons, in nearly all of which lay a boomerang unguessed by that same bungling stupidity.'

In an article, 'The Impossibility of War', which had appeared in the *Overland Monthly* fourteen years earlier, Jack predicted that the days of cavalry charges would soon be over: 'No more open fields; no more decisive victories; but a succession of sieges . . . At the front will be the chess-game; at home the workers feeding the players. All will depend upon the stamina of the civil population.'

His prophecy of a war of attrition was now coming true in northern France, already scarred by trenches and barbed wire as the Allies and Germany became bogged down in a bloody stalemate. Still haunted by the scandal surrounding his alleged authorship of 'The Good Soldier', and recalling his frustrations in Korea, Jack did not volunteer to report on the war, suspecting that again he would not be allowed near the front lines. 'Again I say, the Japanese settled the war correspondent forever, by proving him non-essential,' he told Charmian. 'Look at Davis and the rest, some of the best in the world – eating out their hearts over there. Not for me. If I went, I would be unable to get what I went after. I have learned my lesson. If I ever do go to this war, it will be to fight with England and her allies.'

The most remarkable of his statements was a dismissal of the slaughter in Europe as negligible when compared to the deaths through poverty in peacetime: 'As regards a few million terrible deaths, there is not so much of the terrible about such a quantity of deaths as there is about the quantity of deaths that occur in peace times in all countries of the world, and that occurred in war times in the past. Civilisation at the present time is going through a Pentecostal cleansing that can result only in good for mankind.'

Only a sick man could have described the First World War in such terms. By 1915 Jack was using increasing doses of pain-killers. Just as he had taught himself to write and navigate, he had now learned how to inject himself by reading medical text-books. And so, as humanity bled itself dry, Jack numbed his pain, spending many days in a morphine haze.

Charmian, his Eternal Kid, was called on to play her final role. She had been his sparring partner, his sexual liberator, his co-adventurer.

Now she became his nurse. She too learned how to use the hypodermic syringe, and she patiently sat by him as he raged long into the night against the Hun, and the injustices he himself had suffered. At a moment's notice she would run to his bedside and massage his bloated ankles until he fell asleep. 'Getting old, getting old,' he would say through gritted teeth as she rubbed his small feet.

Yet still he would not take care of himself. In 1902 he had weighed a trim 170 pounds. Now, aged thirty-nine, he was over two hundred. He could feel his heart murmur, and would hold his hand to it in mock protest, but still, despite a constant cough, he continued to chain-smoke sixty Russian Imperiales a day.

Preoccupied by his physical decline, he read medical text-books, discussing his symptoms with Charmian *ad nauseam*. It didn't take a medical genius to make a diagnosis: Jack had, as George Sterling put it, 'worn down as perfect a human machine as the world seldom sees' through a lifetime of excess. He took a subscription to the *American Journal of Urology and Sexology*, and began to amass a library on venereal diseases. His symptoms seemed similar to the ones he read about in *Diagnosis of Diseases of the Brain and of the Spinal Cord*: 'severe and persistent headache, vomiting, and optic neuritis'. Would he meet the same fate as Maupassant and Nietzsche, two of his idols, who had died of tertiary syphilis?

What definitely had begun to kill him was uraemia, possibly exacerbated, as Andrew Sinclair has argued, by the mercury-based drug Salvarsan, which was widely used to treat syphilis. Although Salvarsan was at first hailed as a miracle drug, it had serious side-effects. Many patients died due to its toxicity, and often treatment was a race to determine which would die first, the disease or the patient. According to Sinclair, Jack had used the drug after returning from Australia, where doctors had prescribed an arsenic-based compound to cure his skin ailments. Since then, its toxic effect may have been compounded by his poor diet and growing dependency on pain-killers.

The common signs of uraemia are headaches lasting several days, attacks of nausea, insomnia, sudden temper fits and loss of balance. Jack would soon show all these symptoms, mistakenly ascribed by some later detractors to excessive drinking and madness. In fact, because of the disease, he was now able to drink relatively little, as his body could no longer process alcohol. Whether he liked it or not, his years of heavy drinking were over.

As Jack's kidneys gradually failed, poisons began to accumulate in his body, causing agonising pain which required greater doses of pain-killers to alleviate it. In the years before dialysis, there was no hope of recovery, and no denying that the 'noseless one' was close at hand.

16

The Noseless One

Darn the wheel of the world! Why must it continually
turn over? Where is the reverse gear?
                                        JACK LONDON

JACK STOOD at the foot of an endless staircase and watched the dark
figure move towards him. He had seen it before, he told Charmian,
but only in his dreams. Now, imperial and ominous, it haunted his
waking hours, drawing closer and closer. All he could do was watch
and wait. The dark figure on the stairs was surely his nemesis, the
ultimate superman to whom he would soon have to surrender himself.

Isolated on his mountain top, everything and everybody seemed to
be closing in on him. If an old friend or a family member upset him
by accident, he became resentful. He wrote bilious letters to creditors
and critics, and became involved in a legal dispute with neighbours,
including Charmian's aunt Ninetta Eames, after damming a nearby
stream to provide the Beauty Ranch with irrigation. Charmian would
find her husband with his head in his hands, cursing friends, foe and
family. 'What am I to think?' he asked her one morning. 'Are they
all alike? Every person I've done anything for – and I've not been a
pincher, have I? – has thrown me down: near ones, dear ones – and
the rest.'

'Some of us are still standing by,' she reassured him.

'Oh, I don't mean you, of course, nor Eliza. But the exceptions
are so rare – friend and stranger alike.'

'No man who ever made money and played Santa Claus to many
has escaped your fate,' she said. 'Be careful, or you'll find yourself
nursing a persecution mania.'

Of his most recently published novel, *The Little Lady of the Big House*, Jack had claimed: 'Except for my old-time punch, which is in it from start to finish, it will not be believed that I could write it – it is so utterly fresh, so absolutely unlike anything I have ever done.'

Yet even George Sterling condemned the novel as mediocre. The *Atlantic Monthly*, which had published the brilliant 'An Odyssey of the North' back in January 1900, gave it a particularly damning review: 'Is this perverted gusto the half-surrender of one more artist to the baser demands of his market? Or the resort of a thinker too sophisticated for the old naive and cleansing intensities, too undisciplined for the new impersonal meanings of things?'

Jack had, it appeared, fallen from dizzying heights to rock bottom. André Tridon, writing in the *New Review*, thought he knew why: 'Read *John Barleycorn* and you will soon enough discover what ails him. He will tell you himself, and the tragedy is that he does not even seem to know how far gone he is.'

Jack protested that, just as they had failed to understand or even recognise the underlying 'motifs' of *The Sea Wolf* and *Martin Eden*, the critics had misconstrued *The Valley of the Moon*, *Burning Daylight* and particularly *The Little Lady of the Big House*. True, he had cast himself (along with Charmian) as characters, but he had then preached against their mistakes. In a letter to Mary Austin, he claimed that visionary artists had always been misunderstood: 'As I remember it, the prophets and seers of all times have been compelled to sit alone except at such times when they were stoned or burned at the stake.'

Some of Jack's readers were beginning to find fault. Lady Isobel Ryder, an English aristocrat, urged him to take the 'higher way' as 'a safe writer for the young'. Alexander Cotter wrote expressing his dismay at the first magazine instalment of *The Little Lady of the Big House*, which, he said, he had tossed in the fire. He felt that his 'idol had fallen – and it certainly fell with a crash! . . . Have you poisoned the Muses, or did the manna of sleepy Sonoma Valley get you? . . . Write like you used to – write something with a kick to it.' Jack replied defiantly: 'Let me tell you right here that I am proud, damn proud of *The Little Lady of the Big House*.'

The sales figures for his recent novels, however, indicated that the muses had indeed deserted Jack. He had lost touch with current trends in American fiction. *The Mutiny of the* Elsinore sold 49,181 copies; *The Star Rover* 30,634; and *The Little Lady of the Big House* just 21,679.

These totals paled into insignificance beside those of ex-dentist Zane Grey, author of the western *Riders of the Purple Sage* (1912), and of former lightbulb salesman Edgar Rice Burroughs, whose *Tarzan of the Apes* (1914) was an overnight sensation, selling millions of copies.

The project Jack most cared about – the Beauty Ranch – was still a monumental liability. 'It is dreadfully hard for me to get my friends to understand just what the ranch means to me,' he had told Brett in 1914. 'It does not mean profit, at all. My fondest hope is that somewhere in the next six or seven years I shall be able to break even on the ranch. The ranch is to me what actresses, racehorses, or collecting postage stamps, are to some other men ... Next to my wife, the ranch is the dearest thing in the world to me. Heavens! I sit up nights over that ranch.'

By early 1915, however, Jack was spending more nights sitting aboard the *Roamer*, which he kept moored near Vallejo, twenty miles from the ranch on San Pablo Bay, than pacing his sleeping-porch. Faced with a barrage of lawsuits connected to his failed grape-juice venture and another unsuccessful enterprise, the Fidelity Loan & Mortgage Company, on whose board he had served as a director, Jack was teetering as never before on the brink of bankruptcy. On 26 January, from on board the *Roamer*, he wrote to Walter S. Kerr, a struggling playwright who had sought his advice:

> I am afraid to go home for fear of having summons served on me. I have been and am being sued right and left. What complicates my serious situation is that ... I am taking care of many people and am running a number of households, all of which people and households are entirely and absolutely dependent on me for food and shelter ... It is sink or swim with me at the present time, and at present time I am floundering hard.

In early February, a severe attack of inflammatory rheumatism forced Jack to take to his bed for several days. Maudlin and depressed, he yearned more than ever for the affirmation of his daughters' love. On 4 February, after learning that a planned assignment to report on

the opening of the Panama Canal had been cancelled, he wrote to
Joan, now fifteen:

> Now I want to sing to you a song:
>   You are my daughter
>   You do not know, yet, what that means
>   Have you no intellectual stir, no mental prod, no heart
> throb,
>   Impelling you to get acquainted with your dad?
>   Oh, my dear, I am very old, and very wise, and I can set
> you four-square to this four-square world . . .

Soon, even the backwaters of San Pablo Bay were too close to the
problems he confronted back at the Beauty Ranch. On 24 February,
a few days after learning that Mabel Applegarth had died of tuberculosis at the age of forty-one, the Londons left for Hawaii aboard the
steamer the *Matsonia*.

Jack's very first landfall as a young sailor had been Hawaii. Now,
on his Pacific paradise, he hoped he could enjoy a life of leisure, far
from the painful memories and setbacks that depressed him in California. Besides, he deserved a good rest. He was to spend all but a
few months of the time that remained to him in a series of rented
cottages in Honolulu.

'There was scant exertion in his habit of life in the palm-furnished,
breezy bungalow of wide spaces, and the deep gardens of hibiscus and
lilies,' Charmian recalled. 'Too little exertion. Too seldom was the
blue-butterfly kimono changed for swimming suit or riding togs; too
often, from the water, I cast solicitous eyes back to the hammock,
where, out of the blue-figured robe, a too-white arm waved to show
that he was watching me put to use the strokes in which he had
coached me.'

The Crowd of Jack's youth was now usurped by middle-aged
bankers and plantation-owners who lionised him as the author whose
articles had helped make Hawaii a tourist destination for the rich. In
praising Hawaii, Jack had stressed that it was off-limits to those without money. He had warned the American working classes to stay at
home: there was already fierce competition for jobs among the immigrant Japanese and Chinese. The controversy over leprosy was con-

veniently forgotten when Jack lauded the island's idle rich for their kindness to the poor and their hospitality towards him and Charmian.

In Jack's odyssey from ragged-trousered revolutionary to ally of Hawaii's ruling oligarchy lay the future of American socialism. He had the good life in his own lifetime, and had become too impatient to wait for his comrades to catch up. Hiding his sickly skin from the tropical sun, he played high-stakes poker with the bosses, took long siestas and whiled away his evenings watching Charlie Chaplin movies in a local cinema.

His health continued to deteriorate. In March 1916 he woke in the middle of the night in excruciating pain. Local doctors diagnosed kidney stones. Jack's body was slowly filling with poisons from pyorrhoea, a condition related to uraemia. He was told to stop eating raw fish and placed on a strict diet.

Remarkably, Jack kept up his thousand words a day, even when racked with pain. Since 1913 he had written under contract, selling all his fiction in serial form to William Randolph Hearst's *Cosmopolitan* magazine. The $2000 he received each month from Hearst had met his expenses on the ranch, but had not gone far towards paying off mortgages of over $50,000. Then, in October 1915, *Cosmopolitan* had asked Jack to novelise a screenplay, *Hearts of Three*, by Charles Goddard, offering him the huge sum of $25,000, ten times the advance he had received from Century two years earlier for *John Barleycorn*. Jack completed the project a few months after arriving in Hawaii. Finally, he was able to clear his long-standing debts.

By 1916 he was also receiving thousands of dollars for selling motion-picture rights to Hollywood. No other author in America had such a vast back-catalogue of cinematic material: he had published an astonishing forty books in just sixteen years, from which he had earned over a million dollars. Having settled the copyright lawsuits which had cost him several thousand dollars, Jack was beginning to see returns from the films of his works, over $20,000 according to one estimate. *The Sea Wolf, Burning Daylight, Valley of the Moon*, 'Odyssey of the North' and *John Barleycorn* had all transferred with reasonable financial success to the screen. Although the war had seriously affected publishing in Europe, Jack also received royalties from books which had been translated into several foreign languages. In Russia, Germany and Scandinavia in particular, his fiction had won a wide audience.

There was another stream of income. By 1916, Jack had built up a business which brought in revenue from the most unlikely sources. Not only had he put his name to a brand of cigar and a breath-freshening mint, he had also appeared in advertisements for a New York tailor and in many other promotions. The exposure helped sell books and brought audiences to see the films of his best-sellers, and in the process had made him the most recognised writer in American history.

While in Hawaii, apart from *Hearts of Three*, Jack worked on a couple of dog stories, *Jerry of the Islands* and *Michael, Brother of Jerry*. Hoping to resurrect the ghosts of White Fang and Buck, he knocked the two novellas off in a couple of months for quick cash. Once again he took the side of the dog against cruel and callous man. He would not live to see the books' publication in 1917, nor the growth of Jack London Clubs, inspired by the popular reaction to them, and devoted to preventing cruelty to animals.

The hero of *Jerry of the Islands* is a pedigree Irish terrier trained to chase 'niggers' – a 'white man's dog'. *Michael, Brother of Jerry* is notable for a scene in which a trainer tries to break a bear by attaching rings to its ear and nose. Time and time again the bear rips off the rings, until finally the trainer complains that there 'ain't nothing left to make fast to'.

It was also in Hawaii, of all places, that Jack produced his most moving call to arms, the introduction to *The Cry for Justice: An Anthology of the Literature of Social Protest*, edited by Upton Sinclair. Sinclair, who would later run for Governor of California, considered it one of the finest things Jack ever did, and said that some paragraphs 'might be carved upon his monument'. It was an elegy to Jack's idealism – to the beliefs that had blazed so fiercely in his youth.

> He, who by understanding becomes converted to the gospel of service, will serve truth to confute liars and make of them truth-tellers; will serve kindness so that brutality will perish; will serve beauty to the erasement of all that is not beautiful. And he who is strong will serve the weak that they may become strong. He will devote his strength, not to the debasement

and defilement of his weaker fellows, but to the making of opportunity for them to make themselves into men rather than into slaves and beasts . . . We know how gods are made. Comes now the time to make the world.

Although his own prose appeared becalmed to most critics, Jack had lost none of his talent for recognising good writing. Throughout his final months in Hawaii he continued to devour books by the armful; it was the one habit of his life, aside from his thousand words a day, which had not been self-destructive. He had always recognised the genius of Joseph Conrad's writing, and the power and vitality which had characterised his own best work. It was in Hawaii that he read *Victory*, Conrad's personal favourite and perhaps his greatest examination of 'the darkness and grandeur that fight for dominance in the human soul'. Unable to help himself, Jack wrote to congratulate one of the twentieth century's undisputed masters.

Honolulu, T.H.
June 4, 1915
  Dear Joseph Conrad
The mynah birds are waking the hot dawn about me. The surf is thundering in my ears where it falls on the white sand of the beach, here at Waikiki, where the green grass at the roots of the coconut palms insists to the lip of the wave-wash. This night has been yours – and mine.
  I had just begun to write when I read your first early work. I have merely madly appreciated you and communicated my appreciation to my friends through all these years. I never wrote you. I never dreamed to write to you. But Victory has swept me off my feet, and I am inclosing herewith a carbon copy of a letter to a friend at the end of this lost night's sleep.
  Perhaps you will appreciate this lost night's sleep when I tell you that it was immediately preceded by a day's sail in a Japanese sampan of sixty miles from the Leper Settlement of Molokai (where Mrs. London and I had been revisiting old friends) to Honolulu.
  On your head be it.

Aloha (which is a sweet word of greeting, the Hawaiian greeting, meaning 'my love be with you').
Jack London.

Conrad responded:

I am immensely touched by the kindness of your letter – that apart from intense satisfaction given me by the approval of an accomplished fellow-craftsman and a true brother in letters – of whose personality and art I have been intensely aware for many years. A few days before it reached me Percival Gibbon (a short-story writer and a most distinguished journalist and war corresp.) and I were talking you over endlessly, in the quiet hours of the night. Gibbon, who had just returned after 5 months on the Russian front, had been taking you in bulk, soaking himself in your prose. And we admired the vehemence of your strength and the delicacy of your perception with the greatest sympathy and respect. I haven't seen your latest yet. The reviews such as come my way are enthusiastic. The book is in my home but I wait to finish a thing (short) I am writing now before I sit down to read you. It'll be a reward for being a good industrious boy. For it is not easy to write here nowadays. At this very moment there is a heavy burst of gunfire in Dover. I can hear the quick firers and the big guns – and wonder what it is. The night before last a Zep passed over the house (not for the first time) bound west on that raid on London of which you have read already in your papers . . . Keep me in your kind memory and accept a grateful and cordial handgrasp.

The long, lazy days in Hawaii provided time for Jack to write fan letters, and for reflection. When he looked back over his life, he could at least congratulate himself that he had seen the view from the mountain top, no matter how far he had since fallen. Always he had spoken his mind. There had never been a man above him. He had become the first working-class writer in America whose books were read by his own class. Yet he had moved too far from his roots. On the Beauty Ranch he had become isolated from the great social upheavals and cultural changes of his time, but not from the emotional poverty of an imagined past.

Like Buck and White Fang, Jack had moved uneasily between civilisation and the wild. His most engaging human characters had been the downtrodden and oppressed: prisoners, hoboes, labourers, Indian women, Mexican revolutionaries, and others for whom the American Dream was also a cruel fantasy. Like the subjects of his best fiction, Jack had yet to find his place in the sun.

When he asked himself what he still believed in, he realised he was not sure. What he did know was that Marxism alone had not been the answer. For all its tantalising promise, ideology had not nourished his soul. As the Pacific now washed at his feet, he began to look elsewhere. But first he must purge himself of the past. The process began on 7 March 1916, when he marched into Charmian's room in their cottage.

'Take a letter – please!' As fast as she could type, he dictated the following:

Honolulu, March 7, 1916

Dear Comrades:

I am resigning from the Socialist Party, because of its lack of fire and fight, and its loss of emphasis upon the class struggle.

I was originally a member of the old revolutionary up-on-its-hind-legs, a fighting, Socialist Labor Party. Since then, and to the present time, I have been a fighting member of the Socialist Party. My fighting record in the Cause is not, even at this late date, already entirely forgotten. Trained in the class struggle, as taught and practised by the Socialist Labor Party, my own highest judgment concurring, I believed that the working class, by fighting, by never fusing, by never making terms with the enemy, could emancipate itself. Since the whole trend of Socialism in the United States during recent years has been one of peaceableness and compromise, I find that my mind refuses further sanction of my remaining a party member. Hence, my resignation.

Please include my comrade wife, Charmian K. London's resignation with mine.

My final word is that liberty, freedom and independence are royal things that cannot be presented to nor thrust upon race or class. If races and classes cannot rise up and by their own strength of brain and brawn, wrest from the world liberty, freedom and independence, they never in time can come to these royal possessions . . . and if such royal things are kindly presented to them by superior individuals, on silver platters, they will not know what to do with them, will fail to make use of them, and will be what they have always been in the past . . . inferior races and inferior classes.

Yours for the Revolution,
Jack London

When Jack had got the letter out of his system and had cooled down, Charmian asked him, 'What will you call yourself henceforth? Revolutionist? Socialist? What?'

'I am not anything, I fear,' he replied. 'I am all these things. Individuals disappoint me more and more, and more and more I turn to the land.'

Few in the Socialist Party were surprised by Jack's resignation, given his views on the Mexican revolution and the war in Europe. Nor was he alone in his criticism of the party. Like Jack, Eugene Debs had warned as early as 1911 that the party was in danger of being 'permeated and corrupted with the spirit of bourgeois reform to an extent that will practically destroy its virility and efficiency as a revolutionary organisation'.

The party replied to Jack's resignation in a snide article, 'How You Can Get Socialism', which appeared in the *New York Call* on 27 March 1916:

The Socialist Party never spends much time in lamenting over those who occasionally quit its ranks, nor will it do so now . . . London is a fighter. Good. For some reasons not stated, he realised his fighting record in the cause is a closed chapter. He has of late found the party too peaceable for his taste. He quits it and goes elsewhere to find a battlefield. Doubtless this

sounds odd to us and to most party members. Yet doubtless
London is sincere. The reasons may be local or personal, or
both. We don't know Glen Ellen, and we do know Jack
London. The name of the place does sound rather too idyllic
to harmonise with the author of *The Sea Wolf* and *The Call
of the Wild*.

We can only assure him that, however tediously peaceable
membership in Glen Ellen may be, the workingmen in mine
and shop and factory who make up the rank and file of
the Socialist Party are fighting – not always an exhilarating,
romantic, spectacular fight – not always the sort of fight that
makes good copy for the magazines or good films for the
movies – but the steady, unflinching, uncomplaining, unboast-
ing, shoulder to shoulder and inch-by-inch fight that uses the
fighters up one by one and sends them to soon-forgotten
graves, but that gains ground for those who fill up the ranks
as they fall, that undermines the enemy's defences and wears
him down and keeps on wearing him down until the time
comes for breaking his line and making the grand dash that
shall end the war.

Live long, Friend London, and keep the pugnacious spirit,
that, when the way to victory has been prepared by the unher-
alded millions, you may be with us once more on that dramatic
day. We shall go on doing our best to hasten it for you.

For what remained of his life, Jack would grow increasingly bitter
about such criticisms. A few months after his resignation he wrote of
his former comrades: 'They deny I ever struck a blow or did anything
for the Cause, at the same time affirming that all the time they knew
me for what I was – a Dreamer.'

Jack had lost faith not so much in socialism as in the working
class's ability to bring it about. On 21 September 1916 he wrote to
the Secretary of the party: 'I gave a quarter of a century of the flower
of my life to the revolutionary movement, only to find that it was as
supine under the heel as it was a thousand centuries before Christ
was born. Will the proletariat save itself? If it won't, it is unsavable.'

As Jack saw it, the middle-class apologists for capitalism had subverted the movement, arguing as they did for progress through gradual and democratic change. Yet every comrade with half a brain knew the only sure way to end poverty, disease and suffering was for a man to stand up and fight. But why should Jack wait for history to prove him right? He had done his best, fought his fight. (Ironically, he would die just one year before the 1917 Russian revolution.)

Besides, he had discovered a new philosophy of life, one which he could now use as a tool for understanding the passions and demons that had underpinned his socialism, and plenty else besides. At the very moment he had closed the book on Marxism, he had opened another: Carl Jung's *Psychology of the Unconscious* (1916). Later, he heavily underlined a passage in Dr Beatrice Hinkle's introduction to the book: 'the character and intelligence which makes it possible for him to submit himself to a facing of his naked soul, and to the pain and suffering which this entails'.

According to Clarice Statz, Jack had first come into contact with psychoanalysis in 1912 when he read Sigmund Freud's *Selected Papers on Hysteria*. Three years earlier Freud had made a lecture tour of America, drawing large crowds despite the fact that he spoke in German. He was accompanied by Jung, his devoted disciple. The two were to split in 1913, after several disagreements about Freud's theories on infantile sexuality. Freud, Jung felt, had extended sexuality too far. It was Jung with whom Jack agreed, or rather Jung who spoke to his soul.

Due to Jung, the journey that had taken Jack via Marx and Darwin to Spencer and Nietzsche was to end in profound self-awareness. 'Mate-Woman,' he told Charmian one evening after discussing Jung with her, 'I tell you I am standing on the edge of a world so new, so terrible, so wonderful, that I am almost afraid to look over into it.'

For Jack, Jung had arrived in the nick of time. With a mixture of pride and elation he read about the power of myth and the 'collective unconscious', a reservoir of age-old images buried deep in the mind, which he felt he himself had tapped in moments of genius: 'The hidden treasure upon which mankind ever and anon has drawn, and from which it has raised up its gods and demons, and all those potent and mighty thoughts without which. man ceases to be man.'

Jack's entire writing career, it must now have seemed to him, had been a fumbling in the dark, a striving to call up imagery from a prehistoric psyche, to create mythology and to transcend the dull logic of consciousness. Now, at the eleventh hour, he may have realised where the power of Buck's visions had come from, and how he could have written his best prose without knowing at the time how he had been able to do so. Whether through prose, John Barleycorn or by following the adventure path, he had been trying to channel his 'libido': the natural energy which primarily serves the purposes of life, but also fuels creative work. If this energy is blocked, self-destruction and neurosis often follow. When Jack had given his libido full rein through art, it had inspired his best work.

Knowing the end was near, Jack turned to analysis as a means of confession. Charmian recalled that he 'went to startling lengths in the risky game of playing with souls . . . The test of my endurance was severe, for Jack required so greatly of me in the capacities of wife, lover, friend, even confessor, for he withheld nothing – nothing, I repeat – of what he was passing through; and my responsibility, it may be guessed, was almost more than I could bear.'

Jack began to realise that at least some of his political ire had been fuelled by his rage at his mother's refusal to show him love. He had been Flora's only child, yet she had shown him no affection. She had made him lie on the kitchen table when she conducted séances. She had invoked dead spirits to damn him. Now, finally, Jack could see the reasons for his ravenous appetites, and his lifelong quest for fame and wealth, as well as his weakness for alcohol. He had been searching for the affirmation and self-esteem that had been denied him as a child.

Armed with this new self-knowledge, Jack began to analyse his life. He made plans for a sexual biography based on his reading of Freud and Jung. A note made on his night-pad in January 1916 reads: 'My Biography – The Dark Abysm of Sex – rising to the glory of the Sun God. All darks and deeps and fluxes of the abysmal, opening itself in God, basing itself on hell.'

There were also notes for a more conventional autobiography, 'A Sailor on Horseback', which would be the reminiscences of a farmer, not a writer, who had opted for a life of adventure rather than art. Also on his night-pad were jottings outlining a novel, 'Bastard of

Youthful Attempt', in which a young man would overcome the shame of his illegitimacy and discover love through his half-sister. Another confessional project was 'How We Die', which would focus on five men struggling to come to terms with their lives as they neared death.

Finally recognising his own talent for mythology, Jack also planned to go to Norway to research a book on Norse legends, and made a start on a novel about a half-caste woman which would reflect the relatively harmonious racial integration he had witnessed on Hawaii.

Through the drugs he took to kill his physical pain, Jack may have experienced moments of revelation. The opium, in particular, may have opened new doors of perception during a final rush of creativity. In 'The Kanaka Surf', a short story which appeared in the posthumous collection *On the Makaloa Mat*, published in 1919, he made extensive reference to the effects of the drug on a sick and disillusioned super-man, Lee Barton. While Lee sits at home knocking back highball after highball, ill from opium, his wife Ida consorts with other men. He rages against the mediocrities who have blighted his life, who have never 'glimpsed the shining ways nor the mortals that tread them', and obsesses about his wife's infidelity:

> Was, then, woman the utterly unmoral creature as depicted by the German pessimists? he asked himself, as he tossed under his reading lamp unable to sleep or read. At the end of an hour he was out of bed and into his medicine case, and took a heavy sleeping-powder. An hour later, afraid of his thoughts and the prospect of a sleepless night, he took another powder. At one-hour intervals he twice repeated the dosage. But so slow was the action of the drug that dawn had broken ere his eyes closed.

One afternoon Ida and Lee are swimming in the Kanaka surf when, as had happened to Jack in 1915, Lee is attacked by cramp and begins to sink, pulling Ida beneath the waves with him. The couple struggle before Ida persuades Lee to relax and yield to the undertow. Finally they reach the shore safely, their love for each other reaffirmed.

Were the Bartons Jack and Charmian? Charmian's diary hints that Jack was no longer able to make love. Late one night, after a moonlight swim, she noted: 'Oh, those dreams of magic nights. I shall never feel that I have not loved them when I had them.' She also spent many evenings enjoying Hawaii's social whirl without Jack because of his ill-health. The tension between Ida and Lee Barton has another echo in notes which Charmian would later make for a planned autobiographical novel, 'Charmette': 'Perhaps, in her marriage, when her husband is unfaithful, and she finds that he has been for years, she lets him think she too is playing the game.'

'The Kanaka Surf' was an act of exorcism as well as autobiography, and typical of Jack's writing after his discovery of Jung. Due in part to both Jung and the poppy seeds, many of his final stories had a spare lyricism reminiscent of his earliest and best work. The last story he wrote, 'The Water Baby', was almost as affecting as *The Call of the Wild*. Its narrator, John Lakana – 'London' in Hawaiian – is stranded with a hangover in the fishing boat of an elderly Polynesian, Kohokumu. 'When I am really old,' says the fisherman, 'I shall be reported as drowned in the sea ... In truth, I shall have returned to the arms of my mother, there to rest under the heart of her breast until the second birth of me, when I shall emerge into the sun a flashing youth of splendour like Maui himself when he was young.'

'The Water Baby' not only invoked Jung's notion of the mother image, it also showed that Jack was consciously injecting Jungian symbolism into his work. Finally, he was realising that his genius had always lain in the mists and shadows of his mind. It was no machine, no box of cogs. In Jung, above all, Jack found a way to stare down the noseless one, to accept himself as he grew to accept the inevitability of his death. 'Jack chose death, or shall we say another form of rebirth,' Charmian later wrote. 'He went like the conqueror, not the vanquished. He went with the illuminated smile of one who has chosen well.'

On 25 July 1916, a dinner attended by forty of his friends was held in Jack's honour. Petals, fragrant lilies and exotic fruit covered a long table. The place-cards were embossed with the royal coat of arms of Hawaii. Jack, now known as a *kamaaina* – an old-timer – sat at one end beside 'Princess Cupid', formerly Queen Lydia Liliukokalani, who had been deposed from the Hawaiian throne in 1893. Charmian sat at the other end of the table beside the Mayor of Honolulu and 'Prince Cupid', Jonah Kuhio Kalanianaole. After several speeches, Hawaiian singers chanted a hula in praise of Jack. The next morning, weighed down by garlands, 'Keaka Lanaka' and his wife waved goodbye to a crowd of well-wishers as they boarded the *Matsonia*, bound for California.

They arrived at the Beauty Ranch on 3 August. Eliza was the first to suspect that his return marked the beginning of the end. 'Our Jack has not come back to us,' she told a friend. Mustering what little strength he had left, he accompanied George Sterling and Jimmy Hopper to the Bohemian Club High Jinks, but returned to the Beauty Ranch after a few days depressed that a play of his had been rejected for the annual presentation of a new work.

The Acorn Planter, faithfully published by Brett, was Jack's 'final testament' to his agrarian dream. The play begins in 'the morning of the world' and ends with 'the celebration of the death of war and the triumph of the acorn planters'. Its hero is Red Cloud, who is killed by a group called the Sun Men, but comes back to life and returns the California soil to its original fertility. The play failed to impress the businessmen of the Bohemian Club's selection committee, perhaps because it appeared overly sentimental. Its rejection deeply affected Jack, who now clung to his faith in the soil with the urgent sincerity of a dying man.

The following month his rheumatism flared up again while he was visiting the Sacramento Fair. His shire horse, Neuadd Hillside, and a shorthorn bull, Roselawn Choice, won Grand Championships. But misfortune continued to blight Jack's 'ranch of good intentions'. On the morning of 23 October, Charmian found him still lying in bed at nine o'clock.

'Come here and sit beside me,' he said. 'I have bad news for you – your Great Gentleman is gone.' He began to cry. Wiping the tears from his face, he blurted: 'I'm not ashamed, Mate-Woman.'

The previous evening Neuadd Hillside had suffered a rupture and died. Jack had doted on the horse more than on any other animal, casting him in *The Little Lady of the Big House* as Mountain Lad, the symbol of Eros. As Kevin Starr has argued, Neuadd Hillside had come to represent his final hopes for the Beauty Ranch, and perhaps even for life itself.

His last remaining 'bribes for living' were the women in his life. While he remained estranged from Flora, who had not visited the Beauty Ranch in over a decade, he was closer than ever to its manager, Eliza, who had recently divorced and could now devote all her energies to her beloved stepbrother. He had also forgiven Joan for siding with her mother against him. His mistake, he realised, had been to treat his children as adults, with the same gruff insensitivity he had suffered from his own mother. He now replied sympathetically to Joan's letters asking for a pair of skates or a ticket to a play. 'Most adolescent yearnings I suppressed, a few greatly daring hints went unnoticed,' she recalled. 'As time passed I grew embarrassed and then humiliated by the need to make these endless petty requests. The solution seemed eminently reasonable to me: Bess and I were older now, Daddy must increase Mother's allowance.'

In mid-October, Joan decided to broach the subject over lunch with her father in Oakland. 'How very ill he must have been,' she later recalled, 'for how else to explain the totally unexpected violence of his reaction? He was furiously angry, and although I immediately withdrew my proposal, he insisted upon discussing it further. I struggled desperately to hold back my tears, but he saw them.'

After the meal, Jack walked with Joan and her sister in silence down Twelfth Street to the Orpheum Theater, where he was to meet Charmian and some friends. In front of the theatre, Jack kissed his daughters calmly, then stepped towards the glass doors that led into the lobby. With one hand on the door, he looked back, then pushed open the door and went inside. He would never see his children again.

On 10 November 1916, the noseless one jabbed and found his range. Jack passed a kidney stone. He was barely able to walk when Anthony Hopkins of the Gaumont News Reel Company visited the ranch a week later to film a short documentary.

Hopkins's film presented the Londons as contented country gentry. Despite several sleepless nights tending to Jack, Charmian was filmed galloping confidently across the Beauty Ranch. Jack was shown driving a manure-spreader in white breeches and Baden-Powell hat. In another scene, he clutched a pig, grinning like a boy holding his first pet. It was a deeply moving image, final testimony to Jack's lifelong efforts to keep his chin up in the face of overwhelming odds.

But there was no disguising his bloated stomach, or a face disfigured by poisons which his kidneys could no longer process. By now, Jack's uraemia was in its final stages. He would often become manic and pound the table at dinner with a clenched fist. And he would fall asleep suddenly, or go silent for long periods.

'Afraid to say a word that would bring on a berserker rage,' Joseph Noel later wrote, '[George Sterling] fell into the habit of taking a pack of cards with him and he would play solitaire by the hour on the other side of the table from the man he loved above everybody he had ever known . . . The only concern he had was to restore things to their old footing. He succeeded in doing this only intermittently.'

Jack remained a fierce advocate of American intervention in the First World War – to the extent that he sent a monthly cheque for $50 to the family of an Englishman, Harry Strange, who had felt obliged to serve his country but could not support his family if he did so.

When he was asked by the *New York World* to name his choice for president in the November 1916 election, Jack replied that he did not support either of the candidates, Republican Charles Hughes or Democrat Woodrow Wilson. His preference was for Theodore Roosevelt, who was not running, and who had been defeated in 1912 when he ran on the Progressive 'Bull Moose' Party's ticket. 'MY CHOICE FOR PRESIDENT IS THEODORE ROOSE-VELT,' Jack wired the paper on 27 October, 'WHOM NOBODY IN THIS FAT LAND WILL VOTE FOR BECAUSE HE EXALTS HONOUR AND MANHOOD OVER THE COWARDICE AND PEACE-LOVINGNESS OF THE WORSHIPPERS OF FAT.'

When the duck season opened in late October, Jack ate two large birds, canvasback or mallard, each day. It was a diet fit for a suicide – 'a sure ticket for the grave', as Charmian later described it. But at least, as he gorged himself to death, he sounded like his old self. 'I am the sailor on horseback!' Charmian remembered him saying, as if he knew the phrase, which he had used so often before, was now his epitaph. 'Watch my dust! . . . Oh, I shall make mistakes amany; but watch my dream come true.'

His final dream was to see the Beauty Ranch become the utopian community he had envisaged on returning from the South Seas. He wanted to provide first-class facilities for his workers, and even a school for their children. He would make an idyll for others, even if the Beauty Ranch had become a living hell for himself.

Nursing Jack had become so exhausting by mid-November 1916 that Charmian feared she was having a nervous breakdown. But still she would not leave his side, day or night. She knew as she mopped his brow deep in the night that she was all that remained between him and death. He fought the agony of his poisoned body because she urged him on. She gave him hope when there was none.

Jack's final dedication to her, scrawled on the flyleaf of *The Turtles of Tasman*, the last of his books he would hold in his hands, read:

> Dearest Mate,
> After it all, and it all, here we are, all in all, all in all.
> Sometimes I just want to get on top of Sonoma Mountain to shout to the world about you and me.
> Arms ever round and around.
> Mate Man.
> The Ranch, Oct 6, 1916.

In another gesture, Jack gave his 'Mate-Woman' an 'exquisite tiny wrist-watch'.

'What shall I have engraved on it?' she asked.

'Oh, "Mate from Wolf", I guess,' he replied.

'The same as when we exchanged engagement watches?'

'Why, yes, if you don't mind,' he said. 'I have sometimes wished you would call me "Wolf" more often.'

On 21 November 1916, Jack woke up vomiting. He did not take his daily tour around the Beauty Ranch. To help himself sleep, he took a drug. He woke again in the early evening. Eliza arrived to discuss ranch affairs. She could see that Jack's nerves were shot. The pain of his uraemia had tipped him over the edge. He was completely obsessed by his idea of turning the Beauty Ranch into an autarky whose residents he would care for from cradle to grave.

'There are enough children on the ranch to open a school,' he told Eliza. 'The ranch people can have their homes here, trade here at better prices, be born here, grown up here, get their schooling here, and if they die they can be buried on the Little Hill . . . No, I haven't in mind a reform colony. I only look forward to making the place self-sustaining for every soul upon it.'

Eliza promised to carry out his plans. Eliza. His dear stepsister. The one woman who had always understood him, always supported him, helped him with money and encouragement. Her words now haunted him more than ever: 'Jack, you are the loneliest man in the world. The things your heart wanted, you've never had.' Only she knew how he had fought for years to hide the disappointment.

Jack smiled at her. Then he stood, lifted his eyeshade, and hugged her.

Absorbed in his discussions with Eliza, he had forgotten his dinner, now lying cold on a nearby table.

'Your duck was perfection half an hour ago,' said Charmian, 'but I'm afraid it's far from that now.'

He was not interested in the still-bloody duck. He did not want to listen to his favourite gramophone records of Handel's Largo and the Funeral March from Wagner's *Siegfried*. The Wolf did not even want to play with his pet dog, a fox terrier called Possum. All he wanted was to talk about his plans for his utopian community.

After half an hour, his exuberance faded as the pain-killers wore off. He became argumentative, baiting Charmian in search of a quarrel. Then he picked up two wooden boxes of books and placed them next to his untouched dinner.

'Look,' he said, 'see what I've got to read tonight?'

'You don't need to do it,' she pleaded. 'You make all this work for yourself.'

Jack lay down beside Charmian on a couch.

'You're all I've got,' he said softly. 'I've told you before. You must understand.'

'I do understand,' she soothed. 'I understand that there's too much for you to do, and that you're straining too hard to get it done. Something will snap if you don't pull up. You're tired, tired almost to death . . . We can't go on this way.'

Jack's eyeshade hid his eyes. But Charmian could see his drooping lips, thin lips which had once been full. For an hour he lay in her arms, saying little. Finally, turning slightly, he put his arms around her neck as if clinging to life itself.

'I'm so worn out,' he said. 'I'm going to turn in.'

He rose stiffly and made for the door. Suddenly, he turned and looked back at her.

'Thank God,' he said, 'you're not afraid of anything.'

Then he left the room. Possum followed at his master's heels. When Jack reached his room, he decided to make a few notes. At the suggestion of his London agents, Hughes Massie, he was writing an outline for a fifty-thousand-word autobiography. On the notepad he kept beside his bed, he scribbled:

Socialist autobiography
Martin Eden and Sea Wolf, attacks on Nietzschean philosophy, which even the socialists missed the point of . . .

His last written words were to his daughter:

Dear Joan,
Next Sunday, will you and Bess have lunch with me at Saddle Rock, and, if weather is good, go for a sail with me on Lake Merrit?
If weather is not good, we can go to a matinee of some sort. Let me know at once . . .
Daddy

Jack put the letter in the basket for his latest Korean manservant, Sekine, to post the next day. Then he opened a book – *Around Cape Horn: Maine to California in 1852 by Ship*, by James W. Paige. When Charmian returned from a stroll at around nine, she noticed the light still burning in her husband's room. Glancing in, she saw him propped up in bed. His eyes were closed, his chin rested on his chest. She decided not to disturb him and returned to her own sleeping-porch.

Sekine and Eliza woke her shortly before eight o'clock the next morning.

'Yes, what is it?'

'Sekine could not wake Jack,' said Eliza quietly. 'I think you'd better come in and see what you can do.'

Charmian threw on a shawl and sprinted to Jack's sleeping-porch. The Wolf was doubled up, lying on his side, his face dark blue, his breathing very heavy. Two empty vials of morphine lay on the floor. Charmian sent for hot coffee and tried to pour it down his throat. At 8.30, two local doctors arrived from Sonoma, summoned by Eliza. One of them spotted the morphine vials and assumed that Jack had injected himself with a lethal overdose. He asked his assistant to bring him a stomach pump and an antidote for morphine poisoning.

Whatever it took, they must keep his heart pumping. Jack was hauled to his feet and walked around his sleeping-porch. They poured more coffee down his throat, massaged his limbs and shook him. Someone even yelled that a dam on the Beauty Ranch had burst, in the hope of shocking him back to life. Whenever Jack looked as if he might return, Charmian called out: 'Mate, Mate, come back.'

All day, they tried to bring him back. But it was no use. He was drowning in his own poisons – in the toxic fluids that had seeped into his very consciousness. Even if they did find a lifeline, Jack would not reach for it. He wanted to drift off into permanent sleep, it seemed, and who could blame him? Even death would be better than limping on for a few more years, subsisting on a diet of vegetables and warm milk, unable to control his bowels, with agonising pain his constant companion. He had always wished he had become a prize-fighter, not a writer. Time now to leave the ring.

'To me the idea of death is sweet,' he had once told Charmian. 'Think of it – to lie down and go into the dark out of all the struggle and pain of living – to go to sleep and rest, always to be resting . . . when I come to die, I will be smiling at death, I promise you.'

The shadows were lengthening on the grass. His ranch-hands were huddled in quiet groups watching as the doctors tried to revive him. Soon, the sun began to set on his Beauty Ranch, his manzanita groves, his ten-thousand-year-old redwood trees, and the stone ruins of Wolf House, built to last a thousand years. Finally, Jack was laid on a mattress on his wife's sleeping-porch overlooking his Valley of the Moon. He began to beat the mattress with a loosely clenched right fist. There was a smile on his ashen face. He died at 7.45 that evening. He was just forty years of age. According to his death certificate, the cause of death was 'Uraemia following renal colic. Duration one plus ten days. Contributor chronic Interstitial Nephritis. Duration three years.'

Later that night, on the waterfront of his youth and along the alleys of the Barbary Coast, the paper-boys were the first to tell the world. The next day, the news of his death pushed even the slaughter in France off front pages around the globe. The *New York Times* eulogised his peerless contribution to American letters, but made no mention of his socialism. The left-wing press belatedly praised his efforts on behalf of the Cause, and forgave him for living in 'Dreamland', as Emma Goldman once described the Beauty Ranch. Jack's most passionate mission – to leave the land better for his having been – was completely ignored.

After almost two days of deep sleep – her first in years – Charmian had Jack's body laid in a casket, having dressed him in his favourite grey suit, similar to the one he wore when they first met. She was struck by how much smaller he looked in his coffin than in life. The 'death-wagon' arrived, and Jack was taken to Oakland to be cremated in a simple, non-religious service, attended by Bess and his daughters, his mother, and his closest friend, George Sterling. In a gesture of goodwill towards Bess and the girls, Charmian stayed away.

The service began with the Reverend B. Payne delivering a eulogy written by Sterling:

> Oh, was there ever a face of all the dead
> In which too late the living could not read
> A mute appeal for all the love unsaid –
> A mute reproach for careless word and deed? . . .
> Unfearing heart, whose patience was so long!
> Unresting mind, so hungry for the truth!
> Now hast thou rest, gentle one and strong,
> Dead like a lordly lion in its youth . . .

Before Jack's casket was closed and he disappeared for ever into the flames, his valet Sekine slipped a loving message into the breast pocket of the Master's jacket. 'Your Speech was silver,' it read, 'now your Silence is golden.'

*   *   *

Jack had always said he would rather be ashes than dust. In that wish, at least, he got his heart's desire. At sunset on 26 November 1916, a copper cylinder containing his remains was interred on a small knoll overlooking the Valley of the Moon. Oak leaves drifted across his grave as George Sterling, Charmian, Eliza and a few workmen walked silently away. To this day, a large red boulder from the ruins of Wolf House marks the end of Jack's 'adventure path'.

17

Life After Death

Our Jack is dead! He who arose from us and voiced our wrongs; who sang our hopes, and bade us stand alone, nor compromise, nor pause; who bade us dare reach out and take the world in our strong hands. Comrade! Friend! Who let the sunshine in upon dark places. Great ones may not understand, nor grant you now the measure of your mede; but, in the days to come, all men shall see. Father of *Martin Eden* and *The Iron Heel* – yes, men shall know when we arise and fight to victory!

International Socialist Review, April 1917

TWO DAYS before he died on 21 January 1924, Lenin asked his wife, Natasha Krupskaya, to read to him. The book she picked up was by Jack London. The story she read was 'Love of Life', first published in 1905. 'It was a very fine story,' she later wrote. 'In a wilderness of ice, where no human being had set foot, a sick man, dying of hunger, is making for the harbour of a big river. His strength is giving out, he cannot walk but keeps slipping, and beside him there slides a wolf – also dying of hunger. There is a fight between them: the man wins. Half-clad, half-demented, he reaches his goal. That tale greatly pleased Ilyich. Next day he asked me to read him more Jack London. But London's strong pieces of work are mixed with extraordinarily weak ones. The next tale happened to be quite another type – saturated with bourgeois morals . . . Ilyich smiled and dismissed it with a wave of the hand. That was the last time I read to him.'

From the moment of his own death, Jack provoked wildly differing critical appraisal, as he had all his life. According to his *New York Times* obituary, he had 'truly amazing powers of observation and interpretation, and though he often dealt with the impossible, he rarely, if ever missed what in art is far more important than possibility – plausibility'. But to others he was 'an ephemeral sensation as regards all but a handful of his stories', who 'mastered the outward circumstances of life, and then played with the toys'.

That Jack enjoyed in his own lifetime, as J.B. Priestley put it, 'enormous prestige, quite out of proportion to the literary merit of his story-telling', should be no surprise. He was first and foremost a commercial writer, and proud of it. 'He was writing for money and for little else, and he studied his market like a broker,' commented the *Cambridge History of American Literature* in 1918. 'Earlier literature was aristocratic – it was written for the refined few; the latest literature is democratic – it is written for the mass, and the mass is uncritical and unrefined. Its demands are gross: sensation, movement, physical thrill. London gave the mass what it demanded, every sensation which the brutal underworld he knew had afforded him.'

Money came first, art second. And to sell books, he realised quickly, he also had to sell himself. In so doing, he became a legend in his own time. He understood intuitively that what he did mattered as much as what he wrote.

'No writer in our century,' Upton Sinclair would write in 1956, 'has known greater acclaim than an idolising public accorded Jack London at the peak of his popularity. Whenever he made a public appearance, vast crowds swarmed to hear him speak. He was one of a very few whose work drew an enormous following in the popular magazines, and was equally admired by serious literary critics, sociologists, and philosophers. He had legions of friends in every country, and an unmatched zest for living. An unparalleled story-teller, London was also a social philosopher of the first rank, spearheading many of the great social and industrial reforms which by mid-century have become the law of our land.'

The first full assessment of Jack's life came from his wife, Charmian, whose two-volume biography *The Book of Jack London* appeared in the early 1920s. But it was not until the publication in 1938 of Irving Stone's *A Sailor on Horseback* that a serious attempt was made to bring Jack back to life. Dismissed by many academics as a 'biographical novel', Stone's book did however recognise that London's life was his best story, and succeeded in igniting renewed interest in his work.

It was another three decades before Jack London finally became respectable in academic circles, thanks to the efforts of several lifelong enthusiasts, notably Franklin Walker, Russ Kingman, King Hendricks and Earle Labor. His critical standing received a further boost in 1976, the centennial year of his birth, when several academic papers appeared. Andrew Sinclair's biography *Jack*, published in 1977, subverted many of the myths which Charmian had been content to leave intact. In 1988 Clarice Statz produced *American Dreamers*, an exhaustive study of Jack and Charmian's relationship.

In 1990 the Jack London Society was formed at the University of San Antonio in Texas, and soon numbered respected scholars from around the globe among its members. As one of them, Earle Labor, has put it, 'the continuing interest in London among foreign scholars – in China, Japan, and India, as well as Europe – confirms his status as a significant figure in world literature, and *The Call of the Wild* – now translated into more than eighty different languages – is America's best claim to a great world novel.'

That he is now so exalted by such academics is only one of the many ironies of Jack London's life. While he was alive he took every opportunity to lambast academia. He detested what he saw as the snobbish and patronising attitudes of East Coast literary critics, and had no time for the men in morning suits who sought to replicate the ancient privileges and civilisation of Europe rather than embrace the unbounded possibilities that lay on the shores of the Pacific.

Jack cared nothing for their verdict or that of posterity. It was in the soil on his Beauty Ranch that he saw his legacy. It was not in literature, but in blades of grass that he placed his last faith. His greatest hope was that his fellow Californians would leave the land better than they found it. It is perhaps just as well that he did not live to see the effects of corporate greed and unchecked urban growth. Were he alive today, he might write impassioned calls to arms advocating environmental activism and a return to class-based politics. Indeed, the excesses of capitalism which he so despised have not gone away. If anything, they have worsened in recent years.

While he was alive Jack always wanted to be first, to outshine his peers. In death, he got his wish. His Beauty Ranch may have been a monument to his ego, but it was also intended as a model of organic farming. Today, it has been preserved in all its glory as a state park. Most of the sixty-five thousand eucalyptus Jack planted still stand, as do the ruins of Wolf House, undisturbed since that fateful night in 1913. His vineyards now produce some of the finest wines in Sonoma County. Every bottle bears his favourite image – a wolf's head.

Jack urged Americans to look for salvation in wide open spaces, not the canyons of Wall Street, and led by example. He predated contemporary agriculturalists in his conviction that progress lay in mankind's rethinking of its relationship with the land. Many of the methods he introduced are now common practice on organic farms. He developed the first liquid manure and hollow block silos in California and pioneered the cultivation of crops such as alfalfa. In his efforts to regenerate the soil on his Beauty Ranch he was decades ahead of his time.

As a journalist, Jack's impassioned study of poverty in London's East End, *The People of the Abyss*, provided one of the models for a style of reporting that would later be dubbed 'the new journalism', and was in many ways a forerunner of George Orwell's *Down and Out in Paris and London*. The burning indignation expressed in much of his reporting has inspired many campaigning journalists. Through his articles about surfing, he helped introduce the sport to America. He is still a cult hero among well-read surfers from Waikiki beach in Hawaii to St Ives in Cornwall. He was one of the first writers to turn the natural drama of sport into stirring fiction.

Other men with fire in their belly who could also wield a pen owe Jack at least grudging respect, if not a debt. It was not John Dos Passos, Thomas Wolfe, John Steinbeck or Jack Kerouac who wrote the first book about drifting across America, but Jack London, with *The Road*. Ernest Hemingway's spare and forceful prose is reminiscent of Jack London at his best, as are his escapades in France, Italy, Spain and Cuba. It was Jack, however, who first personified the writer as man of action, who truly lived out what he wrote.

If Jack's life was a journey through the intellectual fashions and political prejudices of his time, it was also a quest to realise its ideals. As the English critic Stephen Graham has written, Jack was 'a bugle, an awakener, an annunciator, a wall-shatterer, a herald of the dawn

. . . He intuitively understood the spirit of California and the West, and spoke for her.'

Above all, it is as a uniquely Californian icon that Jack remains so fascinating. Many of his passions were prototypically Californian, including his 'boosterism' of the Golden State. At his most idealistic, he saw America's most diverse and beautiful region as a new Eden, a place where sunshine, hard graft and access to open space guaranteed the good life.

'Like most Californians,' Irving Stone has written, 'he wanted to do everything at the top of his might: work, play, laugh, love, relax, conquer, create. He was independent, self-willed, difficult to lead around by the nose; moody, volatile, often ornery, pig-headed, tempestuous, sadistic. Like most native Californians he despised mental and physical cowardice, had great personal courage . . . Since everything around him was so strong and so vast and so rich, he had boundless confidence in himself, positive that everything that sprang from the California soil was the greatest on earth.'

On the shores of Jack's Pacific, everything seemed possible. In the shadow of Sonoma Mountain, he wanted to live for a hundred years and yet still toast every dawn. He firmly believed that the future belonged to California – the land of perpetual opportunity, where he and his fellow pioneers could remake America. The west promised freedom from the squalid cities of the east and their claustrophobic values. In California, Americans could re-invent themselves as whatever they pleased. Jack was the living proof.

That millions around the globe still read his books is testament not only to the brilliance of his descriptive imagery. That *Martin Eden, The Call of the Wild, The Sea Wolf, White Fang* and *John Barleycorn* are now regarded as modern classics is not only evidence of his gifts as a story-teller. Above all, what keeps Jack London alive – long after death – is the passion and energy with which he lived, and which still sustains his best prose.

Epilogue

After Jack's death, his daughters Joan and Bess continued to live with their mother. To her credit, Charmian chose to interpret Jack's will generously, providing them with gifts and financial help. Their mother Bess, however, remained vehemently opposed to Charmian.

Joan London never quite escaped the shadow of her childhood. Her 1938 biography, *Jack London and his Times*, was in most respects a remarkably balanced account of her father's life, but it was also infused with some of the bitterness towards Jack instilled in her by her mother. Until her death in 1971, Joan remained committed to left-wing causes, writing a biography of another radical icon, the farm labourers' activist Cesar Chavez, and lecturing about Jack.

Bess, or Becky as she was known, was just nineteen months younger than Joan, yet her opposite in temperament. She grew up to be a fun-loving, easy-going woman, who spent her last years in Glen Ellen and would lovingly refer to her father as 'Daddy' until the day she died in 1991.

Eliza Shepard remained superintendent of the Beauty Ranch until her death in 1939. A remarkable woman, she was honoured by many civic organisations for her work on behalf of the Red Cross and the American Legion. The legacy of her careful management of the Beauty Ranch can still be seen today at what is now the Jack London State Park. Her grandson, Milo Shepard, is now the executor of the Jack London estate.

Charmian did not remarry, and spent the rest of her life, until her death in 1955, carefully bolstering the image of Jack London at home and abroad. She travelled extensively throughout Europe, where Jack's popularity was, if anything, even greater after his death than while he was alive. She also remained politically active, never abandoning the views she had shared with Jack.

NOTES

ABBREVIATIONS

AS – Anna Strunsky
BJL – Charmian Kittredge, *The Book of Jack London* (two
    volumes)
CK – Charmian Kittredge
DCK – The Diaries of Charmian Kittredge
HL – The Huntington Library
JL – Jack London
JLT – Joan London, *Jack London and his Times*
LJL – King Hendricks, Earle Labor and Irving Shepard
    (eds), *The Letters of Jack London* (three volumes)

FOREWORD: The Valley of the Moon

xvi 'technological miracles' LJL, p.xiv,
xvii 'a living writer' Stephen Graham,
    'Jack London', *English Review*, 33

8 'Just wait!' ibid, p. 320
8 'My mistake' ibid, p. 322
8 'a princely ego' ibid, p. 320
9 'You are' ibid, p. 326
9 'Oh, have no' BJL 2 p. 326

CHAPTER 1: Aloha Hawaii

4 'The world of adventure' quoted
    Irving Stone, *Sailor on Horseback*,
    p. 329
4 'I'm all right' BJL 2, p. 326
5 'Personality is' quoted Andrew
    Sinclair, *Jack*, p. 213
5 'I assure you' JL to Ethelda Hesser,
    21 September 1915, LJL, p. 1503
6 'Accumulation of wealth' Karl
    Marx, *Das Kapital* Vol 1
6 'Keep flat' BJL 2, p. 314
7 'Relax' JL, 'The Kanaka Surf', *On
    the Makaloa Mat*
7 'You're so little' BJL 2 p. 313
7 'Sometimes I think' ibid, p. 329
7 'Great God' JL to Mabel
    Applegarth, 30 November 1898,
    LJL, pp. 23–6
8 'night and day' BJL 2, p. 325
8 'Radical!' ibid, p. 335

CHAPTER 2: The Cruel Seas

10 'fighting for' JL, 'The Apostate'
11 'My wages were' JL to Mabel
    Applegarth, 30 November 1898, LJL,
    p. 25
12 'badge of shame', Joseph Noel,
    Footloose in Arcadia, p. 17
14 'I was a sick' JL, *John Barleycorn*,
    Chapter 4
16 'the procession' JL, 'The Apostate'
16 'In the saloons' JL, *John Barleycorn*,
    Chapter 5
17 'adopted twin' ibid, Chapter 6
18 'raw and naked' BJL 1, p. 91
19 'remained in the' Herbert Asbury,
    The Barbary Coast
20 'maundering fancy' JL, *John
    Barleycorn*, Chapter 12
20 'fine, a splendid' ibid
21 'I often think' ibid, Chapter 14
21 'Heavens!' ibid

19 'remained in the' Herbert Asbury, *The Barbary Coast*

20 'maundering fancy' JL, *John Barleycorn*, Chapter 12

20 'fine, a splendid' ibid

21 'I often think' ibid, Chapter 14

21 'Heavens!' ibid

21 'It made toward' ibid, Chapter 15

22 'the woodwork' JL, *The Sea Wolf*, Chapter 4

22 'sledge-hammer' Ninetta Eames, 'Jack London', *Overland Monthly*, May 1900

23 'In my grasp' JL, *The Cruise of the Snark*, Chapter 1

24 'It was my first' JL, *John Barleycorn*, Chapter 16

24 'covered with hides' JL, *The Sea Wolf*, Chapter 17

25 'My child life' JL to CK, 18 June 1903, LJL, p. 366

CHAPTER 3: On the Road

28 'the drinking' JL, *John Barleycorn*, Chapter 18

28 'read the books' ibid

28 'It was humdrum' ibid

29 'The life there' ibid

29 'Each mighty sea' *San Francisco Morning Call*, 12 November 1893

30 'the largeness' ibid

30 'Louis was handsome' JL, *John Barleycorn*, Chapter 18

31 'I believed' ibid, Chapter 20

32 'the adventure path' ibid

32 'every once in a while' JL, 'Road-Kids and Gay-Cats', *The Road*

33 'keeping warm' Alan Schroeder, *Jack London*, p. 42

33 'The issue is' quoted Theodore Zinn, *A People's History of the United States*, p. 275

34 'The whip hissed' JL, 'Pictures', *The Road*

36 'march the lock-step' JL, 'How I Became a Socialist', *The War of the Classes*

36 'On June 29' Prison Records, Erie County Penitentiary

36 'magnificently jingled', JL, *John Barleycorn*, Chapter 21

36 'no spring chicken' JL, 'The Pen', *The Road*

37 'handsome young mulatto' ibid

37 'I'd have liked' ibid

38 'down in . . . terrible scare' quoted JLT, p. 90

CHAPTER 4: The Boy Socialist

40 'I was working' JL, *John Barleycorn*, Chapter 21

40 'The whole history' Karl Marx, *The Communist Manifesto*

42 'spiritual blue eyes' JL, *Martin Eden*, Chapter 1

42 'pale gold flower' ibid

42 'They bristled' ibid, Chapter 2

43 'Where do you' ibid, Chapter 12

43 'to listen to' ibid

46 'I didn't want' JL, *John Barleycorn*, Chapter 22

47 'Go to hell' quoted Georgia Loring Bamford, *The Mystery of Jack London*, pp. 28–9

48 'dominating quality' James Hopper, manuscript, Bancroft Library

48 'here was all' JL, *Martin Eden*, Chapter 13

48 'mastered by curiosity' ibid

49 'Spencer asserted' Charles Child Walcutt, *American Writers*, pp. 462–3

49 'Do you know' *San Francisco Bulletin*, 28 February 1914, p. 3

52 'I was never' W.H. Chaney to JL, 4 June 1897, Irving Stone Collection, Bancroft Library

53 'the cause of' W.H. Chaney to JL, 14 June 1897 Irving Stone Collection, Bancroft Library

54 'Heavens, how' JL, *John Barleycorn*, pp. 220–1

55 'The Lover's Liturgy' *The Raven*, February 1901

CHAPTER 5: The White Silence

57 'Floundered into' Pierre Berton, *Klondike Fever*, p. 46

58 'Early in' James S. Easby-Smith, 'The Real Klondike', *Cosmopolitan*, 24 (November–April 1897–8), p. 228

58 'Klondike!' quoted Pierre Berton, *Klondike Fever*, p. 119

59 'the warmest' BJL 1, p. 222

60 'Oh, dear John' ibid

60 'I had let' JL, *John Barleycorn*, Chapter 25

60 'Hurray for' *San Francisco Examiner*, 26 July 1897

60 'We lay several' JL to Mabel Applegarth, 8 August 1897, LJL, p. 11

61 'like mosquitoes' JL, 'Which Make Men Remember', *The God of His Fathers*

62 'Keep on the ridge' JL, 'Through the Rapids on the Way to Klondike', *Home*, June 1899

63 'When we struck' ibid

63 'Their speed' JL, *Smoke Bellew*, p. 83

63 'There's no drama' Rex Beach, *Personal Exposures*, quoted Pierre Berton, *Klondike Fever*, p. 203

64 'world of silence' JL, *Burning Daylight*

65 'smoke-tarnished' Emil Jensen, 'With Jack London at Stewart River', HL

66 'It was in' JL, autobiographical sketch for Macmillan, HL

66 'When a man' JL, 'In a Far Country', *The Son of The Wolf*

67 'a wild, picturesque' quoted Pierre Berton, *Klondike Fever*, p. 318

68 'The crowded room' JL, *A Daughter of the Snows*, pp. 114–15

69 'His face was' quoted Russ Kingman, *A Pictorial Biography of Jack London*, p. 77

69 'home-made' JL, 'From Dawson to the Sea', *Buffalo Express*, 4 June 1899

70 'The three of us' ibid

70 'a vast area' ibid

70 'put up netting' JL, 'Yukon River Diary', 8–30 June 1898, HL

71 'strapping bucks' JL, 'From Dawson to the Sea', *Buffalo Express*, 4 June 1899

71 'so engrossed' ibid

72 'tawny beasts' ibid

72 'than an Eldorado' JL, 'Yukon River Diary', 18 June 1898, HL

72 'Leave St Michael' JL, journal entry, 30 June 1898, quoted BJL 1, p. 258

73 'I never realised' JL to Con Gepfert, 5 November 1900, LJL, p. 217

CHAPTER 6: Superman

74 'Critics have complained' JL, *John Barleycorn*, Chapter 26

75 'the Indian seems' JL, 'Yukon River Diary', 16 June 1898, HL

76 'I have just' JL to the editor, *San Francisco Bulletin*, 17 September 1898, LJL, p. 19

76 'If I die' JL to Mabel Applegarth, 30 November 1898, LJL, p. 26

77 'Egoism is' quoted George Seldes (ed.), *The Great Thoughts*, pp. 308–12

77 'Such an individual' Richard Tarnas, *The Passion of the Western Mind*, pp. 370–1

78 'To be a man' JL, *The War of the Classes*

78 'In 1899' quoted JLT, p. 191

78 'perfect combination' Barbara W. Tuchman, *The Proud Tower*, p. 160

78 'The White Man's Burden' by Rudyard Kipling reproduced by permission of A.P. Watt Ltd on behalf of The National Trust

79 'As for myself' JL to Elywn
   Hoffman, 27 October 1900, LJL,
   p. 216
79 'There is no' JL to Cloudesley Johns,
   30 March 1899, LJL, p. 59
79 'the chief qualification' JL, *Martin
   Eden*
80 'Well, well' JL to Mabel Applegarth,
   quoted JLT, p. 194
80 'I had my name' JL, *John Barleycorn*,
   Chapter 25
80 'I could see' Frank Atherton,
   unpublished manuscript, HL
81 'I was at' JL, introduction to *A
   Selection of Black Cat Stories*, HL
81 'Then you don't' JL, *John Barleycorn*,
   Chapter 25
82 'I would rather' quoted Russ
   Kingman, *A Pictorial Biography of
   Jack London*, p. 97
83 'About the loneliest' JL to Mabel
   Applegarth, 25 December 1898, LJL,
   p. 31
84 'It was a great' JL to AS, 1901, LJL,
   pp. 261–3
85 'To bear his' JL, 'An Odyssey of the
   North', *The Son of the Wolf*
85 'His work is' Cornelia Atwood Pratt,
   'Out of the East and the North', *The
   Critic*, 37, pp. 162–3
85 'Pennsylvania born' JL to Houghton
   Mifflin & Co, 31 January 1900, LJL,
   pp. 148–51
86 'With one foot' JLT, p. 171
86 'That's the way' ibid, p. 194
87 'Good easy reading' Frank Munsey,
   'The Publisher's Desk', *Munsey's*,
   April 1899
88 'corrupt new' Richard Ruland and
   Malcolm Bradbury, *From Puritanism
   to Postmodernism*, p. 222
89 'a romantic popular' Richard Ruland
   and Malcolm Bradbury, *From
   Puritanism to Postmodernism: A
   History of American Literature*, p. 244
89 'coarseness and strength' quoted Dr
   Alan Axelrod and Charles Phillips,

*What Every American Should Know
About American History*, p. 218
89 'Of course' JL to Cloudesley Johns,
   22 December 1900, LJL, pp. 224–8
90 'rather be ashes' quoted Russ
   Kingman, *A Pictorial Biography of
   Jack London*, p. 274
90 'I should like' JL to Cloudesley
   Johns, 4 February 1901, LJL, p. 239
90 'Jack London is' *San Francisco
   Evening Post*, 26 January 1901
91 'wonderful and' JL (with AS), *The
   Kempton–Wace Letters*, quoted JLT,
   p. 223
91 'seven sturdy' Rose Wilder Lane,
   'Life and Jack London', *Sunset*,
   October 1917–May 1918
91 'slender and' Joseph Noel, *Footloose
   in Arcadia*, pp. 50–1
92 'You know I' JL to Ninetta Eames,
   3 April 1900, LJL, p. 178
93 'We are greatly' S.S. McLure to JL,
   quoted Irving Stone, *Sailor on
   Horseback*, p. 141

CHAPTER 7: Howling at the Moon

95 'a pretty little' Joseph Noel,
   Footloose in Arcadia, p. 147
95 'receiving a male' Emma Goldman,
   Living My Life
95 'a young man' AS to CK, 17
   January 1919, BJL 1, p. 323
96 'He systematised' Hal Waters,
   'Anna Strunsky and Jack London',
   American Book Collector, 17
   (November 1966), p. 30
96 'I too was' JL to AS, 21 December
   1899, LJL, pp. 135–6
96 'Our friendship' JLT, p. 217
97 'A young Jewess' JL to Cloudesley
   Johns, 17 October 1900, LJL, p. 214
97 'No, I am not' JLT, p. 223
97 'love is a disorder' JL (with AS),
   The Kempton–Wace Letters, p. 87
97 'toils of an' ibid, p. 25

98 'Jack London' Arnold Genthe, *As I Remember*, p. 49

98 'I never saw' Finn Frolich, interview with Irving Stone, Irving Stone Collection, Bancroft Library

100 'You are handling' JL to Cloudesley Johns, 16 June 1900, LJL, pp. 191–3

100 'If I see' JL to Cloudesley Johns, 10 March 1900, LJL, pp. 167–9

101 'the hot-house breeds' JL, *A Daughter of the Snows*

101 'In spite of' Nathaniel Hawthorne, *Wilshire's* magazine, 62 (February 1903), pp. 84–7

101 'The sharp-beaked' JL, *A Daughter of the Snows*

102 'I do not' JL to Cloudesley Johns, 12 December 1899, LJL, p. 133

102 'Socialism is not' JL to Cloudesley Johns, 23 June 1899, LJL, p. 89

102 'And, O Anna' JL to AS, 6 January 1901, LJL, p. 235

102 'save the mother' Joan London, *Jack London and his Daughters*, p. 3

102 'just when' JL to AS, 26 December 1900, LJL, pp. 228–9

102 'a great novel' Cresmer Collection, University of Southern California

103 'the ideal poet' Gertrude Atherton, *My San Francisco*, p. 100

103 'Our first dinner' Joseph Noel, *Footloose in Arcadia*, p. 80

104 'cannibal sandwich' ibid, p. 86

104 'The smells alone' ibid, p. 89

104 'Don't let them' ibid, p. 90

105 'You think' ibid, p. 92

105 'Here is' ibid, p. 94

108 'that what the' JLT, p. 236

108 'It's money' JL to Cloudesley Johns, 1 March 1900, LJL, p. 164

109 'If cash comes' JL to Cloudesley Johns, 21 November 1899, LJL, p. 129

109 'I dined yesterday' JL to AS, 5 January 1902, LJL, pp. 269–70

109 'the very best' George Brett to JL, 3 December 1902, HL

111 'Mr Brett' Donald Sheehan, *This was Publishing*, p. 56

111 'god's own mad' BJL 1, p. 11

111 'cordial and' *San Francisco Chronicle*, 30 June 1904, p. 9

111 'It was her' quoted Irving Stone, *Sailor on Horseback*, p. 165

112 'Dear, Dear You' JL to AS, 10 June 1902, LJL, pp. 297–8

112 'the cruellest woman' JL to AS, 25 August 1902, LJL, pp. 306–7

CHAPTER 8: The Abyss

114 'A man does' JL to Cloudesley Johns, 8 November 1901, LJL, p. 258

114 'Concerning myself' JL to Cloudesley Johns, 12 July 1902, LJL, p. 301

115 'A week from' JL to AS, 31 July 1902, LJL, pp. 303–4

115 'Drive me' JL, *The People of the Abyss*, Chapter 1

116 'The London Abyss' ibid, Chapter 19

116 'I am worn' JLT, p. 240

116 'the paradise of' JL, *The People of the Abyss*, Chapter 17

117 'giddy battles' ibid, Chapter 6

118 'the most splendid' ibid, Chapter 12

118 'Out all night' JL to AS, 25 August 1902, LJL, p. 307

118 'How often' JL to George and Carrie Sterling, 22 August 1902, LJL, p. 306

119 'Their faces' JL, *The People of the Abyss*, Chapter 20

119 'Of all my' JL to Leon Weilskov, 16 October 1916, LJL, p. 1590

119 'If this is' JL, *The People of the Abyss*, Chapter 24

120 'has written' C.F.G. Masterman, *London Daily News*, 28 November 1903

120 'snobbishness' quoted JLT, p. 297

120 'Henceforth' JL to AS, 29 September 1902, LJL, p. 313

120 'Anyway, if I' quoted Russ Kingman, *A Pictorial Biography of Jack London*, p. 115

121 'On the train' JL to Arthur T. Vance, 18 July 1906, LJL, pp. 593–5

121 'Oh, it was' JL to AS, 15 October 1902, HL

121 'a wrinkled sack' quoted Irving Stone, *Sailor on Horseback*, pp. 170–1

121 'I want to get' JL to George Brett, 21 November 1902, LJL, pp. 317–22

122 'I hope that' George Brett to JL, 3 December 1902, HL

122 'Once I am' JL to George Brett, 21 November 1902, LJL, pp. 317–22

122 'jerked from' JL, *The Call of the Wild*, Chapter 2

123 'His muscles became' ibid

124 'There is an' ibid, Chapter 3

124 'remove few' George Brett to JL, 19 February 1903, HL

125 'The most virile' Russ Kingman, *A Pictorial Biography of Jack London*, p. 125

125 'struck the chord' Richard O'Connor, *Jack London: A Biography*, p. 176

125 'dreamland of' Granville Hicks, *The Great Tradition*, p. 194

125 'Except for' Kenneth S. Lynn, 'Disturber of Gentility', *New York Times Book Review*, 14 February 1965

125 'dominant primordial', JL, *The Call of the Wild*, Chapter 3

125 'In describing' Roderick Nash (ed.), *The Call of the Wild 1900–1916*, p. 2

125 'I was unconscious' JLT, p. 252

126 'When the long' JL, *The Call of the Wild*, Chapter 7

CHAPTER 9: Behind Enemy Lines

129 'an enchanted little ' Joan London, *Jack London and his Daughters*, p. 1

130 'sycophants, well' JLT, p. 256

130 'upward of' Joseph Noel, *Footloose in Arcadia*, p. 149

131 'a rusty foghorn' Herman Scheffauer to CK, 8 June 1926, HL

131 'She's devoted' Joseph Noel, *Footloose in Arcadia*, p. 150

132 'laughter a little' JLT, pp. 260–1

132 'Ask people' JL to CK, 18 June 1903, LJL, p. 366

133 'Yes, I have' BJL 2, p. 62

133 'Yes, we must' JL to CK, 1 September 1903, LJL, p. 382

134 'I'm leaving you' Irving Stone, *Sailor on Horseback*, p. 183

134 'When I say' JL to CK, 10 November 1903, HL

135 'Ah, my love' CK to JL, 12 September 1903, HL

135 'I had all' JL to CK, 27 October 1903, LJL, p. 397

135 'Sometimes' CK to JL, 12 September 1903, HL

136 'Mr Jack London' *Chicago Record Herald*, 12 August 1903

136 'It will soon' JL to AS, 23 July 1904, LJL, p. 436

136 'the very highest' JL to AS, 14 August 1903, LJL, p. 378

136 'Remember' JL to CK, 24 September 1903, LJL, p. 389

138 'the most admired' Richard O'Connor, *Jack London: A Biography*, p. 205

139 'Well, concerning' JL to CK, 13 February 1904, LJL, p. 412

140 'physical wreck' Robert Dunn, *World Alive*, pp. 117–18

140 'the combination' JL, *San Francisco Examiner*, 3 March 1904

140 'I am profoundly' JL to CK, 6 May 1904, LJL, p. 427

141 'after a good' Robert Dunn, *World Alive*, pp. 117–18

141 'Jack's front false' Frederick Palmer, *With My Own Eyes*, p. 238

141 'the most inherently' Frederick
Palmer, *With Kuroki in Manchuria*,
p. 242

142 'dressed in European' *San Francisco
Examiner*, 26 February 1904

142 'Perfect rot' JL to CK, 29 March
1904, LJL, p. 421

142 'These men' *San Francisco
Examiner*, 1 May 1904

142 'an international incident', Robert
Dunn, *World Alive*, p. 117

143 'I want to say' ibid

143 'They may be' Frederick Palmer,
With My Own Eyes, p. 242

143 'the menace to' JL, 'The Yellow
Peril', *San Francisco Examiner*, 25
September 1904, p. 45

143 'cursed the entire' Edmund Peluso,
quoted Richard O'Connor, *Jack
London: A Biography*, pp. 220–1

143 'What the devil' ibid

CHAPTER 10: Yours for the
Revolution

145 'I fear you' quoted Irving Stone,
Sailor on Horseback, pp. 202–3

146 'Absurd is hardly' AS, *San Francisco
Chronicle*, 30 June 1904, p. 9

146 'a figment of' quoted Richard
O'Connor, *Jack London: A
Biography*, p. 225

147 'I saw you' quoted Irving Stone,
Sailor on Horseback, p. 208

147 'I realise Mate's' DCK, 8 March
1905, HL

147 'I am not' CK to Blanche
Partington, 8 March 1907, Blanche
Partington Collection, Bancroft
Library

147 'So good' DCK, 15 July 1905, HL

148 'No, I am' JL to George Sterling, 1
June 1905, LJL, pp. 487–8

148 'certain inadvertancies' Ninetta
Eames, 'Jack London', *Overland
Monthly*, May 1900, pp. 417–25

149 'a beast with' JL, *The Game*, p. 117

149 'struck him' JL, *The Sea Wolf*,
Chapter 12

150 'came in like' ibid, Chapter 21

150 'life is a' ibid, Chapter 6

150 'Underneath we' ibid, Chapter 5

150 'I had never' ibid, Chapter 12

150 'a great Man-Comrade' JL to CK,
July 1903, LJL, p. 370

151 'was as the' JL, *The Sea Wolf*,
Chapter 14

151 'a delicate, ethereal' ibid, Chapter 23

151 'Truly she was' ibid, Chapter 36

151 'The "love" element' Ambrose
Bierce to George Sterling, 18
February 1905, Special Collections,
Stanford University Libraries

152 'the critics' JL, 'Experiences',
manuscript notes, HL

152 'a rattling good' Ambrose Bierce to
George Sterling, 18 February 1905

152 'a complex of' quoted Russ
Kingman, *A Pictorial Biography of
Jack London*, p. 141

153 'a loaded revolver' AS, *The Masses*,
p. 14

153 'I meditated' JL, *John Barleycorn*,
Chapter 28

153 'The things' ibid

154 'Anglo-Saxon ' BJL 2, p. 188

155 'I am really ' JL to George Sterling,
28 May 1905, LJL, pp. 485–6

155 'no matter how' George Brett to JL,
12 June 1905 HL

155 'I'm going to' JL to George Brett, 5
December 1904, LJL, p. 454

156 'I have been' George Brett to JL, 22
October 1906, Utah State
University; quoted LJL, p. 630

156 'a nature faker' Theodore
Roosevelt, interview with Edward B.
Clark, *Everybody's Magazine*, June
1907

156 'President Roosevelt' JL, *Collier's*, 8
September 1908

157 'a non-existent' Thomas
Williamson, *Far North Country*,
pp. 73–4

157 'The sin' Arthur Stringer, 'The Canada Fakers', *Canada West*, 4 October 1908, p. 1140

157 'a horrible land' Cornelia Atwood Pratt, 'Out of the East and the North', *Critic*, 37, July–December 1900, p. 162

157 'London's novels' Barry Lopez, *Of Wolves and Men*, p. 218

157 'In all his' Stephen Graham, *The Death of Yesterday*, p. 58

158 'If Slocum could' BJL 2, pp. 62–3

158 'Oh, by the way' JL to George Brett, 1 August 1905, LJL, pp. 504–5

159 'Socialism deals with' JL, *The War of the Classes*, Preface

160 'except that' Alvin A. Teeney, *Charities*, 15 (1905), p. 403

160 'I was a' JL, *John Barleycorn*, pp. 256–7

160 'I'm not a' *Oskaloosa* (Iowa) *Herald*, 3 November 1905

161 'You must not' *Common Sense*, 14 January 1905, p. 1

161 'You are drones' 'Jack London and Silk-Stocking Society', *Miner's Magazine*, 13 April 1905, p. 12

162 'a natural' JL, *The Iron Heel*, Chapter 1

162 'Pyschologically speaking' Earle Labor and Jeanne Campbell Reesman, *Jack London*, p. 65

162 'The gown' JL, *The Iron Heel*, p. 39

162 'When you reach' ibid, pp. 96–7

163 'dim, ferocious' ibid, pp. 326–7

163 'out of his' Philip Foner, *Jack London: American Rebel*, p. 95

164 'If they find' quoted ibid.

164 'as a work' H. Addington Bruce, 'More Books on Socialism', *Outlook*, 89, May–August 1908, p. 338

165 'that particular genius' JLT, pp. 313–15

165 'The fact is' ibid

165 'London could' Sonia Orwell and Ian Angus (eds), *The Collected Essays,*

Journalism and Letters of George Orwell, p. 25

165 'Genuine blood-red' 'They All Wear Red to Hear Jack London', *New York Times*, 20 January 1906

166 'strode down' ibid

166 'Consider the' 'Revolution', *War of the Classes*

166 'were inflamed' Upton Sinclair, *Cup of Fury*, p. 53

167 'Grant married us' DCK, 19 November 1905, HL

168 'I'll get married' *San Francisco Call*, 21 November 1905, p. 4

168 'Fame depends' Joseph Noel, *Footloose in Arcadia*, p. 149

168 'the Socialist apostle' quoted Richard O'Connor, *Jack London: A Biography*, p. 240

168 'ugly-faced girl' BJL 2, p. 87

168 'Throw on' ibid, p. 115

CHAPTER 11: The Voyage of the *Snark*

170 'his canvas' Gordon Thomas and Max Morgan Witts, *The San Francisco Earthquake*, p. 65

171 'pillar of fire' BJL 2, p. 125

171 'That night' ibid, p. 127

171 'At nine o'clock' JL, 'The Story of an Eye-Witness', *Collier's*, 5 May 1906

172 'Yesterday morning' BJL 2, p. 127

173 'San Francisco is' JL, 'The Story of an Eye-Witness', *Collier's*, 5 May 1906

173 'Spare no expense' BJL 2, p. 143

174 'sagging a little' Mary Austin, 'George Sterling at Carmel', *American Mercury*, 11 (1927), p. 69

174 'George Sterling' Arnold Genthe, *As I Remember*, pp. 75–6

175 'Jack London' *New York Times*, 9 March 1907

175 'There isn't a' BJL 2, p. 147

176 'I won't be' JL to Arthur T. Vance, LJL, p. 678

176 'Don't get the' 'Jack London Tells of Social Revolution', *New York Call*, 28 January 1912

176 'bold black eyes' BJL 2 p. 155

176 'Will God have' ibid

176 'Just try me' Osa Johnson, *I Married Adventure*, p. 44

176 'When it comes' JL to Martin Johnson, 17 November 1906, LJL, pp. 632–4

178 'the type of' Frank Pease, *Seven Arts Magazine*, 1 (December 1916–April 1917), p. 523

178 'He was excited' Joan London, *Jack London and his Daughters*, p. 67

178 'chequebook' Irving Stone, *Sailor on Horseback*, p. 236

179 'played the most' Martin Johnson, *Through the South Seas with Jack London*, p. 50

179 'Consider them both' Herman Melville, *Typee*

180 'More trust' JL, *The Cruise of the Snark*, Chapter 2

180 'I have seen' Martin Johnson, *Through the South Seas with Jack London*, p. 53

181 'One whole afternoon' JL, *The Cruise of the Snark*, Chapter 4

181 'He would get' Martin Johnson, *Through the South Seas with Jack London*, p. 72

182 'ethereal creature' JL, *Martin Eden*, Chapter 1

182 'They were numskulls' ibid, Chapter 40

183 'Down, down' ibid, Chapter 46

184 'Jack London created' *San Francisco Chronicle*, 18 August 1907, p. 46

185 'mildewed' A. Grove Day, *Jack London in the South Seas*, p. 51

185 'So utterly, agedly' JL, *The Cruise of the Snark*, Chapter 14

185 'I thought it' BJL 2, p. 139

185 'It was like' JL, 'To Build a Fire', *Lost Face*

186 'He is impassive' JL, *The Cruise of the Snark*, Chapter 6

186 'Get off that' ibid.

187 'Don't let me' A. Grove Day, *Jack London in the South Seas*, pp. 55–6

187 'the pit of' JL, *The Cruise of the Snark*, Chapter 7

187 'greeted in' A. Grove Day, *Jack London in the South Seas*, p. 67

187 'the audience' CK, *The Log of the Snark*, p. 45

188 'In the eery' ibid

188 'write us up' JL, *The Cruise of the Snark*, Chapter 7

188 'a sneak' *Honolulu Sunday Advertiser*, 22 May 1910

189 'a living ravage' JL, 'The Sheriff of Kona', *The House of Pride*

189 'monsters' JL, 'Koolau the Leper', *The House of Pride*

CHAPTER 12: The Heart of Darkness

190 'gaunt and' Martin Johnson, *Through the South Seas with Jack London*, pp. 151–2

191 'wedged between' JL, *The Cruise of the Snark*, Chapter 9

191 'Fallible and frail' ibid, Foreword, pp. 6–7

191 'the delightful' CK, *The Log of the Snark*, p. 80, HL

192 'a placid harbour' JL, *The Cruise of the Snark*, Chapter 10

193 'All this strength' ibid

194 'The air was' ibid

194 'the heavens roll' quoted A. Grove Day, *Jack London in the South Seas*, p. 104

195 'a covert attack' Ninetta Eames to George Brett, 11 July 1907

195 'There is one' JL to Ninetta Eames, 25 July 1907, LJL, p. 700

195 'that woman' Ninetta Eames to JL, 11 July 1907, quoted LJL, p. 701

196 'I think Jack' DCK, 6 February
    1908, HL
197 'What does' JL, *The Cruise of the
    Snark*, p. 181
198 'How did they' CK, *The Log of the
    Snark*, p. 208, HL
198 'I wouldn't have' ibid, p. 210
199 'teak-hulled' JL, *The Cruise of the
    Snark*, pp. 260–80
200 'Bristling with' CK, *The Log of the
    Snark*, p. 814, HL
200 'She's not going' JL, *The Cruise of
    the* Snark, Chapter 15
200 'Like vultures' ibid
201 'dull and crusty' DCK, 19 July 1908,
    HL
201 'an orgy of' DCK, 21 July 1908 HL
203 'Bunster had' JL, 'Mauki', *South
    Seas Tales*
204 'The black will' JL, 'The Inevitable
    White Man', *South Seas Tales*
204 'must have a' JL, 'The Terrible
    Solomons', *South Seas Tales*
204 'When one considers' JL, *The
    Cruise of the* Snark, Chapter 10
206 'The skin peels' CK, *The Log of the
    Snark*, p. 357, HL
206 'I am sending' JL to Bess London,
    27 October 1908, LJL, p. 769
207 'the future belongs' JL, 'Strike
    Methods: America and Australia,'
    Sydney Star, 14 January 1909
208 'too willing' *Socialist*, 12 March 1909
208 'God knows' JL to the editor,
    Socialist, March 1909, LJL,
    pp. 795–6
208 'Am boxing' JL to George and
    Carrie Sterling, 2 May 1909, LJL,
    p. 800
209 'unutterably weary' quoted Richard
    O'Connor, *Jack London: A
    Biography*, p. 275

CHAPTER 13: King of the Castle

210 'out of his' *The Bookman*, 30
    November 1916, pp. 278–80

211 'This is a' quoted Philip Foner,
    Jack London: American Rebel,
    p. 104
211 '*Martin Eden*' Jonathan Harold
    Spinner, *Michigan Academician*,
    III, summer 1970, p. 48
212 'I'm darned' quoted Russ Kingman,
    A Pictorial Biography of Jack London,
    p. 160
213 'trivial in plot' *Boston Evening
    Transcript*
213 'I, in the' quoted Russ Kingman, *A
    Pictorial Biography of Jack London*,
    p. 118
213 'a new country' JL, *The Valley of the
    Moon*, pp. 413–14
214 'grading the land' JL to Geddes
    Smith, 31 October 1916, LJL,
    pp. 1600–1
214 'I believe' JL to Frederick H.
    Robinson, *Medical Review of
    Reviews*, 5 September 1913, LJL,
    p. 1226
215 'Depend on me' JL to William
    English Walling, 30 November
    1909, LJL, p. 844
215 'I have been' *San Francisco
    Chronicle*, 8 January 1911, p. 78
216 'I am trying' JL to Hartwell S.
    Shippey, 7 February 1913, LJL,
    p. 1122
217 'Oh they won't' Adela Rogers
    St John, *Final Verdict*, pp. 354–7
217 'despised and mistrusted' Joan
    London, *Jack London and his
    Daughters*, p. 167
217 'declaring war' ibid, p. 169
217 'In reply to' JL to Bess Maddern, 8
    January 1911, LJL, pp. 969–71
219 'we three' BJL 2, p. 186
220 'ranch of good intentions' Bailey
    Millard, 'Jack London, Farmer', *The
    Bookman*, 1916
220 'Sometime, when' JL to Eileen
    Moretta, 18 October 1911, LJL,
    pp. 1039–40
220 'he was always' BJL 2, p. 205

221 'mouth parched' JL, *John Barleycorn*, Chapter 34

221 'This is what' BJL 2, p. 218

222 'The plucked bird' JL to Elizabeth Kleber, 5 November 1914, LJL, pp. 1386–7

222 'figure the horses' BJL 2, p. 205

222 'I dream of' JLT, pp. 336–7

224 'survived where' JL, *John Barleycorn*, Chapter 17

224 'a supreme organic' JL, *Burning Daylight*

226 'a ghostly' Fred Lockley, 'Impressions and Observations of the *Journal* Man', *Oregon Journal*, 5 January 1913

226 'Oh, it's only' BJL 2, p. 222

226 'sew on the' quoted Richard O'Connor, *Jack London: A Biography*, p. 284

227 'The anarchists' BJL 2, p. 184

227 'Oh, don't say' ibid. p. 224

227 'soft, pretty ways' ibid. p. 250

227 'A man finds' Adela Rogers St John, *Final Verdict*, pp. 354–8

228 'In a few' *Daily Journal*, Willows, California, 31 August 1911

228 'Why should I' JL, notes in Josiah Flynt, *My Life*, p. 293, HL

229 'not fancy' quoted Kevin Starr, *Californians and the American Dream*, p. 235

229 'Boy or girl' BJL 2 p. 189

229 'Anglo-Saxon' ibid. p. 188

230 'More babies' quoted DCK, 3 July 1910, HL

230 'How many' CK to 'Fannie', 1 July 1910, HL

230 'I had the' *San Francisco Examiner*, 23 June 1910

231 'someday, somehow' 29 July 1910, LJL, pp. 916–18

231 'This young man' *San Francisco Call*, 2 August 1910, p. 4

231 'the ocean will' quoted Richard O'Connor, *Jack London: A Biography*, p. 305

231 'Damn Ambrose' JL to CK, 29 July 1910, LJL, p. 915

231 'Here you are' quoted Richard O'Connor, *Jack London: A Biography*, pp. 307–8

232 'Jack looked' BJL 2, p. 197

233 'weren't dry' JL to George Brett, 18 October 1911, LJL, p. 1037

234 'I am on' JL to Doubleday, 20 September 1911, LJL, p. 1026

235 'Almost any passage' BJL 2, p. 230

CHAPTER 14: Whiskey and Rye

236 'I have been' JL to W.G. Beecroft, 7 February 1913, Utah State University

237 'house in order' Joseph Noel, *Footloose in Arcadia*, p. 220

237 'Don't forget' BJL 2 p. 232

237 'unmistakable emphasis' Joseph Noel, *Footloose in Arcadia*, p. 221

237 'with little dabs' ibid. p. 223

237 'Arthur Rimbaud' ibid. p. 224

238 'the best place' *Oakland Tribune*, BJL 2 p. 236

239 'Never was such' Gertrude Atherton, *Ancestors*, p. 369

239 'London's failure' Kevin Starr, *Californians and the American Dream*, p. 261

239 'Wait until' BJL 2 p. 239

240 'deep down' JL, 'The Terrible and the Tragic in Fiction'

240 'moody, often' Earle Labor and Jeanne Campbell Reesman, *Jack London*, p. 67

240 'Jack's shaved head' CK, Dirigo Journal, 1 March 1912, HL

240 'I drink very' BJL 2 p. 245

240 'That is what' ibid

241 'Jack is swinging' CK, Dirigo Journal, 16 April 1912, HL

241 'grinning the tops' DCK, 16 March 1912 HL

242 'Cape Horn on' BJL 2 p. 241

242 'I listened' BJL 1, pp. 42–3

243 'What's the matter' CK, Dirigo Journal, 17 June 1912, HL

243 'almost forgotten' BJL 2 p. 244

243 'old acquaintance' ibid

244 'In the working-class' JL, *Novels and Social Writings*, p. 1144

244 'My face changed' BJL 2, p. 255

244 'Allan and I' DCK, 4 March 1913, HL

245 'As for Hamilton' JL to CK, 19 November 1912, LJL, pp. 1100–1

245 'I am the proudest' DCK, 10 March 1913, HL

245 'Three characters' JL to Roland Phillips, 14 March 1913, LJL, p. 1135

246 'the natural expression' JL (with AS), *The Kempton–Wace Letters*, p. 203

246 'snapped with' JL, *The Valley of the Moon* Chapter 30

246 'London has written' *New York Times Review of Books*, 9 November 1913, p. 607

247 'Jack London' 'A Tireless Romancer', *Current Opinion*, 54 (1913), p. 490

247 'from 1910' Carolyn Johnston, *Jack London: An American Radical?*, p. 163

247 'a story about' Kevin Starr, *Californians and the American Dream*, p. 227

247 'girlish and sweet' JL, *The Little Lady of the Big House*

248 'good stuff' ibid, p. 95

248 'She beat me' ibid, p. 382

248 'Sleepy, sleepy' ibid, p. 392

249 'There is a' JL to Eliza Shepard, 2 December 1913, Utah State University

249 'I shall appear' *Los Angeles Express*, May 1913

249 'Gruff and businesslike' Hobart Bosworth, 'My Jack London', *Mark Twain Quarterly*, Fall/Winter 1949

249 'Jack and Charmian' ibid

250 'If they get' BJL 2, p. 255

250 'in every court' Joseph Noel, *Footloose in Arcadia*, pp. 238–9

250 'When we turned' JL to CK, 1 February 1914, LJL, p. 1296

251 'Oh, I know' JL to CK, 29 January 1914, LJL, p. 1295

251 'Young writing men' Will Irwin, *The Making of a Reporter*, p. 84

252 'the messenger of' JL, *John Barleycorn*, Chapter 35

252 'a classic of' John Sutherland, introduction to The World's Classics edition of *John Barleycorn* (Oxford, 1989), p. 24

252 'I achieved' JL, *John Barleycorn*, Chapter 34

253 'Jack had hurtled' Upton Sinclair, *Cup of Fury*, p. 164

253 'vivid and palpitating' *San Francisco Examiner*, 3 October 1913, p. 22

254 'I am absolutely' *New York Times*, 3 November 1915, p. 1

254 'As a tract' 'Notes', *Nation*, 97 (July–December 1913), p. 190

254 'That the work' Upton Sinclair, *Cup of Fury*, p. 165

254 '*John Barleycorn* is' quoted Russ Kingman, *A Pictorial Biography of Jack London*, p. 241

254 'but one freedom' JL, *John Barleycorn*, Chapter 38

254 'No, I decided' ibid, Chapter 39

255 'the most beautiful' 'The House that Jack Built', *National Parks Magazine*, 35 (November 1961) p. 5

255 'It would serve' Mark Twain, quoted Joseph Noel, *Footloose in Arcadia*, p. 168

CHAPTER 15: Twilight of the Idol

256 'What's the use' BJL 2 p. 261

258 'The key-note' JL to Roland Phillips, 26 March 1914, LJL, p. 1315

258 'pretty picayune world' BJL 2, p. 375

259 'What do you' JL to Joan London, 24 August 1913, LJL, pp. 1218–19

259 'Daddy was deadly' Joan London, *Jack London and his Daughters*, p. 173

259 'Everything he had' ibid, p. 175

260 'In reply to' JL to Joan London, 24 February 1914, LJL, pp. 1298–1301

263 'exciting, excessively' *Outlook*, 108 (September–December 1914), p. 846

263 'You are right' JL to Charles L. Marriott, 24 June 1913, HL

264 'far more interested' BJL 2, p. 269

264 'The soil is' JL to Geddes Smith, 31 October 1916, LJL, pp. 1600–1

264 'disheartenment with' CK, 13 December 1916

264 'Napoleon of the pen' AS, *The Masses*

265 'I'm going to' BJL 2, p. 281

266 'Now I may' ibid, p. 289

266 'Young Men' 'The Good Soldier', *International Socialist Review*, 14 (1913–14), p. 199

266 'We socialists' JL, 4 February 1911, LJL, pp. 980–1

267 'stupid anarchs' quoted JLT, p. 351

267 'shake down' quoted Philip Foner, *Jack London: American Rebel*, p. 116

268 'foments all the' ibid

268 'Let's go and' Ford Madox Ford, 'Jack London', *Living Age*, January 1917

269 'peaked, yellow' Robert Dunn, *World Alive*, p. 202

269 'cleaned out' Richard O'Connor, *Jack London: A Biography*, p. 361

269 'desperate, cautious' BJL 2, p. 299

270 'That an eminent' JLT, p. 352

270 'flattering good' 'Appeal to Reason', 10 April 1915

270 'a tragic sellout' JLT, p. 353

271 'I can only' JL to H. Braam, 11 December 1914, LJL, pp. 1389–90

271 'God help them' BJL 2, p. 346

271 'Belgium is' JL to Thomas Hall Caine, 16 November 1914, LJL, p. 1388

271 'snapped' BJL 2, p. 345

272 'No more open' JL, 'The Impossibility of War', *Overland Monthly*, March 1900

272 'Again I say' BJL 2, pp. 301–2

272 'As regards' ibid, p. 347

273 'Getting old' ibid, pp. 305–6

273 'worn down' Joseph Noel, *Footloose in Arcadia*, p. 270

273 'severe and persistent' W.R. Gowers, *Diagnosis of Diseases of the Brain and of the Spinal Cord*, p. 195

CHAPTER 16: The Noseless One

275 'What am I' BJL 2, p. 375

276 'Except for my' JL to Roland Phillips, 14 March 1913, LJL, p. 1135

276 'Is this perverted' Wilson Follett, 'Sentimentalist, Satirist and Realist: Notes on Some Recent Fiction', *Atlantic Monthly*, 118 (July–December 1916), p. 495

276 'Read *John Barleycorn*' JLT, p. 358

276 'As I remember' JL to Mary Austin, 5 November 1915, LJL, p. 1513

276 'higher way' Lady Isobel Ryder to JL, 7 March 1915, HL

276 'idol had fallen' Alexander Cotter to JL, 22 May 1915, HL

276 'Let me tell' JL to Alexander Cotter, 18 June 1915, LJL, p. 1471

277 'It is dreadfully' JL to George Brett, 7 October 1914, LJL, p. 1377–8

277 'I am afraid' JL to Walter S. Kerr, 26 January 1915, LJL, p. 1415

278 'Now I want' JL to Joan London, 4 February 1915, LJL, pp. 1419–20

278 'There was scant' quoted *Our Hawaii: Islands and Islanders* (New York, 1922), p. 338

280 'white man's dog', JL, *Jerry of the Islands*, p. 289

280 'ain't nothing' JL, *Michael, Brother of Jerry*, p. 309

280 'might be carved' quoted Philip
    Foner, *Jack London: American Rebel*,
    p. 118
280 'He, who by' Upton Sinclair (ed.),
    *The Cry for Justice: An Anthology
    of the Literature of Social Protest*
281 'The mynah birds' JL to Joseph
    Conrad, 4 June 1915, LJL,
    pp. 1467–8
282 'I am immensely' Joseph Conrad to
    JL, 10 September 1915, LJL, p. 1468.
    Reproduced by permission of the
    Trustees of the Joseph Conrad
    Estate
283 'Take a letter' BJL 2, p. 336
283 'I am resigning,' JL to the Members
    of Local Glen Ellen Socialist Labor
    Party, 7 March 1916, LJL, pp. 1537–8
284 'What will you' BJL 2, p. 337
284 'permeated and corrupted' Eugene
    V. Debs, 'The Danger Ahead',
    International Socialist Review,
    January 1911
285 'They deny' quoted Philip Foner,
    Jack London: American Rebel, p. 128
285 'I gave a' JL to William Davenport,
    21 September 1916, Utah State
    University
286 'the character and' Carl Jung,
    Pyschology of the Unconscious, HL.
    Also quoted BJL 2, p. 355
286 'Mate-Woman' BJL 2, p. 323
286 'The hidden treasure' Carl Jung,
    Two Essays on Analytical Pyschology
287 'went to startling' BJL 2, p. 325
287 'My Biography' JL, notes on
    nightpad, 1916, HL
288 'glimpsed the shining' JL, 'The
    Kanaka Surf', *On the Makaloa Mat*
289 'Perhaps' CK, 'Charmette', HL
289 'When I am' JL, 'The Water Baby',
    On the Makaloa Mat
289 'Jack chose death' quoted Clarice
    Statz, *American Dreamers*, p. 314
290 'Our Jack has' BJL 2, p. 352
290 'the morning of' JL, *The Acorn
    Planter*

290 'Come here and' BJL 2, p. 371
291 'Most adolescent' Joan London,
    Jack London and his Daughters,
    p. 177
291 'How very ill' ibid
292 'Afraid to say' Joseph Noel,
    Footloose in Arcadia, p. 258
292 'My choice' JL to *New York World*,
    27 October 1916, LJL, pp. 1598–9
292 'a sure ticket' BJL 2, p. 372
292 'I am the sailor' ibid, p. 267
293 'exquisite tiny' ibid, p. 73
293 'There are enough' ibid, p. 383
294 'Jack, you are' quoted Irving Stone,
    Sailor on Horseback, p. 327
294 'Your duck was' BJL 2, p. 382
295 'Socialist autobiography' JL, notes
    on nightpad, 1916, HL
295 'Next Sunday' JL to Joan London,
    21 November 1916, LJL, p. 1604
296 'Yes, what' BJL 2, p. 386
296 'Mate, Mate' ibid, p. 388
296 'To me the' ibid, p. 75
297 'death-wagon' ibid, p. 388
297 'Oh, was there' quoted Russ
    Kingman, *A Pictorial Biography of
    Jack London*, p. 275
297 'Your Speech was' BJL 2, p. 340

CHAPTER 17: Life After Death

299 'It was a' N.K. Krupskaya,
    Memories of Lenin, pp. 208–9
299 'truly amazing' *New York Times*, 24
    November 1916
300 'an ephemeral' Frederick Lewis
    Pattee, *Cambridge History of
    Literature*, quoted JLT, p. 380
300 'mastered the outward' Waldo
    Frank, *Our America*, p. 37
300 'enormous prestige' J.B. Priestley,
    Literature and Western Man, quoted
    Richard O'Connor, *Jack London: A
    Biography*, p. 405
300 'He was writing' William Peterfield
    Trent et al, *The Cambridge History
    of American Literature*, p. 392

300 'No writer' Upton Sinclair, *Cup of Fury*, p. 11

301 'the continuing' Earle Labor and Jeanne Campbell Reesman, *Jack London*

302 'a bugle' Stephen Graham, *The Death of Yesterday*, pp. 53–61

303 'Like most Californians' Irving Stone, *Sailor on Horseback*, p. 292

BIBLIOGRAPHY

Gertrude Atherton, *Ancestors* (New York, 1907)

Gertrude Atherton, *My San Francisco* (Indianapolis, 1946)

Dr Alan Axelrod and Charles Phillips, *What Every American Should Know About American History* (1992)

Georgia Loring Bamford, *The Mystery of Jack London* (Oakland, 1931)

Pierre Berton, *Klondike Fever* (New York, 1958)

A. Grove Day, *Jack London in the South Seas* (New York, 1971)

Robert Dunn, *World Alive* (New York, 1956)

Philip Foner, *Jack London: American Rebel* (New York, 1947)

Waldo Frank, *Our America* (New York, 1919)

Arnold Genthe, *As I Remember* (New York, 1941)

Emma Goldman, *Living My Life* (New York, 1970)

W. R. Gowers, *Diagnosis of Diseases of the Brain and of the Spinal Cord* (New York, 1885)

Stephen Graham, *The Death of Yesterday* (London, 1930)

King Hendricks, Earle Labor and Irving Shepard (eds), *The Letters of Jack London* (three volumes, Stanford, 1988)

Granville Hicks, *The Great Tradition* (New York, 1933)

Will Irwin, *The Making of a Reporter* (New York, 1942)

Martin Johnson, *Through the South Seas with Jack London* (New York, 1913)

Osa Johnson, *I Married Adventure*

Carolyn Johnston, *Jack London: An American Radical?* (Westport, Connecticut, 1984)

Carl Jung, *Pyschology of the Unconscious* (1916)

Russ Kingman, *A Pictorial Biography of Jack London*

Charmian Kittredge, *The Book of Jack London* (two volumes, London, 1992)

Charmian Kittredge, *The Log of the* Snark

N. K. Krupskaya, *Memories of Lenin* (New York, 1930)

Earle Labor and Jeanne Campbell Reesman, *Jack London* (revised edition, New York, 1994)

Joan London, *Jack London and his Daughters* (Berkeley, 1990)

Joan London, *Jack London and his Times*

Roderick Nash (ed.), *The Call of the Wild 1900–1916* (New York, 1970)

Joseph Noel, *Footloose in Arcadia* (New York, 1940)

Richard O'Connor, *Jack London: A Biography* (Boston, 1964)

Sonia Orwell and Ian Angus (eds), *The Collected Essays, Journalism and Letters of George Orwell* (New York, 1968)

Frederick Palmer, *With Kuroki in Manchuria* (New York, 1904)

Frederick Palmer, *With My Own Eyes* (Indianapolis, 1933)

Adela Rogers St John, *Final Verdict*

Richard Ruland and Malcolm Bradbury, *From Puritanism to Postmodernism: A History of American Literature* (Harmondsworth, 1991)

Alan Schroeder, *Jack London*

George Seldes (ed.), *The Great Thoughts* (New York, 1985)

Donald Sheehan, *This was Publishing* (Bloomington, 1952)

Andrew Sinclair, *Jack* (London, 1977)

Upton Sinclair (ed.), *The Cry for Justice: An Anthology of the Literature of Social Protest* (Philadelphia, 1915)

Upton Sinclair, *Cup of Fury* (New York, 1956)

Kevin Starr, *Californians and the American Dream* (Oxford, 1973)

Clarice Statz, *American Dreamers* (New York, 1988)

Irving Stone, *Sailor on Horseback* (Cambridge, Massachusetts, 1938)

Anna Strunsky, *The Masses*

Richard Tarnas, *The Passion of the Western Mind* (New York, 1991)

Gordon Thomas and Max Morgan Witts, *The San Francisco Earthquake* (New York, 1971)

William Peterfield Trent et al, *The Cambridge History of American Literature* (New York, 1918)

Barbara W. Tuchman, *The Proud Tower* (New York, 1966)

Charles Child Walcutt, *American Writers* (New York, 1974)

Thomas Williamson, *Far North Country* (New York, 1944)

Theodore Zinn, *A People's History of the United States* (New York, 1995)

INDEX

TELECOMMUNICATIONS
IN TURMOIL